AF521893

Walid Raad

Walid

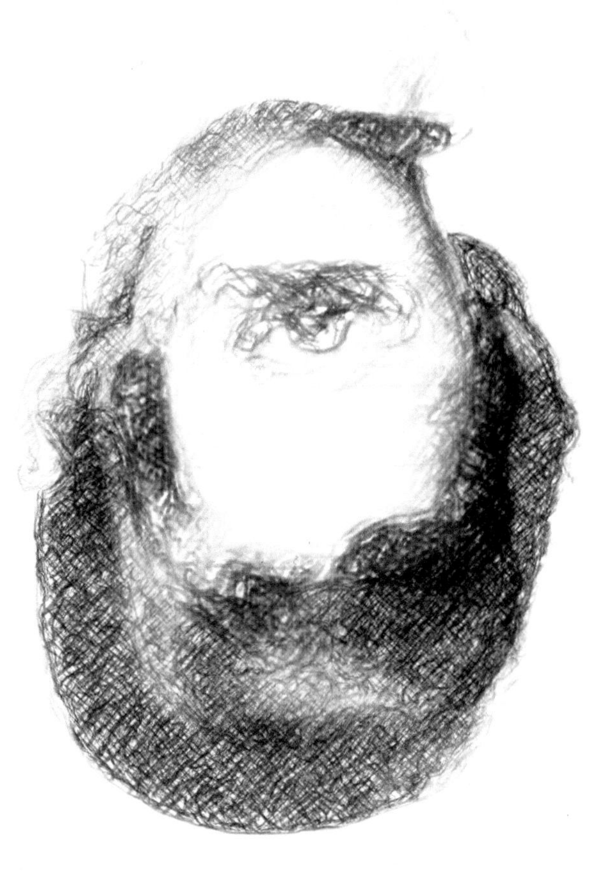

Invited to contribute a text to this book, Walid Raad researched art magazines, newspapers, journals, catalogues, and other sources—all published over the last twenty years in Arabic, English, and French—to find quotations from about fifty people: Lebanese artists, architects, historians, writers, curators, and gallerists, mostly from his own generation. Raad chose quotations from statements he wishes he had made himself or would never make himself. Culled from over 1,400 pages of text, the voices featured here include Amhad Beydoun, Tony Chakar, Joana Hadjithomas, Khalil Joreige, Bernard Khoury, Rabih Mroué, Ghassan Salhab, Lina Saneh, Christine Tohme, Jalal Toufic, Fawwaz Traboulsi, Akram Zaatari, and others.

I Thought I'd Escape My Fate, But Apparently

Walid Raad

Walid Raad wishes to thank: Tarek Abou El Fetouh, Samar Abou-Zeid, Dennis Adams, Haig Aivazian, Hoor Al Qasimi, Rheim Alkhadi, Anthony Allen, Eric Alliez, Shaina Anand, Ayreen Anastas, Zeina Arida, Joumana Asseili, Doug Ashford, Kader Attia, Nayla Audi, Negar Azimi, Hervé Bachelez, Hala Barakat, Saleh Barakat, Pedro Barbosa, Karl Bassil, Stefanie Baumann, Omar Berrada, Scott Berzofsky, Sven Age Birkeland, Doris Bittar, Iwona Blazwick, Achim Borchardt-Hume, Robert Bordo, Saskia Bos, Sabine Breitwieser, James Brookens, Matthew Burns, Frank Caccio, Alberto Caputo, Carlos Chahine, Tony Chakar, Paula Chakravartty, Catherine Chalmers, Carla Chammas, Stefanie Carp, Virginia Carter, Carolyn Christov-Bakargiev, Hélène Chouteau-Matikian, Mack Cole-Edelsack, Marie Collin, Stuart Comer, Lynne Cooke, Paula Cooper, Tamara Corm, A. S. Bruckstein Çoruh, Suzanne Cotter, Matthew Cox, Fereshteh Daftari, Catherine David, Jacqui Davis, Christian de Vietri, David Deitcher, Renaud Detalle, Nitasha Dhillon, David Diao, Katherine Dieckmann, Corinne Diserens, Gina Diwan, Sandi Dubowski, Rana Nasser Eddin, Galit Eilat, Chad Elias, Georgia Elrod, Okwui Enwezor, Octavian Esanu, Charles Esche, Mike Essl, Reem Fadda, Solange Farkas, Dana Farouki, Raphael Fleuriet, David Frankel, Christine Frisinghelli, René Gabri, Ryan Garrett, Jim Gettinger, Nadim Ghorra, Alan Gilbert, Basar Girit, Day Gleeson, Lizzie Gorfain, Gene Gort, Lynn Gumpert, Hans Haacke, Linda Haacke, Francesca Habsburg, Joana Hadjithomas, Christian Hanussek, Aaron Harrow, Kristoffer Hayes, Sharon Hayes, Steven Henry, Nikolaus Hirsch, Claire Hsu, Gabe Huck, Laura Hunt, Amin Husain, Ryan Inouye, Amal Issa, Zaza Jabre, Ana Janevski, Tom Jennings, Gonçalo Jesus, Alexis Johnson, Eungie Joo, Khalil Joreige, Lamia Joreige, Mireille Kassar, Alexandre Kazerouni, Tom Keenan, Hicham Khalidi, Kristine Khouri, Bernard Khoury, Nathalie Khoury, Clara Kim, Rachel Kim, Jack Kirkland, Adam Kleinman, Moukhtar Kocache, Silvia Kolbowski, Prem Krishnamurthy, Theresa Kubasak, Carin Kuoni, Anne-Catherine Kunz, Susan Lee, Frie Leysen, Matthias Lilienthal, Maria Lind, Charles Lindsay, Marcella Lista, Nadine Lockyer, Glenn Lowry, Aleksey Lukyanov-Cherny, Joshua Mack, Sergio Mah, Guy Mannes-Abbott, Bartomeu Mari, Debi Martini, Mores McWreath, Lutz Meyer, Adam Michaels, Sean Miller, Naeem Mohaiemen, Joe Montgomery, Leora Morinis, Margaret Morton, Rabih Mroué, Anthony Nahas, Nabil Nahas, Raya Nahas, Hammad Nassar, Nicolette Nauman, Anna Nowak, Christine Osinski, Willie Osterman, Anne Pasternak, Rebecca Perl, Tina Perlmutter, Jack Persekian, Christine Peters, Nataša Petrešin-Bachelez, Katarina Pierre, Deborah Pope, Jean-Marc Prevost, Tristram Pye, Laura Quinn, Alessandro Rabottini, Lakhena Raingsan, Joseph Raouch, Annie Ratti, Marwan Rechmaoui, Markus Reymann, Anthony Reynolds, Shelley Rice, Grace Robinson-Leo, Irit Rogoff, Andrew Ross, Celesta Rottiers, Wes Rozen, Beatrix Ruf, Ghalya Saadawi, Tony Salamé, Jayce Salloum, Rasha Salti, Brad Samuels, Lina Saneh, Marc Sapir, Joseph Sarkis, Michka Nahas Sarkis, Kirsten Scheid, Britta Schmitz, Sven Christian Schuch, Ulrich Semler, Andrée Sfeir, Avinoam Shalem, Gregory Sholette, Suha Shoman, Sharan Sklar, Christophe Slagmuylder, Kaja Silverman, Herman Sorgeloos, Carol Squiers, Ashok Sukumaran, Rayyane Tabet, Ana Luiza Teixeira de Freitas, Luiz Augusto Teixeira de Freitas, Christine Tohme, Nato Thompson, Jalal Toufic, Jimmy Traboulsi, Rysiek Turbiasz, Fabienne Verstraeten, Anton Vidokle, Andrea Viliani, Gordana Vnuk, Jeff Wallen, Brian Wallis, Miguel Wandschneider, Eyal Weizman, Kaelen Wilson-Goldie, Sylvie Winckler, Ann Wolf, Brian Kuan Wood, Regina Wyrwoll, Loretta Yarlow, Akram Zaatari, Daniela Zyman

and

professors, students, and/or colleagues at Ashkal Alwan's Home Workspace, the Rochester Institute of Technology, University of Rochester, Hampshire College, Queens College (CUNY), Gulf Labor, G.U.L.F., the Arab Image Foundation, and The Cooper Union for the Advancement of Science and Art

and

Finbarr Barry Flood, Kristin Poor, Lucien Samaha, and Katerina Stathopoulou

and

Eva Respini

and

Anthony Allen, Paula Cooper, Anthony Reynolds, and Andrée Sfeir

and

Lynn, Petra, Vera, Myrna, Ghanem, Mansour, Eileen, Hilda, Selim, Carla, and Christina.

Acknowledgments

A project of this scope would have been impossible without the assistance of many dedicated and talented people, both within and outside The Museum of Modern Art. My heartfelt appreciation goes to Glenn D. Lowry, Director, a champion of the show since its inception and a critical sounding board when I needed it. At the ICA/Boston, I am deeply grateful to Jill Medvedow, Ellen Matilda Poss Director, who warmly welcomed me and this project to Boston.

I am honored by the generous support provided for the exhibition by The Andy Warhol Foundation for the Visual Arts; The Jill and Peter Kraus Endowed Fund for Contemporary Exhibitions; MoMA's Wallis Annenberg Fund for Innovation in Contemporary Art through the Annenberg Foundation; The Contemporary Arts Council of The Museum of Modern Art; Oya Eczacıbaşı; A. Huda and Samia Farouki; Elham and Tony Salamé, Aïshti Foundation Beirut; Basil and Raghida Rahim; Maya and Ramzy Rasamny; and Rana Sadik and Samer Younis. I am also deeply grateful for the research and travel support provided by The International Council of The Museum of Modern Art.

Walid Raad has depended for its success on its lenders, listed on page 191. The Museum of Modern Art is grateful to these individuals and institutions for their willingness to make important works available to a larger viewing public.

I very much appreciate the collaboration of the exhibition's tour partners. At ICA/Boston: Jill Medvedow, Director, and Abigail Anne Newbold, Exhibitions Manager; and at the Museo Jumex, Mexico City: former Director Patrick Charpanel, interim Director Julieta González, Deputy Director Rosario Nadal, and Exhibition Coordinator Andrea de la Torre.

I thank Finbarr Barry Flood, William R. Kenan Jr. Professor of the Humanities, Institute of Fine Arts and Department of Art History, New York University, for his illuminating essay in this book. Special thanks are due to Kristin Poor, Museum Research Consortium Fellow in the Museum's Department of Photography, for her contributions. In MoMA's Department of Publications, I am grateful to Christopher Hudson, Publisher; Chul R. Kim, Associate Publisher; David Frankel, Editorial Director; and Marc Sapir, Production Director. My praise and thanks go to Adam Michaels, Prem Krishnamurthy, and Grace Robinson-Leo at Project Projects for their design of the book.

This project would certainly have been impossible without the support of the artist's galleries: Paula Cooper Gallery, New York, and Sfeir-Semler Gallery, Beirut/Hamburg. I am especially grateful to Anthony Allen, Associate Director, Paula Cooper Gallery, and to Andrée Sfeir.

An exhibition is the work of many people. I am thankful for the support of Quentin Bajac, The Joel and Anne Ehrenkranz Chief Curator of Photography; Peter Reed, Senior Deputy Director for Curatorial Affairs; Ramona Bronkar Bannayan, Senior Deputy Director, Exhibitions and Collections; and Stuart Comer, Chief Curator, Department of Media and Performance Art. In the Department of Photography I appreciate the assistance of Marion Tandé, Department Manager, and Megan Feingold, Department Coordinator, and the contributions of curatorial interns Chelsea June Airey and Gökcan Demirkazik.

Erik Patton, Associate Director of Exhibition Planning and Administration, and Rachel Kim, Assistant Coordinator, Exhibition Planning and Administration, provided counsel on the organizing of the show. Susan Palamara, Registrar, and Victoria Manning, Assistant Registrar, skillfully handled the transport and registration. Lee Ann Daffner, Andrew W. Mellon Foundation Conservator of Photographs, provided deft stewardship of the exhibition's objects. Mack Cole-Edelsack, Exhibition Designer, and Matthew Cox, Assistant Production Manager, conceived an elegant exhibition design. I am grateful to Rob Jung and Sarah Wood, Manager and Assistant Manager of Art Handling and Preparation, and to the preparators who helped with the show's physical implementation. Additional thanks are due to Aaron Louis, Director of Audio Visual, and Aaron Harrow, AV Design Manager. Special thanks are owed to the team that oversaw the complex logistics of Raad's performances: Lizzie Gorfain, Performance Producer; Nancy Adelson, Deputy General Counsel; LJ Hartman, Director of Security; Sonya Shrier, Assistant Director, Visitor Services; Melissa Falkenham, Manager of Group Services; and Carrie McGee, Assistant Director of Community and Access Programs.

Other professionals at the Museum who deserve special acknowledgment include: Kim Mitchell, Chief Communications Officer; Margaret Doyle, Director of Communications; Todd Bishop, Senior Deputy Director for External Affairs; Lauren Stakias, Director of Exhibition and Program Funding; Wendy Woon, Deputy Director for Education; Pablo Helguera, Director of Adult and Academic Education; Sarah Kennedy, Associate Educator, Public and Studio Programs; and, in the Department of Graphic Design and Advertising, Claire Corey, Production Manager; Ingrid Chou, Associate Creative Director; and Vanessa Lam, Senior Designer.

Very warm and sincere thanks are due to Katerina Stathopoulou, Curatorial Assistant in the Museum's Department of Photography, for her invaluable contributions to the exhibition and catalogue. She was truly my partner in this exhibition and I am deeply grateful to her.

My first and final thanks are reserved for Walid Raad. I am deeply honored to have worked closely with such a brilliant and thoughtful artist. I learned an enormous amount from Walid and his work, which has profoundly moved and inspired me.

This book is dedicated to my family.

—Eva Respini
Barbara Lee Chief Curator
Institute of Contemporary Art/Boston

Foreword

In an age of increasing Western engagement with art from across the globe, it is a pleasure to present the first American museum survey of one of contemporary art's most critical figures, Walid Raad. Several years ago I had the opportunity of traveling with Raad in the United Arab Emirates, where we encountered an advertisement for a commercial bank stating "Pre-write history." This slogan precipitated a lengthy conversation about what history means in a region with various and often conflicting accounts of past, present, and future. No one has thought more about this problem than Raad; the construction of history—how it is made, received, visualized, and understood—is a central theme for him. A Lebanese national who fled his war-torn country in 1983, Raad emerged in the 1990s with work that asked urgent questions about the power of images and information within the context of the trauma of war. His work generates a host of questions about our fundamental understanding of lived experiences and a palpable sense of art as urgent.

The Museum of Modern Art committed to Raad early in his career, acquiring major works in 2003 and 2004 and including his art in group exhibitions such as *Without Boundary: Seventeen Ways of Looking* (2006), *Color Chart: Reinventing Color 1950 to Today* (2008), *Greater New York 2005* at MoMA PS1, and several collection installations throughout the last decade. This exhibition, which surveys his output in all mediums over the last twenty-five years, is the most comprehensive in any museum to date, introducing the full scope of his work to an American audience for the first time. Raad's art touches on so many areas of curatorial expertise—photography, video, architecture, graphic design, and performance—that it epitomizes the mission of our museum as an institution of cross-disciplinary learning.

I am indebted to MoMA's Board of Trustees for supporting such an ambitious project, and for allowing us, once again, to break new ground. I owe my deepest gratitude to the exhibition's funders: The Andy Warhol Foundation for the Visual Arts; MoMA's Wallis Annenberg Fund for Innovation in Contemporary Art through the Annenberg Foundation; The Jill and Peter Kraus Endowed Fund for Contemporary Exhibitions; The Contemporary Arts Council of the Museum of Modern Art; Oya Eczacıbaşı; A. Huda and Samia Farouki; Elham and Tony Salamé, Aïshti Foundation Beirut; Basil and Raghida Rahim; Maya and Ramzy Rasamny; and Rana Sadik and Samer Younis. I am also grateful to The International Council of The Museum of Modern Art for providing critical research and travel support for the exhibition.

After its presentation in New York, the exhibition will be shown at the Institute of Contemporary Art in Boston and Museo Jumex in Mexico City. I extend my thanks to Jill Medvedow, Ellen Matilda Poss Director of the ICA, and to interim Director Julieta González and former Director Patrick Charpenel of Museo Jumex, for embracing this project. This tour is only possible because the lenders (p. 191) have been willing to part with important works for over a year, and we owe them an enormous debt.

I extend my profound gratitude to Eva Respini for organizing this important exhibition. Before assuming the role of Barbara Lee Chief Curator at the ICA/Boston, Eva served as a curator in MoMA's Department of Photography, organizing exhibitions such as the Museum's major retrospective of Cindy Sherman and its long-overdue survey of the work of Robert Heinecken. I also wish to thank Finbarr Barry Flood, William R. Kenan Jr. Professor of the Humanities, Institute of Fine Arts and Department of Art History, New York University, for his illuminating contribution to this book.

Finally I salute Walid Raad for his extreme generosity and close collaboration in bringing this presentation to its fruition. His works are moving, elegant, and provocative, leading us to reflect deeply on the issues of our time.

—Glenn D. Lowry
Director, The Museum of Modern Art

Published in conjunction with the exhibition *Walid Raad*, at The Museum of Modern Art, New York, October 12, 2015–January 31, 2016, organized by Eva Respini with Katerina Stathopoulou

The exhibition will travel to the Institute of Contemporary Art/Boston, February 24–May 30, 2016, and to the Museo Jumex, Mexico City, October 13, 2016–January 14, 2017.

The exhibition is made possible by The Andy Warhol Foundation for the Visual Arts, The Jill and Peter Kraus Endowed Fund for Contemporary Exhibitions, MoMA's Wallis Annenberg Fund for Innovation in Contemporary Art through the Annenberg Foundation, and The Contemporary Arts Council of The Museum of Modern Art.

Major support is provided by Oya Eczacıbaşı; A. Huda and Samia Farouki; and by Elham and Tony Salamé, Aïshti Foundation Beirut.

With generous funding from Basil and Raghida Rahim, Maya and Ramzy Rasamny, and from Rana Sadik and Samer Younis.

Additional support is provided by the MoMA Annual Exhibition Fund with major contributions from an anonymous donor, The Contemporary Arts Council of The Museum of Modern Art, Glenn and Eva Dubin, The Donald R. Mullen Family Foundation, Inc., The Junior Associates of The Museum of Modern Art, Mimi and Peter Haas Fund, Franz Wassmer, Gary and Karen Winnick, and from Susan and Leonard Feinstein.

Research and travel support for this exhibition was provided by The International Council of The Museum of Modern Art.

This publication was made possible by the Nancy Lee and Perry Bass Publication Endowment Fund.

Produced by the Department of Publications, The Museum of Modern Art, New York

Christopher Hudson, Publisher
Chul R. Kim, Associate Publisher
David Frankel, Editorial Director
Marc Sapir, Production Director

Edited by David Frankel
Designed by Project Projects
Production by Marc Sapir
Printed and bound by Ofset Yapimevi, Istanbul

This book is typeset in Fakt and Lyon. The papers are Arctic Volume 150 gsm and Amber Graphic 130 gsm.

Library of Congress Control Number: 2015942034
ISBN: 978-0-87070-973-9

Published by The Museum of Modern Art
11 West 53 Street
New York, New York 10019
www.moma.org

Distributed in the United States and Canada by ARTBOOK | D.A.P., New York
155 Sixth Avenue, 2nd floor, New York, NY 10013
www.artbook.com

Distributed outside the United States and Canada by Thames & Hudson ltd
181A High Holborn, London WC1V 7QX
www.thamesandhudson.com

Printed in Turkey

Front cover:
Appendix XVIII: Plate 101_A History of Indices. 2009. Pigmented inkjet print, 21½ × 16½" (54.6 × 41.9 cm). The Museum of Modern Art, New York. Sue and Edgar Wachenheim III Endowment

Back cover:
I might die before I get a rifle_Device III. 1993/2002. Pigmented inkjet print, 63" × 6'11" (160 × 210.8 cm). Courtesy the artist and Paula Cooper Gallery, New York

The Museum of Modern Art

Raad

Eva Respini

With a contribution by Walid Raad
and an essay by Finbarr Barry Flood

"I thought I'd escape my fate, but apparently."

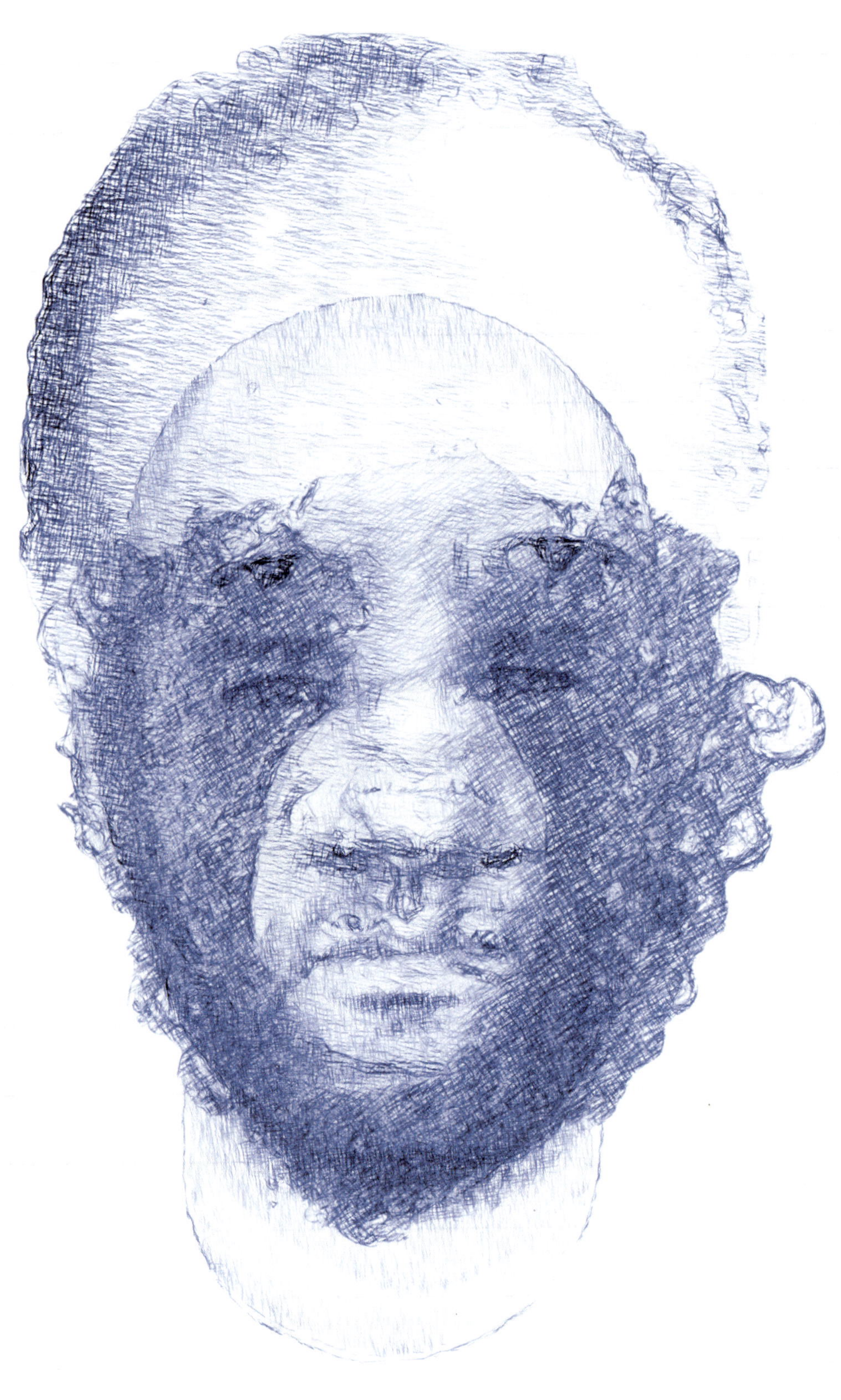

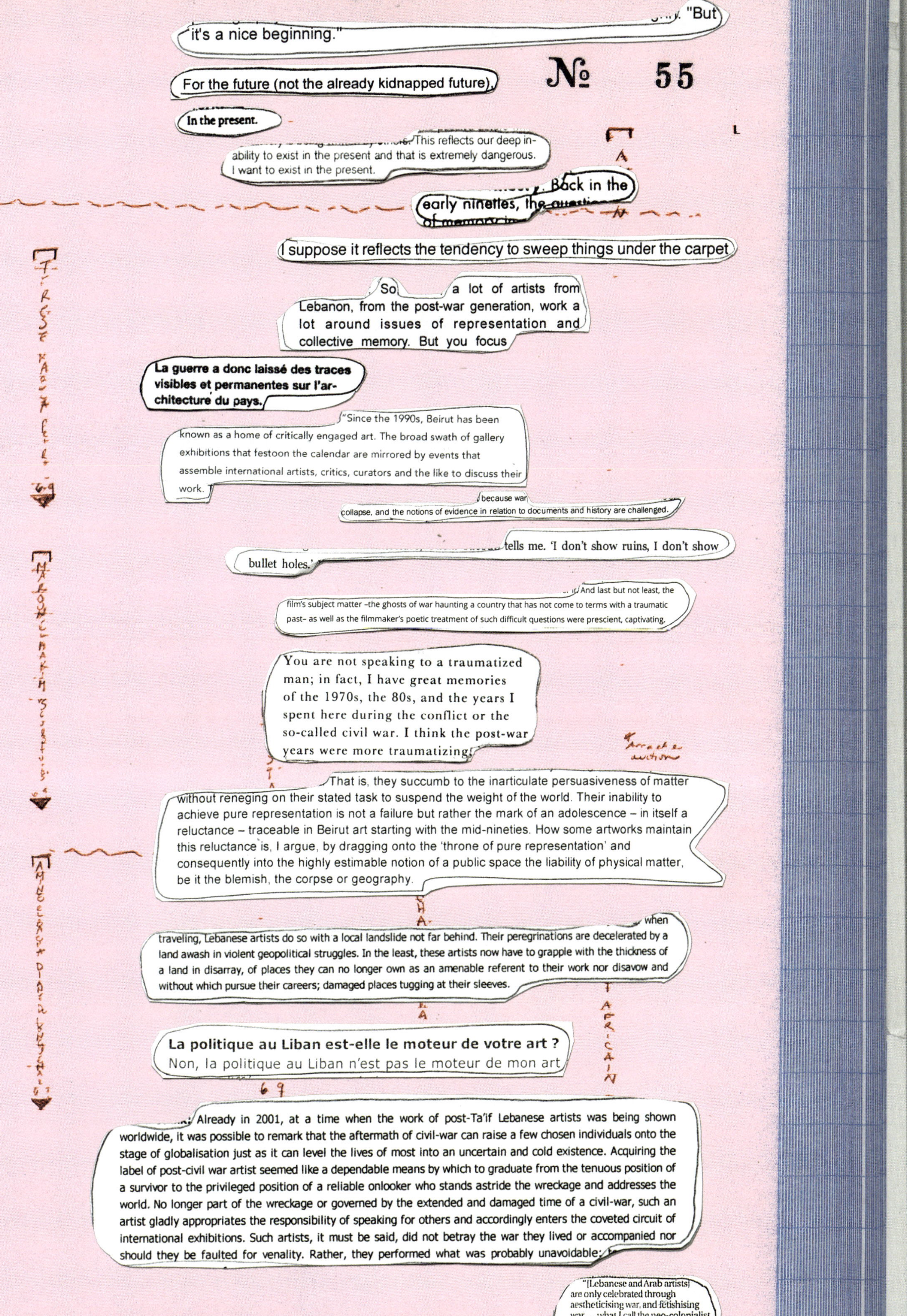

"But it's a nice beginning."

№ 55

For the future (not the already kidnapped future).

In the present.

This reflects our deep inability to exist in the present and that is extremely dangerous. I want to exist in the present.

Back in the early nineties, the

I suppose it reflects the tendency to sweep things under the carpet

So a lot of artists from Lebanon, from the post-war generation, work a lot around issues of representation and collective memory. But you focus

La guerre a donc laissé des traces visibles et permanentes sur l'architecture du pays.

"Since the 1990s, Beirut has been known as a home of critically engaged art. The broad swath of gallery exhibitions that festoon the calendar are mirrored by events that assemble international artists, critics, curators and the like to discuss their work.

because war collapse, and the notions of evidence in relation to documents and history are challenged.

tells me. 'I don't show ruins, I don't show bullet holes.'

And last but not least, the film's subject matter –the ghosts of war haunting a country that has not come to terms with a traumatic past– as well as the filmmaker's poetic treatment of such difficult questions were prescient, captivating.

You are not speaking to a traumatized man; in fact, I have great memories of the 1970s, the 80s, and the years I spent here during the conflict or the so-called civil war. I think the post-war years were more traumatizing.

That is, they succumb to the inarticulate persuasiveness of matter without reneging on their stated task to suspend the weight of the world. Their inability to achieve pure representation is not a failure but rather the mark of an adolescence – in itself a reluctance – traceable in Beirut art starting with the mid-nineties. How some artworks maintain this reluctance is, I argue, by dragging onto the 'throne of pure representation' and consequently into the highly estimable notion of a public space the liability of physical matter, be it the blemish, the corpse or geography.

when traveling, Lebanese artists do so with a local landslide not far behind. Their peregrinations are decelerated by a land awash in violent geopolitical struggles. In the least, these artists now have to grapple with the thickness of a land in disarray, of places they can no longer own as an amenable referent to their work nor disavow and without which pursue their careers; damaged places tugging at their sleeves.

La politique au Liban est-elle le moteur de votre art ?
Non, la politique au Liban n'est pas le moteur de mon art

Already in 2001, at a time when the work of post-Ta'if Lebanese artists was being shown worldwide, it was possible to remark that the aftermath of civil-war can raise a few chosen individuals onto the stage of globalisation just as it can level the lives of most into an uncertain and cold existence. Acquiring the label of post-civil war artist seemed like a dependable means by which to graduate from the tenuous position of a survivor to the privileged position of a reliable onlooker who stands astride the wreckage and addresses the world. No longer part of the wreckage or governed by the extended and damaged time of a civil-war, such an artist gladly appropriates the responsibility of speaking for others and accordingly enters the coveted circuit of international exhibitions. Such artists, it must be said, did not betray the war they lived or accompanied nor should they be faulted for venality. Rather, they performed what was probably unavoidable;

"[Lebanese and Arab artists] are only celebrated through aestheticising war, and fetishising war … what I call the neo-colonialist fantasy of what Lebanon is and what the Arab world is."

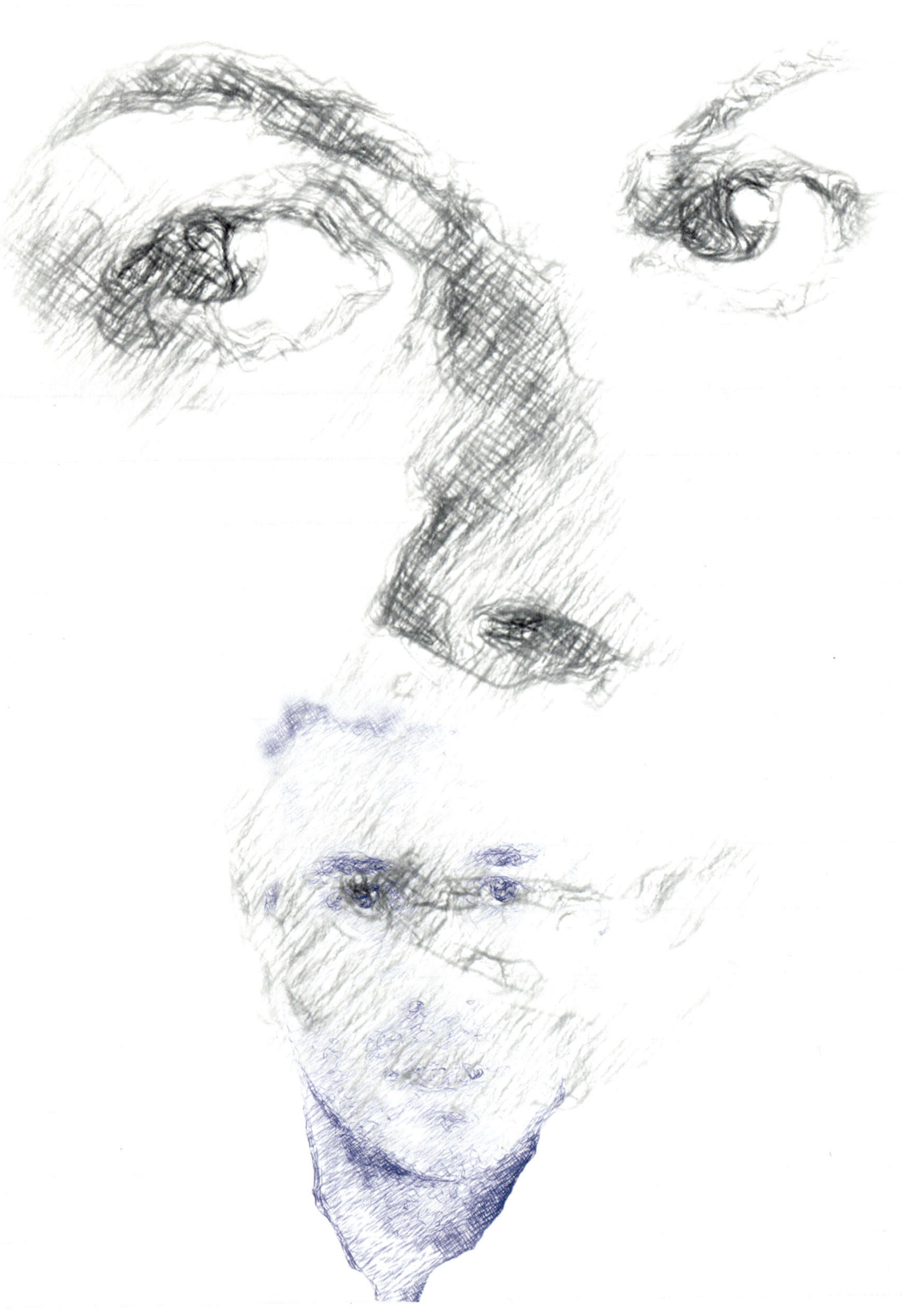

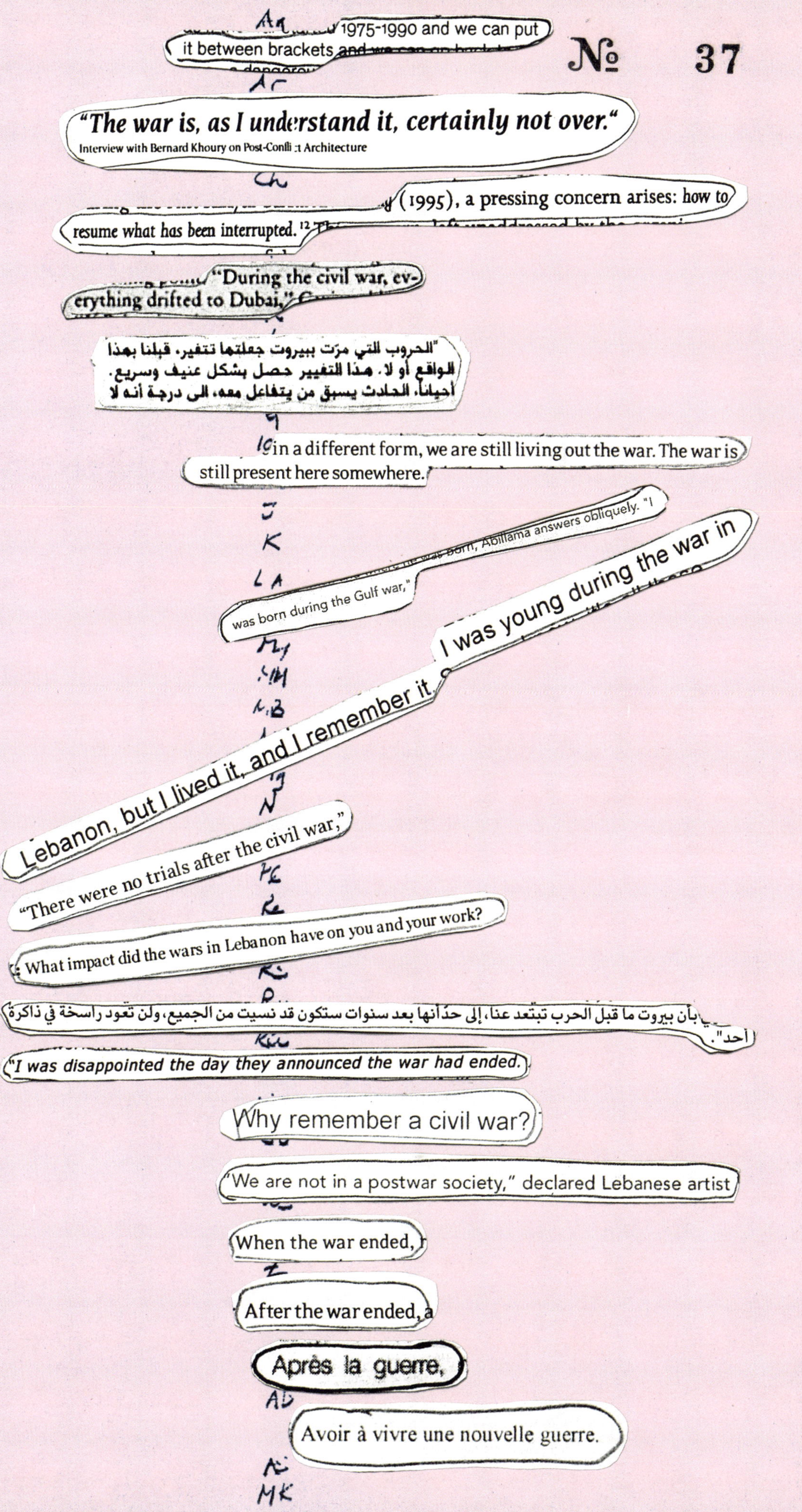
1975-1990 and we can put
it between brackets
"The war is, as I understand it, certainly not over."
Interview with Bernard Khoury on Post-Conflict Architecture
(1995), a pressing concern arises: how to
resume what has been interrupted.
"During the civil war, ev-
erything drifted to Dubai,"
"الحروب التي مرّت ببيروت جعلتها تتغير، قبلنا بهذا
الواقع أو لا. هذا التغيير حصل بشكل عنيف وسريع.
أحياناً، الحادث يسبق من يتفاعل معه، الى درجة أنه لا
in a different form, we are still living out the war. The war is
still present here somewhere.
Abillama answers obliquely. "I
was born during the Gulf war,"
I was young during the war in
Lebanon, but I lived it, and I remember it.
"There were no trials after the civil war,"
What impact did the wars in Lebanon have on you and your work?
بأن بيروت ما قبل الحرب تبتعد عنا، إلى حدّ أنها بعد سنوات ستكون قد نسيت من الجميع، ولن تعود راسخة في ذاكرة
أحد".
"I was disappointed the day they announced the war had ended.
Why remember a civil war?
"We are not in a postwar society," declared Lebanese artist
When the war ended,
After the war ended,
Après la guerre,
Avoir à vivre une nouvelle guerre.

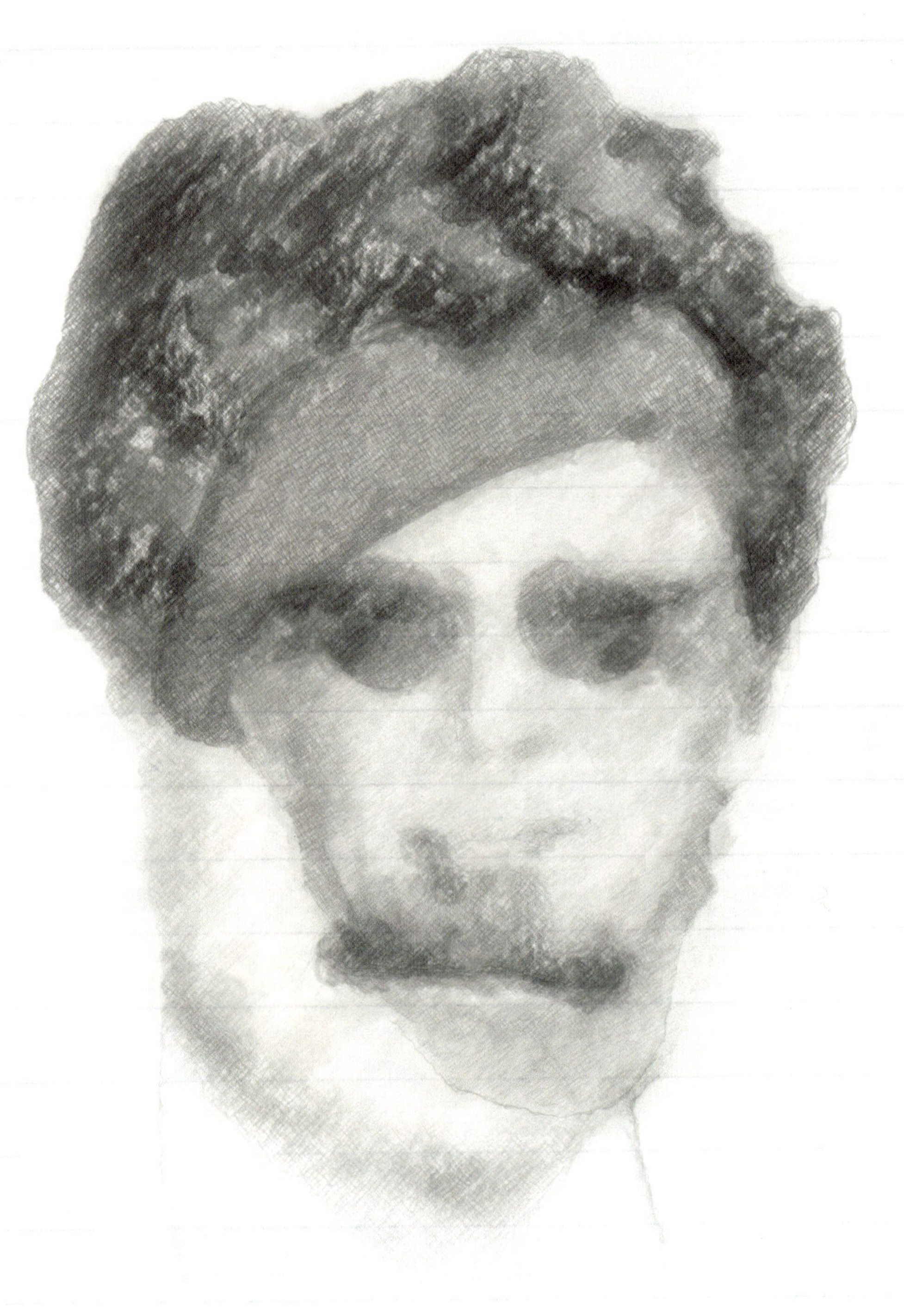

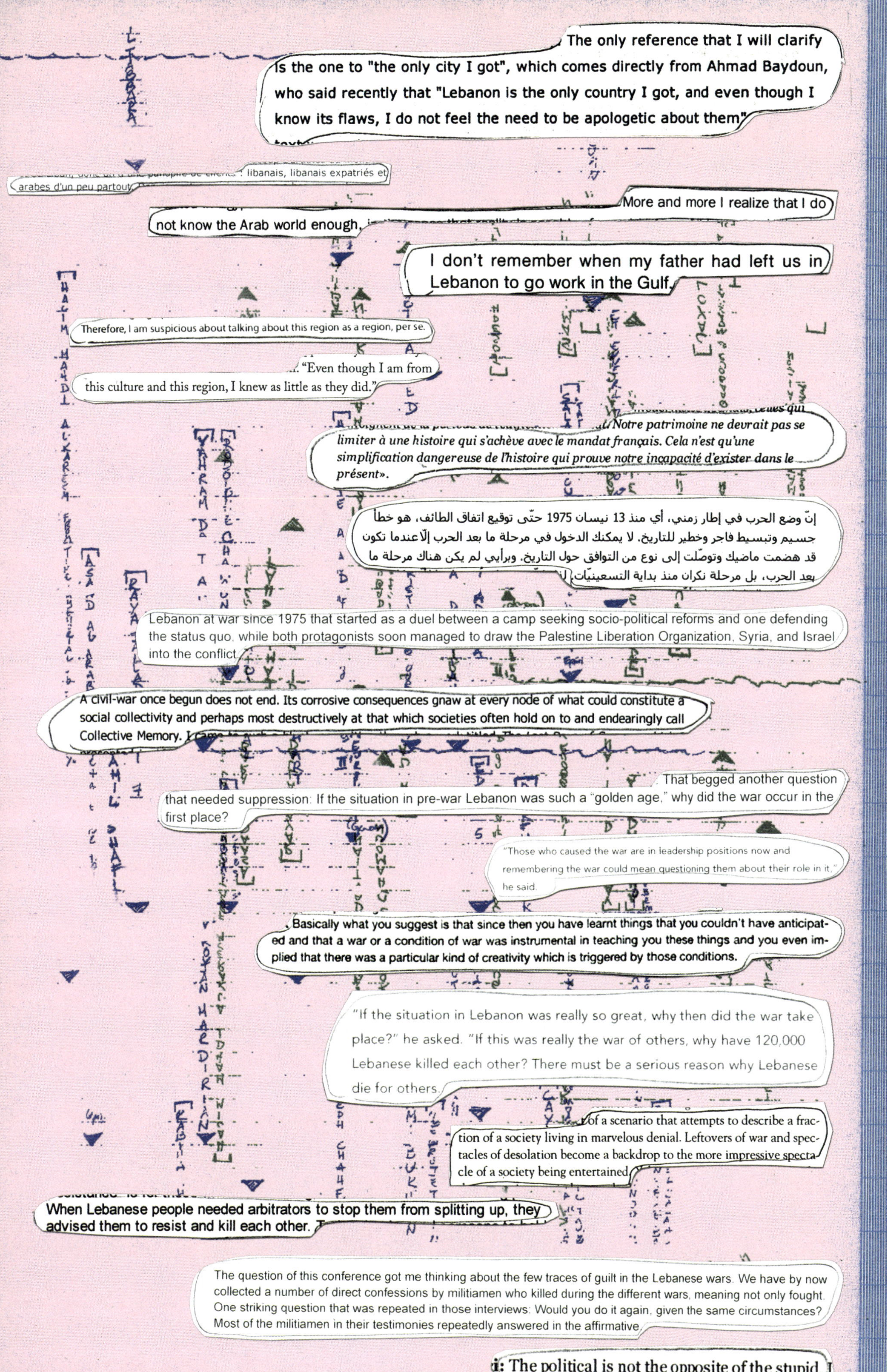

The only reference that I will clarify is the one to "the only city I got", which comes directly from Ahmad Baydoun, who said recently that "Lebanon is the only country I got, and even though I know its flaws, I do not feel the need to be apologetic about them"
libanais, libanais expatriés et arabes d'un peu partout
More and more I realize that I do not know the Arab world enough,
I don't remember when my father had left us in Lebanon to go work in the Gulf.
Therefore, I am suspicious about talking about this region as a region, per se.
"Even though I am from this culture and this region, I knew as little as they did."
Notre patrimoine ne devrait pas se limiter à une histoire qui s'achève avec le mandat français. Cela n'est qu'une simplification dangereuse de l'histoire qui prouve notre incapacité d'exister dans le présent».
إنّ وضع الحرب في إطار زمني، أي منذ 13 نيسان 1975 حتّى توقيع اتفاق الطائف، هو خطأ جسيم وتبسيط فاجر وخطير للتاريخ. لا يمكنك الدخول في مرحلة ما بعد الحرب إلّاعندما تكون قد هضمت ماضيك وتوصّلت إلى نوع من التوافق حول التاريخ. وبرأيي لم يكن هناك مرحلة ما بعد الحرب، بل مرحلة نكران منذ بداية التسعينيّات
Lebanon at war since 1975 that started as a duel between a camp seeking socio-political reforms and one defending the status quo, while both protagonists soon managed to draw the Palestine Liberation Organization, Syria, and Israel into the conflict
A civil-war once begun does not end. Its corrosive consequences gnaw at every node of what could constitute a social collectivity and perhaps most destructively at that which societies often hold on to and endearingly call Collective Memory.
That begged another question that needed suppression: If the situation in pre-war Lebanon was such a "golden age," why did the war occur in the first place?
"Those who caused the war are in leadership positions now and remembering the war could mean questioning them about their role in it," he said.
Basically what you suggest is that since then you have learnt things that you couldn't have anticipated and that a war or a condition of war was instrumental in teaching you these things and you even implied that there was a particular kind of creativity which is triggered by those conditions.
"If the situation in Lebanon was really so great, why then did the war take place?" he asked. "If this was really the war of others, why have 120,000 Lebanese killed each other? There must be a serious reason why Lebanese die for others.
of a scenario that attempts to describe a fraction of a society living in marvelous denial. Leftovers of war and spectacles of desolation become a backdrop to the more impressive spectacle of a society being entertained
When Lebanese people needed arbitrators to stop them from splitting up, they advised them to resist and kill each other.
The question of this conference got me thinking about the few traces of guilt in the Lebanese wars. We have by now collected a number of direct confessions by militiamen who killed during the different wars, meaning not only fought. One striking question that was repeated in those interviews: Would you do it again, given the same circumstances? Most of the militiamen in their testimonies repeatedly answered in the affirmative.
The political is not the opposite of the stupid.

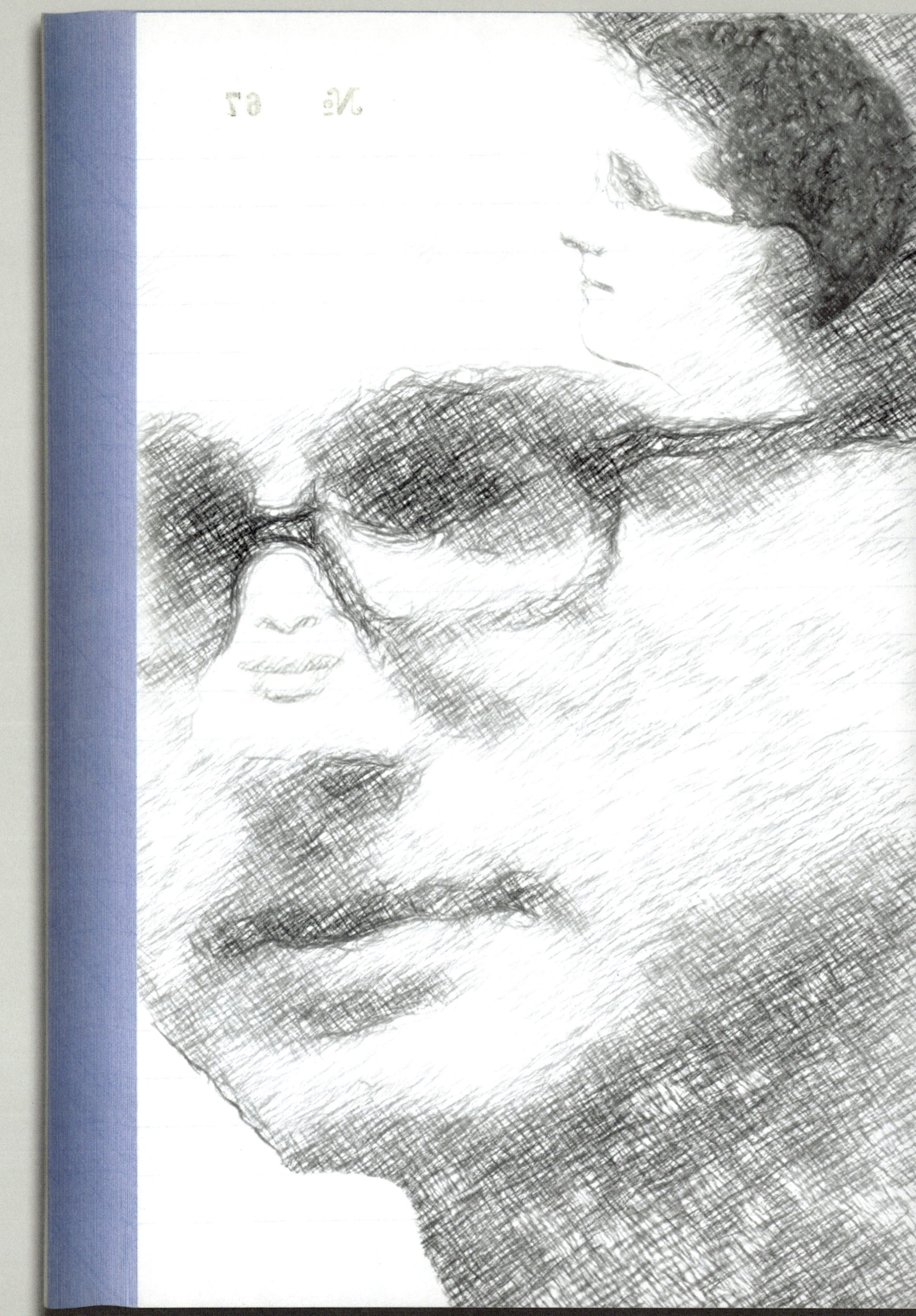
№ 67

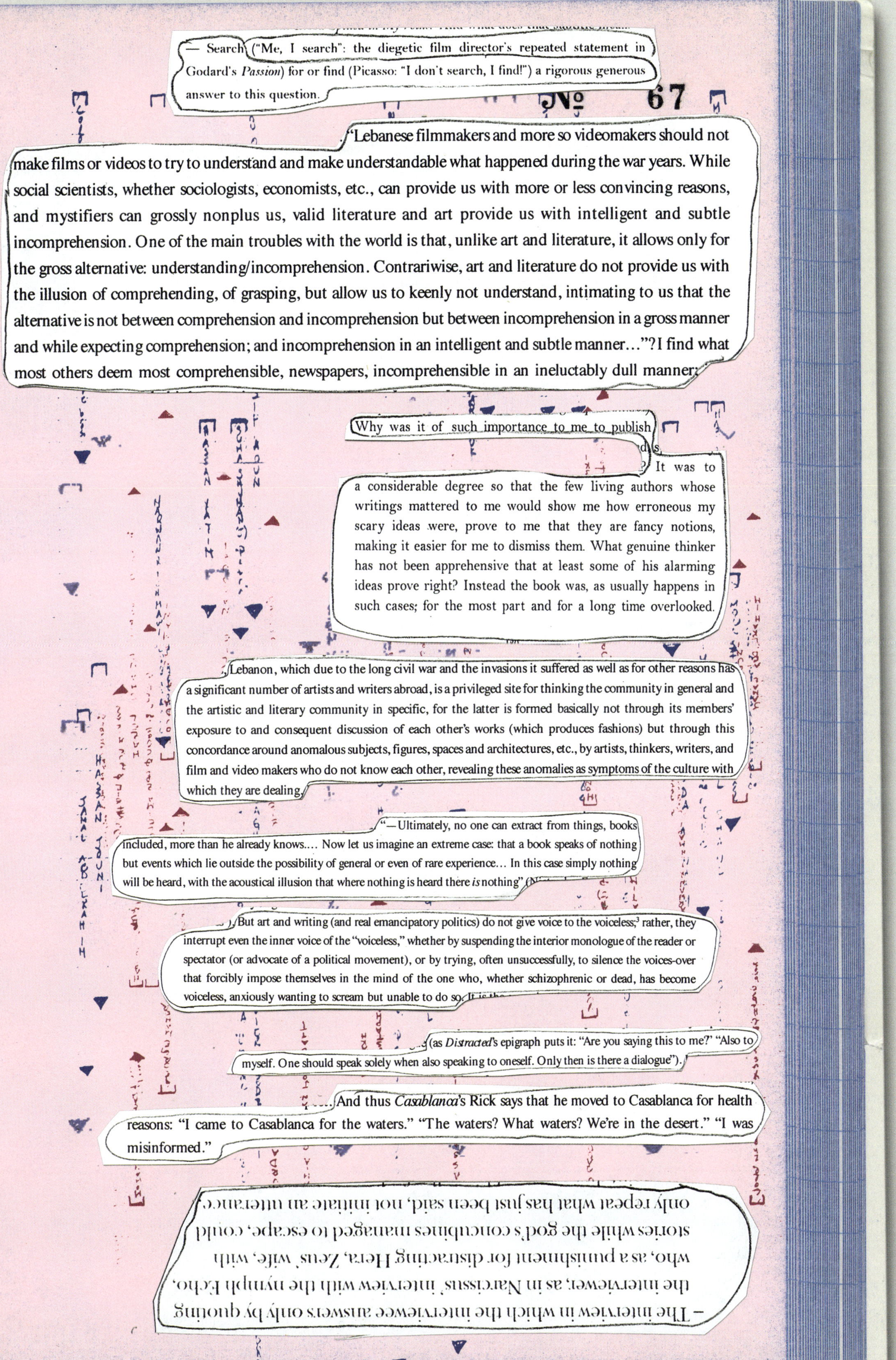

— Search ("Me, I search": the diegetic film director's repeated statement in Godard's *Passion*) for or find (Picasso: "I don't search, I find!") a rigorous generous answer to this question.

№ 67

"Lebanese filmmakers and more so videomakers should not make films or videos to try to understand and make understandable what happened during the war years. While social scientists, whether sociologists, economists, etc., can provide us with more or less convincing reasons, and mystifiers can grossly nonplus us, valid literature and art provide us with intelligent and subtle incomprehension. One of the main troubles with the world is that, unlike art and literature, it allows only for the gross alternative: understanding/incomprehension. Contrariwise, art and literature do not provide us with the illusion of comprehending, of grasping, but allow us to keenly not understand, intimating to us that the alternative is not between comprehension and incomprehension but between incomprehension in a gross manner and while expecting comprehension; and incomprehension in an intelligent and subtle manner…"?I find what most others deem most comprehensible, newspapers, incomprehensible in an ineluctably dull manner;

Why was it of such importance to me to publish … It was to a considerable degree so that the few living authors whose writings mattered to me would show me how erroneous my scary ideas were, prove to me that they are fancy notions, making it easier for me to dismiss them. What genuine thinker has not been apprehensive that at least some of his alarming ideas prove right? Instead the book was, as usually happens in such cases; for the most part and for a long time overlooked.

Lebanon, which due to the long civil war and the invasions it suffered as well as for other reasons has a significant number of artists and writers abroad, is a privileged site for thinking the community in general and the artistic and literary community in specific, for the latter is formed basically not through its members' exposure to and consequent discussion of each other's works (which produces fashions) but through this concordance around anomalous subjects, figures, spaces and architectures, etc., by artists, thinkers, writers, and film and video makers who do not know each other, revealing these anomalies as symptoms of the culture with which they are dealing.

"—Ultimately, no one can extract from things, books included, more than he already knows.… Now let us imagine an extreme case: that a book speaks of nothing but events which lie outside the possibility of general or even of rare experience… In this case simply nothing will be heard, with the acoustical illusion that where nothing is heard there *is* nothing"

But art and writing (and real emancipatory politics) do not give voice to the voiceless;[3] rather, they interrupt even the inner voice of the "voiceless," whether by suspending the interior monologue of the reader or spectator (or advocate of a political movement), or by trying, often unsuccessfully, to silence the voices-over that forcibly impose themselves in the mind of the one who, whether schizophrenic or dead, has become voiceless, anxiously wanting to scream but unable to do so.

(as *Distracted*'s epigraph puts it: "Are you saying this to me?' "Also to myself. One should speak solely when also speaking to oneself. Only then is there a dialogue").

And thus *Casablanca*'s Rick says that he moved to Casablanca for health reasons: "I came to Casablanca for the waters." "The waters? What waters? We're in the desert." "I was misinformed."

— The interview in which the interviewee answers only by quoting the interviewer, as in Narcissus' interview with the nymph Echo, who, as a punishment for distracting Hera, Zeus' wife, with stories while the god's concubines managed to escape, could only repeat what has just been said, not initiate an utterance.

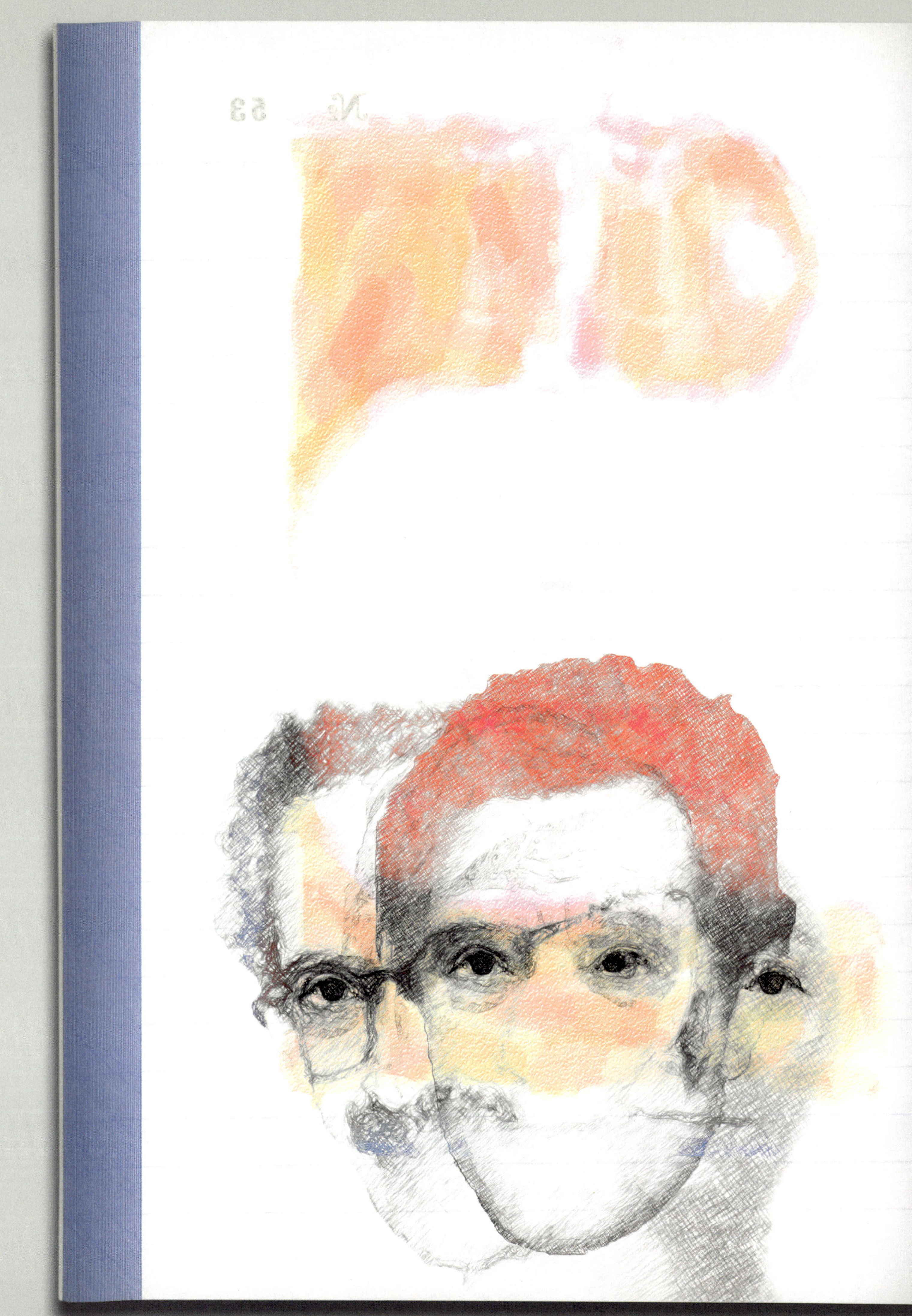

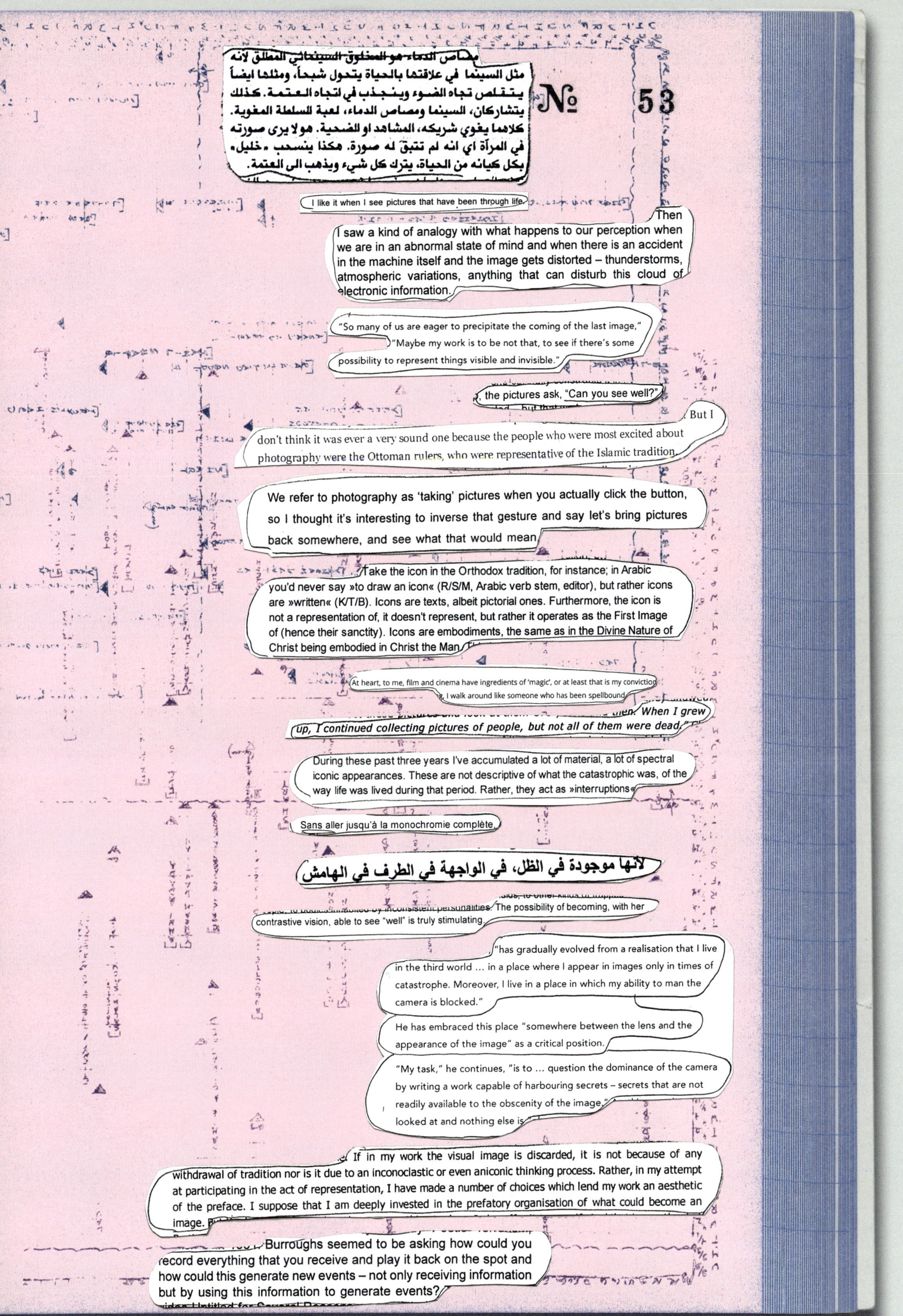

مصاص الدماء هو المخلوق السينمائي المطلق لانه
مثل السينما في علاقتها بالحياة يتحول شبحاً، ومثلها ايضاً
يتقلص تجاه الضوء وينجذب في اتجاه العتمة. كذلك
يتشاركان، السينما ومصاص الدماء، لعبة السلطة المغوية.
كلاهما يغوي شريكه، المشاهد او الضحية. هو لا يرى صورته
في المرآة اي انه لم تتبقَ له صورة. هكذا ينسحب «خليل»
بكل كيانه من الحياة، يترك كل شيء ويذهب الى العتمة.

№ 53

I like it when I see pictures that have been through life.

Then I saw a kind of analogy with what happens to our perception when we are in an abnormal state of mind and when there is an accident in the machine itself and the image gets distorted – thunderstorms, atmospheric variations, anything that can disturb this cloud of electronic information.

"So many of us are eager to precipitate the coming of the last image," "Maybe my work is to be not that, to see if there's some possibility to represent things visible and invisible."

the pictures ask, "Can you see well?"

But I don't think it was ever a very sound one because the people who were most excited about photography were the Ottoman rulers, who were representative of the Islamic tradition.

We refer to photography as 'taking' pictures when you actually click the button, so I thought it's interesting to inverse that gesture and say let's bring pictures back somewhere, and see what that would mean.

Take the icon in the Orthodox tradition, for instance; in Arabic you'd never say »to draw an icon« (R/S/M, Arabic verb stem, editor), but rather icons are »written« (K/T/B). Icons are texts, albeit pictorial ones. Furthermore, the icon is not a representation of, it doesn't represent, but rather it operates as the First Image of (hence their sanctity). Icons are embodiments, the same as in the Divine Nature of Christ being embodied in Christ the Man.

At heart, to me, film and cinema have ingredients of 'magic', or at least that is my conviction

I walk around like someone who has been spellbound

When I grew up, I continued collecting pictures of people, but not all of them were dead.

During these past three years I've accumulated a lot of material, a lot of spectral iconic appearances. These are not descriptive of what the catastrophic was, of the way life was lived during that period. Rather, they act as »interruptions«

Sans aller jusqu'à la monochromie complète,

لأنها موجودة في الظل، في الواجهة في الطرف في الهامش

The possibility of becoming, with her contrastive vision, able to see "well" is truly stimulating.

"has gradually evolved from a realisation that I live in the third world … in a place where I appear in images only in times of catastrophe. Moreover, I live in a place in which my ability to man the camera is blocked."

He has embraced this place "somewhere between the lens and the appearance of the image" as a critical position.

"My task," he continues, "is to … question the dominance of the camera by writing a work capable of harbouring secrets – secrets that are not readily available to the obscenity of the image,"

looked at and nothing else is

If in my work the visual image is discarded, it is not because of any withdrawal of tradition nor is it due to an inconoclastic or even aniconic thinking process. Rather, in my attempt at participating in the act of representation, I have made a number of choices which lend my work an aesthetic of the preface. I suppose that I am deeply invested in the prefatory organisation of what could become an image.

Burroughs seemed to be asking how could you record everything that you receive and play it back on the spot and how could this generate new events – not only receiving information but by using this information to generate events?

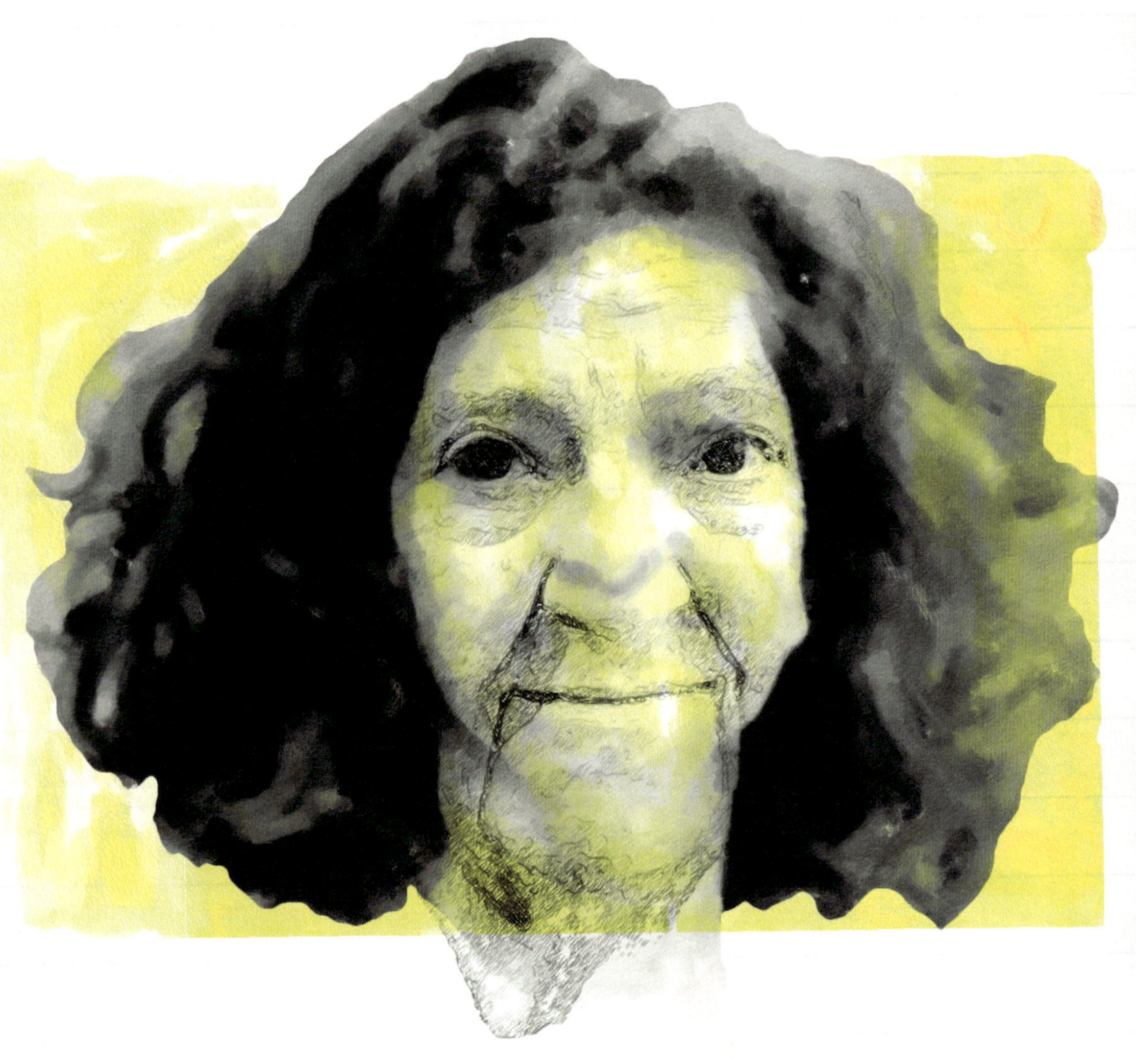

Unlike Syria, Egypt, Iraq or Palestine, and in spite of a so-called historically liberal disposition, Lebanon was not a vanguard home to feminist movements, discourse or activists

№ 24

"Someone else said to her. You are an Arab woman. Where is the tradition in your work? She responded 'Tradition is not what keeps you stationary, like a metal ball chained to a prisoner's leg. I carry (tradition) with me in my heart and soul, and I go.' For him tradition is stones and arches. For her, tradition is something that she holds within her and uses to inform her designs."

كيف تكونين زوجة فضلى؟ هل للمرأة أن تحارب؟

لماذا تغضب المرأة؟ هل للمرأة أن تسامح؟

I have since aspired to become the sort of woman, like her, who will be remembered as exquisitely eccentric, fearlessly singular and tirelessly accomplished.

One, to the best of my knowledge, no other Lebanese painter has grappled with the subject of Asian women, despite their plethora in Lebanese daily life (and the same holds for most of the other arts as well, with rare exceptions

أمام الحضور، أنا مجرمة.

Fuir le travail, oublier un rendez-vous, en avoir soudain marre de me tenir compagnie.

I am known to say that work leads to work

La lenteur du geste, mon énergie servant à accélérer la repartie.

I think that sometimes materials need to ferment and reach maturity.

• To historicize

• To investigate

• To transcribe

• To identify a

• To create

"It was reported,"

Her work is essentially on

Among her works are

is the author of

holds a Ph.D from

She uses

She explores

This project is the first chapter of a longer project

In other words, I am not asking a

As I am asked to reflect on t

Between what exactly?

It just gets better, sharper, more radical and less inhibited.

as I said above, the intention is to complicate, not to simplify or explain

These are all very complex issues

I realize that t

Great question, thank you!

Yes, I agree.

Yes. Thank you.

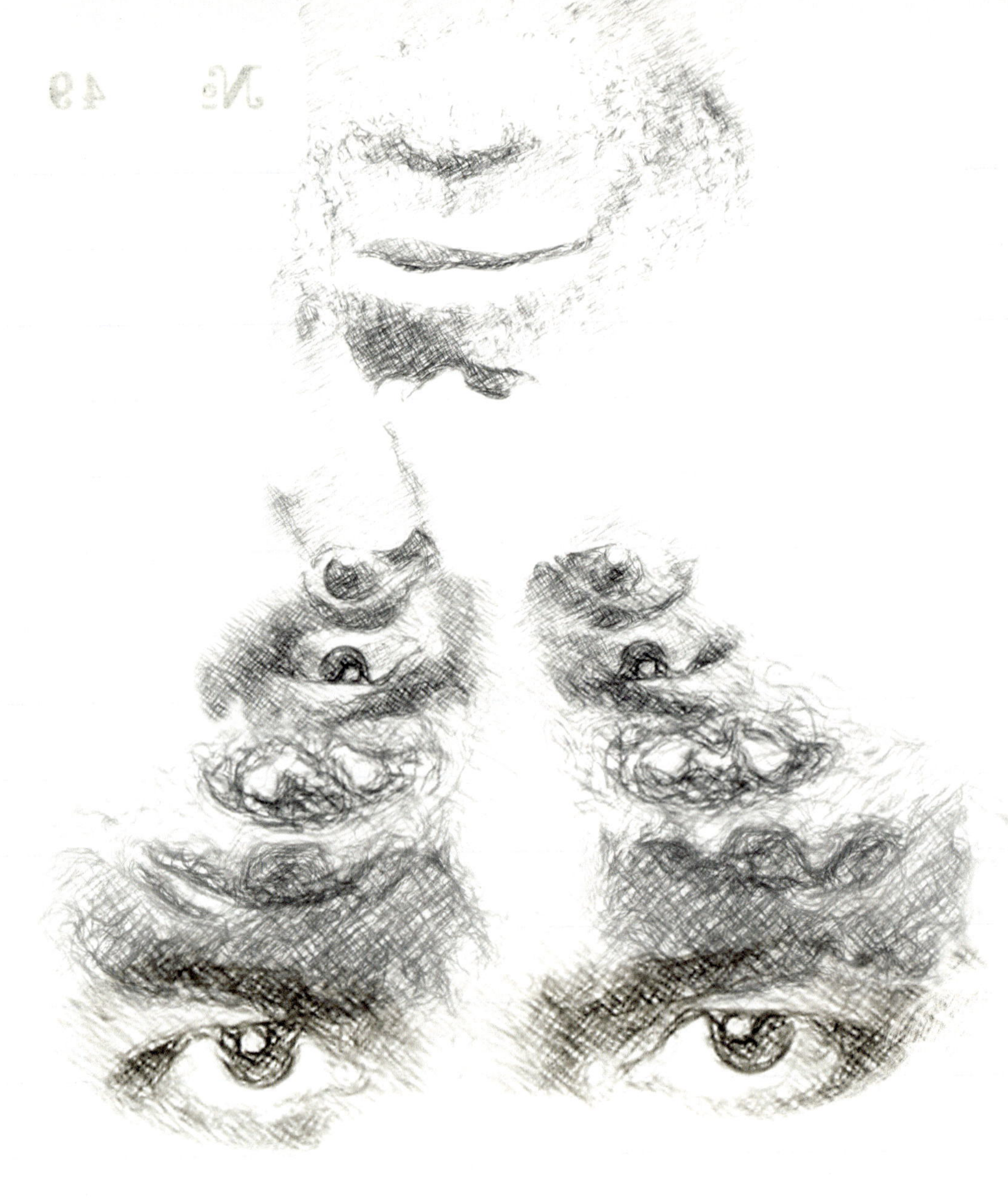
№ 49

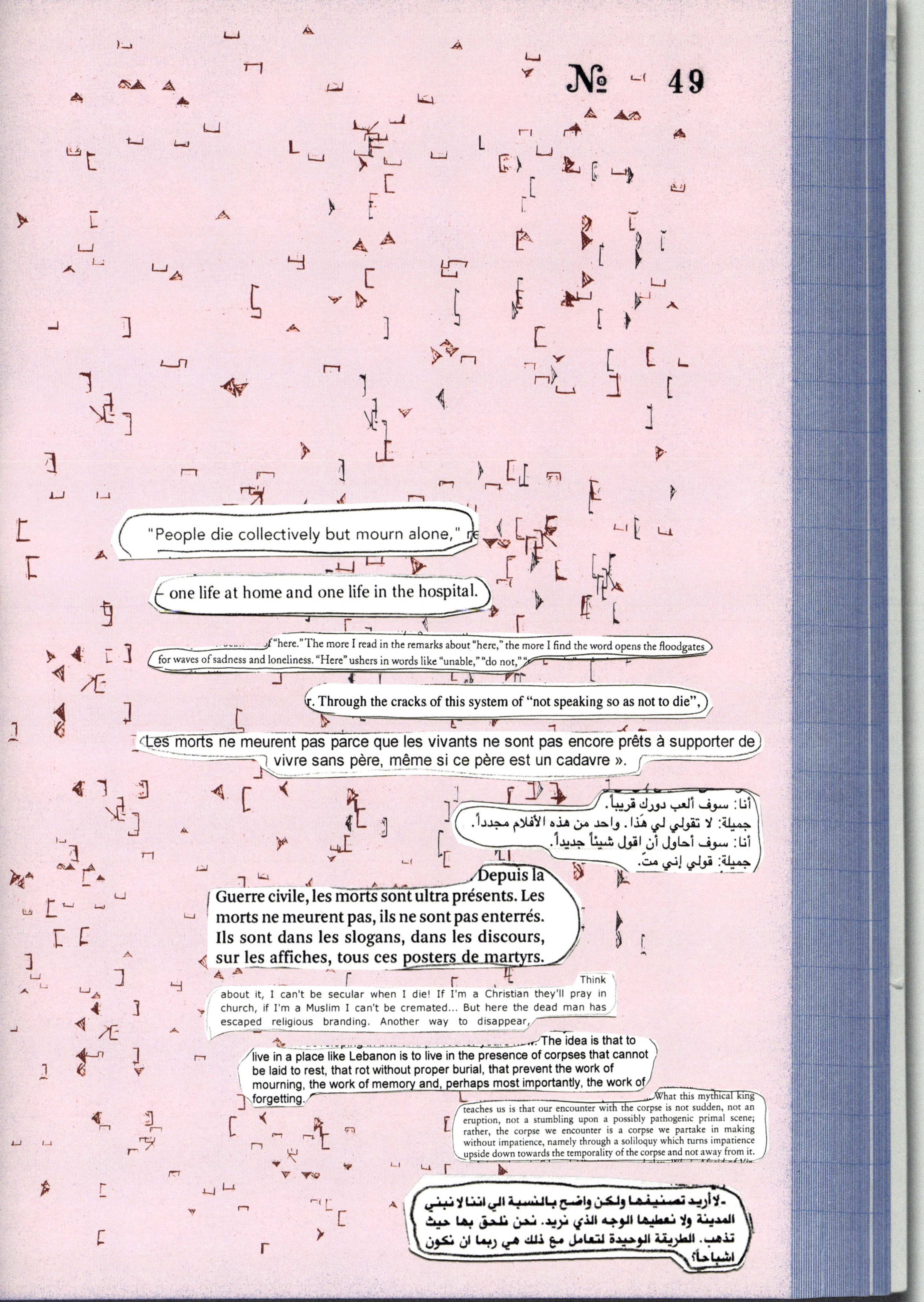
№ 49
"People die collectively but mourn alone,"
one life at home and one life in the hospital.
"here." The more I read in the remarks about "here," the more I find the word opens the floodgates for waves of sadness and loneliness. "Here" ushers in words like "unable," "do not,"
. Through the cracks of this system of "not speaking so as not to die",
Les morts ne meurent pas parce que les vivants ne sont pas encore prêts à supporter de vivre sans père, même si ce père est un cadavre ».
أنا: سوف ألعب دورك قريباً.
جميلة: لا تقولي لي هَذا. واحد من هذه الأفلام مجدداً.
أنا: سوف أحاول أنِ اقول شيئاً جديداً.
جميلة: قولي إني متّ.
Depuis la Guerre civile, les morts sont ultra présents. Les morts ne meurent pas, ils ne sont pas enterrés. Ils sont dans les slogans, dans les discours, sur les affiches, tous ces posters de martyrs.
Think about it, I can't be secular when I die! If I'm a Christian they'll pray in church, if I'm a Muslim I can't be cremated... But here the dead man has escaped religious branding. Another way to disappear,
The idea is that to live in a place like Lebanon is to live in the presence of corpses that cannot be laid to rest, that rot without proper burial, that prevent the work of mourning, the work of memory and, perhaps most importantly, the work of forgetting.
What this mythical king teaches us is that our encounter with the corpse is not sudden, not an eruption, not a stumbling upon a possibly pathogenic primal scene; rather, the corpse we encounter is a corpse we partake in making without impatience, namely through a soliloquy which turns impatience upside down towards the temporality of the corpse and not away from it.
-لاأريد تصنيفها ولكن واضح بالنسبة الي اننا لا نبني المدينة ولا نعطيها الوجه الذي نريد. نحن نلحق بها حيث تذهب. الطريقة الوحيدة لتعامل مع ذلك هي ربما ان نكون اشباحاً؟

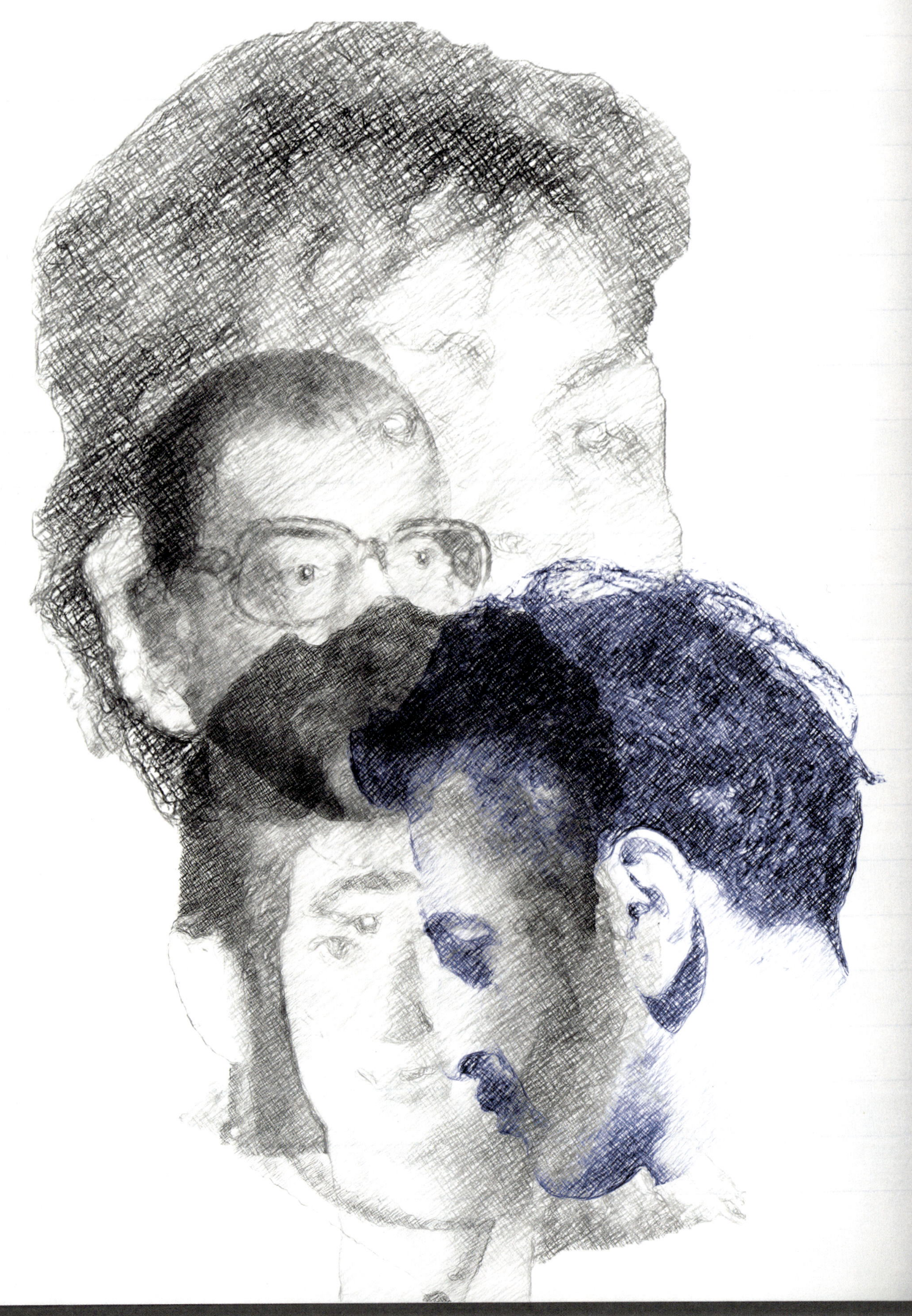

№ 15

art Moreover, portraiture was the first type of "modern" painting to inhabit Lebanon, indeed to form the notion of a nation called Lebanon made up of fully autonomous, rational individuals deserving of nationhood status. Yet since the 1930s, or three-quarters of a century ago, that form of figural painting has fallen completely out of favor to be replaced first by landscapes and types, and later by abstraction

By 2003, one could speak of an inflation concerning contemporary Lebanese art. The contradictions were conspicuous. Lebanese art was marking the calendar of the international art circuit at a time when the socio-political situation in the country was regressing alarmingly. Artists, it seemed, could do nothing

But it's not true. Nobody in the region is supposed to have watched Maya Deren's films when they came out, but they did. The first post-independent films in Algeria? So radical. The first post-independent films in Morocco? Crazy

ذلك الخطّ الصغير الذي يتيح للسطر الواحد أن يتّسع لأربعين كلمة، وللصفحة أن تتّسع لسبعين سطراً هو، في ما يتهيّأ لي، المساوي الشكلي، أو الرمزي، لأن أقول، لنفسي أوّلاً، إن ما أخطّه على الورقة ليس سهل الكتابة، ولا سهل القراءة من ثمّ، ذاك أنّ الخطّ الذي هو غاية في الصغر يتطلبّ إجهاداً للنظر، ينبغي أن يساويه إجهاد مماثل في النظر المقابل، نظر قارئيها

another interview with an artist and art critic, who was a Lebanese nationalist, another art critic and writer who was an Arab nationalist, then became a progressive leftist, a collector who was part of elite ruling Beiruti family but was more interested in Iraqi and Arab art, not Lebanese art, a gallerist whose experience is during the war, which is outside of our time bracket.

Such has certainly been the situation during the past fifty years of interpreting art in Lebanon. "Traditional," "European," "Arab," "universal," "Ottoman," "modern," "Islamic," "nationalist," and "individual" notions of art were called upon by different actors to promote various projects designed to

All signs suggest an imminent flourishing in the study of contemporary Arab art.[1]

Because Lebanon is joining the biennale's national pavilions 112 years into the history of the event - late in the game, as it were - and because it is doing so at a time of grave political crisis in the country - when the concept of the nation has once again been called rather roughly, even violently into question - this exhibition does not seek to represent

"As an artist you do everything in English," "From grant applications to press releases."

Out of Breath

Statements from a round-table discussion between four Lebanese artists and intellectuals

is a visual artist and filmmaker who lives

is the Director of

is the Editor-in-Chief

sits on the editorial board

currenty editing

is a Consulting Editor

is an Advisor to the

Where are the Palestinian painters of the Nakba and Intifada, such as Suleiman Mansour and Ismael Shammout, or the Lebanese artists of Arab nationalism and communism, such as Saloua Raouda Choucair, Aref Rayyes, and Seta Manoukian? The polymaths, Jabra Ibrahim Jabra, Abdel-Rahman Munif, and Fateh Mudarris? Is it that they were asleep

"In Lebanon, for instance," she says, "there's an artist named

Slippery Delays and Optical Mysteries: The Work of Walid Raad

Eva Respini

An encounter with Walid Raad's work can be a profoundly moving experience, shaking the very foundations of what we believe to be true. For Raad, the opposition between fiction and nonfiction does not apply. Fact in his work incorporates fantasy and imagination while fiction is grounded in real events, dates, and statistics. Raad's career thus far has had two main chapters, The Atlas Group (1989–2004) and *Scratching on things I could disavow* (2007–); both are large bodies of work that tell a complex composite truth stretching beyond historical fact, and both rely on storytelling and performance to activate imaginary narratives. In both cases, parsing fact from fiction is beside the point.

Raad was born in Lebanon, a republic whose history since its founding, in 1943, is not taught in its schools, and where, during its sixteen-year Civil War (1975–91), sectarian allegiances changed from one day to the next. Having fled the brutal violence of the war, Raad took to photography and theoretical art discourses as a means to reflect on the lived experience of conflict. Investigating how photographs, moving images, documents, and first-person narratives confer authenticity on official histories, be they histories of war or of art, Raad's work weaves elements of the past, the present, and the future to build narratives that question how history, memory, and geopolitical relationships are constructed. A viewer need not know the history of Lebanon or the Middle East to engage with this art; at its heart is a coming-to-terms with the limits of directly capturing history through images or words.

Perhaps it is more productive to think of Raad's work in terms of its *imaginary* dimensions rather than its *fictive* ones. For Raad, the relationship between image and text is key to unlocking how photographs, videos, and documents occupy the public sphere. He activates this relationship, this interdependence, through wall texts written in the first-person voice or in the guise of an imaginary character. His works are further illuminated by frequent lecture/performances wherein Raad adopts the persona of a scholar or artist. It is through these literary acts—the performance monologue or wall-text narrative—that the work truly comes into its own. In fact, its success hinges on our need to believe in official narratives.

To grasp the complexity of Raad's work, it is worth revisiting his formative cultural and artistic influences. Born in 1967 to a Palestinian mother and a Lebanese father, Raad grew up in predominantly Christian East Beirut. As a teenager, he dreamed of being a photojournalist, and his father gave him his first camera and helped him to build a home darkroom. Raad subscribed to European photography magazines such as *Photo*, *Zoom*, and *Photo Reporter*, where he saw the work of Eugène Atget, Henri Cartier-Bresson, Man Ray, Diane Arbus, and Helmut Newton.[1] The escalating violence of the Lebanese Civil War, especially with Israel's invasion of Lebanon in 1982, led to Raad's emigration the following year to the United States, where he finished high school.

After a brief stint in Boston University's premed program, Raad enrolled in photography courses at the Rochester Institute of

Technology (RIT). He was already deeply aware of photography's tenuous claim to veracity and its power as informational currency:

> You don't do street photography in a city at war. . . . [Doing street photography] assumes that you can stay in one place for 20 minutes, adjust your tripod and ensure that there's no sniper or bomb about to go off nearby. It also assumes that the photograph is neutral, the product of a predominantly aesthetic activity. But in a divided city, it's an intelligence document. Especially when people want information about the other side, taking photographs of buildings, streets or residents is very contentious.[2]

In addition to his photography courses at RIT, and perhaps just as important, Raad took classes in Middle Eastern studies and, in exile, began to gain perspective on the Arab world. Of his earlier education in Beirut, he has said, "I never got to learn anything about the history of the Arab world or the history of Lebanon in a serious way. That training was in the United States."[3]

On leaving RIT, Raad enrolled as a doctoral candidate in visual and cultural studies at the University of Rochester, where he was introduced to semiotics, Marxism, and psychoanalysis and was taught by Kaja Silverman, Douglas Crimp, and Norman Bryson. He also eagerly read the theories of race, sexuality, feminism, and postcolonialism written by Edward Said, Gayatri Spivak, and others. Raad's dissertation focused on the captivity of Western hostages in Lebanon in the 1980s, a topic later developed in his 2001 work *Hostage: The Bachar tapes (English version)* (2001; pp. 90–93). Preparing for the dissertation, Raad honed his research skills, combing through archival documents and congressional testimony on the Iran-Contra affair to analyze the literary dimensions of the writings of those in captivity. Occupied with the demands of a PhD, Raad made little art during this time, but the research skills and theoretical literacy he developed then anticipate the artistic strategies that he employs to this day.

An important influence on Raad's artistic formation was his return to Lebanon after the end of the Civil War. In 1992 he took a break from his studies to live in Lebanon for a year (the most time he had spent at home since leaving) and to collaborate with the Canadian-Lebanese artist Jayce Salloum on the documentary *Up to the South* (1993; fig. 1). He and Salloum conducted interviews with fighters, farmers, workers, and intellectuals who had been actively involved in the resistance against the Israeli occupation of South Lebanon (and who therefore had often been called terrorists). Encountering the nascent postwar Lebanese art scene during this year, Raad met the artist Akram Zaatari (fig. 2) and the writer Jalal Toufic, important influences and future collaborators. Raad is now part of the tight-knit generation of Lebanese artists, architects, and filmmakers, among them Toufic, Zaatari, Tony Chakar, Joana Hadjithomas, Khalil Joreige, Lamia Joreige, Bernard Khoury, Rabih Mroué, Marwan Rechmaoui, Walid Sadek, Ghassan Salhab, Mohamed Soueid, and Lina Saneh, who collectively established

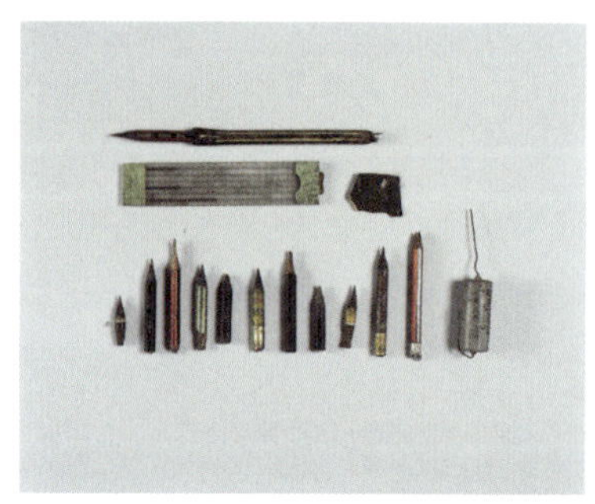

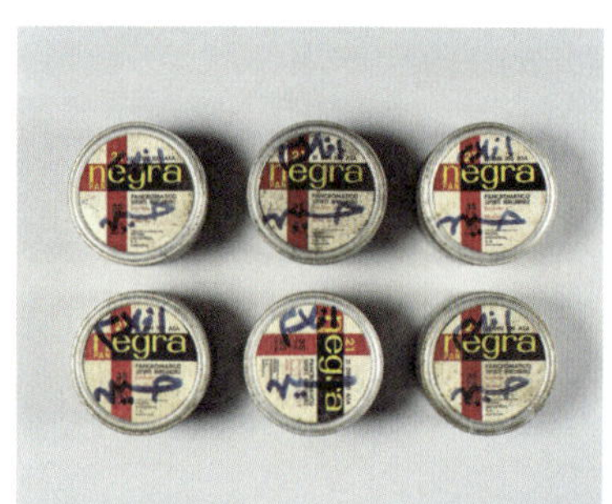

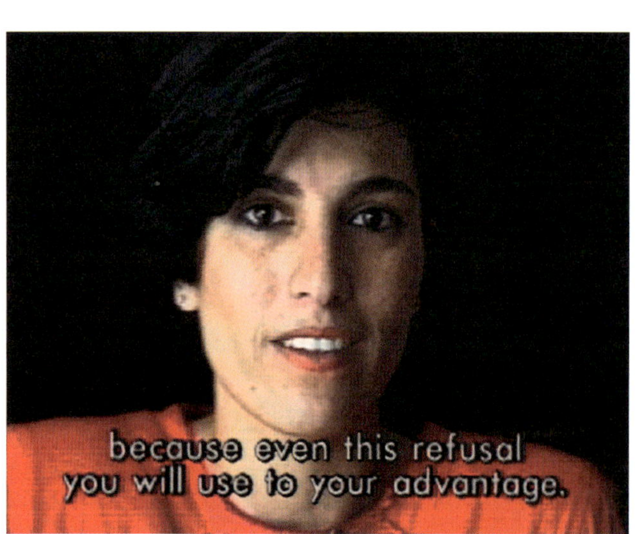

1 Jayce Salloum and Walid Raad. *Up to the South*. 1993. Still from video (color, sound), 1 hour

Beirut as a fertile cultural center in the 1990s.[4] They responded to the aftermath of the war with wide-ranging works probing shared questions about memories, traces, and images of conflict. Khalil Joreige has speculated on these Lebanese artists' fascination with the status of the image: "During the war, every militia had its own media station, television, newspaper or radio. There was a real war of images. Audiences or publics had to learn to deal with these images. We as artists became critical about the use of images. Perhaps interest in art coming from Beirut was due to this sophisticated relationship to images."[5]

The work of many of these Lebanese artists, including Raad, points back to the rich legacy of the twentieth-century artists who explored trauma and memory, from Hannah Höch to Gerhard Richter. Raad's methods are also indebted to Conceptual artists such as Hans Haacke and Michael Asher, to the post-Conceptual inquiries into the lives of institutions exemplified by the work of Ilya Kabakov and Mark Dion, to the postmodern appropriations of Sherrie Levine (fig. 3) and Louise Lawler, and to the performative strategies of Joseph Beuys, Sophie Calle, and others. Raad's formative training in photography, however, is the driving force of his work. He is well versed in the conventions of photographic image-making, and in how those conventions may change or be changed in the aftermath of crisis. His projects continually call into question the still-dominant fiction of photography's objectivity, and insinuate the suspicion that material evidence is insufficient to capture a full understanding of historical events. They extend the same suspicion to other archival materials besides photographs, to the point of generating alternate documents. Beginning in the late 1990s, these strategies, along with a close reading of theory and a quasi-outsider's perspective on the war in Lebanon, coalesced into the fragmentary narratives, documents, and images of the groundbreaking work Raad made under the aegis of The Atlas Group.

The Atlas Group (1989–2004)

It was with The Atlas Group that Raad established the brilliantly daring artistic methodology that he employs to this day. The group presented itself as an organization founded to research and document the contemporary history of Lebanon, specifically the Lebanese Civil War, and as such as maintaining an archive of documents, films, notebooks, photographs, and objects. (Raad himself refers not to the Lebanese Civil War but to the Lebanese civil wars, underscoring the pluralistic nature of the shifting and sometimes conflicting agendas at stake.) Raad, supposedly, was the group's archivist. Each Atlas Group document was attributed to a source, including the colorful historian Dr. Fadl Fakhouri—who, however, was fictional, as was the organization itself.

Raad acknowledged the fictive quality of The Atlas Group from the beginning; in a wall text or performance, for example, he might announce, "We produced and found several documents." (He often uses the plural "we" in discussing The Atlas Group, although he was in fact its sole member.) Yet many failed to perceive or fully grasp the group's imaginary dimension, so

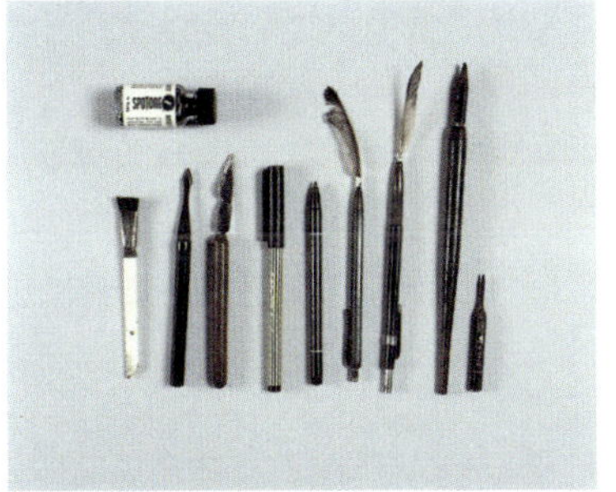
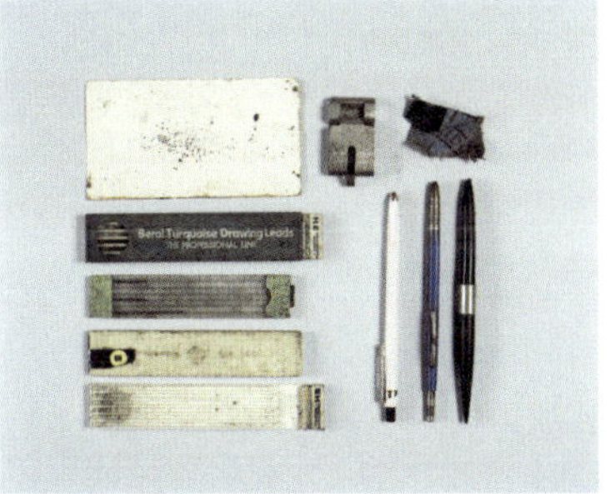
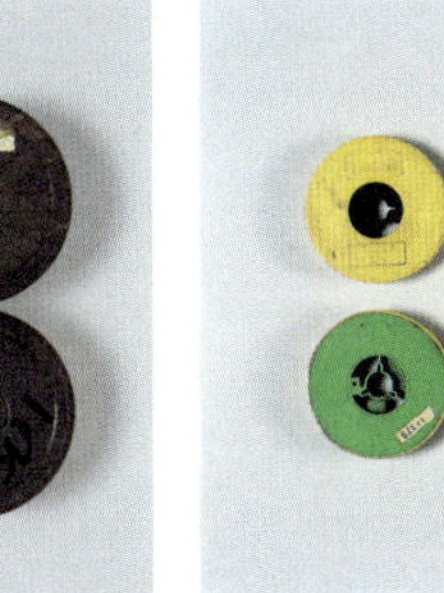
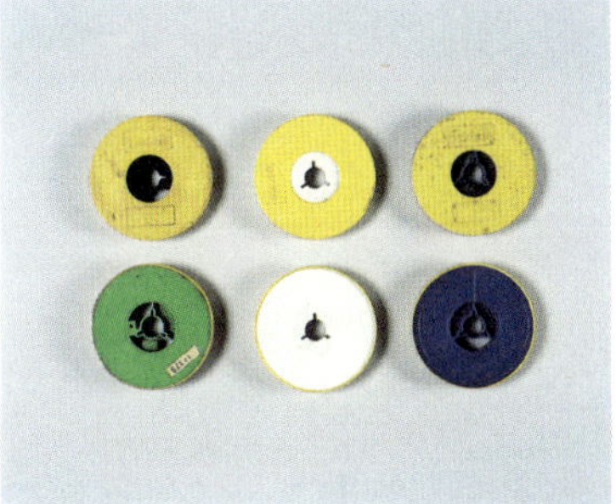

2 Akram Zaatari. *Twenty-Eight Nights and a Poem* (detail). 2010. Twenty-eight chromogenic prints in wooden cabinet, each: 15¾ × 19⁵⁄₁₆" (40 × 49 cm), Super 8 loop, video projection, variable durations

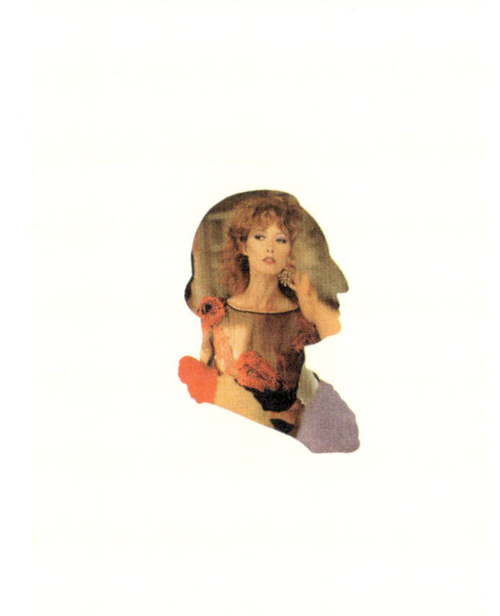

3 Sherrie Levine. *President Collage: 1*. 1979. Cut-and-pasted printed paper on paper, 24 × 18" (61 × 45.7 cm). The Museum of Modern Art, New York. The Judith Rothschild Foundation Contemporary Drawings Collection Gift

strong is our belief in the authority of archives as the repositories of documents that enable and authorize our understanding of history. Raad acknowledges the power of photography's claim to veracity within his own formative training, even while he debunks the fiction of photography's impartiality.[6] Although his intention is not to mislead, the imaginary dimension of his project can be destabilizing. In 2002, at a lecture he gave for the Middle Eastern Studies Association at the CUNY Graduate Center in New York, Raad faced heated questioning from students, and replied, "The Atlas Group proceeds with the consideration that the Lebanese wars are an abstraction. One troubling question is: under what notion of facts can we operate in our construction of 'the history of' the history of Lebanon? How do we approach the facts of the war?"[7] The Atlas Group is less about the Lebanese Civil War than about the limits and possibilities of writing, documenting, and remembering history. Raad's personal experience of the last decade of the war was as an émigré, dealing in partial information, rumor, mediated news reports, and conversations with family members over crackling phone lines. His work is predicated on a reality in which recent events are accessed not only through statistics and facts but equally through experiences, memory, and feelings.

None of the "documents" produced by The Atlas Group is essentially faked: these photographs, texts, and videos are appropriated from original sources, such as newspapers, or from Raad's own street photography. But when Raad rephotographs or scans them and mediates their presentation through story lines, literary titles, narrative wall texts, and engaging performances, they move into the imaginary realm. Raad calls these hybrids "hysterical documents": "they are not based on any one person's actual memories but on 'fantasies erected from the material of collective memories.'"[8] They also look less like documents than like art: featuring formally considered compositions and carefully calibrated colors and marks, each series falls squarely within the legacy of the politically contentious collage and montage aesthetics of Höch and John Heartfield.

Violence is rarely pictured in The Atlas Group archive, which focuses instead on peripheral details such as the gambling habits of historians (*Notebook volume 72: Missing Lebanese wars*, 1989/1998; pp. 60–63). Even human figures are rare, and when they exist, they are microscopic specks in a bucolic landscape (*We are a fair people. We never speak well of one another*, 1994/2013; pp. 102–5). The Atlas Group is seemingly involved in absurdly exhaustive tasks—locating every car bomb detonated during the Civil War, for instance (*My neck is thinner than a hair: Engines*, 1996–2001; pp. 74–77). Serial repetition, a hallmark of the efficiency of photography and the archive, gives way to bizarre and arbitrary obsessions symptomatic of the experiences of war.

Raad's avoidance of overtly picturing violence corresponds to his interest in vernacular photography, such as family albums and commercial studio photography. He was a member of the Beirut-based Arab Image Foundation (AIF), founded in 1997 with the mission of collecting and studying photographs from the Middle East. In 2002, together with Zaatari, a fellow AIF

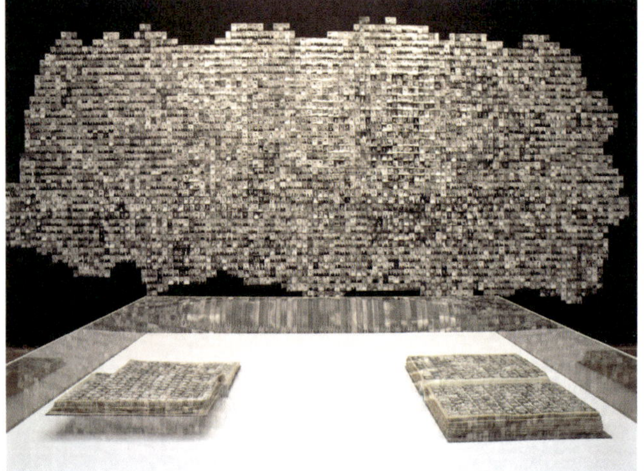

4 Walid Raad, Akram Zaatari, and the Arab Image Foundation. *Mapping Sitting: On Portraiture and Photography*. Installation view, Palais des Beaux-Arts, Brussels, May 4–26, 2002

member, Raad organized the exhibition *Mapping Sitting: On Portraiture and Photography*, drawn from the AIF archive (fig. 4).[9] His interest in the collapse between public and private is reflected in the seemingly superficial, often personal narratives that populate The Atlas Group archives, where they serve as an alternative to the linear construction of the grand historical narrative. The Atlas Group follows the principle that conflict is never a unified entity, and privileges memory and personal experience in the retelling of history.

The Atlas Group takes part in a fertile discourse around the status of the archive. Artists have explored the relationship of photographs to evidence, history, and information since the inception of the medium, but interrogation of the archive, both as subject and format, has intensified in the last two decades, being taken up such artists as Zoe Leonard, Hans-Peter Feldmann, Gerhard Richter, and others. Central to this exploration have been Hal Foster's 2004 article "An Archival Impulse" and Okwui Enwezor's 2008 exhibition *Archive Fever: Uses of the Document in Contemporary Art* at the International Center of Photography, New York, which examined how artists have reinterpreted and appropriated archival documents and systems of organization and logic, ultimately in order to challenge the archive's authority and relevance in the present moment.[10] As Foster points out, this mode of investigation is not new in art,[11] but Raad's work and that of his contemporaries reflect the new realities of the post-Internet age: the easy access to information (if often dubious or unreliable information), the ubiquity of photographic images, the blurring of the distinction between amateur and professional image-makers, and the widespread understanding that any image can be manipulated to support any narrative.

Raad has supplied conflicting narratives about the origins of The Atlas Group, variously describing it as founded by himself or by the Lebanese artist Maha Traboulsi, and in 1967 (Raad's birth year), 1976 (the year after the start of the Civil War), or various years in the 1990s and early 2000s.[12] In fact the group's first incarnations were in "lecture/performances" in Beirut in the late 1990s.[13] Raad was the first artist in Beirut to engage in the format of lecture/performances, which soon became a fertile format for experimentation for a number of artists. Later, Rabih Mroué, who had a background in theater, created lecture/performances that toed the line between fact and fiction, between theater and visual art, bringing this discourse into the realm of theater (fig. 5). At its inception, The Atlas Group archive was virtual, comprising a set of on-screen images that were activated through the performative act of storytelling. The performative element is inscribed in the group's very fabric, from the narratives of the wall texts to the accompanying lecture/performances, which simultaneously illuminate the "documents" and unravel the imaginary dimensions of The Atlas Group.

Raad's performances occur in lecture halls and have been presented in a wide range of contexts, including high-profile art exhibitions such as the Whitney Biennial in New York and documentas 11 and 13 in Kassel, as well as many universities and

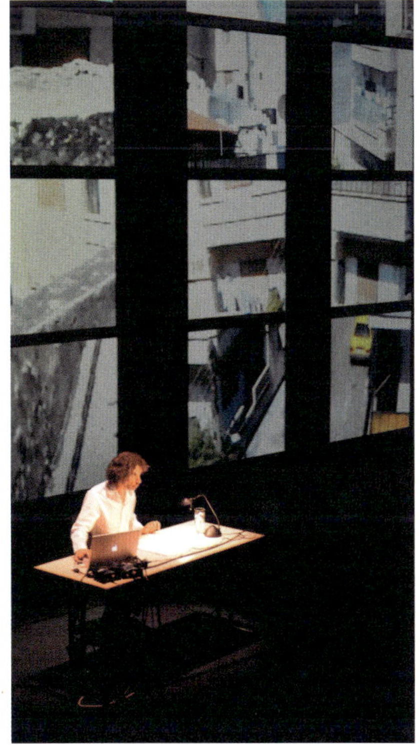

5 Rabih Mroué. *The Pixelated Revolution*. 2012. Nonacademic lecture, dOCUMENTA (13), Kassel, 2012

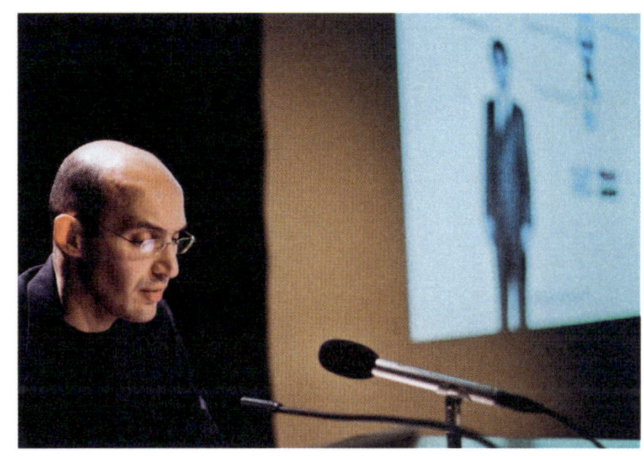

6 Walid Raad. *My neck is thinner than a hair: A history of the car bomb in the 1975–1991 Lebanese Wars_Volume 1*. 2004–5. Performance view, Kunstenfestivaldesarts, Kaaitheater, Brussels, May 12–15, 2004

museums (fig. 6). Presenting himself as an archivist and representative of The Atlas Group, Raad sits at a table furnished with a small lamp, a glass of water, and a laptop computer that he uses to project PowerPoint images onto a screen. The images include handsome diagrams of The Atlas Group's document categorization system as well as the documents themselves. The presentation may sometimes be interrupted by (staged) technical difficulties, and may be followed by an awkward question-and-answer session with the audience, often featuring planted questioners. The legitimacy and authority of the scholar persona are paramount: Raad follows a respectable dress code (dark suit, wire-rimmed glasses) and stages the lecture apparatus carefully. As the performance historian André Lepecki has observed, he also carefully calibrates his Lebanese accent, making it more pronounced over the course of the lecture.[14] The familiar presentation format and staging are upended by Raad's admission at the beginning of the lecture that The Atlas Group is an imaginary organization. But while he clearly distinguishes between documents that he has produced and those attributed to individuals he acknowledges are imaginary, his scholarly authority is such, and the stories of his characters and documents are so compelling, that audiences often fail to hear, or grasp, the imaginary dimensions of the project.

Raad's PhD curriculum at the University of Rochester, like that of American graduate programs in the humanities generally, emphasized spoken and written language as a means of synthesizing and articulating ideas, and he also teaches in the university and art school contexts. The lecture format is part of the very fabric of his art. If his work as The Atlas Group is to be fully appreciated, performance must be recognized as not ancillary to it but central. His performances, with their literary titles, colorful characters, diversions, digressions, and self-referential texts and images, work to demonstrate that the construction of history is unstable, being open to interpretive invention. These lectures can be understood as a performance of memory on levels personal, national, and historiographic. The slippage between authenticity and imagination, the academic decoding of stories and archival documents, is at turns probing, absorbing, and confounding, and resonates deeply with our own experiences of remembering and understanding the images, documents, and stories that are integral to our own lived experiences.

A number of Atlas Group works are attributed to a Dr. Fadl Fakhouri, including *Notebook volume 72: Missing Lebanese wars*, *Notebook volume 38: Already been in a lake of fire* (1991/2003; pp. 84–89), and *Miraculous beginnings/No, illness is neither here nor there* (1993/2003; pp. 68–69). Dr. Fakhouri, an esteemed, recently deceased, fictional historian of the Lebanese Civil War whose papers were donated to The Atlas Group, lends the project an authenticity not typically afforded to artists—yet despite the meticulousness of his documents, an arbitrariness is inscribed within the structure of his authority. Dr. Fakhouri was an avid gambler who filled notebooks with such banal details as the particulars of the bets he placed with fellow

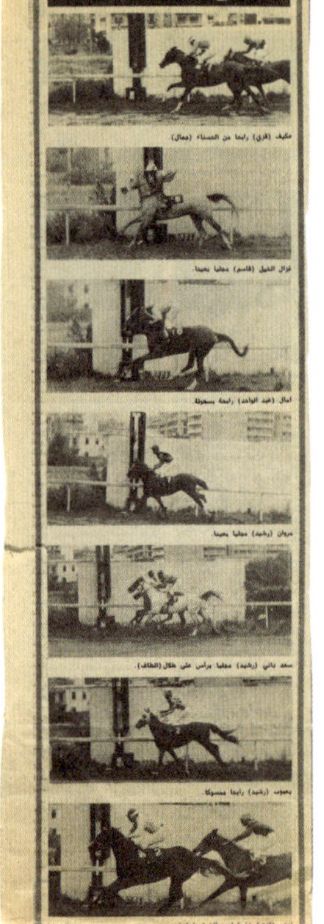
نتائج سباق الخيل

7 Clipping from the Lebanese newspaper *An-Nahar*. N.d.

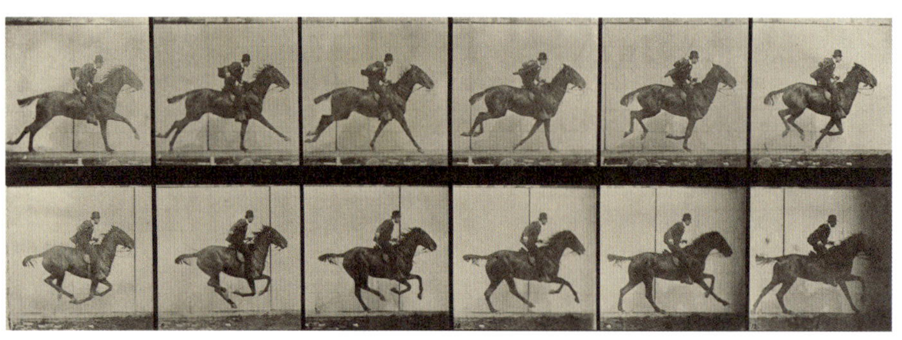

8 Eadweard J. Muybridge. *"Daisy" Galloping, Saddled: Plate 624 from Animal Locomotion (1887)*. 1884–86. Collotype, 5 15/16 × 16 7/8" (15.1 × 42.9 cm). The Museum of Modern Art, New York. Gift of the Philadelphia Commercial Museum

historians who gathered on Sundays at the track.[15] They wagered not on which horse would win, but on a particular margin of error—that is, by how many fractions of a second the track's photographer would miss the exact moment when the animal crossed the finish line. Dr. Fakhouri's lined notepads feature a neatly pasted photograph of one race's winning horse, clipped from the daily newspaper *An-Nahar*; details of the race's distance and duration; and anecdotal descriptions of the historian who won the bet that day ("He was the thief who at night hugs the walls as he walks home. He was the one who said he will not die with his throat cut").[16] *An-Nahar*, a source that Raad continues to use often (in *My neck is thinner than a hair: Engines*, for example), is itself a site for suspicion, since during the Civil War, Lebanon's various militias often used the country's newspapers for propaganda purposes. The photographs in *Notebook volume 72* were indeed clipped from the paper, but years after the war (fig. 7).[17] Raad's project questions the authority ascribed to legitimate sources of information (the newspaper), the arbiters of history (the historian), and the tool that often bears witness (the camera).

Notebook volume 72 details an avoidance of the facts of a singular moment. Rather than bet on the win, the historians bet on the inaccuracy of representation and photography's failure to make crucial events visible. Eadweard Muybridge's famous photographic sequence of a galloping horse (fig. 8), also the result of a wager, was an exercise in proof: his photographs confirmed what the naked eye could not see—that all four of the horse's hooves left the ground at full gallop. Muybridge's photographs showed what *happened*. The photographs in Dr. Fakhouri's notebooks, however, don't show that at all. The images are delayed, and the crucial moment of winning remains unrecorded, unseen, missing. Fakhouri's notebooks are incapable of describing the "decisive moment," the phrase made famous by the celebrated photojournalist Henri Cartier-Bresson. For Raad, this inability is analogous to the limitations of accurately documenting histories of conflict. The viewer's attention is shifted from the center of events (that is, the photo finish) to the margins, underscored by the copious notes in the work's margins. By highlighting what was not there, Raad exposes the gap between an event and the report of it, between an incident and the history written about it.

Another work attributed to Dr. Fakhouri is *Civilizationally, we do not dig holes to bury ourselves* (1958–59/2003; pp. 52–55), a series of small black and white photographs purportedly taken by the scholar during his first and only trip to Europe, in the late 1950s. These self-portraits capture the lone Fakhouri lounging in the hotel rooms, reading in the cafés, and viewing the tourist sites of Paris and Rome. The images being repurposed from family snapshots, the subject is actually Raad's father. The meshing of personal and private through the apparatus of an archive recalls a project by artist Zoe Leonard, *The Fae Richards Photo Archive* (1993–96; fig. 9), about the life of a fictitious African-American starlet of the 1930s who is documented in "vintage" headshots and stills. Conceived as a way

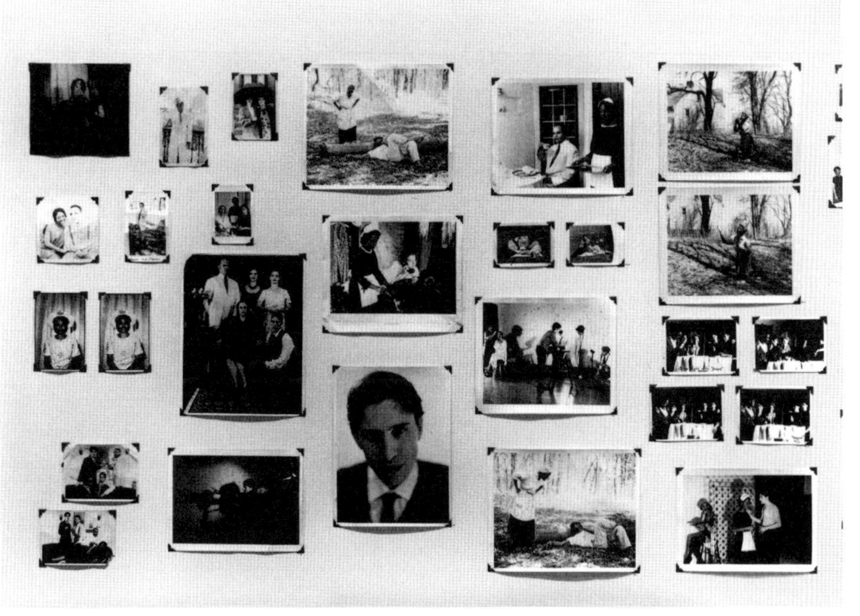

9 Zoe Leonard. *The Fae Richards Photo Archive*. 1993–96. Installation view, Whitney Museum of American Art, New York. Whitney Museum of American Art, New York. Purchase, with funds from the Contemporary Painting and Sculpture Committee and the Photography Committee

to write an unwritten history, the project was created for *The Watermelon Woman* (1996), by filmmaker Cheryl Dunye, who has said that it "came from the real lack of any information about the lesbian and film history of African-American women. Since it wasn't happening, I invented it."[18] Raad similarly uses the conventions of the photographic archive and the family album to create a plausible narrative for Dr. Fakhouri, a historian of the Lebanese Civil War active at a time when such figures were rare or nonexistent.

Not all of The Atlas Group's documents are attributed to invented characters. *Let's be honest, the weather helped* (1998/2006; pp. 78–83) comprises images of notebook pages featuring black-and-white photographs that Raad himself took in Beirut during the Civil War. These images of pockmarked buildings and bombed-out neighborhoods are overlaid with different-sized colored disks that map bullets and shrapnel left after bombings and battles, again collected by Raad himself as a child in Beirut. The colors are linked to the national origins of the ammunitions: in the accompanying text, Raad explains, "It took me ten years to realize that ammunition manufacturers follow distinct color codes to mark and identify their cartridges and shells. It also took me another ten years to realize that my notebooks in part catalogue seventeen countries and organizations that continue to supply the various militias and armies fighting in Lebanon." An upsetting of expected timelines through delays and absences permeates much of Raad's work: whether he took the photographs when he collected the shrapnel or later, and whether the photographs represent the actual places where he collected it, are unimportant. The dating of The Atlas Group works share in this temporal disruption: each work has two dates, the first a fictional, attributed date, the second the actual production date. The first of these dates may go back as far as the 1950s, although the group was not founded, or Raad's project begun, until 1998. Similarly, although 2004 is given as The Atlas Group's end date, Raad has made later works attributed to it (*We are a fair people . . .* , for example), has *pre*dated works, and has on occasion changed the dates of works even after they were published or exhibited. The collapse of past, present, and future in Raad's "documents" is one signal that they cannot be readily consumed as records of past events.

Let's be honest . . . draws from the rich photographic tradition of the documentary survey, most notably Eugène Atget's record of old Paris (fig. 10), made in the late nineteenth and early twentieth centuries. Atget produced thousands of photographs bearing witness to the streets and locales that were disappearing under Baron Haussmann's modernization of Paris. Although made for commercial purposes (the pictures were offered for sale to artists, artisans, and architects), these photographs fascinated the Surrealists and are precursors to the work of August Sander, Walker Evans, and Bernd and Hilla Becher, whose various projects ambitiously catalogue types of people and buildings. Raad's alignment of *Let's be honest . . .* with a recognizable documentary mode gives it an assumption

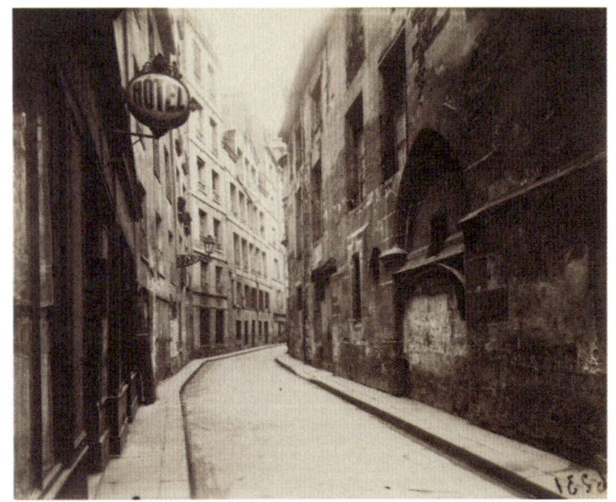

10 Eugène Atget. *Rue de l'Hôtel de Ville*. 1921. Albumen silver print, $6\frac{15}{16} \times 8\frac{11}{16}$" (17.6 × 22.1 cm). The Museum of Modern Art, New York. Abbott-Levy Collection. Partial gift of Shirley C. Burden

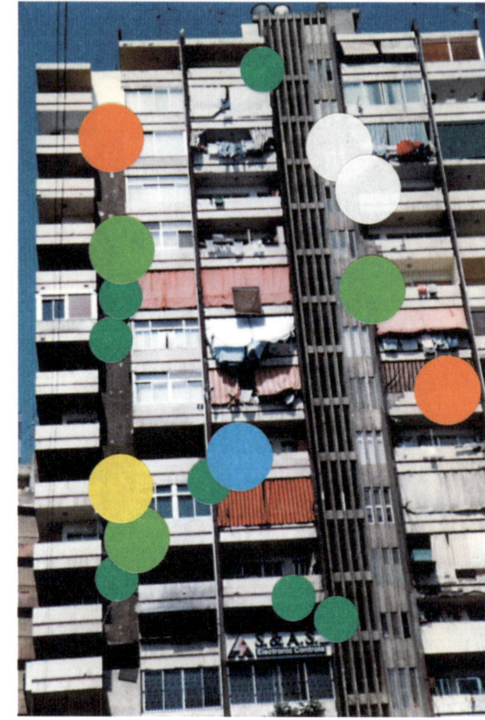

11 Walid Raad. Study for *Let's be honest, the weather helped*. 2000. Color photograph and pressure-sensitive stickers, $4\frac{15}{16} \times 3\frac{3}{8}$" (12.5 × 8.6 cm)

of indexicality. He first produced these works as analogue collages, applying colorful stickers to his street photographs (fig. 11), and then eventually began to develop them as digital images. The formal, almost abstract compositions of the brightly colored disks recall the conceptual works of John Baldessari (fig. 12), who has long added colored disks to the surfaces of found photographs—a humorous punctuation that alters the meaning and role of these ordinary pictures in the cultural realm. The colored disks in Raad's *Let's be honest . . .* similarly introduce a different kind of visual narrative from the documentary mode, one that is more expressive, poetic, even illogical.

The seemingly arbitrary title *Let's be honest, the weather helped* also undermines the claim to veracity inscribed in the work. The weather is a recurring motif for The Atlas Group; the banal staple of small talk, it is neutral and acts as an equalizer, circumscribing the direct address of violence.[19] During Israel's attack on Lebanon in 2006, when Raad and his family ensconced themselves in their home in the Lebanese mountains, he wrote to a friend, "I just woke up and the weather in the mountains is beautiful. Eastern winds have cleared the air all around. It is just beautiful here. The weather again: the best way to naturalize a disaster, to think of something else to write, to think, and to feel."[20]

The weather also plays a role in *Hostage: The Bachar tapes (English version)*. This Atlas Group video focuses on Souheil Bachar, a fictional Lebanese national who, we learn from his testimony, was held hostage in Lebanon in the 1980s and early '90s alongside five Americans—Terry Anderson, Thomas Sutherland, Benjamin Weir, Lawrence Martin Jenco, and David Jacobsen, all actual abductees in Lebanon during that period, kidnapped by the Islamic Jihad group. At least one early U.S. reviewer of *Hostage . . .* speculated about whether Bachar was a real person, but this would not have happened in Lebanon, for he was played by a Lebanese actor well-known and recognizable there.[21] In the video, Bachar notes that all five Americans wrote memoirs of their time in captivity and each began by mentioning the weather. The sea too plays a role: Bachar asks that the subtitles translating his Arabic be shown against a background blue like the Mediterranean (fig. 13), and the video ends with a montage of the sea's crashing waves, with Bachar gazing out at them. The legendary beauty of Lebanon's Mediterranean coast must have made the violence of the Civil War even more incomprehensible as it played out against that backdrop.[22]

Beginning as research for Raad's doctoral dissertation, *Hostage . . .* evolved into an artwork setting imaginary narratives against real historical events. Bachar's testimony, which takes place in a nondescript room with a pinned-up sheet as a backdrop, and with a camera that seems to have been set up on a tripod by either Bachar or his captors, is interspliced with footage of U.S. President Ronald Reagan speaking from the Oval Office and of Oliver North at the Iran-Contra trial. To accompany this found footage an offscreen narrator describes

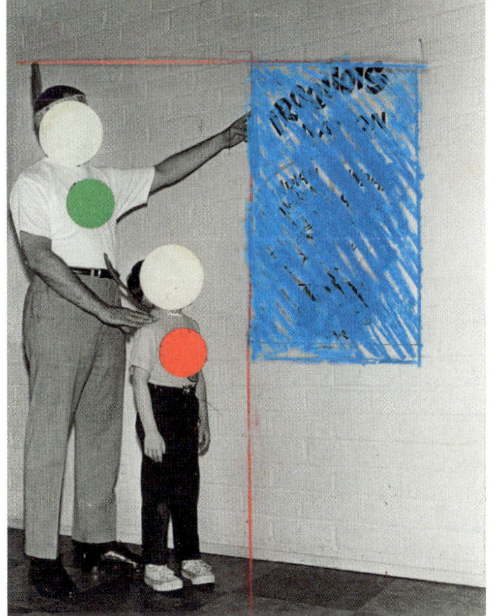

12 John Baldessari. *Untitled*. 1986. Crayon and pressure-sensitive stickers on synthetic polymer sheet overlay on gelatin silver print, 9¾ × 7⅜" (24.8 × 18.7 cm). The Museum of Modern Art, New York. Gift of Brooke Alexander and of the artist

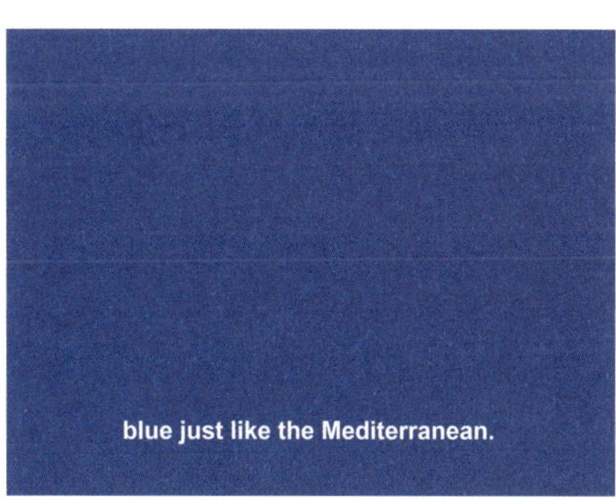

13 Walid Raad. *Hostage: The Bachar tapes (English version)*. 2001. Stills from video (color, sound), 16:17 min. The Museum of Modern Art, New York. Gift of the Jerome Foundation in honor of its founder, Jerome Hill

the kidnappings and their relation to Iran-Contra. Meanwhile there are many ways in which Bachar's story breaks from the published accounts: he describes homoerotic activities on the part of the captives, for instance, that are not known to have taken place. If the hostages' own published accounts constitute the "official" narratives of their captivity, Bachar offers an alternate point of view, challenging their authority and the subjective points of view embedded in such documents.

While researching *Up to the South*, Raad viewed videotapes made by resistance fighters preparing to die—tapes, the artist notes, that often include multiple takes of the same scripted speech.[23] The *Hostage . . .* video evokes these tapes in being frequently interrupted by video noise, bands of color, and other technical disruptions that lend authenticity to its DIY quality. At the same time, though, this noise has its own formal beauty, and further destabilizes the narrative by offering visual breaks in an apparently plausible story. The claim to authority is key to Raad's imaginary documents and characters: just as Dr. Fakhouri lent authority to the archival activities of The Atlas Group, Bachar's firsthand experience as a hostage is necessary to make his account of it convincing.

Secrets in the open sea (1994/2004; pp. 70–73) addresses loss and disappearance through the brilliant blue of the Mediterranean. This is a group of large photographs, supposedly found in a pile of rubble in Beirut in 1993, that appear at first to be monochromes—variations of the color blue—but on close inspection reveal in their margins small black-and-white portraits of individuals who, an accompanying text notes, had drowned, died, or been found dead in the Mediterranean between 1975 and 1991. In fact these group portraits come from newspapers that had originally identified their subjects as attendees at innocuous gatherings such as corporate board meetings.[24] The presence of hidden data beneath the surface of a monochrome recalls On Kawara's monochromatic date paintings, which are linked to world events that are typically invisible to viewers, as the box that houses each painting is lined with the local newspaper for the day the work was made (fig. 14). Similarly, the hidden narratives in Raad's art destabilize our certainty about what we understand to be facts, and ultimately about what we are seeing.

Secrets in the open sea plays deftly on the associations of the color blue, including, as curator Achim Borchardt-Hume writes, "its symbolism of promise (a bright blue sky on a sunny day), neutrality (the helmets of the NATO peace-keeping forces in the Middle East), and Romantic longing (Novalis's blue flower)."[25] Blue is also the hue of a lost or dead video signal. Raad has long been fascinated with color; as a student in Rochester, he was the chemical technician in the school's darkroom and made monochromatic prints there as a personal project, experimenting with the variables affecting the reproduction of colors on photographic papers. At the time, he was also viewing iconic works in the photograph collection of George Eastman House and modernist paintings in Buffalo's Albright-Knox Art Gallery, encounters, he remembers, that along with

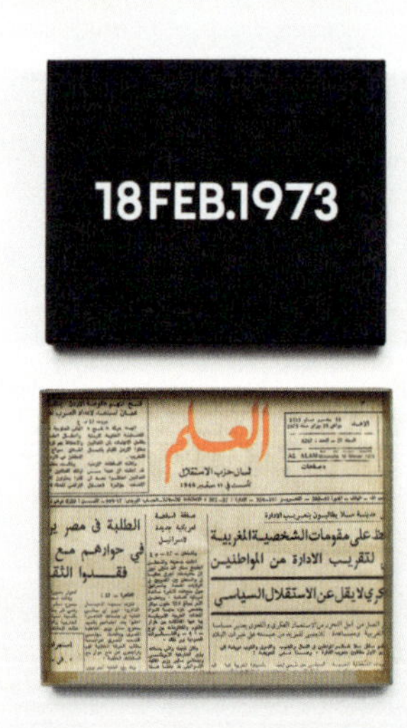

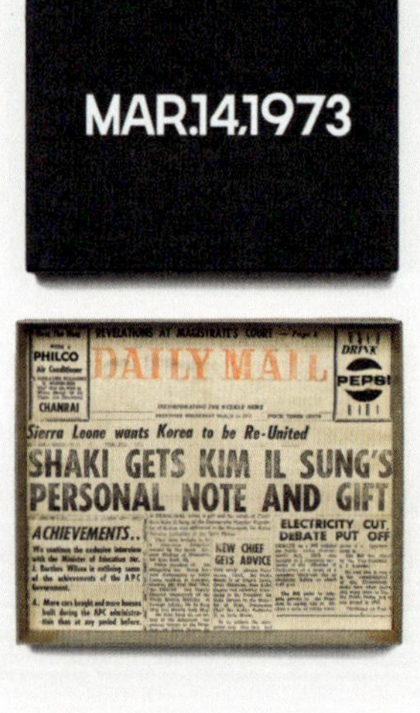

14 On Kawara. Left: *18 FEB. 1973.* "Dimanco." Right: *MAR. 14, 1973.* "Wednesday." Both 1973. Both from the Today series, 1966–2013. Both acrylic on canvas, 8 × 10" (20.3 × 25.4 cm), accompanied by artist-made box and corresponding newspaper clipping

> the daily phone calls to Beirut must have combined into a potent cocktail that, at the time, failed to blend smoothly with the chemical and optical experiments unfolding in my darkroom. For some time, the experiences sat on top of the other, like oil on water. It took another fifteen years for the blend to mix in such works as *Secrets in the open sea*, *We decided to let them say "we are convinced" twice . . .* , and *Let's be honest, the weather helped*.[26]

For Raad, color—and specifically the monochrome—is a way to experience war from a distance.

The Atlas Group gives rise to many shifting chronologies, from the various accounts of its founding to its official conclusion, in 2004. Although Raad has begun to exhibit this body of work as if it were completed, he has revisited the project in recent years, producing new works attributed to the organization. *We are a fair people . . .* is a recent series of color photographs enlarged from slides, their golden palette evoking the 1960s. The original photographs were taken by a relative of Raad's who had traveled the scenic countryside of Lebanon and Syria before the Lebanese Civil War. Into these color images Raad has collaged found black-and-white newspaper photos of militia leaders assassinated or murdered during the Lebanese Civil War, tiny pictures well hidden within the surrounding bucolic landscapes and archaeological sites. Embedded in these works is a sense of unease—something is not quite right. The rough outlines of the collaged elements are a far cry from the seamless Photoshop techniques of today, and the shift in scale between the bodies and the landscape is jarring. What has led Raad to reopen The Atlas Group? Can it be the ongoing civil war in Syria, the deepening crisis in Gaza, or the broadcasting of the increasing violence of ISIS? Although Raad avoids commenting on specific events, at a time of escalating conflict in the Middle East and at home *We are a fair people . . .* signals the continuing importance of investigating the ways in which violence and its image affect our reading and understanding of both historical and current affairs.

Scratching on things I could disavow (2007–)

Scratching on things I could disavow, which Raad began in 2007, is an interrelated series of photographs, videos, sculptures, installations, and performances.[27] While each of the several series within this various and all-encompassing body of work stands individually, taken together they constitute an examination of how art history is being forged within the new infrastructures for art in the Arab world—Abu Dhabi's Saadiyat Island, for example, which will soon house several world-class museums, including branches of the Louvre and Guggenheim, designed by international architects Frank Gehry, Jean Nouvel, Zaha Hadid, and Tadao Ando. New museums, biennials, and galleries are also proliferating in Beirut, Doha, Dubai, Saudi Arabia, and Sharjah. While *Scratching . . .* may seem a departure from the Atlas Group project, in both Raad uses literary and imaginative means to reimagine a history set against the background of the geopolitical, economic, and military conflicts that have shaped the Middle East.

Where The Atlas Group appropriated the logic and look of the archive, *Scratching . . .* takes a more digressive and poetic approach. The methodologies of The Atlas Group, systematic, serial, and repetitive, are supplanted by more subjective relationships. None of the works are presented in grids, as they are in The Atlas Group; the works are all different sizes and no two structures are the same. If in The Atlas Group Raad appropriated the authority of the archive to probe how history is written, read, and remembered, his new line of inquiry uses the conventions of the museum display and the authority of the curatorial voice to introduce a performative space for art.

Performance is the central axis around which *Scratching . . .* revolves—indeed the overall body of work includes a performance, *Scratching on things I could disavow: Walkthrough*, that shares its title. That performance, which is scheduled regularly throughout the run of the MoMA exhibition that this book accompanies, takes the form of a gallery talk, in MoMA's case accommodating forty to fifty visitors who sit on the small stools that the Museum's educators use to seat attendees at their lectures. For this presentation Raad has devised five platform stages, each with a floor based on that of a different art space, ranging from the poured concrete of a contemporary art gallery to a herringbone wood-parquet motif at New York's Metropolitan Museum of Art. The artworks on these stages—the exhibition's galleries—function like props, signaling that the art is just one part of a larger performative project; and the stages are installed in MoMA's Marron Atrium, where they can be viewed from above by visitors to that space's various catwalks, which come to resemble balconies at a theater (fig. 15). Raad's careful delivery, dramatic staging, and the performance's narrative arc are intensely theatrical. He forbids the recording of his performances, for their success, as in theater, relies on the performer's live presence.[28]

The performance begins in front of Raad's video installation *Translator's introduction: Pension arts in Dubai* (2012; pp. 114–21), where the artist launches into an overview of the complex structure of the Artist Pension Trust (APT), a real organization that signals a significant shift in the collection of art and in the speculative practices of the art market. The installation includes a digitally animated chart recalling the famous chart of the development of modern art that Alfred H. Barr, Jr., the founding director of MoMA, published in 1936, as well as later precedents such as Hans Haacke's *Shapolsky et al. Manhattan Real Estate Holdings, a Real-Time Social System, as of May 1, 1971* (1971; fig. 16).[29] Like Haacke's work, Raad's APT chart attempts to track and expose the control of assets, but his diagram is an exercise in digression and uncertainty, and he explicates it like an investigative journalist or even a conspiracy theorist. He next invites his audience to move to another "gallery," where, by tapping his cell phone, he makes the lights fade in one area and come up in another, signaling a new act. His monologue now turns bizarre, as he recounts how an unnamed Arab is physically

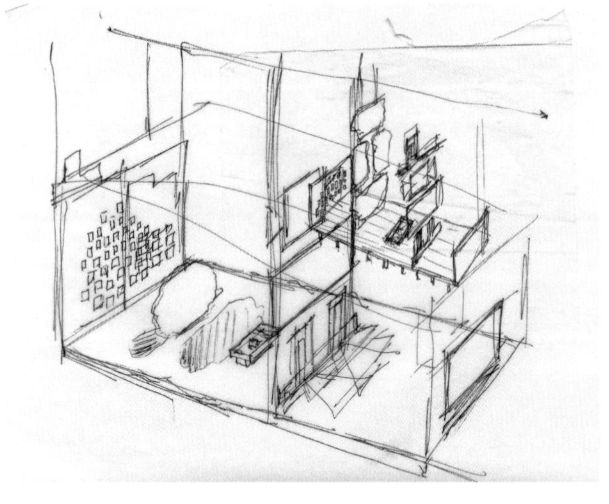

15 Walid Raad. Sketch for *Walkthrough*. 2013. Ink on tracing paper, 8½ × 7" (21.6 × 17.8 cm)

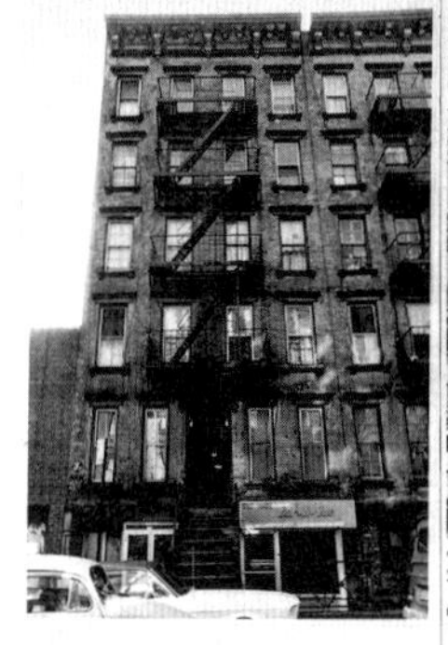

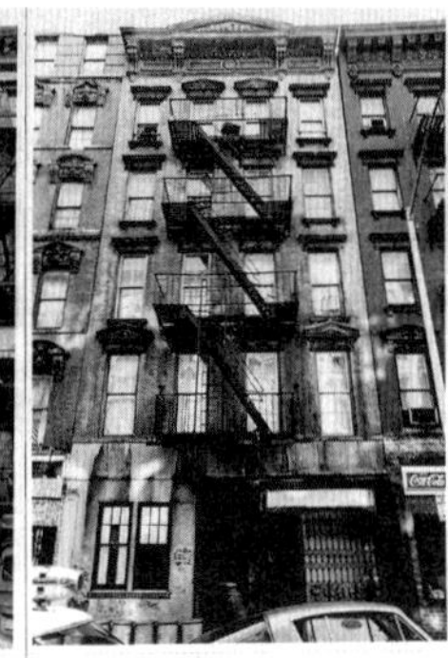

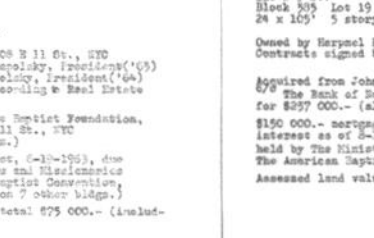

16 Hans Haacke. *Shapolsky et al. Manhattan Real Estate Holdings, a Real-Time Social System, as of May 1, 1971*. 1971 (detail). 2 photo-enlarged maps, each 24 × 20" (61 × 50.8 cm); 142 black-and-white photographs, each 10 × 8" (25.4 × 20.3 cm); 142 typewritten sheets, each 10 × 8" (25.4 × 20.3 cm); 6 charts, each 24 × 20" (61 × 50.8); one explanatory panel, 24 × 20" (61 × 50.8 cm). Whitney Museum of American Art, New York. Purchased jointly by the Whitney Museum of American Art, New York, with funds from the Director's Discretionary Fund and the Painting and Sculpture Committee, and the Fundació Museu d'Art Contemporani de Barcelona

incapable of entering a new museum built at some as yet undefined time in the next ten years (here he focuses our attention on *Section 88_ACT XXXI: Views from outer to inner compartments,* 2010; pp. 122–25) and matter-of-factly reveals that he has received information telepathically from artists in the future (*Index XXVI: Red, blue, black, orange, yellow*, 2010; pp. 132–37).

A number of artists have used the gallery-talk format, perhaps most famously Andrea Fraser, in her fictional persona as a museum docent (fig. 17).[30] Like Raad, Fraser plays with museum practices as a way to question their authority. Where Fraser's work is the talk itself, though (and its reperformance through live and recorded means), Raad's is one part of a complex network of elements (wall color, wall texts, lights, floors). Like his Atlas Group lectures, the *Scratching . . .* performance unlocks the meaning of all of the works that constitute the series.

Scratching . . . is marked by narratives of absence and withdrawal—the shrinking of works of art (*Section 139: The Atlas Group (1989–2004)*, 2008; pp. 128–31), for instance, or their changing over time (*Preface to the third edition*, 2013; pp. 150–51), or empty museum spaces with unenterable doorways (*Section 88: Views from outer to inner compartments*, 2010; pp. 126–27). The idea of withdrawal is inspired by Toufic's concept of "the withdrawing of tradition past a surpassing disaster," as elaborated in his book of the same title.[31] Toufic posits that there are events (the dropping of the atomic bomb on Hiroshima, for example) so devastating that their impact causes certain cultural artifacts—that is, artworks—to "withdraw" (which occasionally means that they become unavailable). Raad, who in *Scratching . . .* seems more like a spiritual medium, or the narrator of a play, than like the scholarly historian of The Atlas Group, for his part creates scenarios wherein works of art are no longer fully available to be seen, read, or experienced.

The recent history of the Middle East has marked the cultural realm with startling violence. In Baghdad in 2003, the National Museum was ransacked and priceless cultural artifacts were lost after the collapse of the regime of Saddam Hussein. In Cairo in 2011, the Museum of Egyptian Antiquities in Tahrir Square was looted during the Arab Spring. In 2013, the minaret of the Great Mosque at Aleppo was destroyed during the Syrian Civil War, and more recently, ISIS forces in northern Iraq have destroyed Shia shrines, Sufi sites, and Mesopotamian relics. This kind of violence affects not only historical sites and institutions but the study of recent art history, particularly of Arab modernism, which flourished in centers like Damascus and Baghdad, where the first Arab biennial was presented in 1974. In the current environment, art historians must struggle to gain access to artworks, documents, and archival materials essential to write the history of the Arab art of the twentieth century.

Recognizing that these realities demand new modes of display and content formation, Raad proposes scenarios that make even extant artworks appear in some ways unavailable to those standing in front of them. *Section 139: The Atlas Group (1989–2004)*, for example, is a retrospective of the works of The Atlas Group, but they are scaled down and installed in a gallery

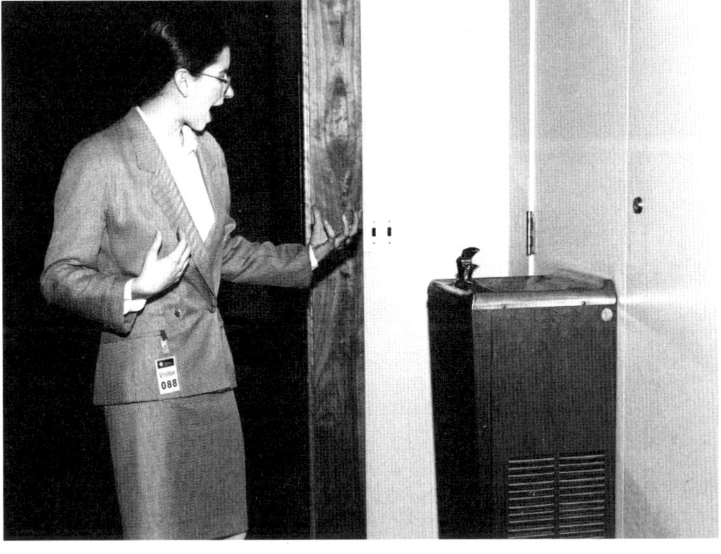

17 Andrea Fraser. *Museum Highlights: A Gallery Talk*. 1989. Performance view, Philadelphia Museum of Art, 1989

model small enough to be unenterable. The accompanying text explains that in 2008, after agreeing to exhibit in a chic new white-cube gallery in Beirut (in the neighborhood of Karantina, site of one of the deadliest massacres of the Lebanese Civil War), Raad found that his works had shrunk to 1/100th of their original size. He insists, though, that the works on view are not miniatures:

> These artworks shrunk once they entered the space. Why, I don't know. Sometimes artists encounter their own works, concepts or forms, and they're no longer available to them. They appear distorted. Something about Beirut's time and space makes an artwork shrink and inaccessible to the artist. This is not a psychological encounter, nor is it a metaphor for some condition.[32]

Museums, galleries, and artists often use architectural models and scaled-down artworks to plan exhibition layouts (including those of Raad's survey at MoMA) before installing them. *Section 139*, though, does not prefigure The Atlas Group but comes after it—it is a literally miniature retrospective of a kind. As such it recalls Marcel Duchamp's *Boîte en valise* (Box in a suitcase, 1935–41; fig. 18), in which the artist reproduced over sixty of his own works at a reduced scale. In *Section 139* Raad re-created his own artworks equally faithfully, down to the videos, which play in the model. Even the frames of the photographs are as meticulously reproduced as the images themselves. Like Duchamp, Raad constructed a mobile museum of his own work, and like the valise, *Section 139* exists in multiple editions, in this case five, so that an Atlas Group retrospective could be theoretically mounted in five different locations simultaneously.

While *Scratching . . .* is grounded in the present conditions of the Middle East, its roots lie in the Conceptual and post-Conceptual art that investigated the legitimacy and relevance of the art museum by appropriating and altering conventional museum practices and modes of display. Perhaps the most famous example is Marcel Broodthaers's *Musée d'Art Moderne, Département des Aigles* (1968–72; fig. 19), an art museum with neither a collection nor a permanent site that appeared in pop-up locations between 1968 and 1971, when it was offered for sale (no buyers were found). Like Broodthaers, Raad adapts the apparatus of the museum display—silkscreen wall texts, the white-cube gallery space, the gallery talk, carefully considered frames and lighting—in order to lean on and play with the authority of the museum.

Scratching . . . should also be considered alongside architects' imaginings of what civic institutions might look like in the future—visionary projects such as the Japanese Metabolism movement's models for living after the devastation of World War II, and Lina Bo Bardi's projects during the period of the military dictatorship that ruled Brazil from 1964 to 1985. For the Museu de Arte de São Paulo (1957–68), Bo Bardi designed not only the building but the display scheme: the museum's paintings

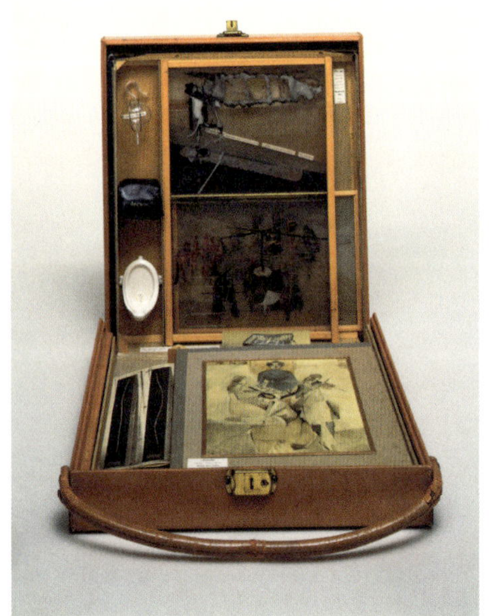

18 Marcel Duchamp. *Boîte en valise (De ou par Marcel Duchamp ou Rrose Sélavy* [From or by Marcel Duchamp or Rrose Sélavy]). 1935–41. Leather valise containing miniature replicas, photographs, color reproductions of works by Duchamp, and one "original" drawing (*Large Glass*, collotype on celluloid, 7½ x 9½" [19 x 23.5 cm]), 16 x 15 x 4" (40.7 x 38.1 x 10.2 cm). The Museum of Modern Art, New York. James Thrall Soby Fund

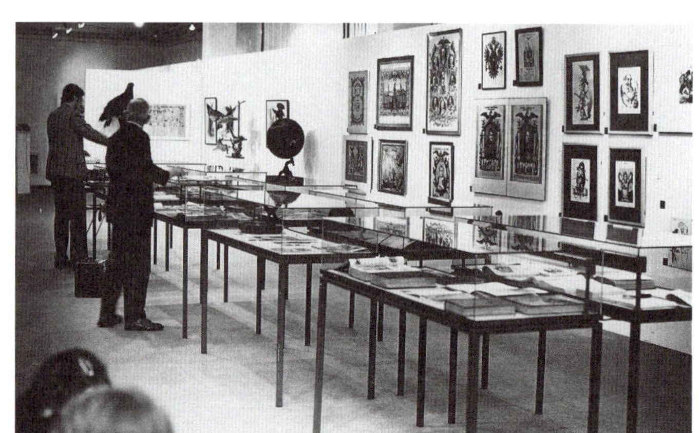

19 Marcel Broodthaers. *Musée d'Art Moderne, Département des Aigles, Section des Figures.* Installation view, Düsseldorf Kunsthalle, May 16–July 9, 1972

were mounted within glass panes (making them viewable from both front and back) that in turn were set on concrete blocks distributed throughout an enormous open gallery without walls (fig. 20). Not only could these individual pods be moved around, but visitors had to create their own paths through them—their own paths through art history. By stripping away the institutional apparatus of sequential rooms of works that the visitor came to in a certain order, Bo Bardi undercut the typical Western form of art history as a chronological series of movements and developments. Working during the turbulent sociopolitical events of mid-century Brazil, she was interested in a populist "pedagogy of the oppressed," a democratization of knowledge.[33] The political gesture inscribed in her system resonates with the multifarious network that is *Scratching . . .*, which suggests, as Bo Bardi's does, that in certain political and social climates the undoing of museums as we know them is a reality. Raad speculates on new, subjective relationships among works of art, systems of display, and cultural entities reflecting the sociopolitical contexts that they occupy.

Scratching . . . encompasses an entire constellation of the ephemera that accompany the production and display of art in today's accelerated art economy. *Appendix XVIII: Plates 22–257* (2008– ; pp. 138–43) is a series of photographs drawn from documents of real exhibitions and art activities in the Arab world: books, catalogues, posters, invoices, invitations. After scanning these documents, though, Raad erased or rearranged their graphic elements, signs, and letters, producing works that although colorful are largely monochromatic. According to his text (pp. 140–41), this realignment is a direct effect of the Lebanese Civil War: "It is clear to me today that these wars also affected colors, lines, shapes, and forms. Some of these were affected in a material way, and, like burned books or razed monuments, were physically destroyed and lost forever; others, like looted treasure or politically compromised artworks, remain physically intact but are removed from view, possibly never to be seen again."

The titles of bodies of work such as *Appendix XVIII*, of course, are appropriated from the language of academic books, which may contain an appendix at the end to supplement or explicate the information that has preceded it. *Appendix XVIII: Plates*, however, is an appendix without an antecedent. *Scratching . . .* also includes several prefaces, an index (*Index XXVI: Red, blue, black, orange, yellow*), and a prologue (*Prologue_Plates I, II, III* (2015; pp. 150–51, 158–59), but the manuscript to which these addenda refer is absent. In breaking the linear sequences of written art history, Raad speculates on a new reality for art that is subject to delays and absences and presented as a decentralized combination of subjective images.

Like much of Raad's work, *Appendix XVIII: Plates* is grounded in traditional photographic practices, and he likens his method to that of a documentary photographer: "I produce an image by 'borrowing' historical facts."[34] The photographs in *Appendix XVIII* constitute a kind of map or catalogue for the new infrastructures of Arab art. *Plates 22–24: A History of Venice I–III*,

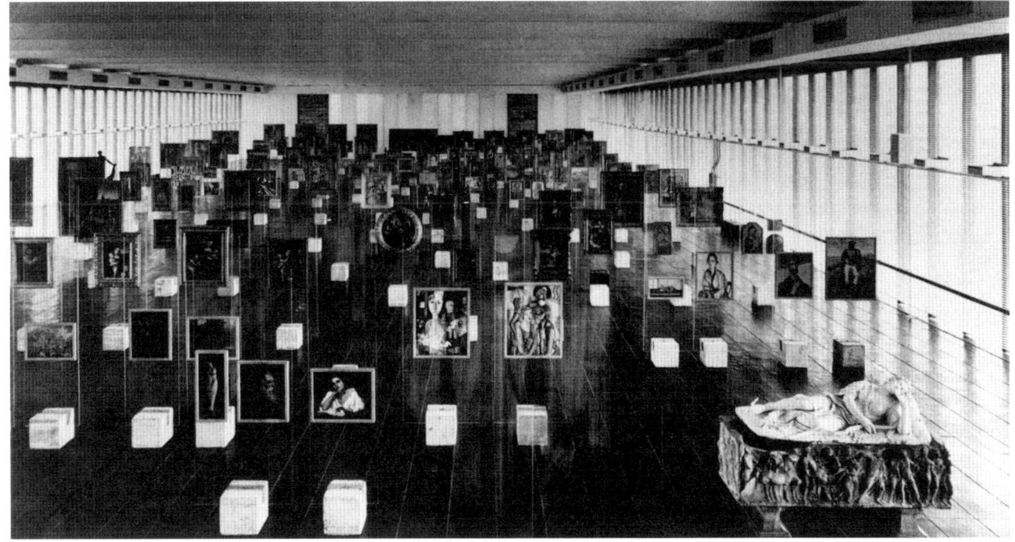

20 Lina Bo Bardi. Museu de Arte de São Paulo (MASP). 1957–68. Interior view of the main gallery with the original display system, c. 1971

for example, is drawn from promotional materials for the Lebanese Pavilion at the Venice Biennale of 2007, the first time Lebanon was represented with its own national pavilion there. Beyond the title, however, this reference is unclear, since the text and graphics have been removed or rearranged, leaving a predominant field of red. Like *Secrets in the open sea*, the monochromes in *Appendix XVIII: Plates* are a site for hidden or encrypted information. As such, they are highly politicized documents.

Where *Appendix XVIII: Plates* appropriates documents from the contemporary-art infrastructures of the Arab world, the several bodies of work in *Scratching . . .* that bear the title *Preface* (there are currently seven of these, numbered from one to seven) largely focus on Islamic art. Raad acknowledges his novice status as a student of Islamic objects: "I don't know that much about Islamic art. All this is very new to me, but some of these objects I see in the display at the Louvre and at the Met—their lines, their forms, and their colors—have been very productive for me."[35] Raad's treatment of these artworks in *Scratching . . .* addresses the slippery nature of their forms and the inability to "see" them within their new contexts. *Preface to the third edition* and *Preface to the fifth edition* (2012–15; pp. 150–51, 154) focus on the Louvre's collection of Islamic art, one of the premier holdings in the West, eventually to be displayed in the new Abu Dhabi museum designed by Nouvel. In 2012, at the invitation of the Louvre, Raad accessed the Paris museum's archives, including pictures from its conservation and curatorial files and object photographs made by in-house photographers. He also photographed the highly publicized new Islamic-art wing, which opened in the fall of 2012. This research produced an exhibition of a video and sculptural installation at the Louvre in 2013 (fig. 21), followed by an ongoing series of intertwined multimedia installations built around imaginary narratives of the Louvre's collection. These works, which continue to be rearranged in various configurations, include *Footnote II* (2015; pp. 150–51), a sculptural installation conceived for the MoMA exhibition.

In *Preface to the third edition* Raad tells the story of the inexplicable transformation of 294 objects from the Louvre during their journey to Abu Dhabi, to take place in the future, sometime between 2016 and 2046:

> While no one will doubt the subsequent changes, the nature and reason of their onset will be contested. Many will attribute them to the weather, asserting that the "corrosion" began soon after the exquisitely crafted, climate-controlled crates were opened in the Arabian Desert. Others will insist they are immaterial and psychological, expressed only in the dreams and psychological disorders of noncitizens working in the Emirate. And a few, the rare few, will speculate that they are aesthetic and came into view only once, in the . . . photographs produced by an artist during her Emirati-sponsored visit to the museum in 2026.

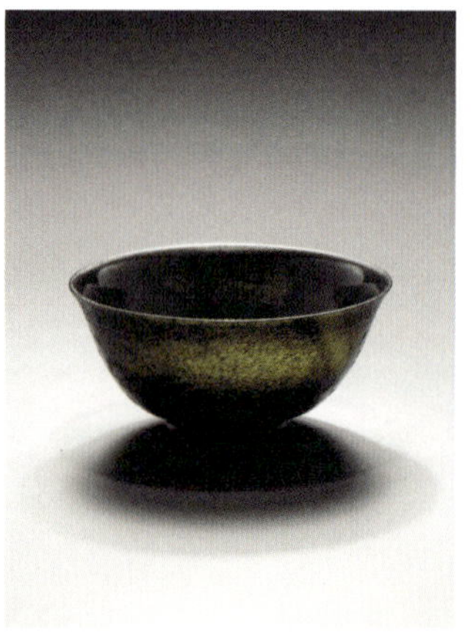

22 Cup with inscribed poem. Iran, 15th century. Jade with traces of gold and incised decoration, 2⅝ × 5 11/16" (6.7 cm × 14.4 cm) diam. Musée du Louvre, Paris

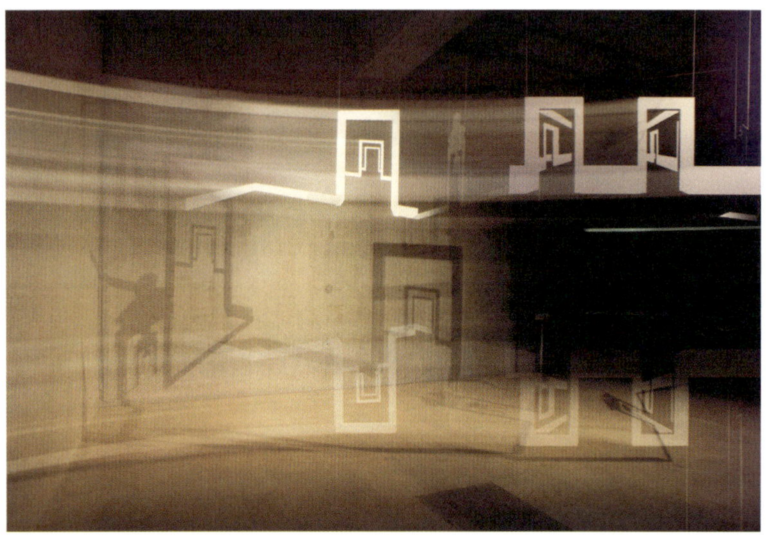

21 Walid Raad. *Préface à la première édition*. Installation view, Pavillon Sully, Musée du Louvre, Paris, January 19–April 8, 2013

The photographs picture this transformation: a fifteenth-century jade wine cup from Iran inscribed with a poem and a design of carved flowers (fig. 22), for example, combines with a late-twelfth-to-early-thirteenth-century sculpture from Iran (fig. 23) to produce a new hybrid (p. 154). The objects seem to have changed skins, as if one object's form had been superimposed on another.

The photographs in *Preface to the third edition* are just one part of an iterative process that is growing increasingly layered as Raad's work develops. In *Preface to the third edition_Acknowledgement* (2014–15; p. 150), for example, Raad's photographs become sculptural objects, their forms being printed with a 3-D printer and recast in plaster, resin, and other materials. The most complex iteration in *Scratching . . .* is surely *Footnote II*, a section of wall wallpapered with a digital collage of archival photographs of the vitrines that the Louvre used to display Islamic art in the 1920s—vitrines, though, that these particular photographs show empty. On the surface of the wallpaper, meanwhile, hang both the photographs from *Preface to the third edition* and the three-dimensional objects derived from them. The wall, then, contains not only all the elements of the objects' transformation but clues to their past histories. Having disappeared from the archival photographs, appeared transformed in Raad's new images, and been remade in other materials in the sculptures, these objects are evidently not fixed; they are elusive, in flux. Their support is also elusive: wallpaper, photographs, and objects are all affixed to a separate wall segment that hangs off the museum wall structure, as if ready to be transported in its entirety to Abu Dhabi.

For Raad, a key idea about these intangible Louvre artworks is that they are "extant but not available. I've always liked the sentence. Toufic has written it. It resonates with me. It's like something is there but not, present but not available."[36] In this context consider the 1990 art theft at the Isabella Stewart Gardner Museum in Boston (Raad's first American landing point). Gardner, the museum's founder, stipulated in her will that the works in the collection had to stay where she had put them; her installation cannot be changed. Today, then, empty frames hang in place of the stolen treasures (fig. 24). These frames signal a hope for the art's eventual retrieval, but also in a way make the stolen works visible to visitors through memory, like sites for their afterimage. Raad's *Preface to the third edition* draws on the idea of placeholders for artworks that are never fully available.

Many of the works in *Scratching . . .* picture not art objects but their effects, such as reflections (*Preface to the second edition*, 2012; pp. 144–47) and shadows (*Preface to the seventh edition*, 2012). Blank walls, polished floors, and empty doorways become active players in works such as *Section 88: Views from outer to inner compartments*, the title of both a video and a sculptural installation. The sculptural work was made for the opening of Mathaf: Arab Museum of Modern Art, in Doha, for which Sheikh Hassan bin Mohamed bin Ali Al Thani of Qatar invited a group of internationally recognized artists affiliated

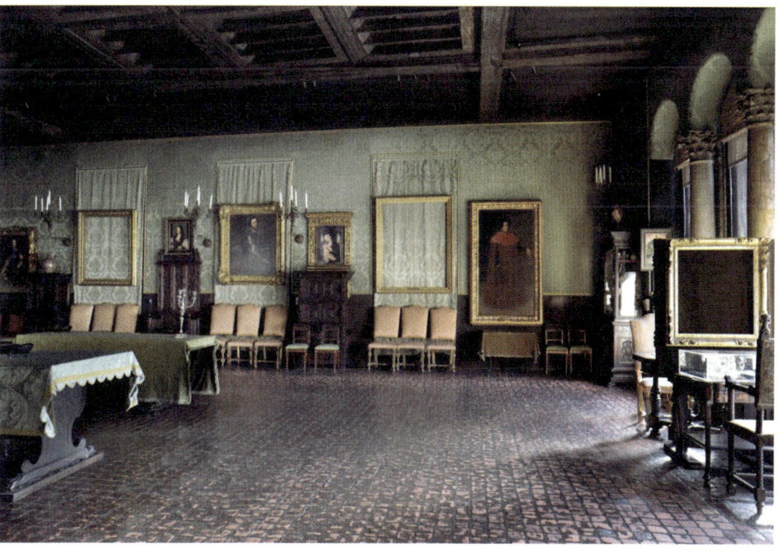

24 The Dutch Room, Isabella Stewart Gardner Museum, Boston

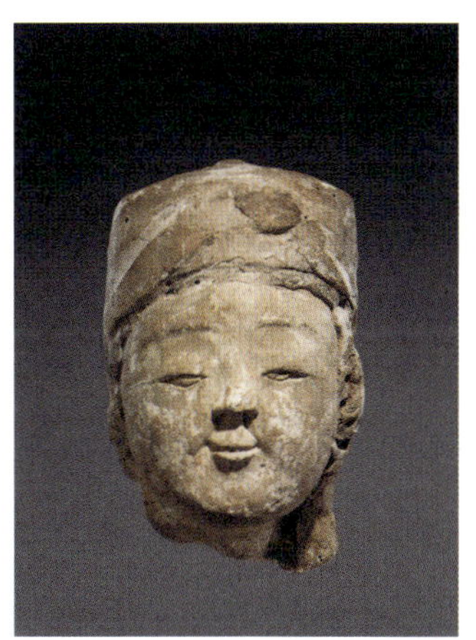

23 Head of a prince. Rayy, Iran, late 12th–early 13th century. Stucco with polychrome traces, 12 13/16" (32.5 cm) high. Musée du Louvre, Paris

with the Middle East to conceive artworks.[37] Raad devised a set of doorways that mimics the architectural style of Western museums of the nineteenth century. Photography remains the artist's primary language even in this sculptural work, for the proportions of the doors are derived from photographs. The doorways, which are fashioned from wood, are like stage sets in that they are only convincing from a frontal vantage point. This setlike quality is enhanced in the MoMA display with theatrical lighting that casts strong shadows, integral parts of the work that function to activate the sculpture as an agent in a story. A related work, *Letters to the Reader (1864, 1877, 1916, 1923)* (fig. 25), Raad's installation at the 2014 São Paulo Bienale, pictures shadows of empty frames on free-standing walls. In both of these projects, familiar elements of museum display—doors, walls, frames (everything but art-works themselves)—play a role in the new spaces of an imaginary museum.

The video titled *Section 88: Views from outer to inner compartments* features museum doorways that slowly fade into each other in silent animation. Created from digitally manipulated photographs of actual museum doorways, including some at both MoMA and The Metropolitan Museum of Art, the video is a virtual hall of mirrors, the rooms and hallways endlessly looping and superimposing. The galleries are empty of both visitors and art. Their walls refer to the preferred display modes of different eras, from the jewel-toned walls of historical museums to the white cube of the modern and contemporary space. An accompanying text (pp. 124–25) tells the story of a newly built museum in an unnamed Arab country, a museum inaccessible to one of the country's citizens—trying to enter, he "hits a wall" and cannot penetrate the museum's façade. The text concludes,

> Within seconds, he is removed from the site, severely beaten and sent to a psychiatric facility.
>
> These events will take place sometime between 2014 and 2024. We will certainly read in newspapers the following day the headline: "Demented Man Disturbs Opening—Claims World Is Flat."

These blank, empty museum spaces might look innocuous and almost serenely abstract, but geopolitical realities are ever present for Raad and are often hidden in plain sight. As I write this essay, labor conditions for the workers constructing the new museums and universities in the Gulf are being reported on critically in the press, and Raad has been active in Gulf Labor, a coalition of artists, writers, and activists trying to publicize them.[38] These realities, as well as the ever shifting conflicts in the region, have intricate roles to play in the renewed interest in the Islamic heritage and the perception of its traditions.

Scratching . . . should not be considered simply as institutional critique. "When thinking politically, my term was never institutional critique, my term was ideology and hegemony,"

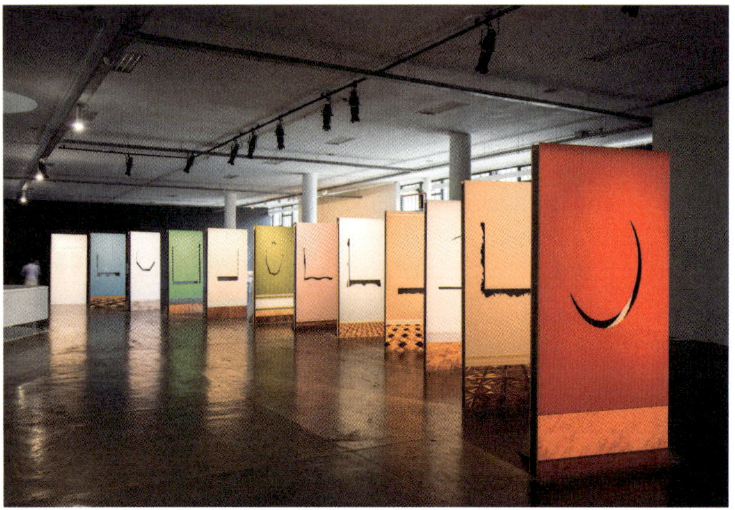

25 Walid Raad. *Letters to the Reader (1864, 1877, 1916, 1923)*. 2014. Installation view, 31st São Paulo Bienal, September 6–December 7, 2014

Raad explains. "Ideology in the sense of, How do ideas become ruling ideas? What is the relationship between ideas, the economy—the superstructure/infrastructure debate—but also ideas, economy, discourse, and the psyche?"[39] Perhaps fantasy and literary digression are the only way to grapple with those complex superstructures. The term proposed by art historian Carrie Lambert-Beatty is *parafictional*, which she uses in relation to recent projects such as Khalil Rabah's natural-history-museum-style display *Palestinian Museum of Natural History and Humankind* (2003–) and Raad's Atlas Group. Lambert-Beatty writes, "Fiction or fictiveness has emerged as an important category in recent art. But, like a paramedic as opposed to a medical doctor, a parafiction is related to but not quite a member of the category of fiction as established in literary and dramatic art. It remains a bit outside."[40] The notion of the parafictional could be extended to precedents such as Ilya Kabakov's seminal series *10 Characters* (1972–75) and *The Man Who Flew into His Picture* (1981–88; fig. 26), which uses fictional characters to explore the ubiquitous language of bureaucracy and the absurdity of daily experience within the old Soviet Union. Raad's imaginary narratives too must be understood within and as a response to the economic, political, and military structures of the contemporary Middle East. Just as the Lebanese Civil War functioned as an ever present abstraction that impacted the reading and understanding of the documents of The Atlas Group, the geopolitical realities, both historical and new, within which Arab art is constructed and read provide the lens through which to view the *Scratching. . .* works.

Raad's art, though, is liberated from fixed historical chronologies, whether the telling of war or the chronology of art. Not just an escape, this disruption offers an alternate vision of how we might understand and remember history. For Raad, the relationship between past and present, personal and public, truth and fiction, are blurred: "The story one tells oneself and that captures one's attention and belief may have nothing to do with what happened in the past, but that's the story that seems to matter in the present and for the future."[41] The optical mysteries, literary digressions, and imaginary dimensions of Raad's art resound well after we encounter them. Through his photographs, videos, and sculptures, he creates compelling scenarios in which we are invited to inhabit the universe that they occupy.

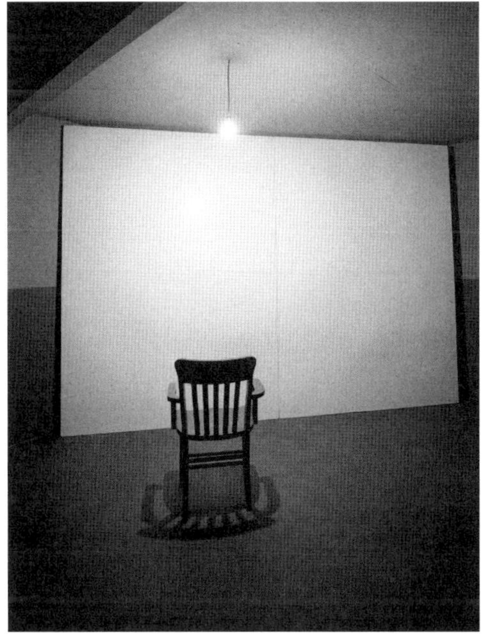

26 Ilya Kabakov. *The Man Who Flew into His Picture.* 1981–88. Installation of painted dry wall, composition board, and painted homasote, containing enamel paint on composition board, ink and colored graphite on paper, photographs, watercolor on paper, painted wood doors, wood chair, painted wood shelf, and painted electric light bulb, dimensions variable. The Museum of Modern Art, New York. Gift of Marcia Riklis, Jerry I. Speyer Fund, and Michael and Judy Ovitz Fund

1
Walid Raad, conversation with the author, March 6, 2014.

2
H. G. Masters, "Those Who Lack Imagination Cannot Imagine What Is Lacking," *ArtAsiaPacific* no. 65 (September/October 2009):130.

3
Raad, quoted in Lee Smith, "Missing in Action: The Art of The Atlas Group/Walid Raad," *Artforum* 41, no. 6 (February 2003):126.

4
A number of influential art and exhibition centers were established in Beirut in the 1990s, including Ashkal Alwan, the Beirut Art Center, and the Ayloul Festival. Curators, critics, and writers both local and international produced exhibitions and publications on the Beirut art scene: see, e.g., *Parachute* no. 108 (October–December 2002); *Tamáss 1: Contemporary Arab Representations. Beirut/Lebanon*, ed. Catherine David (Rotterdam: Witte de With, and Barcelona: Fundació Antoni Tàpies, 2002); and Suzanne Cotter, ed., *Out of Beirut*, exh. cat. (Oxford: Modern Art Oxford, 2006).

5
Khalil Joreige, quoted in Chantal Pontbriand, "Artists at Work: Joana Hadjithomas and Khalil Joreige," *Afterall Online*, September 12, 2013, available online at www.afterall.org/online/artists-at-work_joana-hadjithomas-and-khalil-joreige/#.VMj3KS4sDag (accessed February 26, 2015).

6
Raad, conversation with the author, June 12, 2014.

7
Raad, quoted in Janet A. Kaplan, "Flirtations with Evidence," *Art in America* 92, no. 9 (October 2004):136.

8
Raad, quoted in Alan Gilbert, "Walid Ra'ad," *Bomb* no. 81 (Fall 2002):40.

9
Coproduced by the Arab Image Foundation and the Palais des Beaux Arts, Brussels, the exhibition toured from 2002 through 2006 to venues in several cities, including São Paulo, Athens, Geneva, Singapore, Cologne, and New York.

10
See Hal Foster, "An Archival Impulse," *October* no. 110 (Fall 2004):3–22, and Okwui Enwezor, *Archive Fever: Uses of the Document in Contemporary Art*, exh. cat. (New York: International Center of Photography, and Göttingen: Steidl, 2008).

11
Foster, "An Archival Impulse," p. 3.

12
See Gilbert, "Walid Ra'ad," p. 40.

13
Accounts differ on the timing of Raad's first performance. The artist has said that the first was in Beirut in 1989. See ibid., p. 45.

14
See André Lepecki, "'After All, This Terror Was Not without Reason': Unfiled Notes on the Atlas Group," *TDR* 50, no. 3 (Fall 2006):90, 94.

15
Beirut's racetrack, which remained open intermittently during the war, was in the city center, near the infamous Green Line dividing the city. During the Israeli invasion of Beirut in 1982, the woods around the track were burned and dozens of horses were slaughtered. See Dina Al-Kassim, "Crisis of the Unseen: Unearthing the Political Aesthetics of Hysteria in the Archaeology and Arts of New Beirut," *Parachute* no. 108 (October–December 2002):161, n. 6.

16
See Raad, *Notebook volume 72: Missing Lebanese wars_Plate 135* (1989/1998). Raad collected these quotes, and the titles for his artworks, from the *New York Times* and various other newspapers and magazines. Raad, conversation with the author, April 18, 2014.

17
See Lepecki, "'After All, This Terror Was Not without Reason,'" p. 92.

18
Cheryl Dunye, quoted in Anne Stockwell, "Fall Film Preview: Cheryl Dunye," *The Advocate*, September 17, 1996, p. 69.

19
See, e.g., *Secrets in the open sea* (1994/2004), pp. 70–73 in the present volume.

20
Raad, in Silvia Kolbowski and Walid Raad, *Between Artists* (New York: Art Resources Transfer Press, 2006), p. 36.

21
"I tried Googling Bachar to establish his existence, and all I found were references on The Atlas Group Web site and in writings on Raad's work." Beth Secor, "Walid Raad and his Fake Foundation Show Real Art at the Glassell School," *Houston Press*, October 29, 2008, available online at www.houstonpress.com/2008-10-30/culture/walid-raad-and-his-fake-foundation-show-real-art-at-the-glassell-school/ (accessed March 22, 2015).

22
See also *I only wish that I could weep* (1997/2002; pp. 94–97), which features the purported footage of a Lebanese soldier obsessed with filming the sunset on Beirut's waterfront corniche.

23
Raad, conversation with the author, April 18, 2014.

24
See Janet A. Kaplan, "Flirtations with Evidence," *Art in America* 92, no. 9 (October 2004):137. *Secrets in the open sea* had an earlier iteration, published under the title *Miraculous Beginnings* (now part of the title of a video; see pp. 68–69) in the journal *Public* in 1997. In this version the monochromes were gray and the people identified in the photographs were said to have lived in cities from Detroit to Freetown, Sierra Leone. See Raad, "Miraculous Beginnings," *Public* no. 16 (1997):44–53.

25
Achim Borchardt-Hume, in Raad and Borchardt-Hume, "In Search of the Miraculous," in Borchardt-Hume, ed., *Miraculous Beginnings: Walid Raad* (London: Whitechapel Gallery, 2010), p. 9.

26
Raad, in ibid., p. 12.

27
For more on *Scratching on things I could disavow* see the essay in this volume by Finbarr Barry Flood.

28
Raad sometimes uses a stand-in for the performance *Scratching on things I could disavow*. Actors have included Carlos Chahine, who performed the work at Le Centquatre, Paris, as part of the Festival d'Automne in 2010, and Markus Reymann at Thyssen-Bornemisza Art Contemporary, Vienna, in 2011.

29
The chart appeared on the cover of the exhibition catalogue *Cubism and Abstract Art* (New York: The Museum of Modern Art, 1936).

30
Raad recalls attending one of Andrea Fraser's talks at New York's Whitney Museum of American Art in the 1980s. Raad, conversation with the author, June 12, 2014.

31
Toufic, *The Withdrawal of Tradition past a Surpassing Disaster* (Beirut: Forthcoming Books, 2009), available online at http://www.jalaltoufic.com/downloads/Jalal_Toufic,_The_Withdrawal_of_Tradition_Past_a_Surpassing_Disaster.pdf (accessed March 23, 2015).

32
Raad, quoted in Masters, "Those Who Lack Imagination Cannot Imagine What is Lacking," p. 127.

33
See Roger M. Buergel, "'This Exhibition Is an Accusation': The Grammar of Display According to Lina Bo Bardi," *Afterall* 26 (Spring 2011):51.

34
Raad and Borchardt-Hume, "In Search of the Miraculous," in *Miraculous Beginnings*, p. 14.

35
Raad, quoted in Louisa Buck, "Artist Interview, Walid Raad: A Mediator Between Worlds," *Art Newspaper* no. 242 (January 2013):46.

36
Raad, conversation with the author, June 12, 2014.

37
Preface to the second edition (2012; pp. 144–47) pictures reflections of artworks on a museum floor—the polished concrete floors of the Mathaf museum.

38
See Ariel Kaminer and Sean O'Driscoll, "Workers at N.Y.U.'s Abu Dhabi Site Faced Harsh Conditions," *New York Times*, May 18, 2014. Available online at http://nyti.ms/1gXQSCd (accessed April 1, 2015).

39
Raad, conversation with the author, June 12, 2014.

40
Carrie Lambert-Beatty, "Make-Believe: Parafiction and Plausibility," *October* no. 129 (Summer 2009):54.

41
Raad, quoted in Kassandra Nakas, "Double Miss: On the Use of Photography in The Atlas Group Archive," in *The Atlas Group (1989–2004): A Project by Walid Raad*, ed. Nakas and Britta Schmitz (Cologne: Verlag der Buchhandlung Walther König, 2006), p. 52.

research and document the contemporary history of Lebanon, with particular emphasis on the Lebanese wars of 1975 to 1991. Raad found and produced audio, visual, and literary documents that shed light on this history. The documents were preserved in The Atlas Group Archive, which is located in Beirut and New York and is organized in three types of categories: [cat. A] refers to documents attributed to individuals; [cat. FD] stands for documents attributed to anonymous individuals or institutions; [cat. AGP] is the abbreviation for documents attributed to The Atlas Group itself. The schema reproduced in this book offers a snapshot of the archive and its contents.

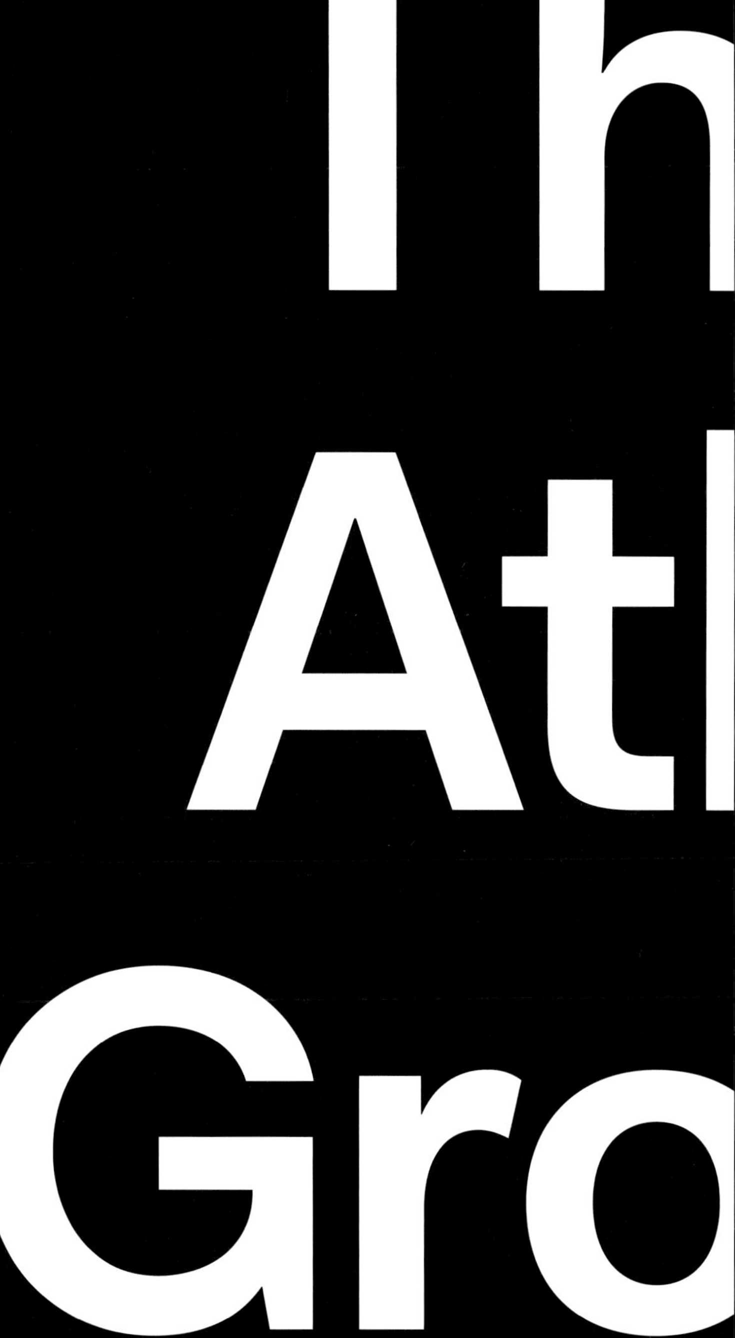

he
las
oup

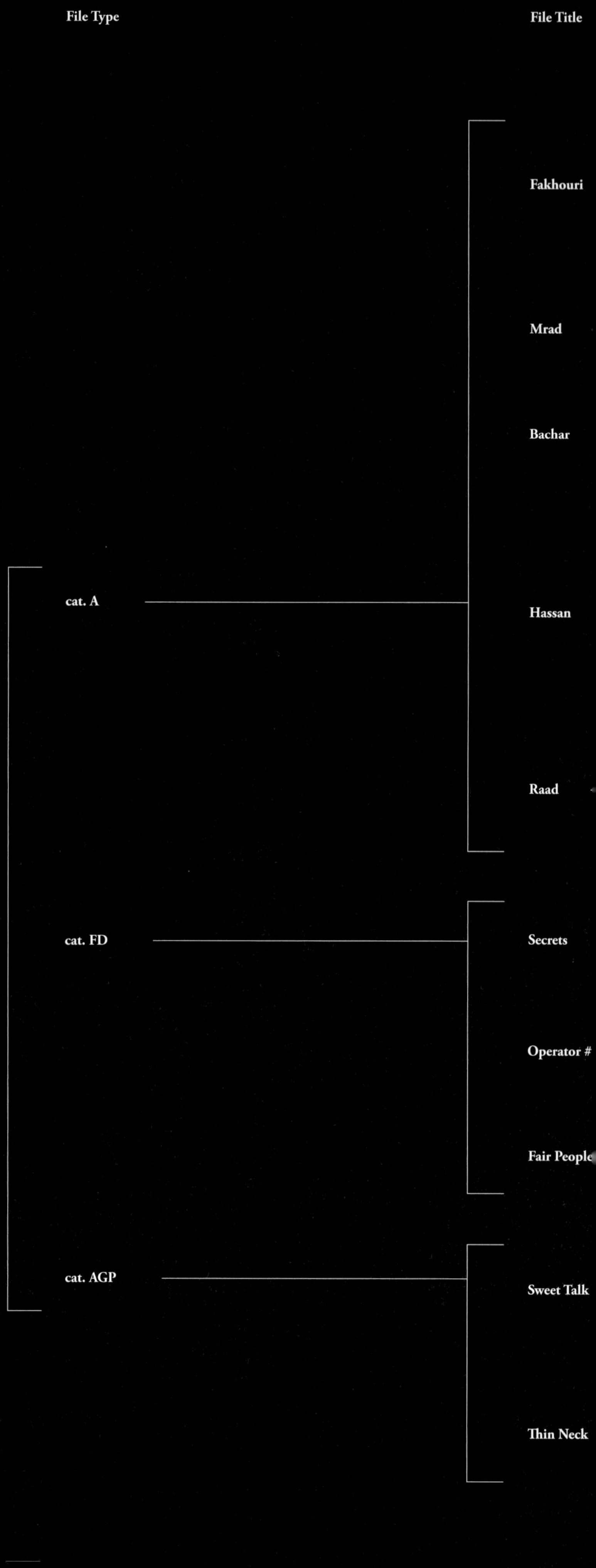

File Type	File Title
cat. A	Fakhouri
	Mrad
	Bachar
	Hassan
	Raad
cat. FD	Secrets
	Operator #
	Fair People
cat. AGP	Sweet Talk
	Thin Neck

File Contents	Document Title
notebooks	Notebook volume 38: Already been in a lake of fire Notebook volume 57: Livre d'or Notebook volume 72: Missing Lebanese wars
films	No, illness is neither here nor there Miraculous beginnings
photographs	Civilizationally, we do not dig holes to bury ourselves
photographs	I might die before I get a rifle
videotapes	Hostage: The Bachar tapes (#17 and #31)_English version
photographs	Hostage: The Bachar Polaroids
photographs	"Oh God," he said, talking to a tree
mixed media	I was overcome with a momentary panic at the thought that they might be right
photographs	We decided to let them say "we are convinced" twice
photographs	Let's be honest, the weather helped
photographs	Secrets in the open sea
videotapes	I only wish that I could weep
photographs	We are fair people. We never speak well of one another
photographs	Better be watching the clouds
photographs	The Hilwé commissions (1992–2004)
photographs	My neck is thinner than a hair: Engines
videotapes	We can make rain but no one came to ask

Civilizationally, we do not dig holes to bury ourselves. 1958–59/2003

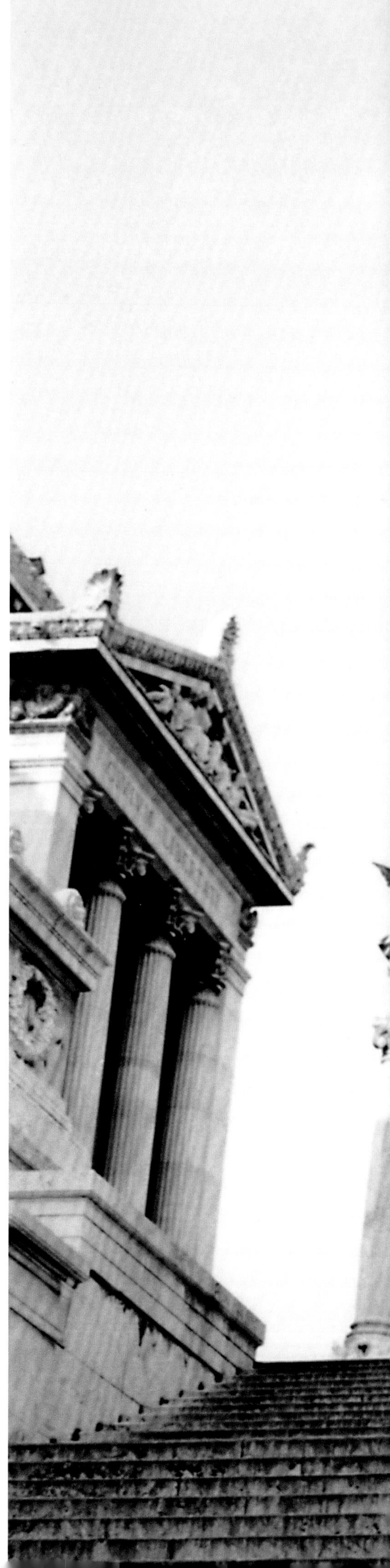

Until his death, in 1993, Dr. Fadl Fakhouri was the most renowned historian of Lebanon. The only available photographs of Dr. Fakhouri consist of twenty-four black-and-white self-portraits that were found in a small brown envelope titled *Civilizationally, we do not dig holes to bury ourselves*. The historian produced the photographs in 1958 and 1959 during his one and only trip outside of Lebanon, to Paris and Rome.

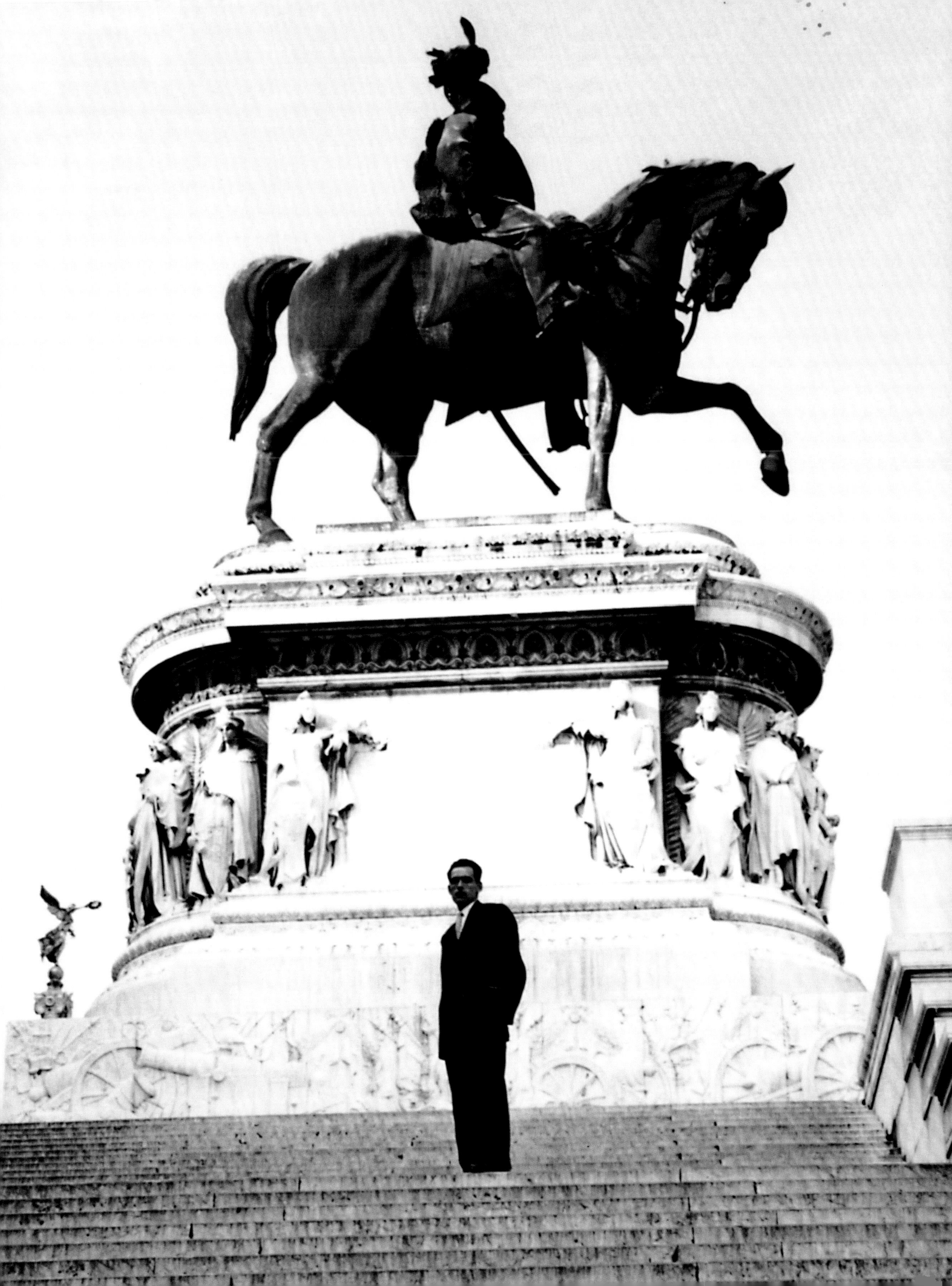

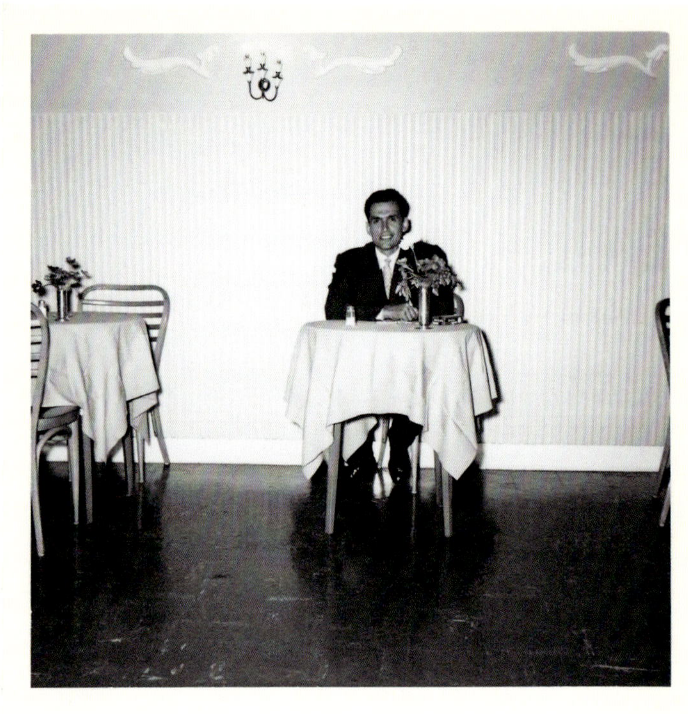

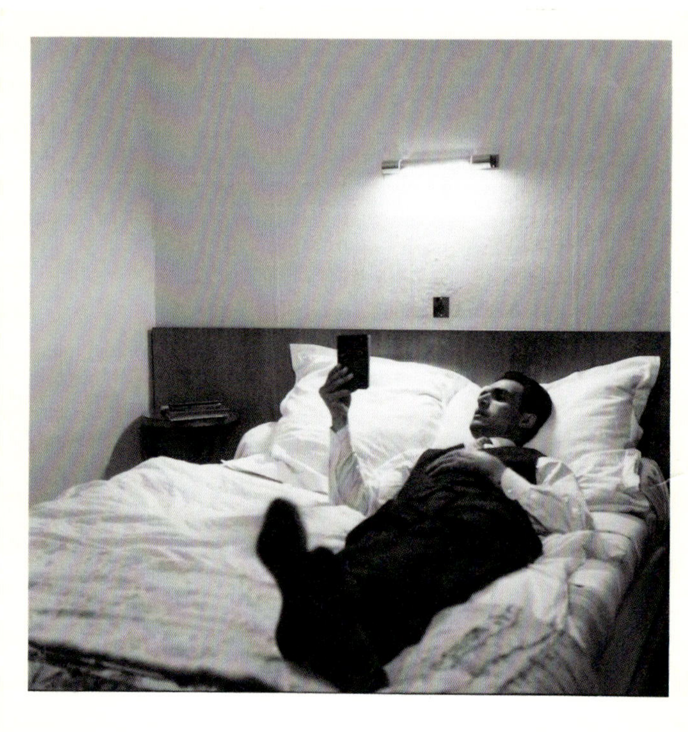

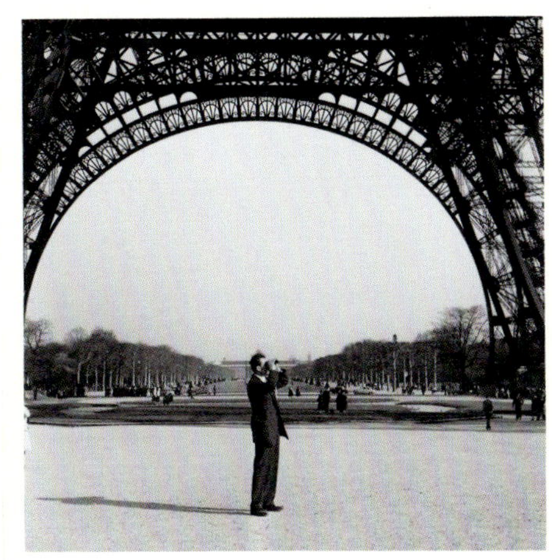
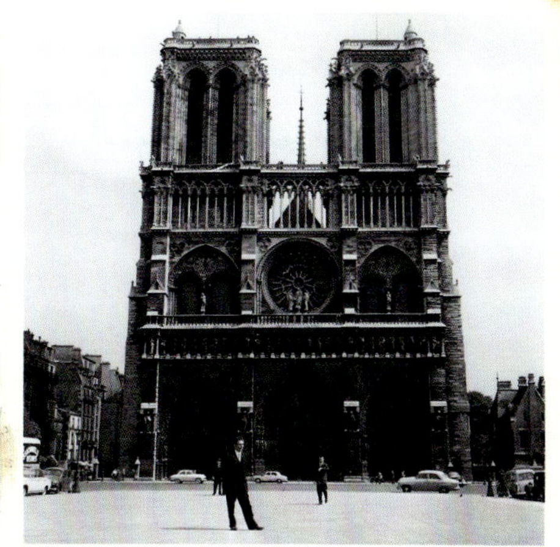
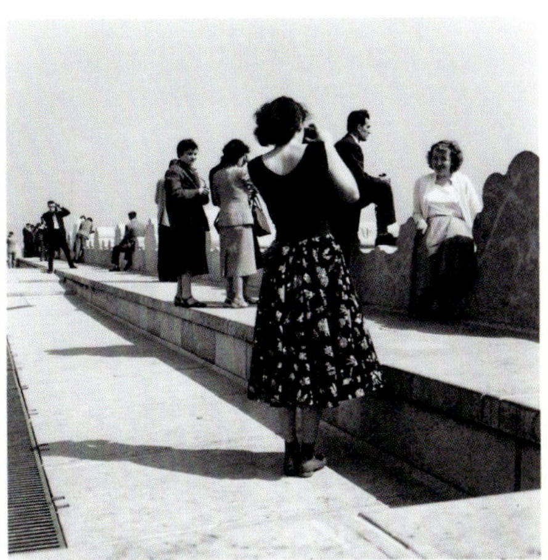
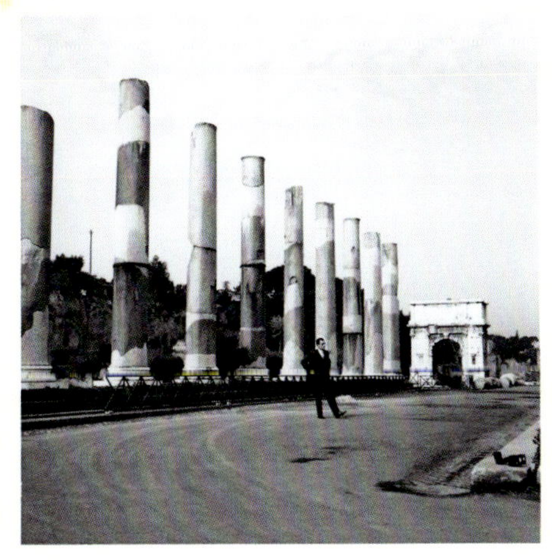
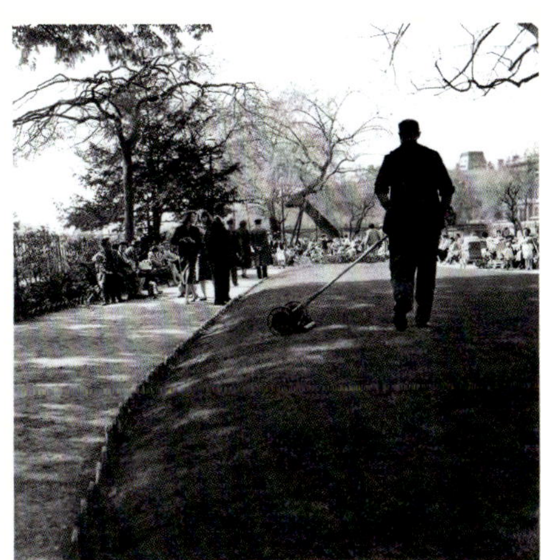
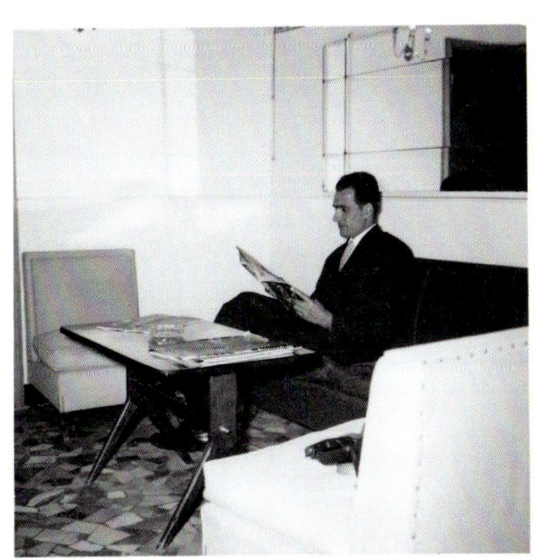

The following photographs are attributed to Walid Raad, who donated them to The Atlas Group in 2002. In the statement accompanying the donation, Raad noted:

In the summer of 1982, I stood along with others in a parking lot across from my mother's apartment in East Beirut, and watched the Israeli land, air, and sea assault on West Beirut. The PLO along with their Lebanese and Syrian allies retaliated, as best they could.

East Beirut welcomed the invasion, or so it seemed, and that much is certain. West Beirut resisted it, or so it seemed, and that much is certain.

One day, my mother even accompanied me to the hills around Beirut to photograph the Israeli army stationed there.

Soldiers rested their bodies and their weapons as they waited for their next orders to attack or retreat.

I was fifteen in 1982, and wanted to get as close as possible to the events, or as close as my newly acquired camera and lens permitted me. Clearly not close enough.

This past year, I came upon the carefully preserved negatives from that time. I decided to look again.

We decided to let them say "we are convinced" twice. It was more convincing this way. 1982/2004

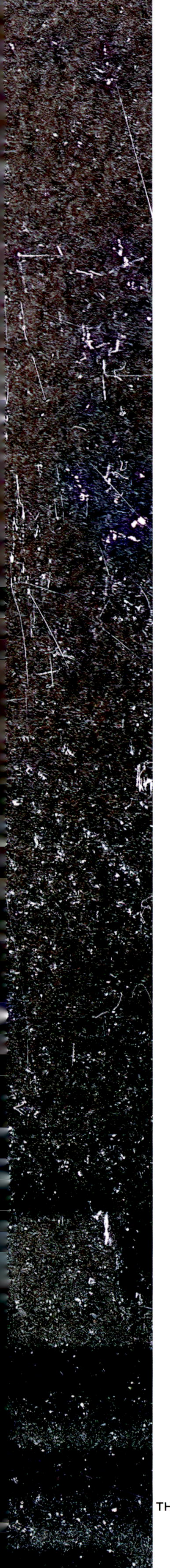
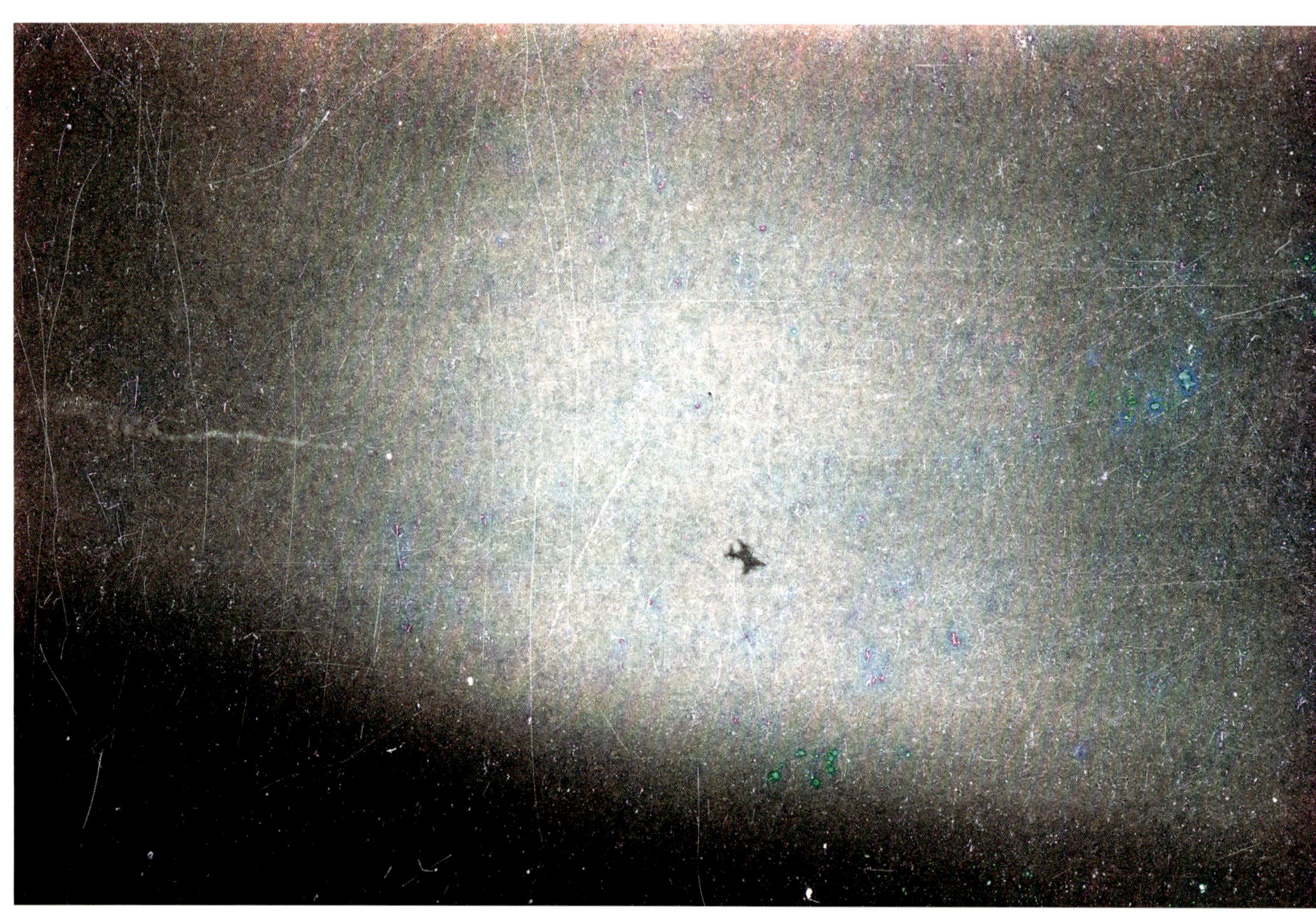

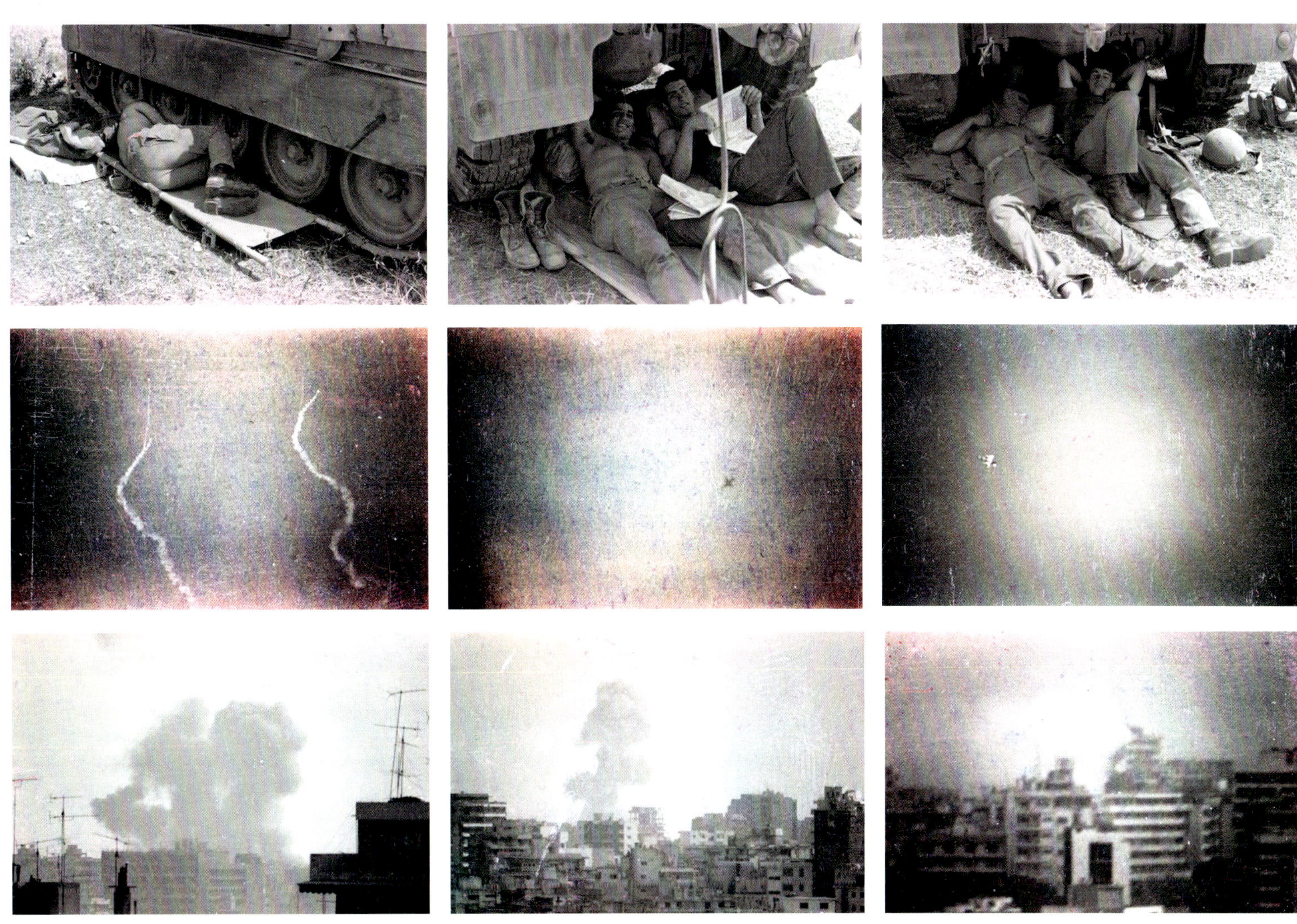

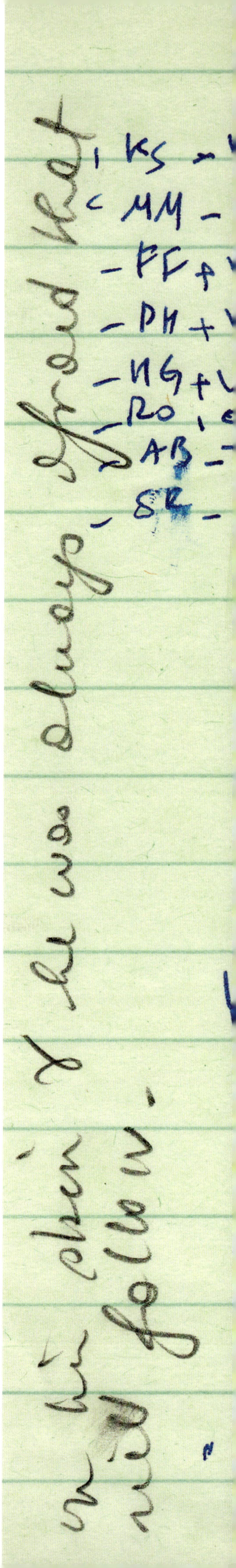

Notebook volume 72: Missing Lebanese wars. 1989/1998

It is a little-known fact that the major historians of the Lebanese wars were avid gamblers. It is said that they met every Sunday at the race track—Marxists and Islamists bet on races one through seven, Maronite nationalists and socialists on races eight through fifteen.

Race after race, the historians stood behind the track photographer, whose job was to image the winning horse as it crossed the finish line, to record the photo finish. It is also said that they convinced (some say bribed) the photographer to snap only one picture as the winning horse arrived. Each historian wagered on precisely when—how many fractions of a second before or after the horse crossed the finish line—the photographer would expose his frame.

Each of the following notebook pages includes a photograph clipped from the post-race-day issue of the newspaper *An-Nahar*. They include Dr. Fakhouri's notations on the race's distance and duration, the winning time of the winning horse, calculations of averages, the historians' initials with their respective bets, the time discrepancy predicted by the winning historian. Written on each page is also a brief paragraph in English. Dr. Fakhouri's widow, Zainab Fakhouri, has attributed these to her husband's habit of including short descriptions of the winning historians in his notebooks.

نتائج سباق الخيل

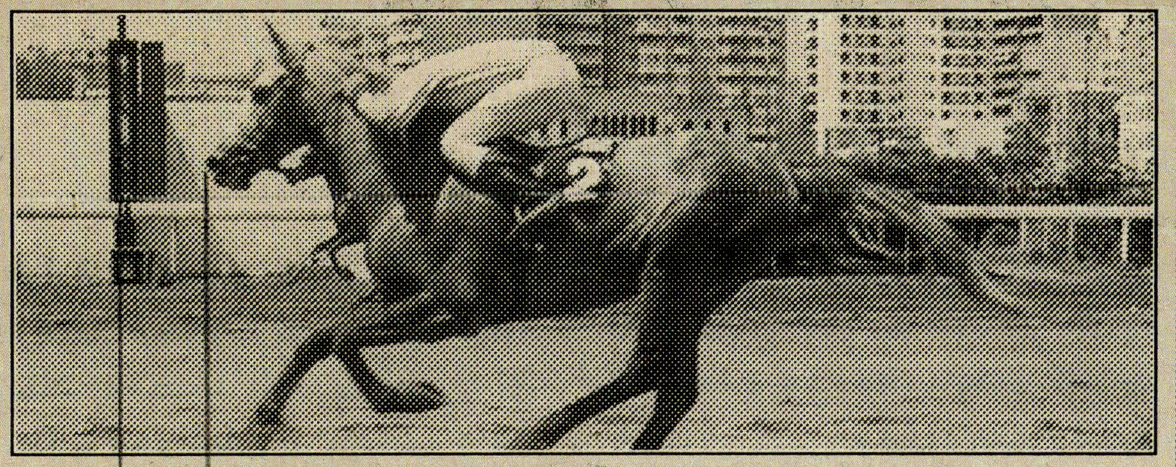

شاعر (سمير) من الخارج مجلياً على مطرب (حوا).

الـ

٦٥ -

٦٠-

الشوط الثاني :

١ درويش ٥٠ كيلو
٢ يعقوب ٦٢ كيلو
٣ من حبيب ٥٧ كيلو
٤ محمد ٥٢ كيلو

والمسافة ١٠٠٠م بـ" دقيقة و٧ ث

٦٧ — ١٠٠٠

Description of the Winning Historian:

What mattered to her most was to avoid anything that might be reminiscent of empathy

Distance Between Horse and Finish Line:

- 17

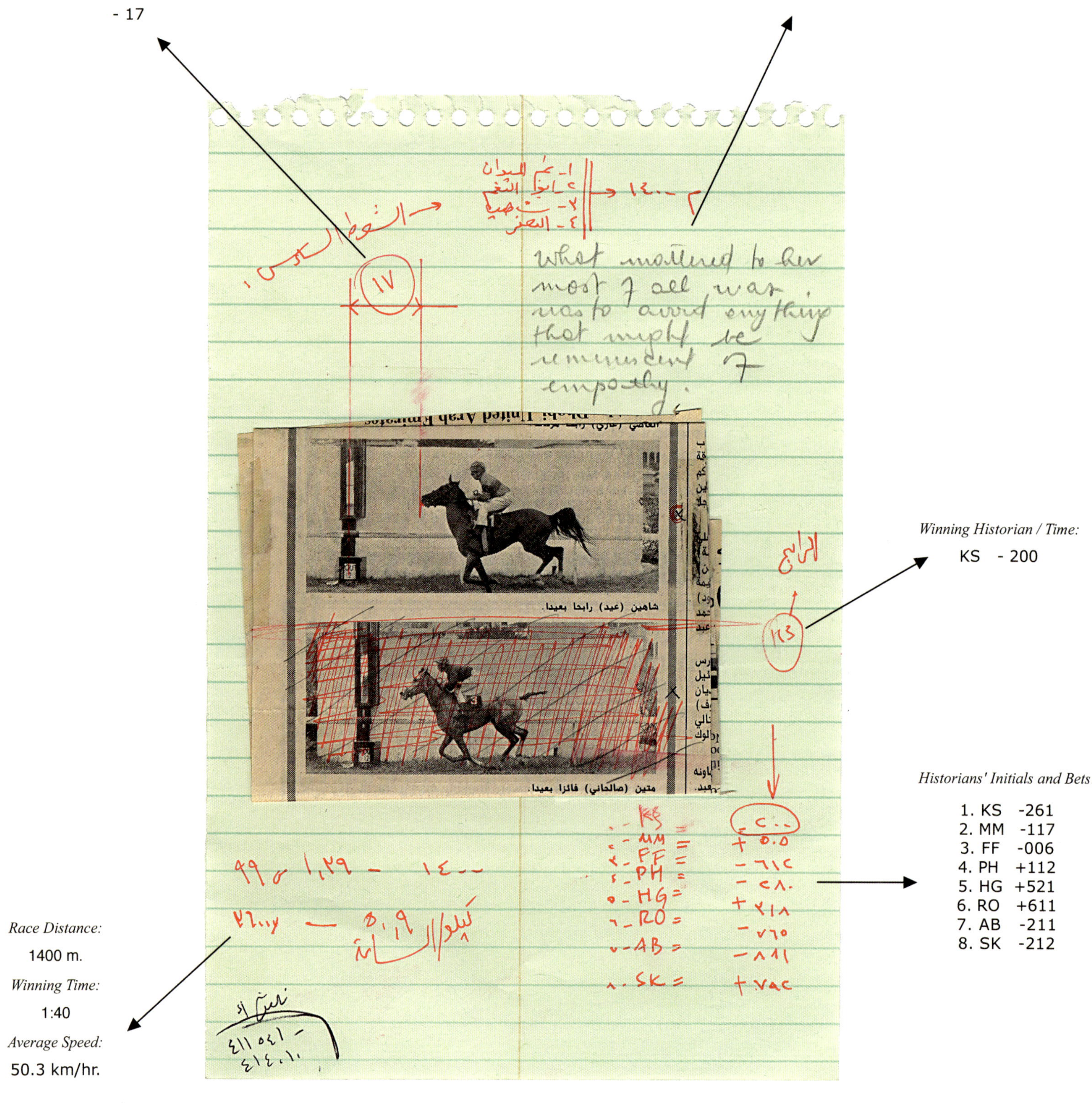

Winning Historian / Time:

KS - 200

Historians' Initials and Bets:

1. KS -261
2. MM -117
3. FF -006
4. PH +112
5. HG +521
6. RO +611
7. AB -211
8. SK -212

Race Distance:

1400 m.

Winning Time:

1:40

Average Speed:

50.3 km/hr.

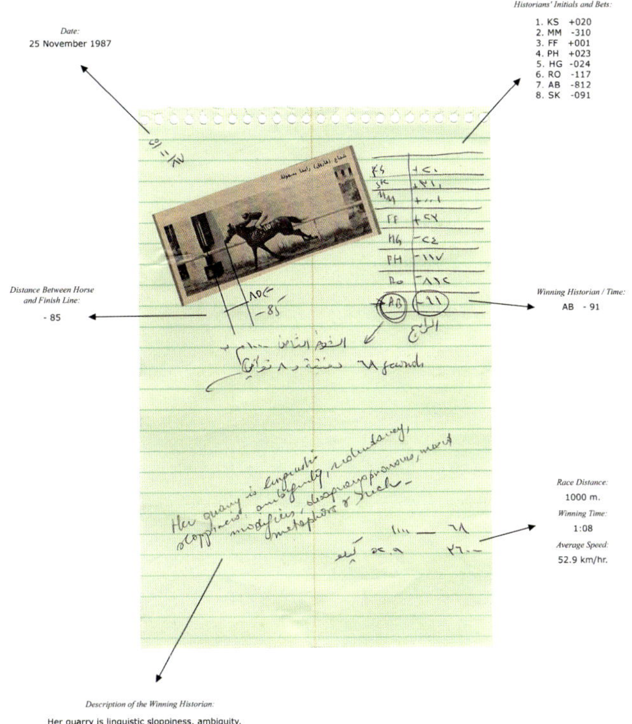

Date:
25 November 1987
Historians' Initials and Bets:
1. KS +020
2. MM -310
3. FF +001
4. PH +023
5. HG -024
6. RO -117
7. AB -812
8. SK -091
Distance Between Horse and Finish Line:
- 85
Winning Historian / Time:
AB - 91
Race Distance:
1000 m.
Winning Time:
1:08
Average Speed:
52.9 km/hr.
Description of the Winning Historian:
Her quarry is linguistic sloppiness, ambiguity, redundancy, modifiers, disagreeing pronouns, mixed metaphors and such

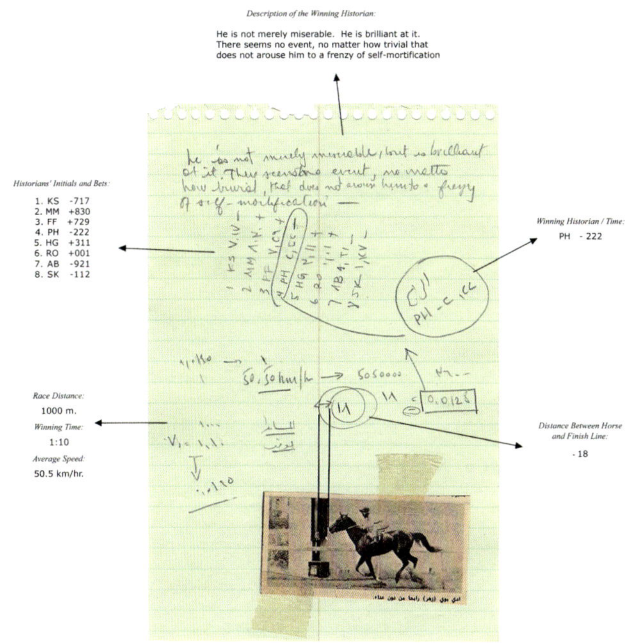

Description of the Winning Historian:
He is not merely miserable. He is brilliant at it. There seems no event, no matter how trivial that does not arouse him to a frenzy of self-mortification
Historians' Initials and Bets:
1. KS -717
2. MM +830
3. FF +729
4. PH -222
5. HG +311
6. RO +001
7. AB -921
8. SK -112
Winning Historian / Time:
PH - 222
Race Distance:
1000 m.
Winning Time:
1:10
Average Speed:
50.5 km/hr.
Distance Between Horse and Finish Line:
- 18

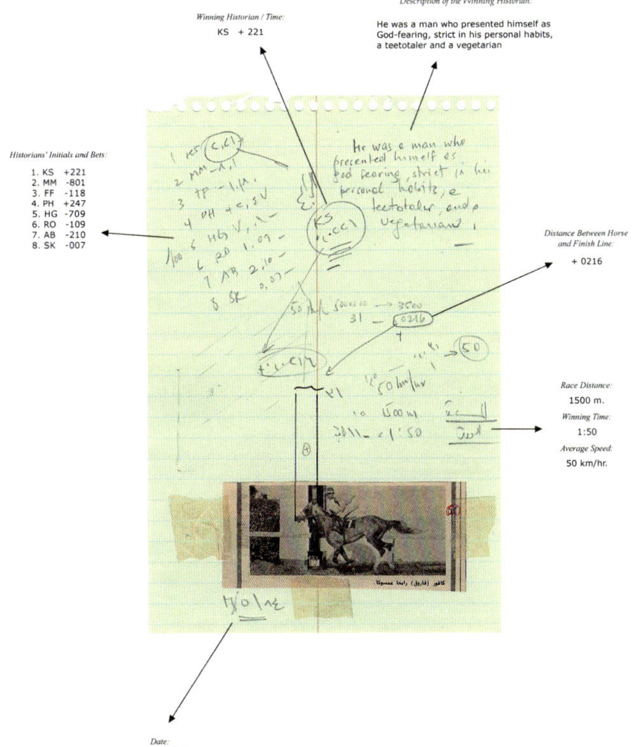

Winning Historian / Time:
KS + 221
Description of the Winning Historian:
He was a man who presented himself as God-fearing, strict in his personal habits, a teetotaler and a vegetarian
Historians' Initials and Bets:
1. KS +221
2. MM -801
3. FF -118
4. PH +247
5. HG -709
6. RO -109
7. AB -210
8. SK -007
Distance Between Horse and Finish Line:
+ 0216
Race Distance:
1500 m.
Winning Time:
1:50
Average Speed:
50 km/hr.
Date:
16 May 1984

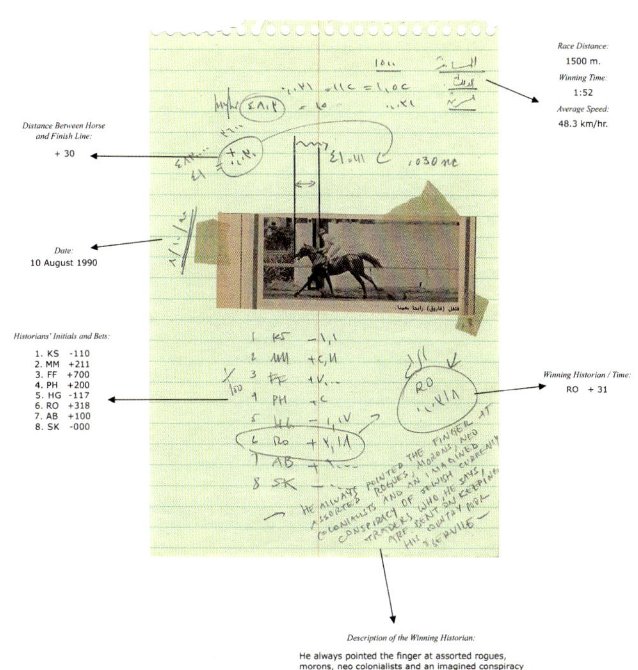

Race Distance:
1500 m.
Winning Time:
1:52
Average Speed:
48.3 km/hr.
Distance Between Horse and Finish Line:
+ 30
Date:
10 August 1990
Historians' Initials and Bets:
1. KS -110
2. MM +211
3. FF +700
4. PH +200
5. HG -117
6. RO +318
7. AB +100
8. SK -000
Winning Historian / Time:
RO + 31
Description of the Winning Historian:
He always pointed the finger at assorted rogues, morons, neo colonialists and an imagined conspiracy of Jewish currency traders who he says are bent on keeping his country poor and servile

I might die before I get a rifle. 1993/2002

The following photographs are attributed to Hannah Mrad, who donated them to The Atlas Group in 1993. In the statement accompanying the donation, Mrad stated:

In 1991, after fourteen years in the Lebanese Communist Party, I was folded into the Lebanese Army's Ammunition and Explosives division. Months into my new assignment, I found myself unable to remember the names of the thousands of explosive devices I was meant to master.

I began to photograph them, hoping that the photographs would aid my memory. They didn't and I was let go. I still blame my photographs for my release.

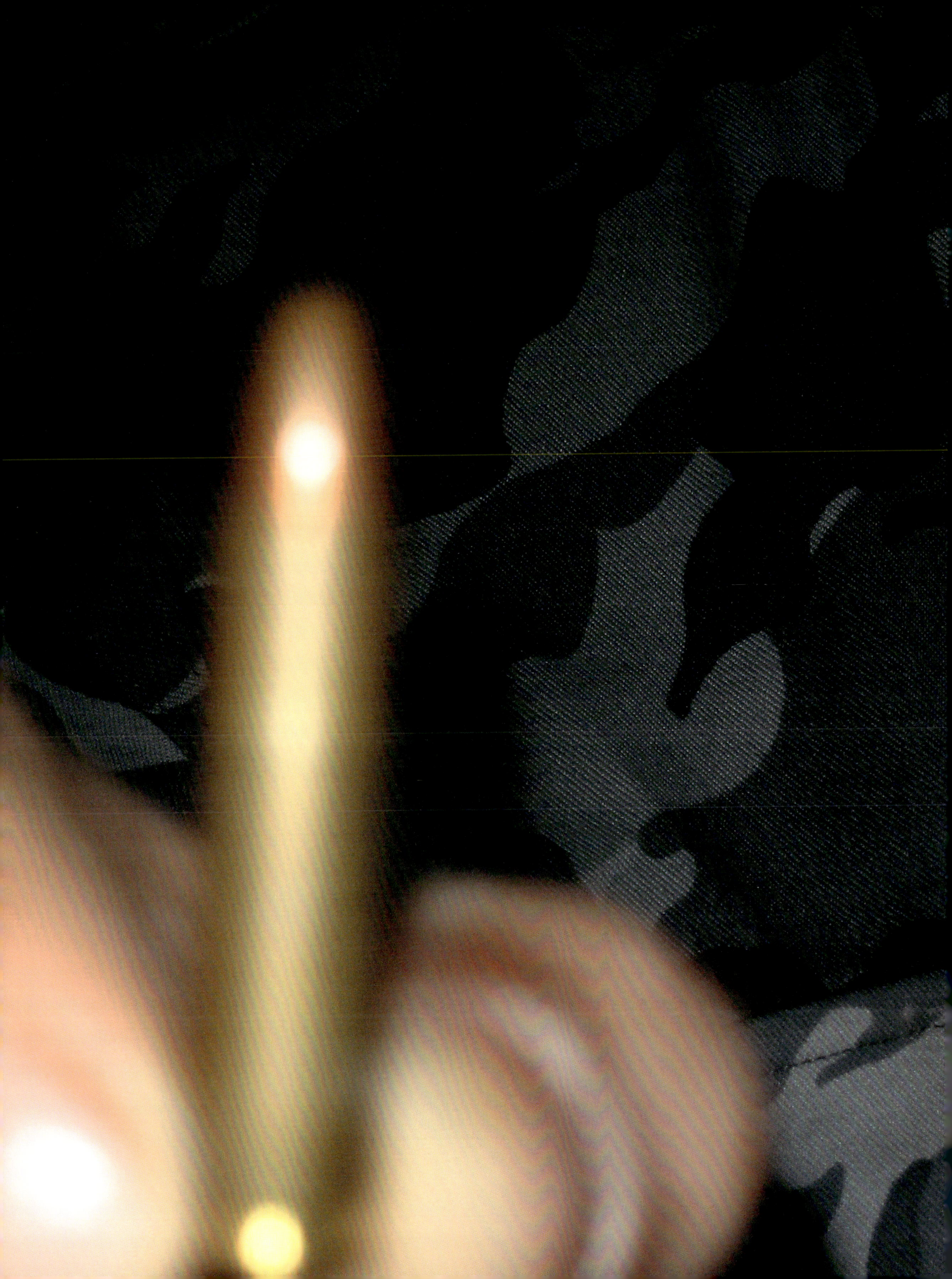

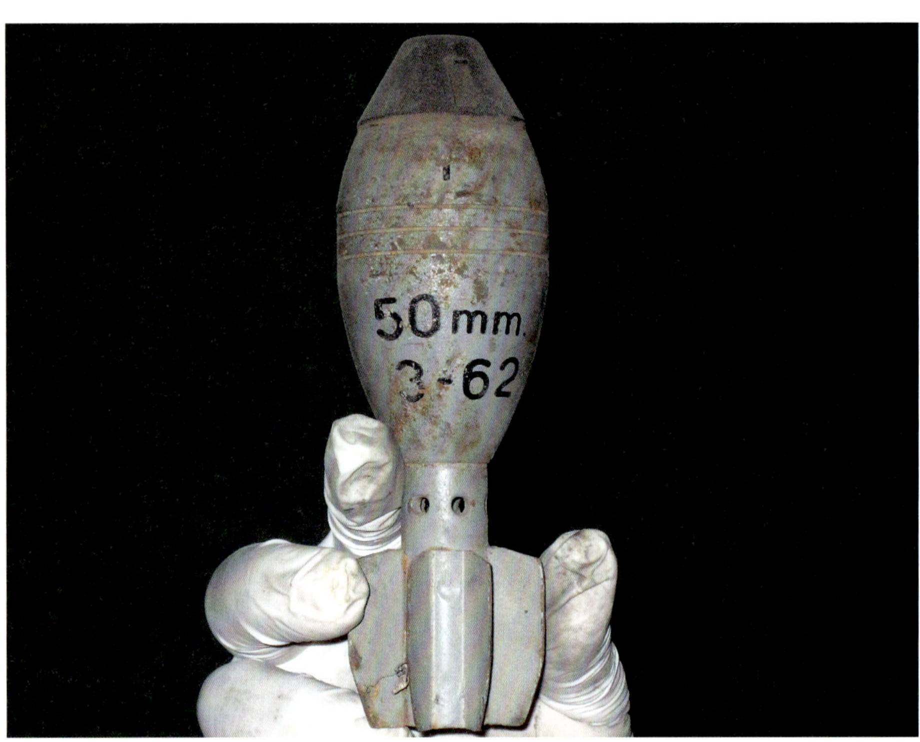
50mm.
3-62

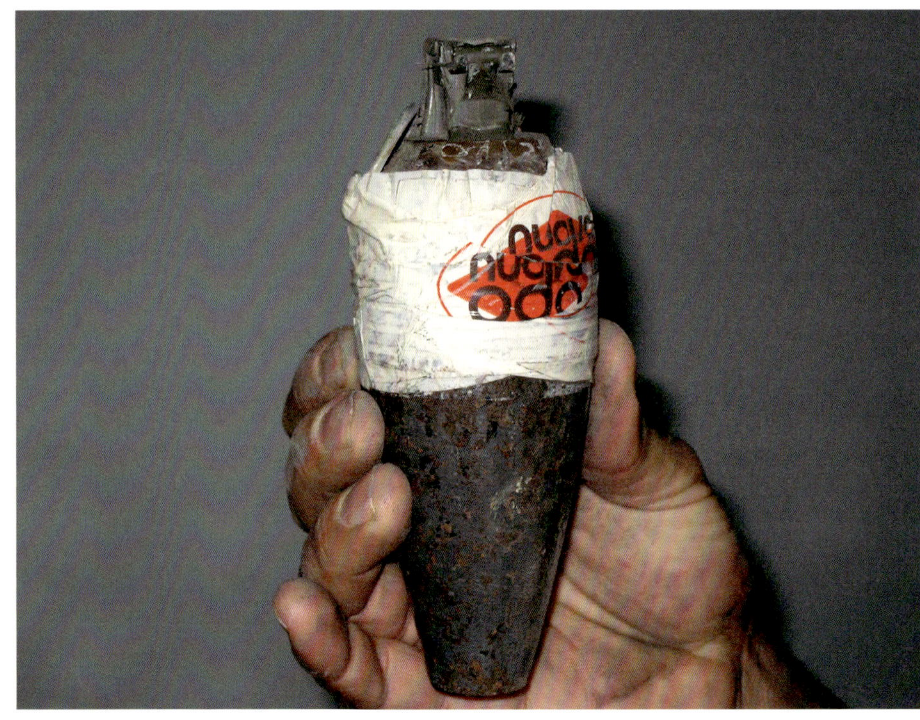

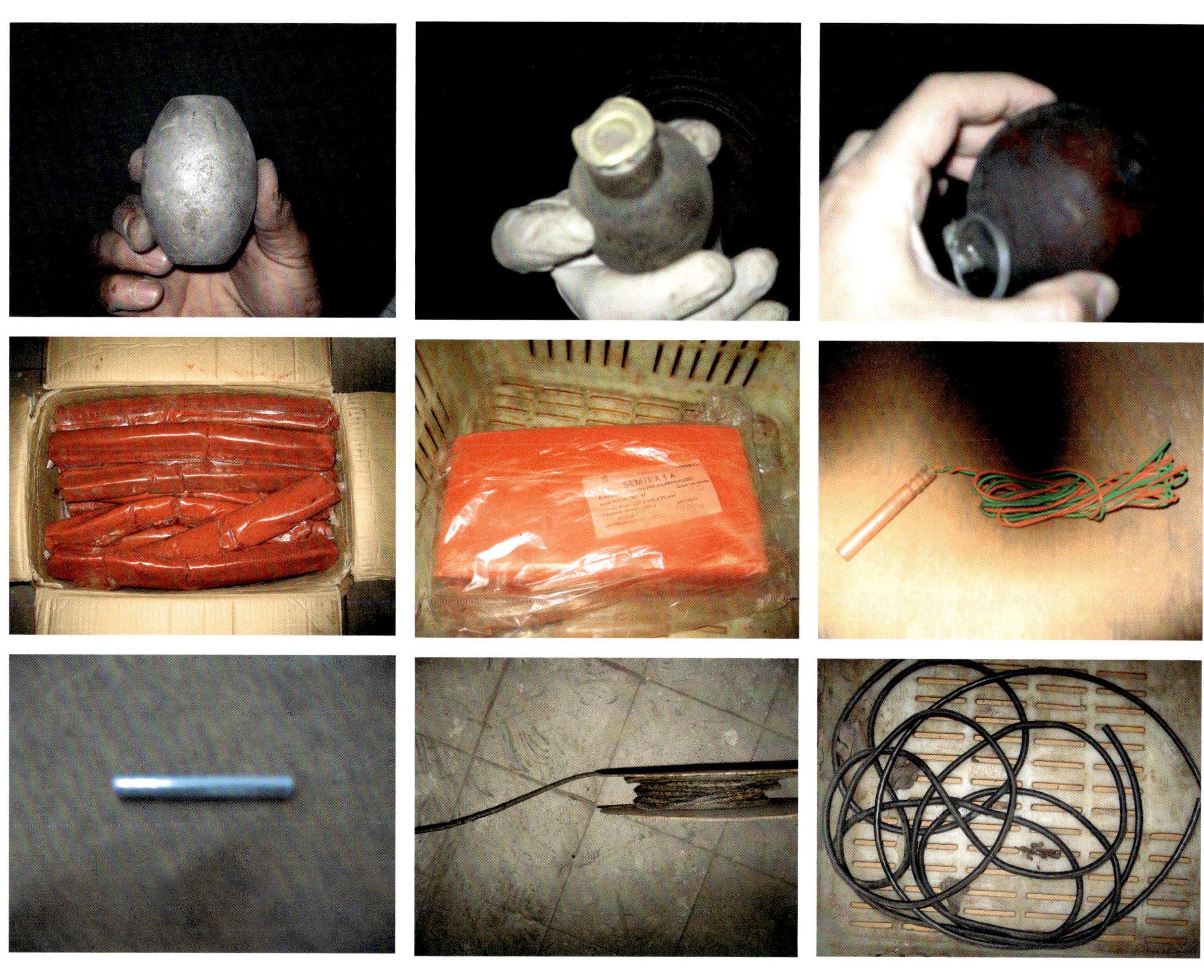
SEMTEX 1 A

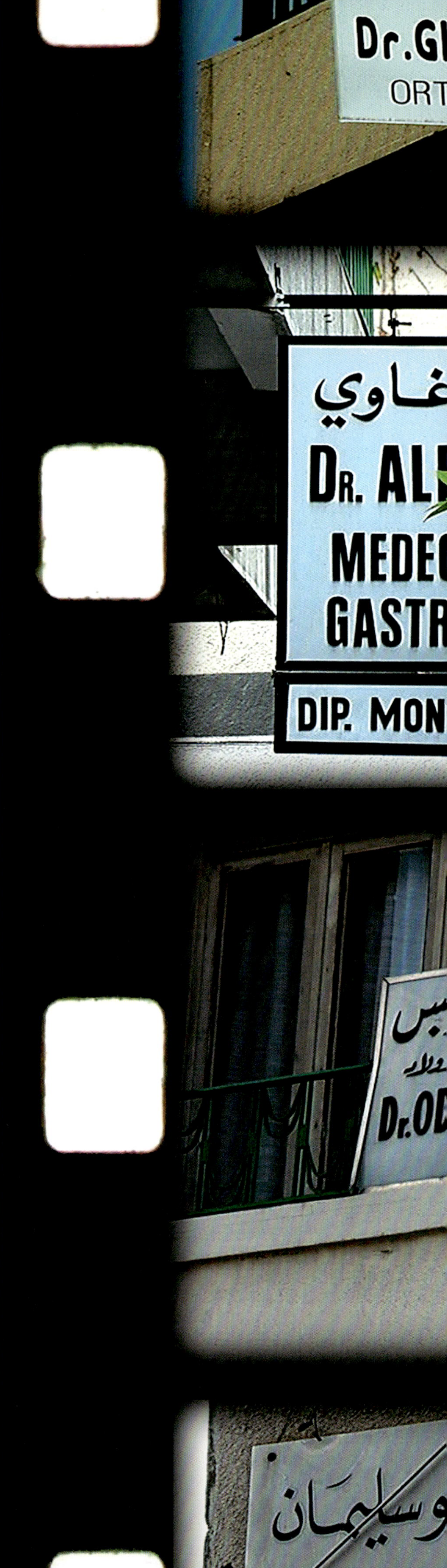

Miraculous beginnings/No, illness is neither here nor there. 1993/2003

Dr. Fakhouri carried with him wherever he went two Super 8-mm film cameras. On one camera he exposed a frame of film every time he thought the Lebanese wars had ended. On the other he exposed a frame of film every time he came across the sign for a doctor's or dentist's office. He titled the two films *Miraculous beginnings* and *No, illness is neither here nor there*.

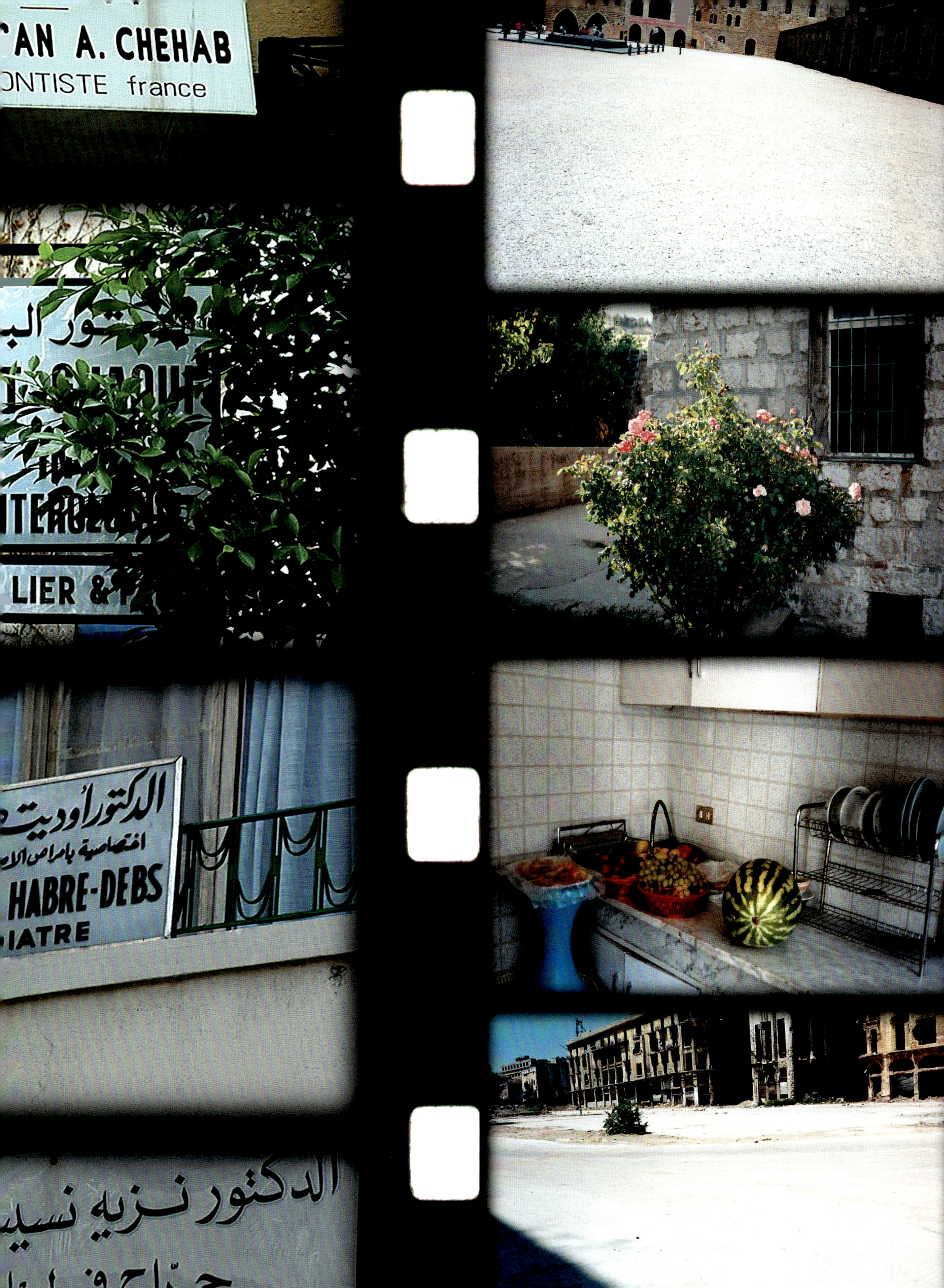
CAN A. CHEHAB
ONTISTE france
LIER &
HABRE-DEBS
IATRE
الدكتور

Secrets in the open sea. 1994/2004

Secrets in the open sea consists of twenty-nine photographic prints that were found buried under the rubble during the 1993 demolition of Beirut's war-ravaged commercial districts. The prints were different shades of blue and each measured 111 × 173 cm. In 1994, the prints were entrusted to The Atlas Group for preservation and analysis. The Atlas Group sent six of the prints to laboratories in France and the UK for chemical and digital analysis.

Remarkably, the laboratories recovered small black-and-white latent images from the blue prints. The small images represented group portraits of men and women. The Atlas Group was able to identify all the individuals represented in the small black-and-white images, and it turned out that they were all individuals who had drowned, died, or were found dead in the Mediterranean between 1975 and 1991.

Plate 18.AG_FD_Secrets.

S18B

S18L

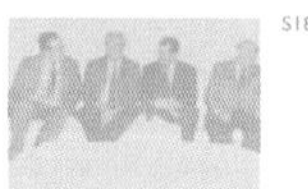

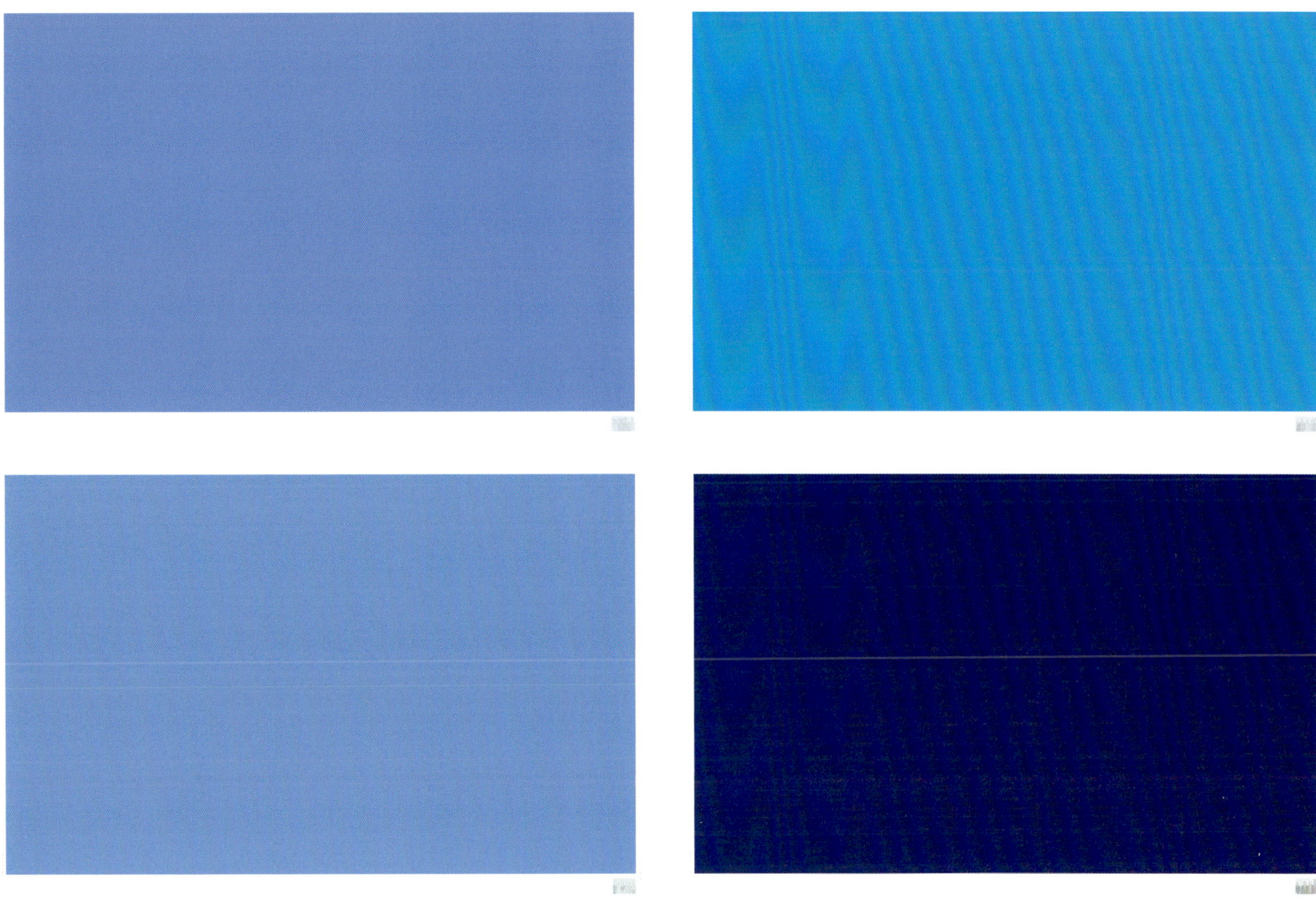

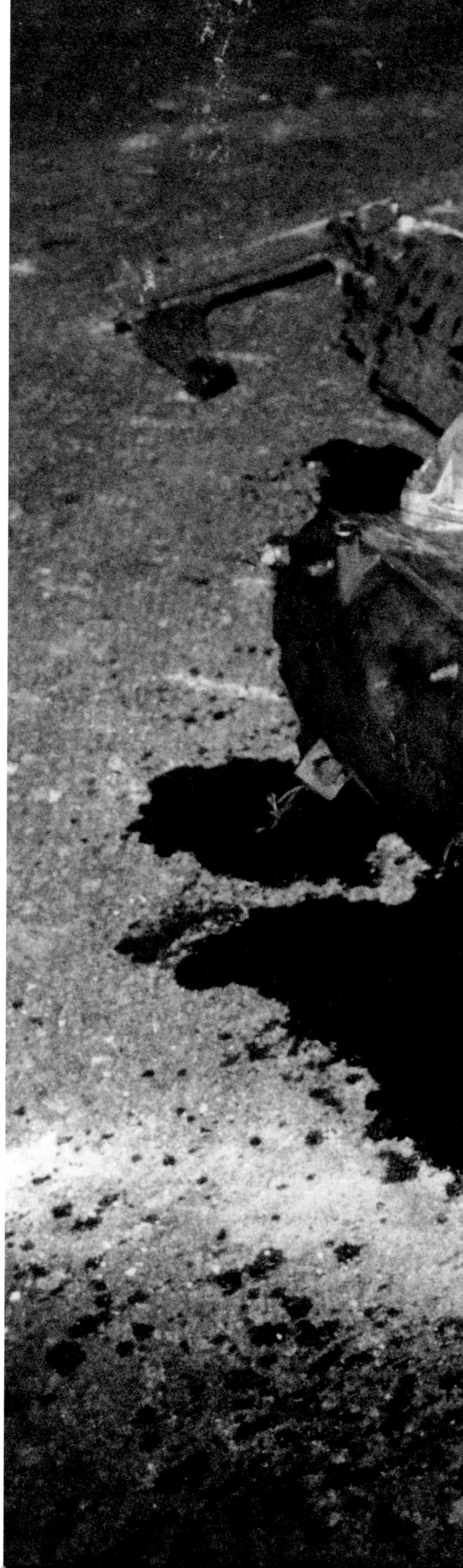

My neck is thinner than a hair: Engines. 1996–2001

My neck is thinner than a hair: Engines is a research project by The Atlas Group about the use of car bombs in the 1975–91 Lebanese wars. With this project The Atlas Group investigates the public and private dimensions of the 3,641 car bombs that were detonated during this period.

The only part that remains intact after a car bomb explodes is the engine. Landing on balconies, roofs, or adjacent streets, the engine is projected tens and sometimes hundreds of meters away from the original site of the bomb. During the wars, photojournalists competed to be the first to find and photograph the engines.

These one hundred photographs were produced by photojournalists and found by Walid Raad in the archives of An-Nahar Research Center (Beirut, Lebanon) and the Arab Documentation Center (Beirut, Lebanon).

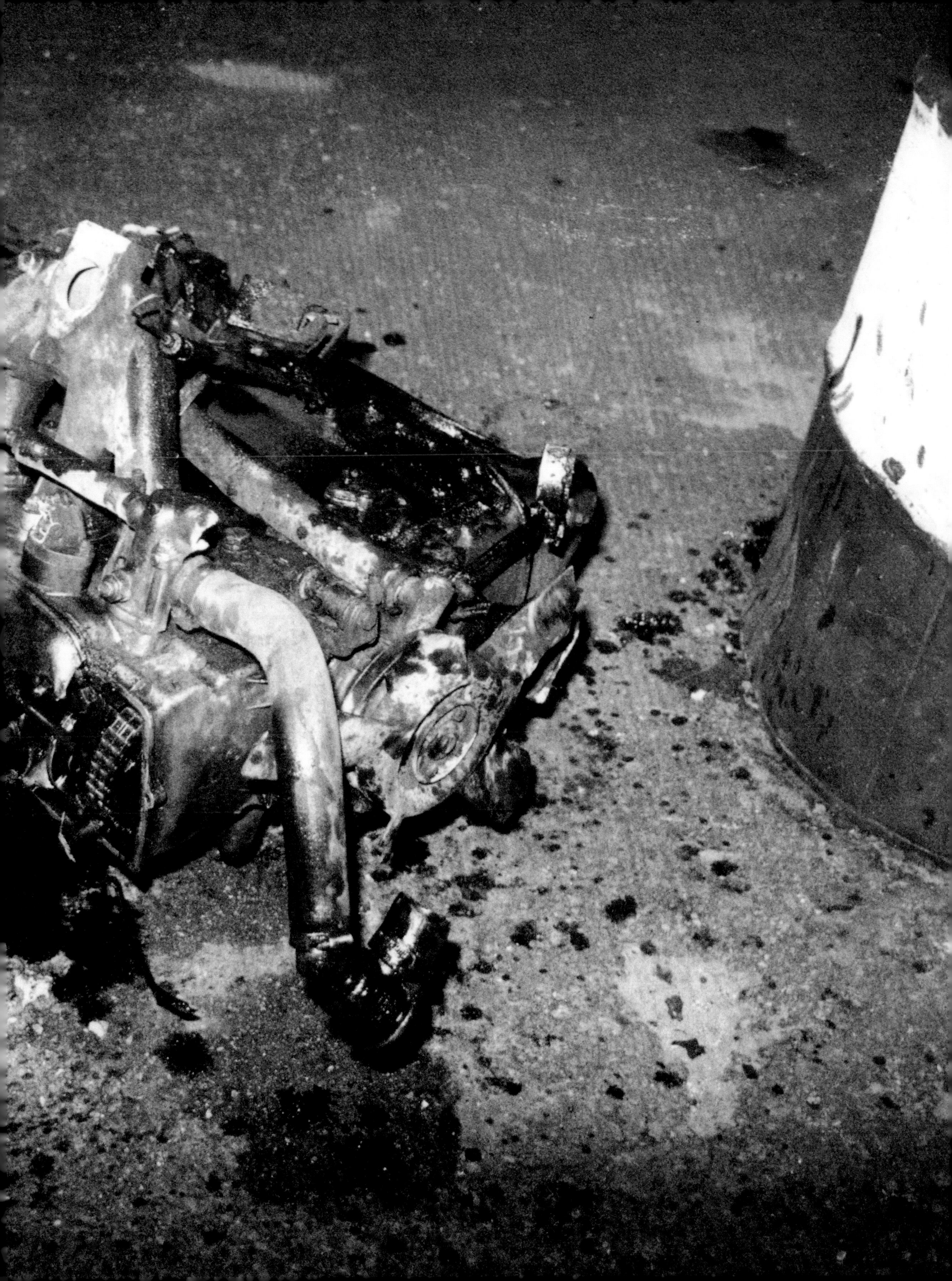

front back

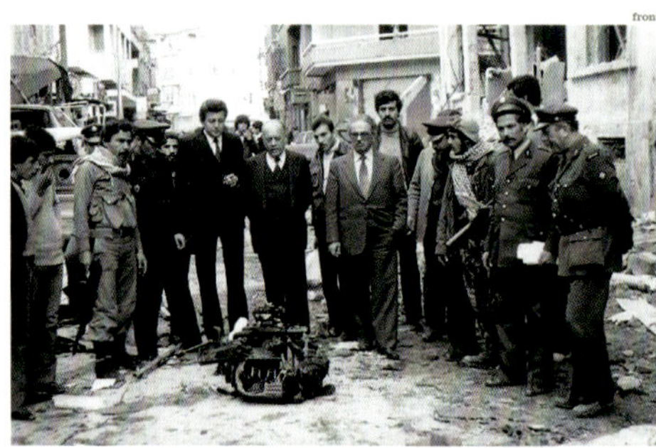

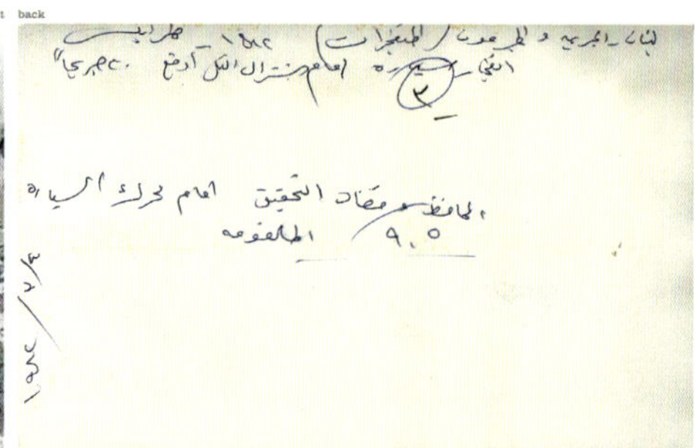

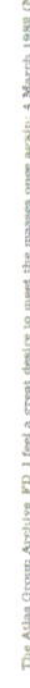

Date: 4 March 1982
Photographer | Original Archive: Unknown | An-Nahar Research Center (Beirut, Lebanon)
Notes on Back: Lebanon_Crimes_Criminals (Explosions)_1982_Tripoli

front back

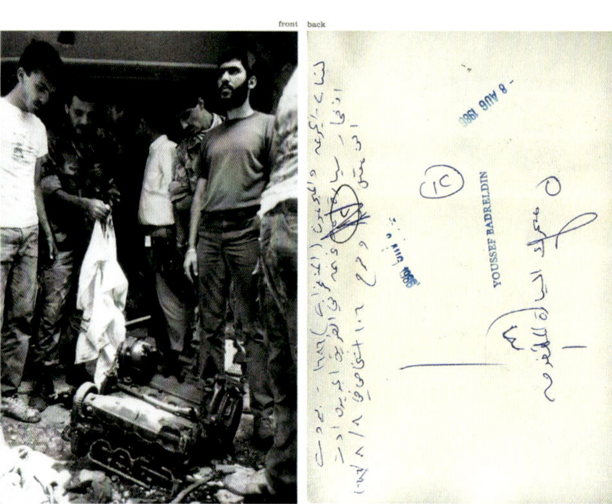

Date: 8 August 1986
Photographer | Original Archive: Yussef Badreldin | An-Nahar Research Center (Beirut, Lebanon)
Notes on Back: Lebanon_Crimes_Criminals (Explosions)_1986_Beirut

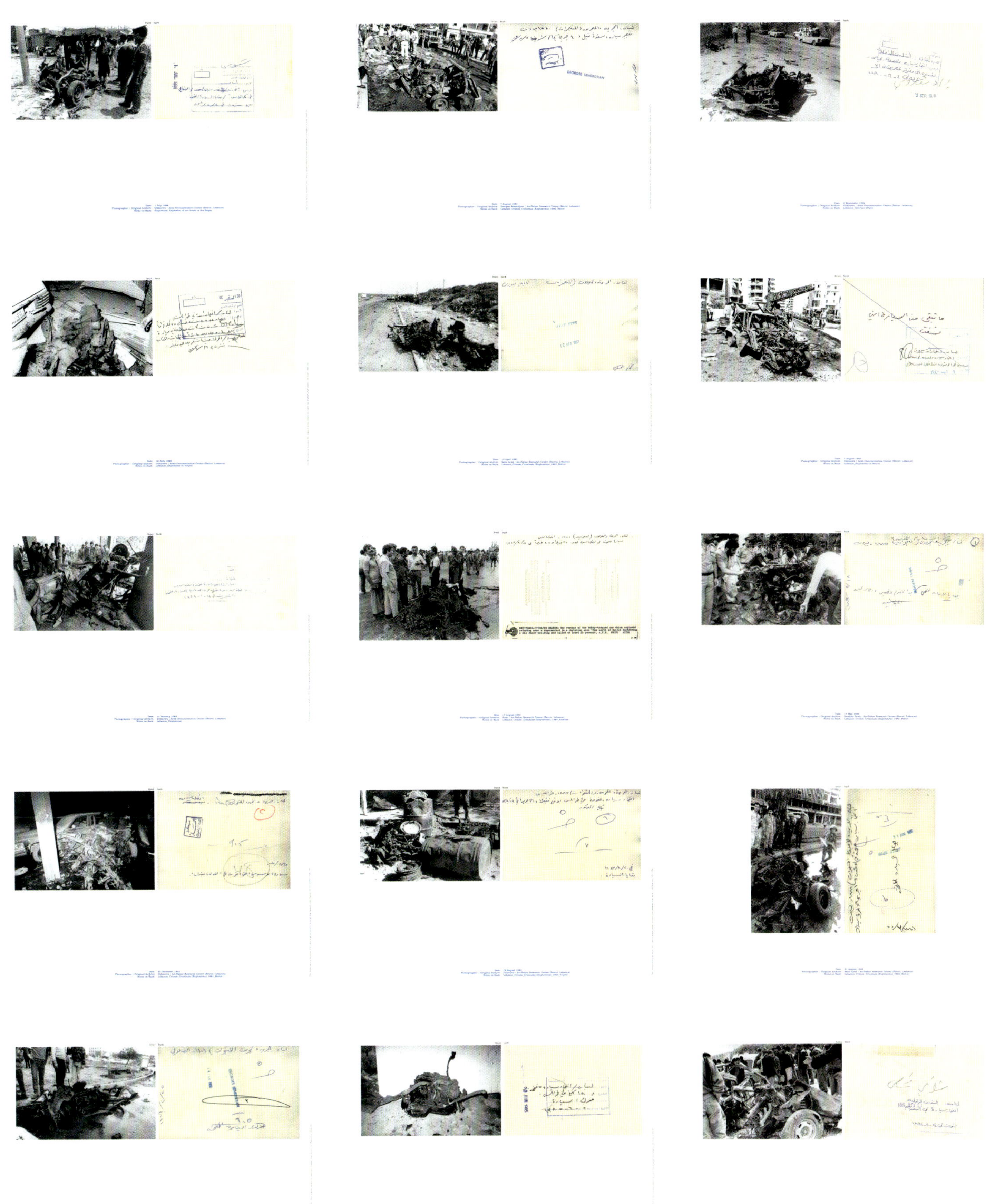

The following plates are attributed to Walid Raad, who donated them to The Atlas Group in 1998. In the statement accompanying the donation, Raad noted:

Like many around me in Beirut in the late 1970s, I collected bullets and shrapnel. I would run out to the streets after a night or day of shelling to remove them from walls, cars, and trees. I kept detailed notes of where I found every bullet and photographed the sites of my findings, covering the holes with dots that corresponded to the bullet's diameter and the mesmerizing hues I found on bullets' tips. It took me ten years to realize that ammunition manufacturers follow distinct color codes to mark and identify their cartridges and shells. It also took me another ten years to realize that my notebooks in part catalogue seventeen countries and organizations that continue to supply the various militias and armies fighting in Lebanon: Belgium, China, Egypt, Finland, Germany, Greece, Iraq, Israel, Italy, Libya, NATO, Romania, Saudi Arabia, Switzerland, the U.K., the U.S.A., and Venezuela.

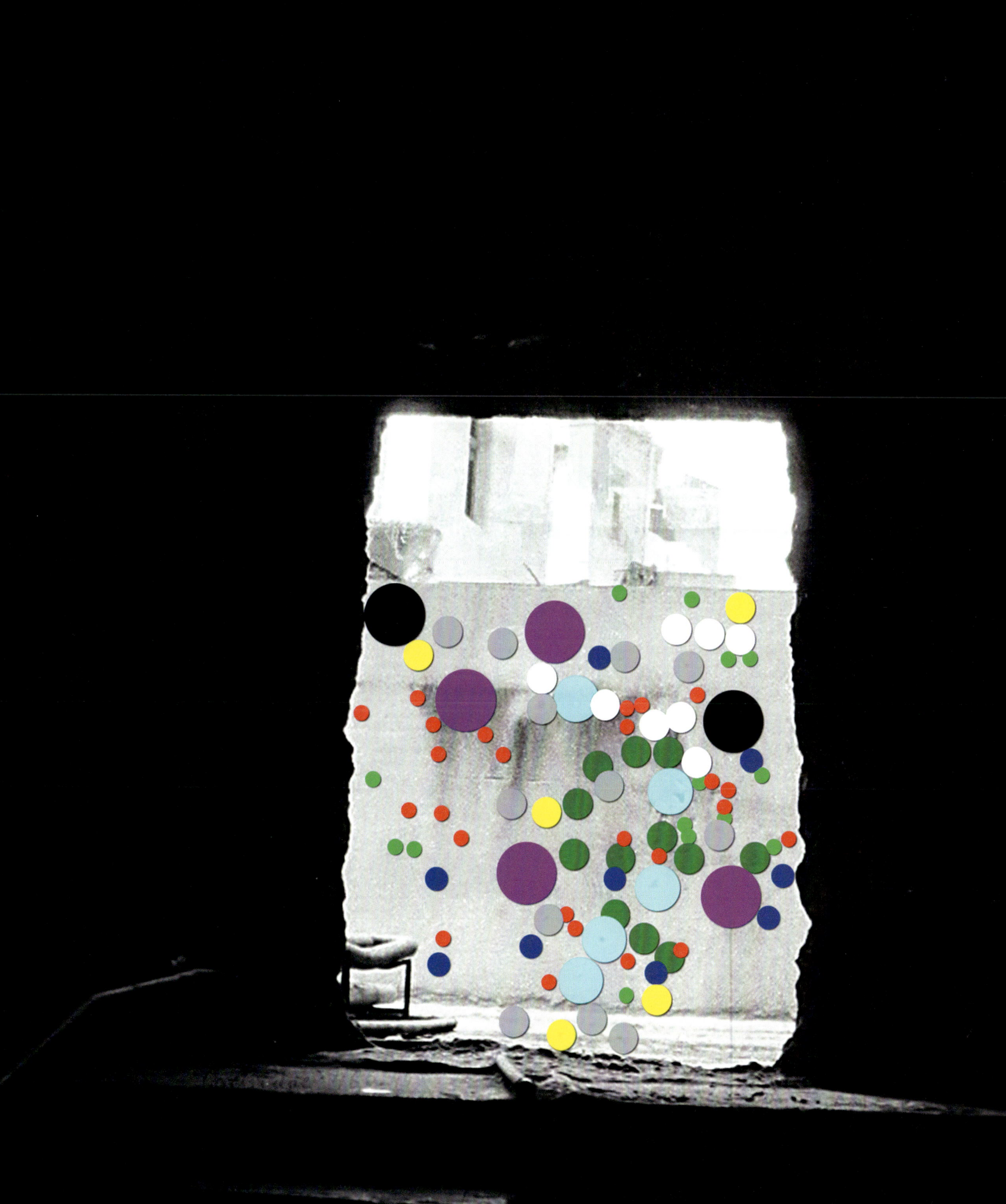

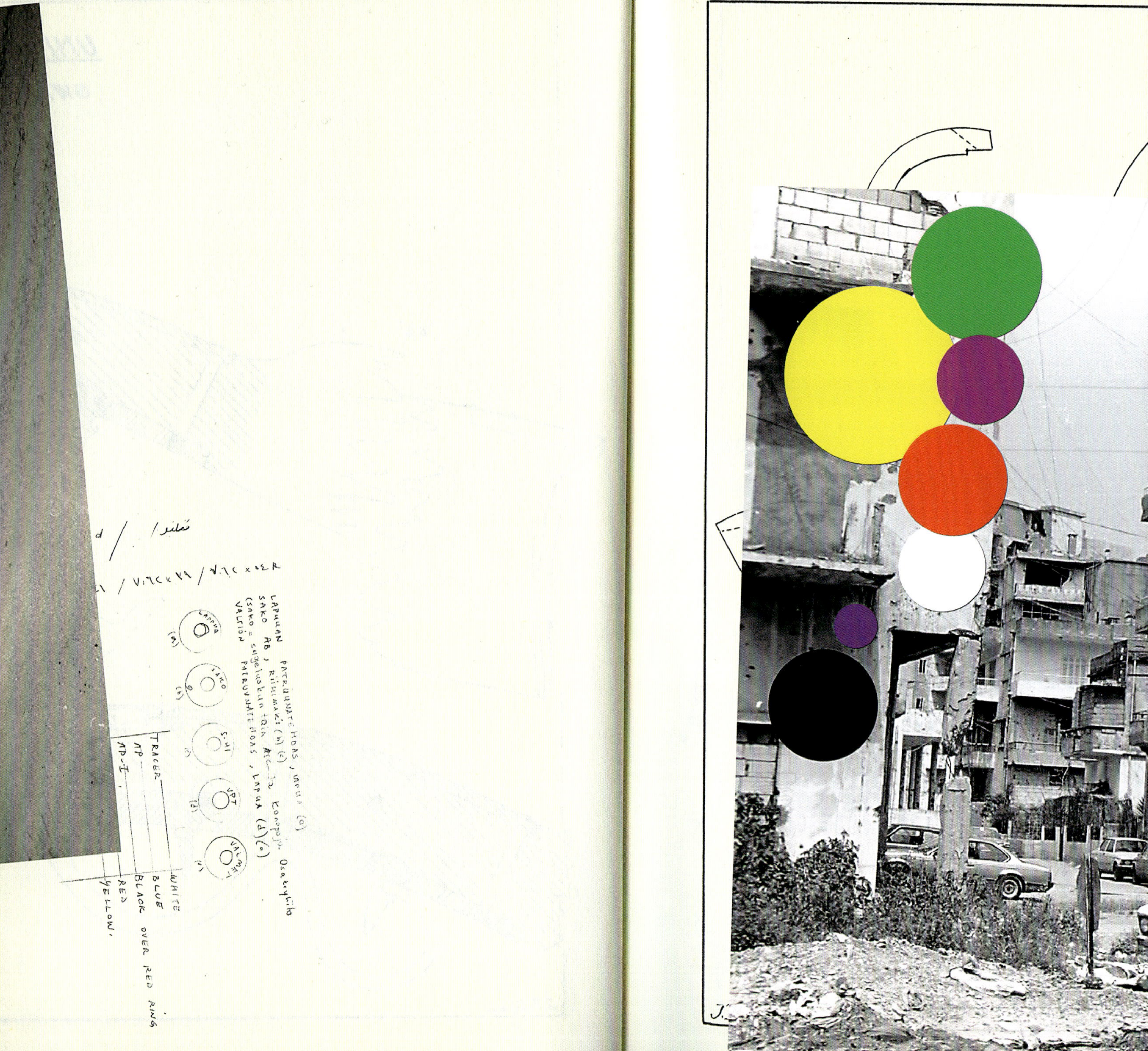

LAPUAN PATRUUNATEHDAS, LAPUA (a)
SAKO AB, RIIHIMAKI (b) (c)
VALTION PATRUUNATEHDAS, LAPUA (d)(e)
LAPPUA
SAKO
VPT
VALMET
TRACER WHITE
AP BLUE
AP-I BLACK OVER RED RING
RED
YELLOW.

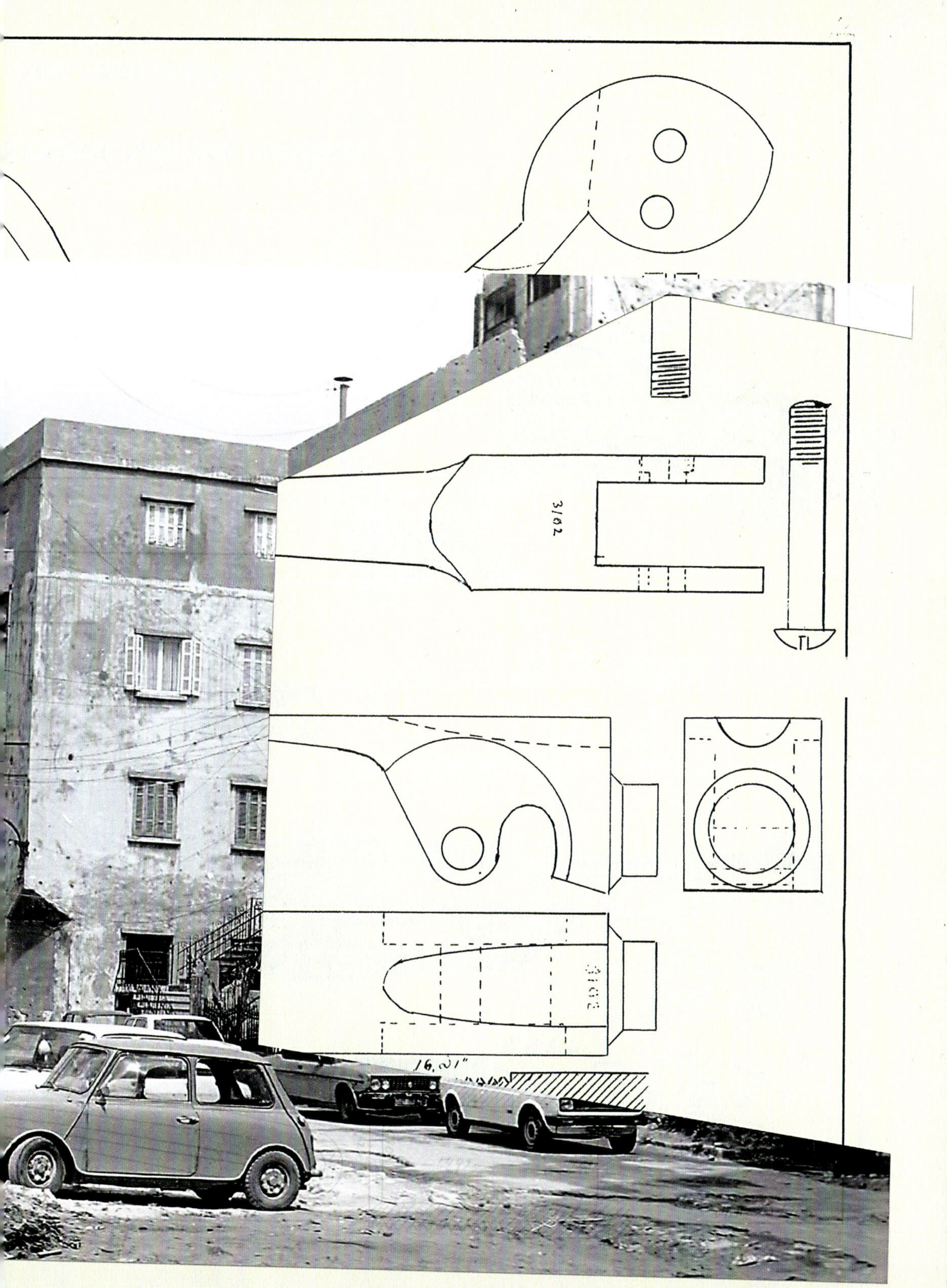

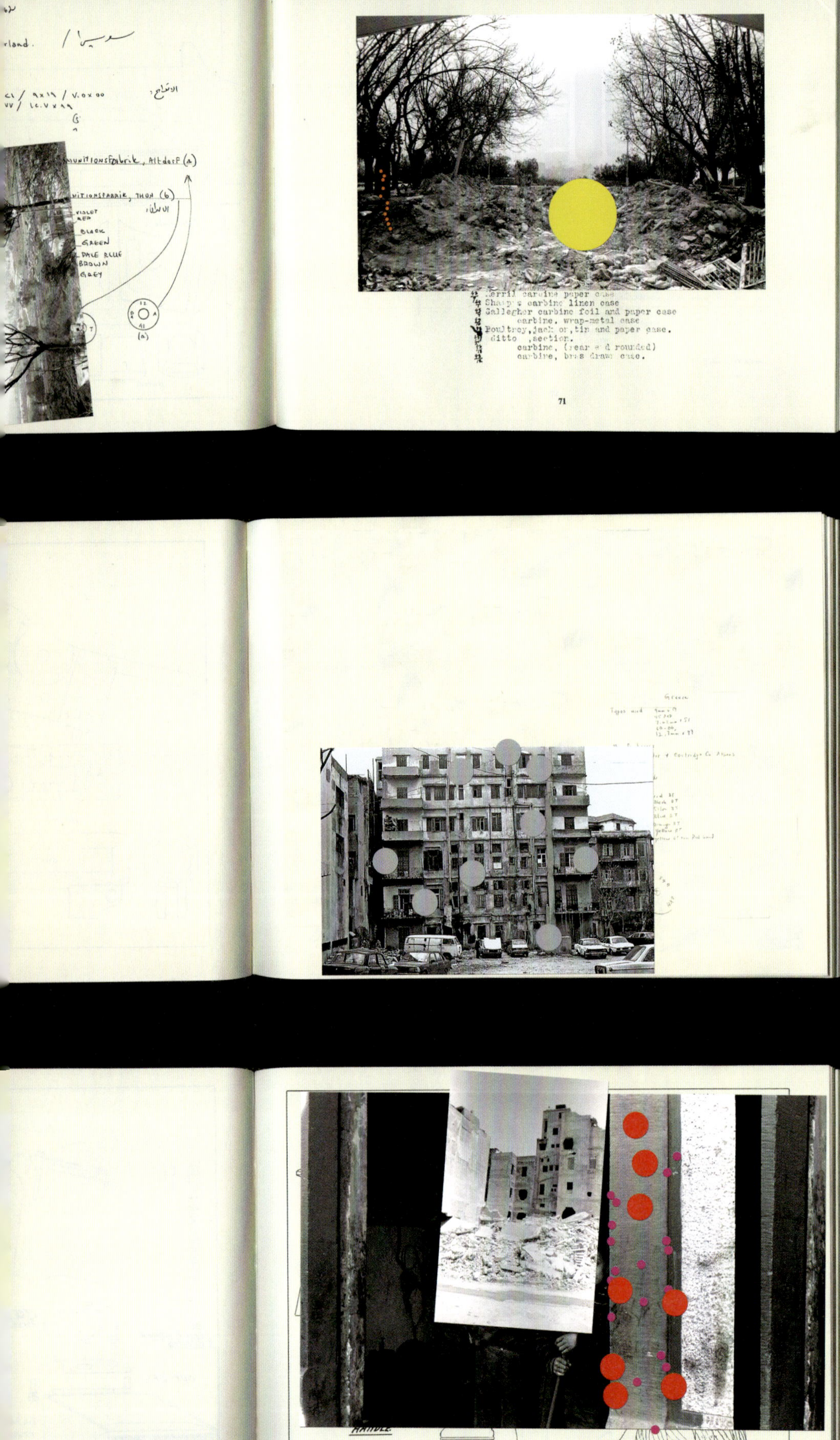

MUNITIONSFABRIK, Altdorf (a)
VIOLET
RED
BLACK
GREEN
PALE BLUE
BROWN
GREY
Sharp's carbine linen case
Gallegher carbine foil and paper case
carbine. wrap-metal case
Poultrey,jack or,tin and paper case.
ditto ,section.
carbine, (rear end rounded)
71

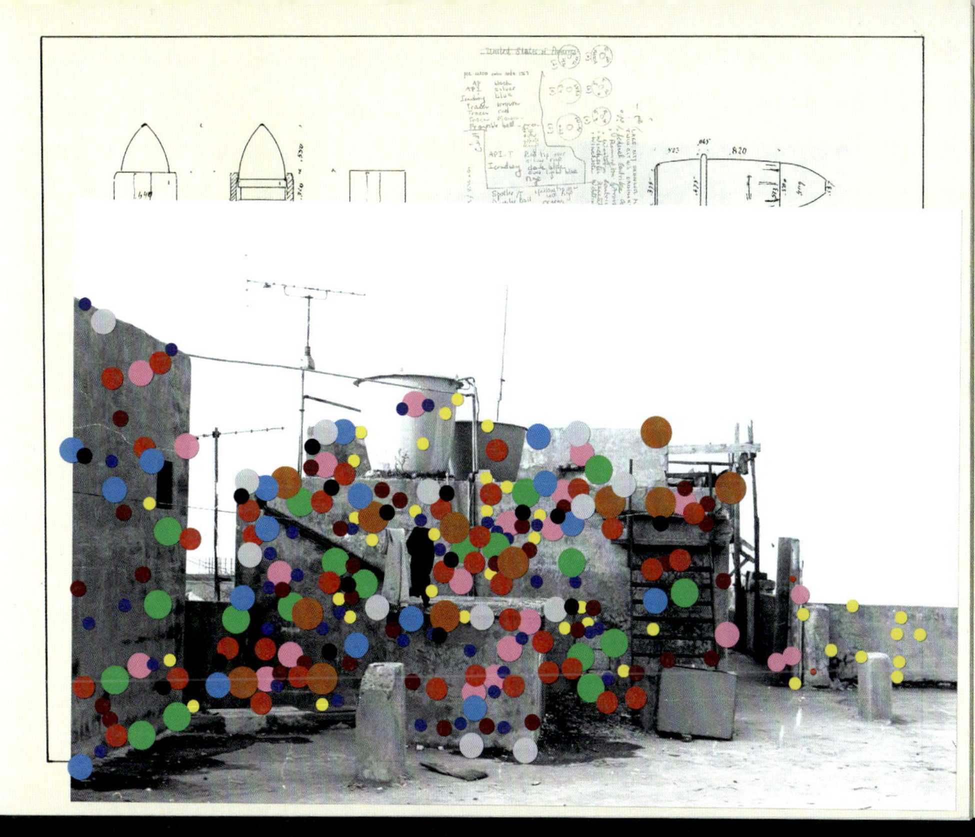

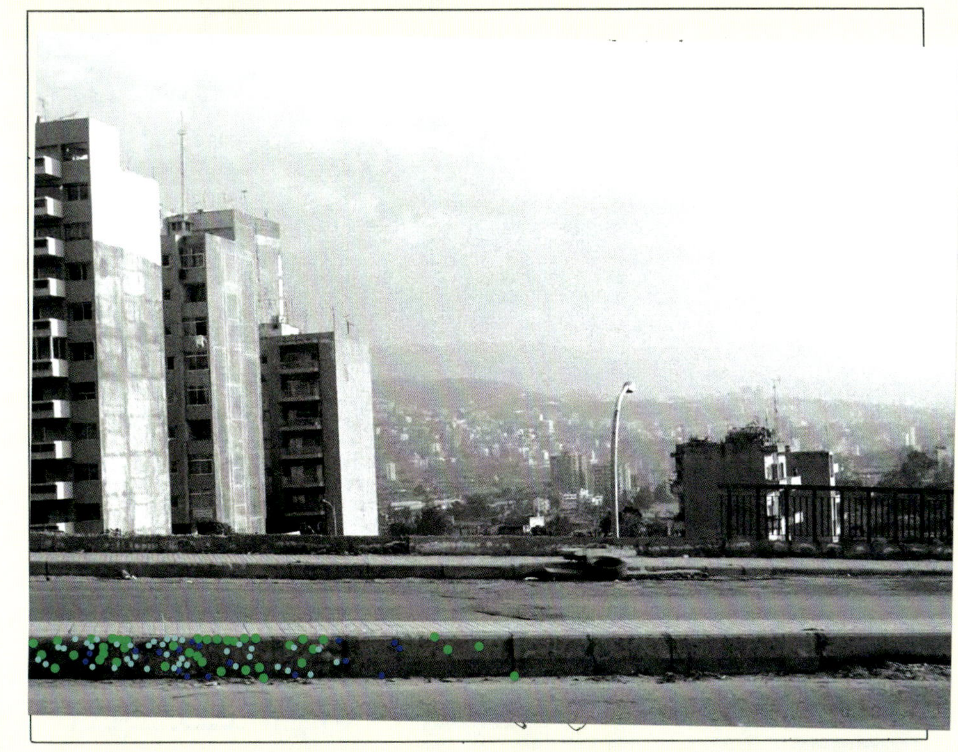

Notebook volume 38: Already been in a lake of fire. 1991/2003

This notebook contains 145 cut-out photographs of cars. They correspond to the exact make, model, and color of every car that was used as a car bomb between 1975 and 1991.

Each of the following notebook pages includes a cut-out photograph of a car that matches the make, model, and color of a car that was used as a car bomb, as well as text written in Arabic that details the place, time, and date of the explosion, the number of casualties, the perimeter of destruction, the exploded car's engine and axle numbers, and the weight and type of the explosives used.

№ 60

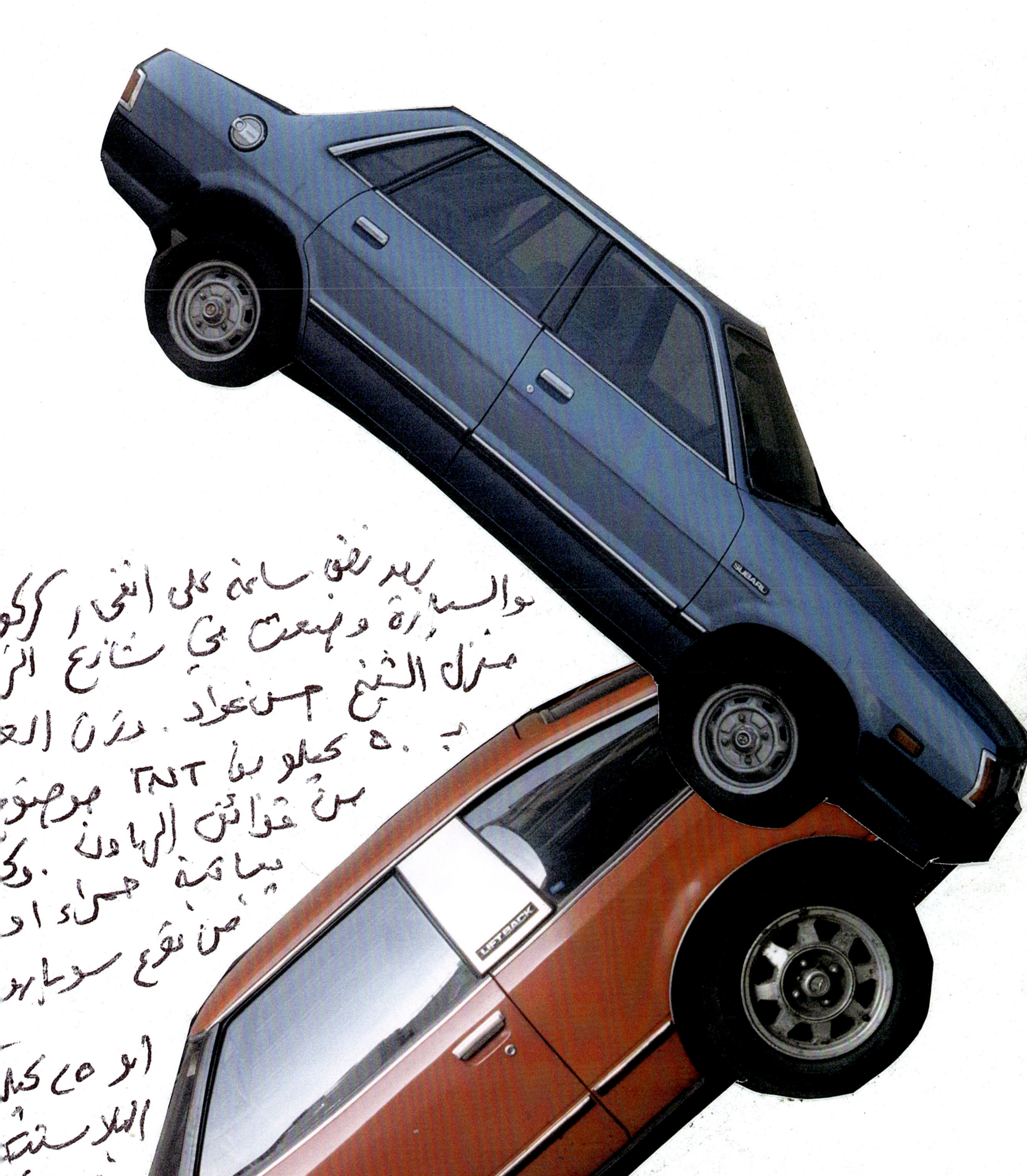
بعد نصف ساعة على انتهاء ركو
والسيارة وضعت في شارع الز
منزل الشيخ حسن عواد. وزن الع
بـ ٥٠ كيلو من TNT موضو
من قوارير الهاون
يابانية حمراء وكـ
من نوع سوبارو
او ٥٠ كيلو
البلاستيك
SUBARU
LIFTBACK

Plate 69

Renault
5
White
March 25, 1986
10:04
Beirut
8 killed
80 injured
75 kg. of TNT
Hexogen
2.4 m. X 0.8 to 1.25 m. crater

№ 69

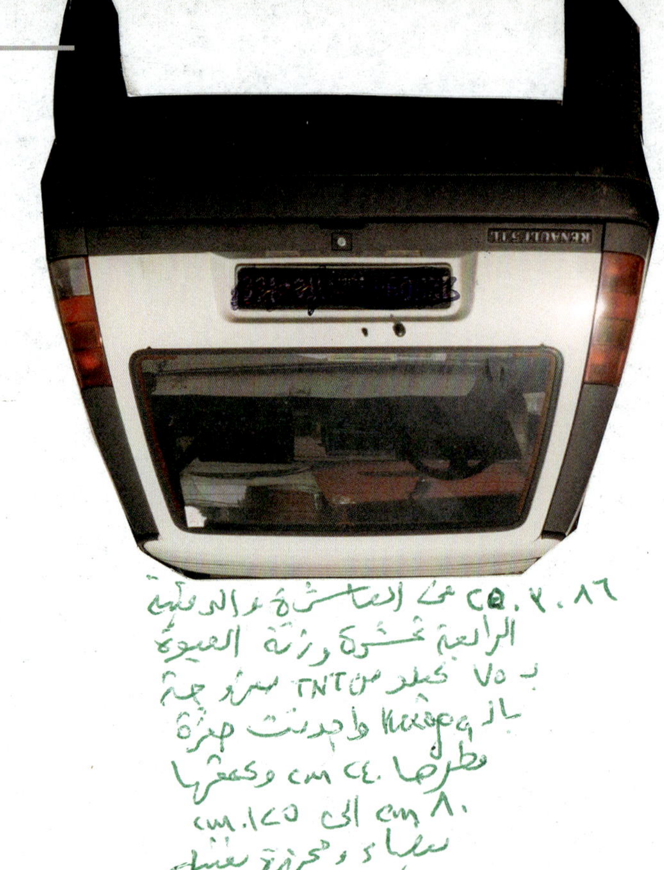

٢٥.٢.٨٦ في العاشرة والدقيقة
الرابعة تحتوي زنة العبوة
ب ٧٥ كيلو من TNT ممزوجة
بال Hexogen واحدثت حفرة
قطرها ٢٤٠ cm وعمقها
٨٠ cm الى ١٢٥ cm
بيضاء ومجهزة بفتيل
٨ قتلى و ٨٠ جريح
رينو 5

Plate 70

BMW
320
White
April 8, 1986
13:04
Jounieh
11 killed
90 injured
75 kg. of TNT
Hexogen

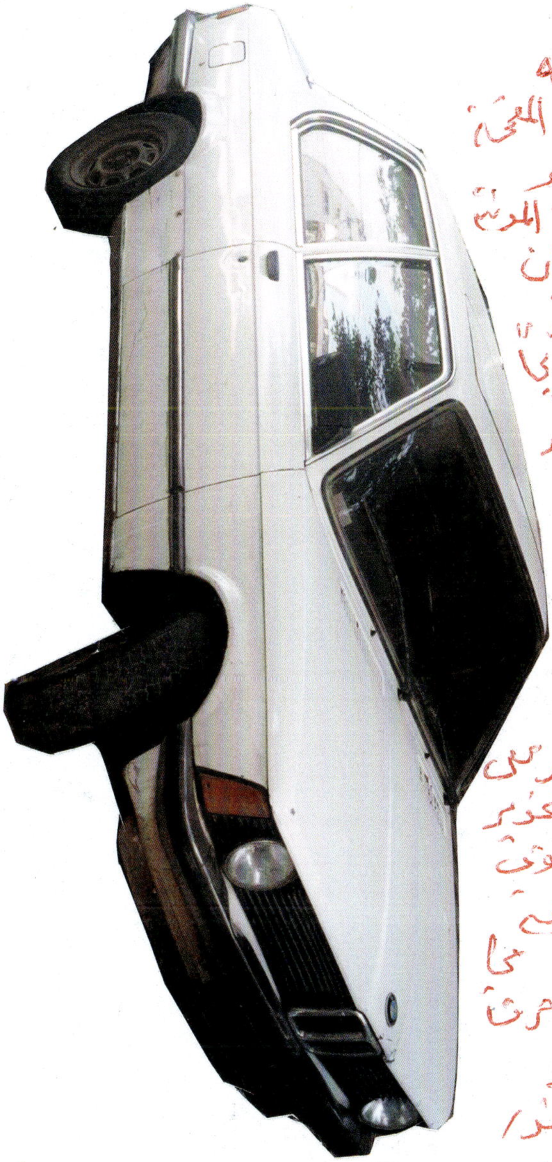

№ 70

4.8.86
جرى مسلسل السيارات المفخخة
يضرب المنطقة الشرقية و
استهدفت هذه المرة المدينة
جونية عاصمة كسروان
وأوقع الانفجار أكثر
من ١١ قتيلاً و ٩٠ جريحاً

حصل الانفجار والربع بعد
الظهر
وتبين أن السيارة
المفخخة أوقفت في
جانب جونية أمام
فرع بنك الاعتماد
المصرفي في شارع [illegible]
تقاطع [illegible] - تحديد
قرب سوق الخضر وسوق
السمك وشالة الجونية
الصغيرة في نطاق الشارع تماما
مواجهة بناية العظم شرقاً
وبناية [illegible] شمالاً
"بـ ام ف" ٣٢٠ وقدرا
زنة العبوة بـ ٧٥ كيلو من Hexogen و TNT ، ومواد حارقة أخرى
ورقم السيارة ٢٩٤٣٣٦

Plate 61

Peugeot
404 or 504
Dark green or light green
August 18, 1985
12:00
Beirut
17 killed
110 injured
35 kg. of Hexogen

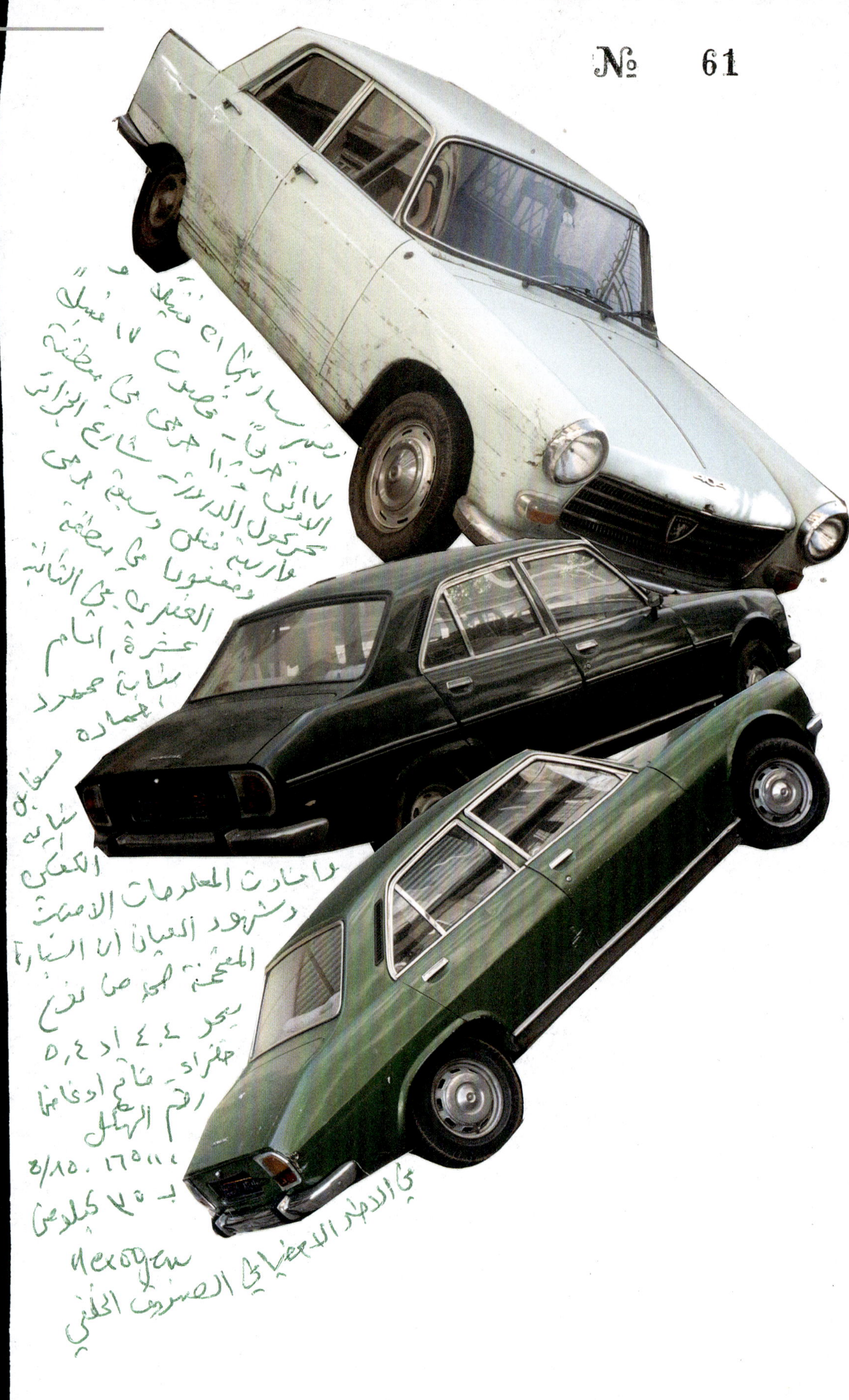

Volvo
Silver
August 20, 1985
12:22
Beirut
56 killed
120 injured
100 kg. of TNT
24 cars destroyed
31 cars damaged
11 buildings destroyed
21 stores destroyed
2.5 m. X 0.4 m. crater

№ 62

٨ - ٢٠ - ٨٥

٥٦ قتيلاً واكثر من ١٢٠ جريحاً بين اهالي منطقة ابي سمراء
ودمار وخسائر مادية جسيمة بـ ١١ بناية سكنية و ٢١
محلاً تجارياً احترق اكثر من ٢٤ سيارة وتضرر ٣١ اخرى.

الثالثة عشرة و٢٢ دقيقة /

وفقاً لقيل الرسمية. في ١٢:٢٢ دوى انفجار مشوه بمنطقة ابي
سمراء، تبين انه ناتج عن زنة ديناميت القاها مجهولون من
سيارة اوتوبيل ريكورد فضية اللون سقفها اسود. بشارع
الهالي. وبعد خمس دقائق انفجرت السيارة المفخخة وهي
VOLVO، فضية
TNT kg 90/100 رقم مركزها ٢٠٨ - ١٩٤٧
واحدثت الانفجار حفرة عمقها ٤٠ سنتمتراً وقطرها متر ونصف المتر.

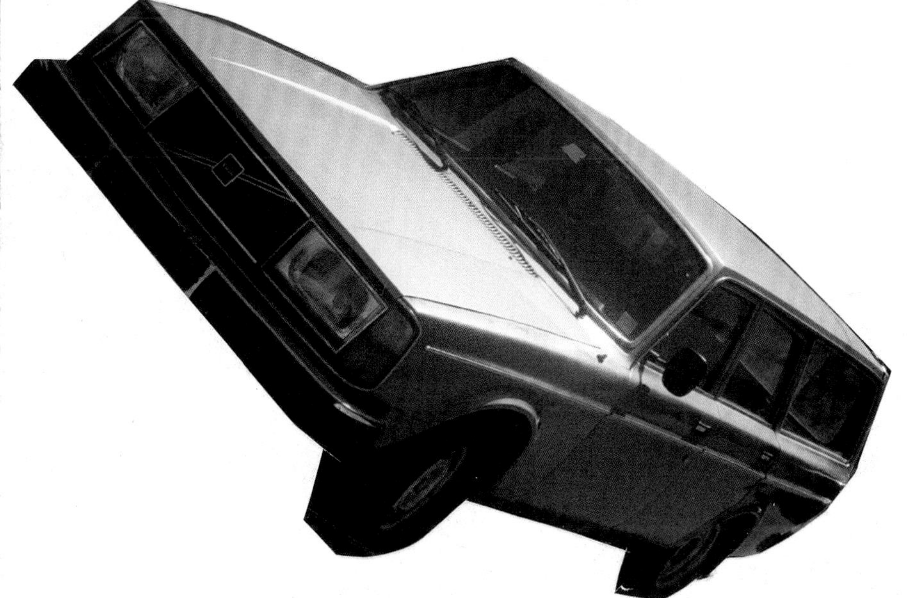

Hostage: The Bachar tapes (English version). 2001

Hostage: The Bachar tapes (English version) is attributed to Souheil Bachar and is about the abduction and detention in Lebanon in the 1980s and early 1990s of Western men like Terry Anderson and Terry Waite by "Islamic militants." This episode directly and indirectly consumed Lebanese, U.S., French, German, and British political and public life, and precipitated a number of high-profile political scandals like the Iran-Contra Affair in the United States.

In *Hostage: The Bachar tapes (English version)* this crisis is examined through the testimony of Souheil Bachar, who was held hostage in Lebanon between 1983 and 1993. What is remarkable about Souheil's captivity is that he was held for three months in 1985 in the same cell as five American men: Terry Anderson, Thomas Sutherland, Benjamin Weir, Martin Jenco, and David Jacobsen.

In 2000, Souheil collaborated with The Atlas Group to produce fifty-three videotapes about his captivity. Tapes #17 and #31 are the only tapes he makes available outside of Lebanon. In the tapes, Souheil addresses the cultural, textual, and sexual aspects of his detention with the Americans.

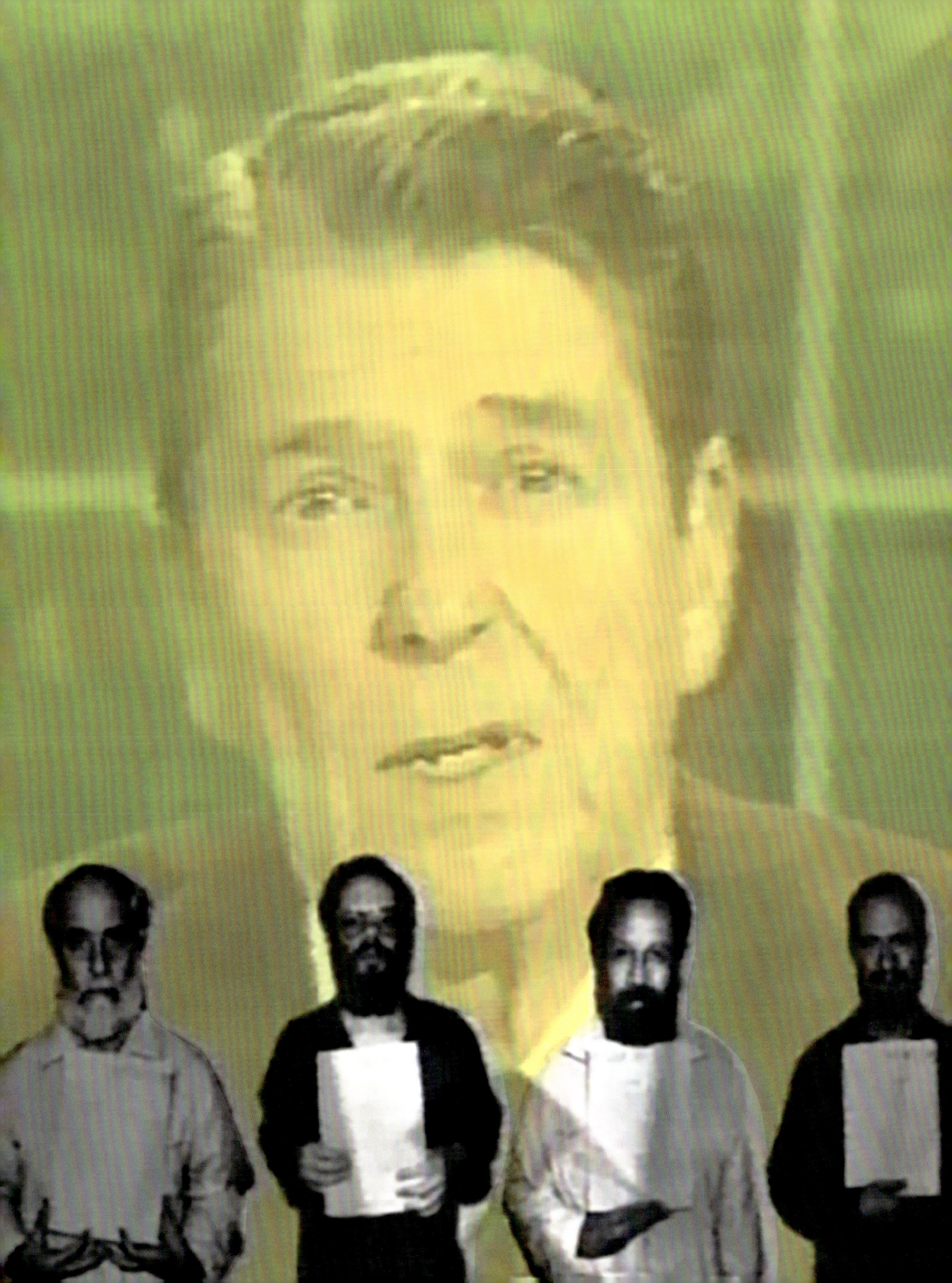

Please translate what I say in the following tapes into
the official language of the country where the tapes are screening.

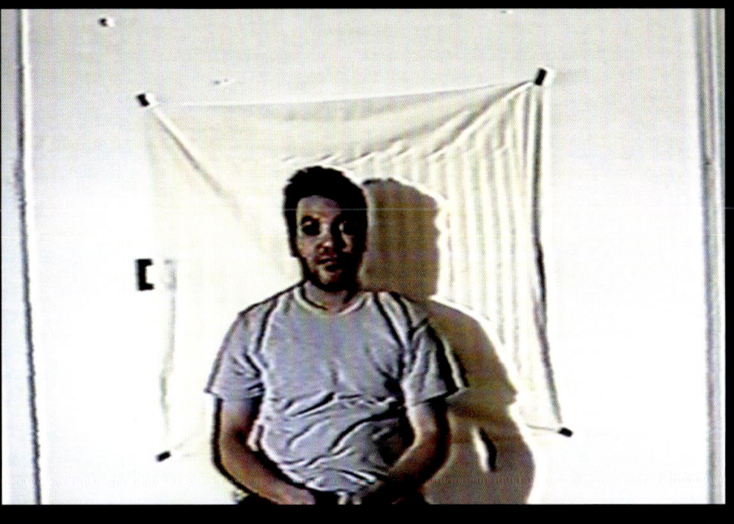

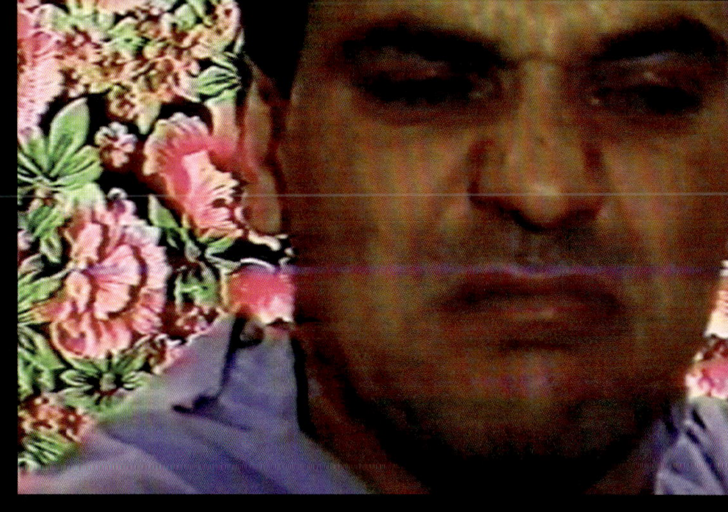

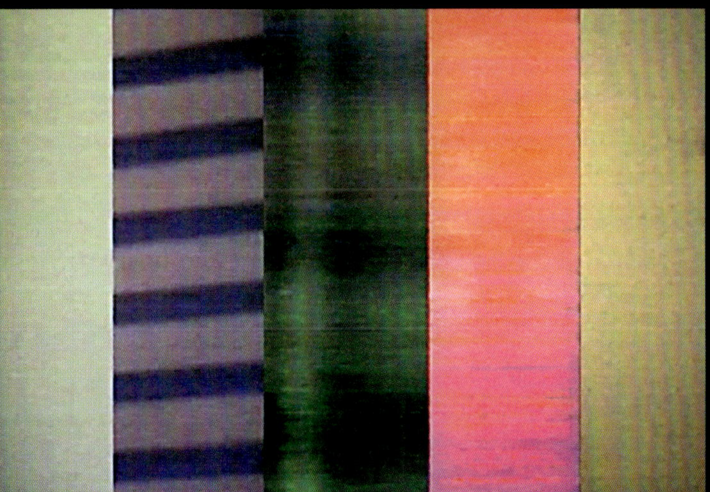

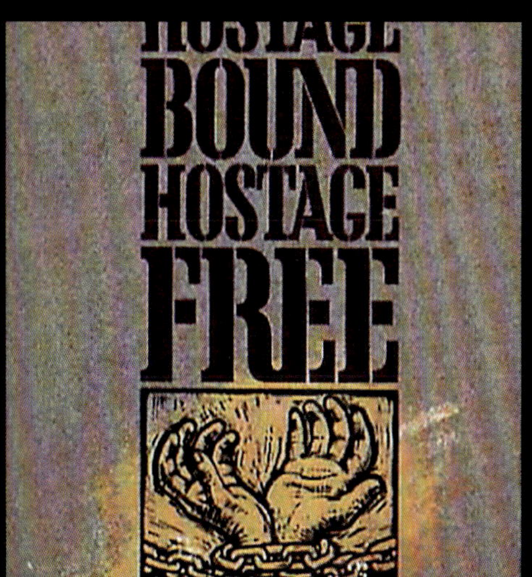

I only wish that I could weep. 1997/2002

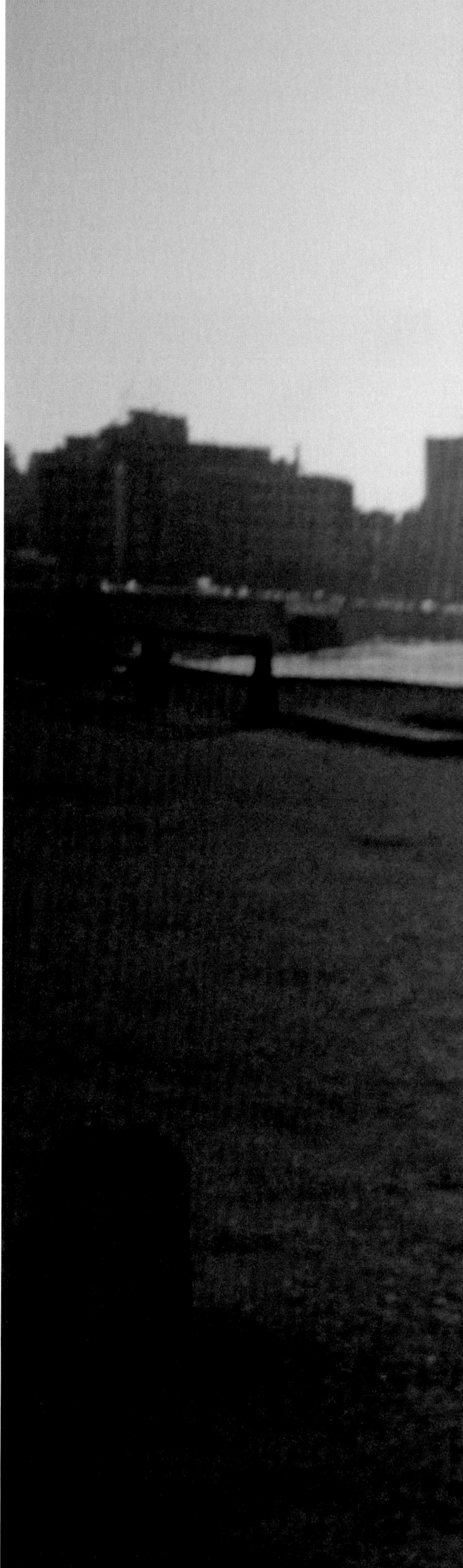

This document is attributed to Operator #17, a Lebanese Army intelligence officer who was assigned to monitor the Corniche, a seaside boardwalk in Beirut. From 1997 on, the officer decided to videotape the sunset instead of his assigned target. This videotape recounts the operator's story and concentrates on the footage he was permitted to keep after his dismissal.

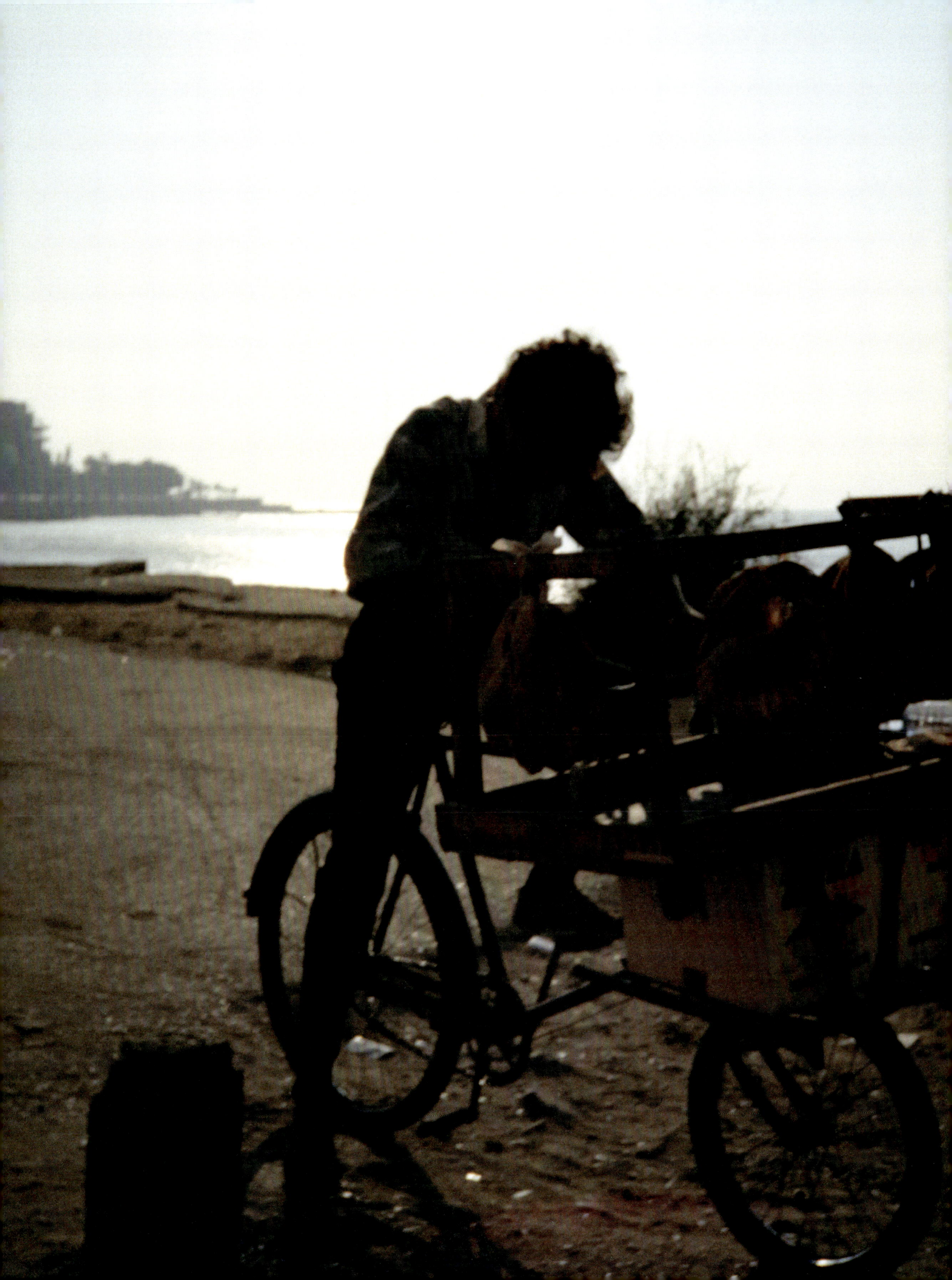

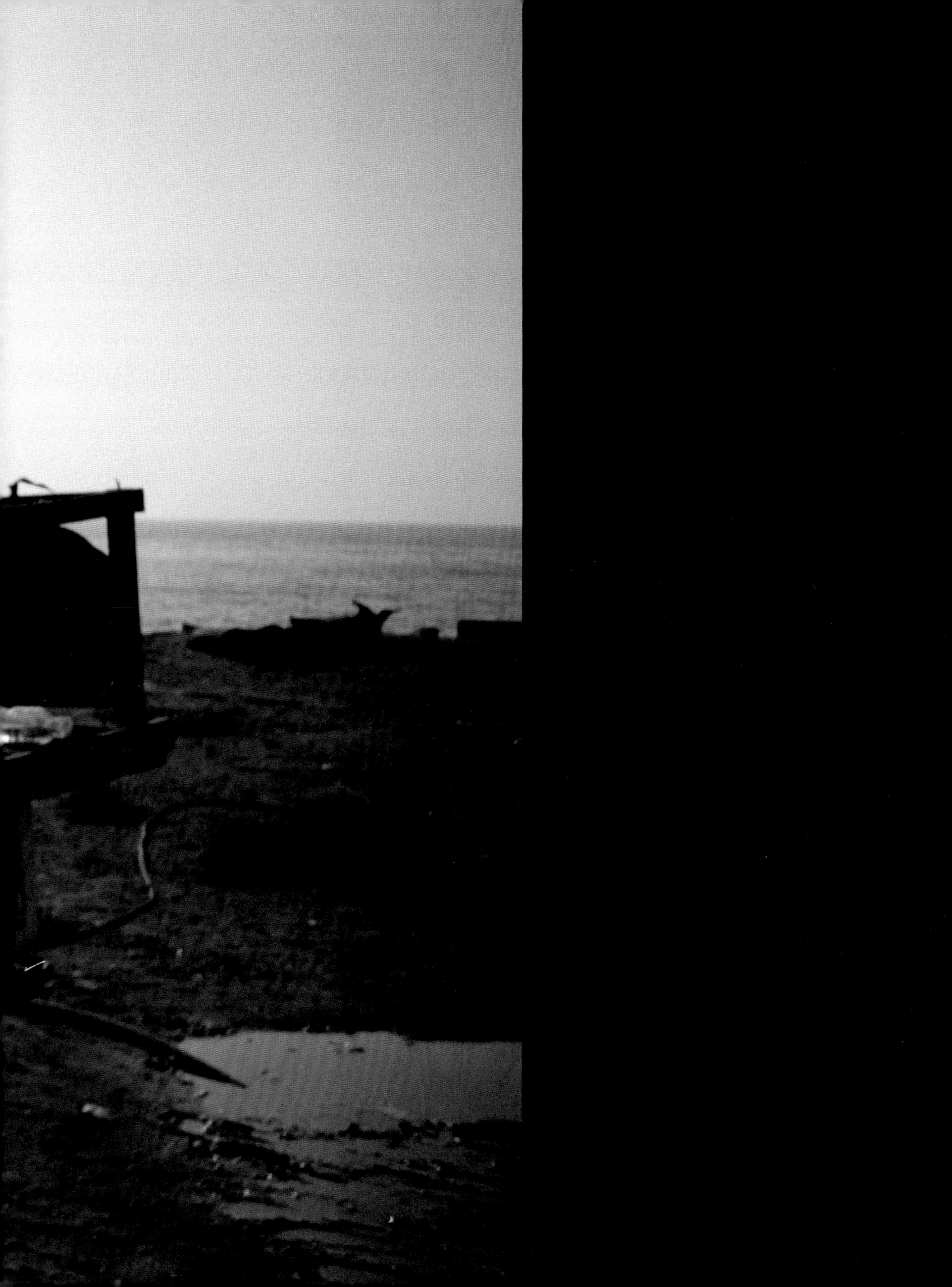

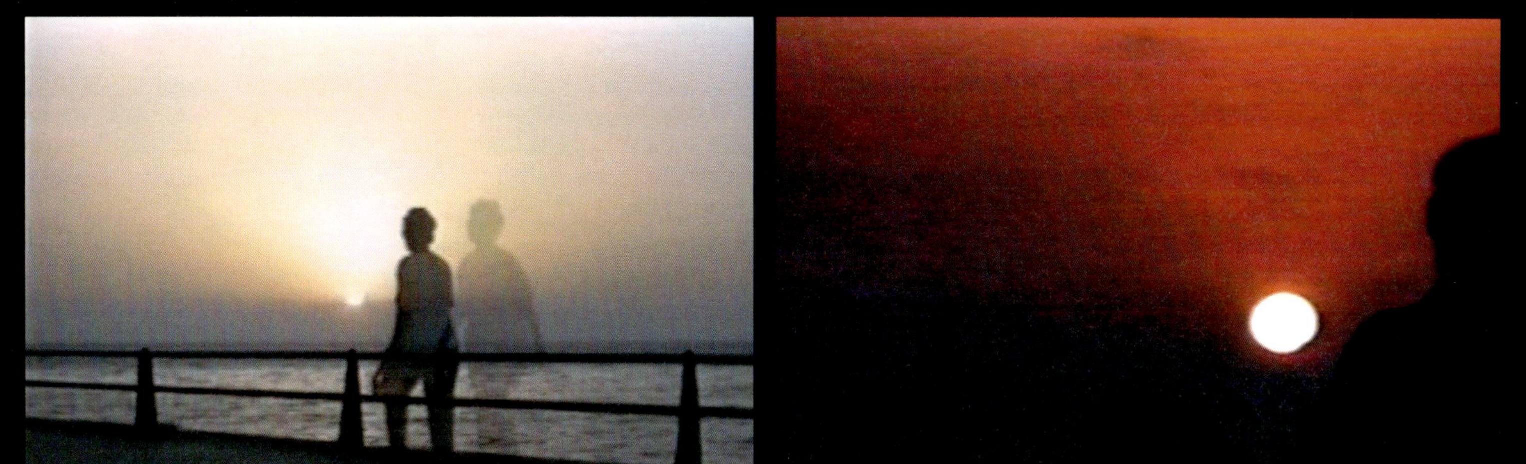

Oh God, he said, talking to a tree. 2004/2008

The following prints are attributed to Nahia Hassan, who donated them to The Atlas Group in 2004. Until her dismissal in 1994, Hassan was a senior topographer in the Lebanese Army's Directorate of Geographic Affairs. Her tasks included the investigation of all missile attacks on Lebanese soil.

In her time off, and as an amateur painter, Hassan painted hundreds of small watercolors of the plumes of smoke, debris, and fire produced by the missiles she tracked. Moreover, and consistently over her twenty-five-year career, she sent the paintings as thank-you gifts to the officers and enlisted men and women who served with her. While some reprimanded her for her insensitivity and others commended her for her formal mastery, few turned down Hassan's painted gifts.

The following are thirty-one such turned-down thank-you gifts.

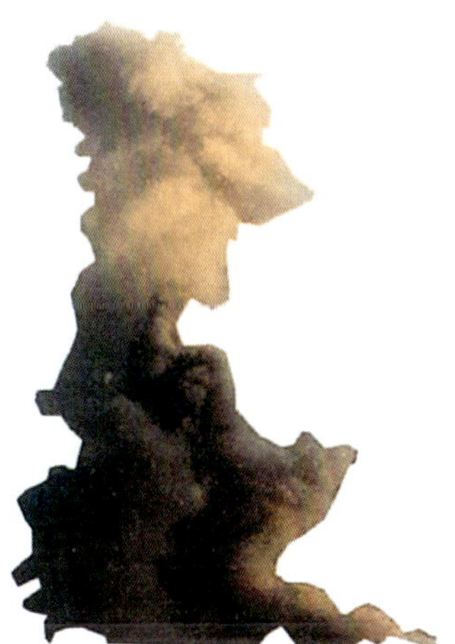

Beirut_August 6, 2006

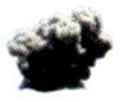

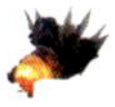

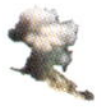

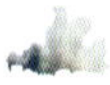

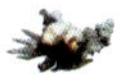

We are a fair people. We never speak well of one another. 1994/2013

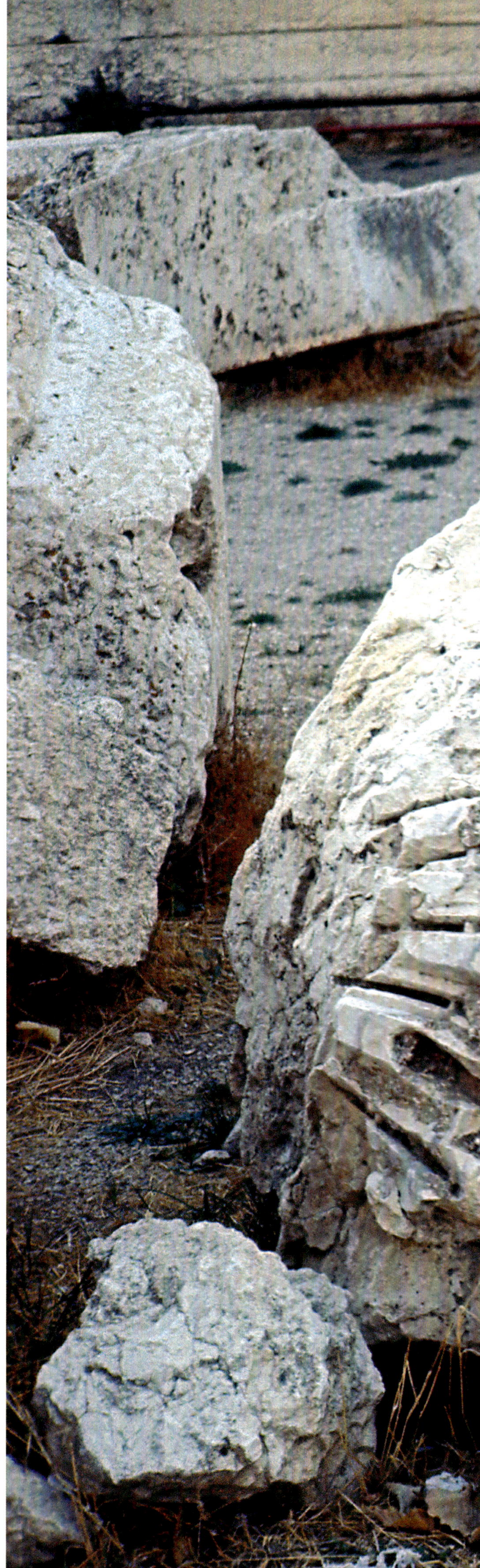

The following photographs were donated to The Atlas Group in 1994. The anonymous donation was accompanied by the following statement:

I always wondered why my father feared the land as he did. Family excursions to the mountains or ancient sites left him shaken and pale. An avid photographer, he photographed our outings and would spend hours alone in his workshop, hunched over his slides with tweezers and a magnifying glass, consumed by what he was seeing or doing. I recently and finally managed to see the slides in question. It goes without saying that my father was clearly seeing things.

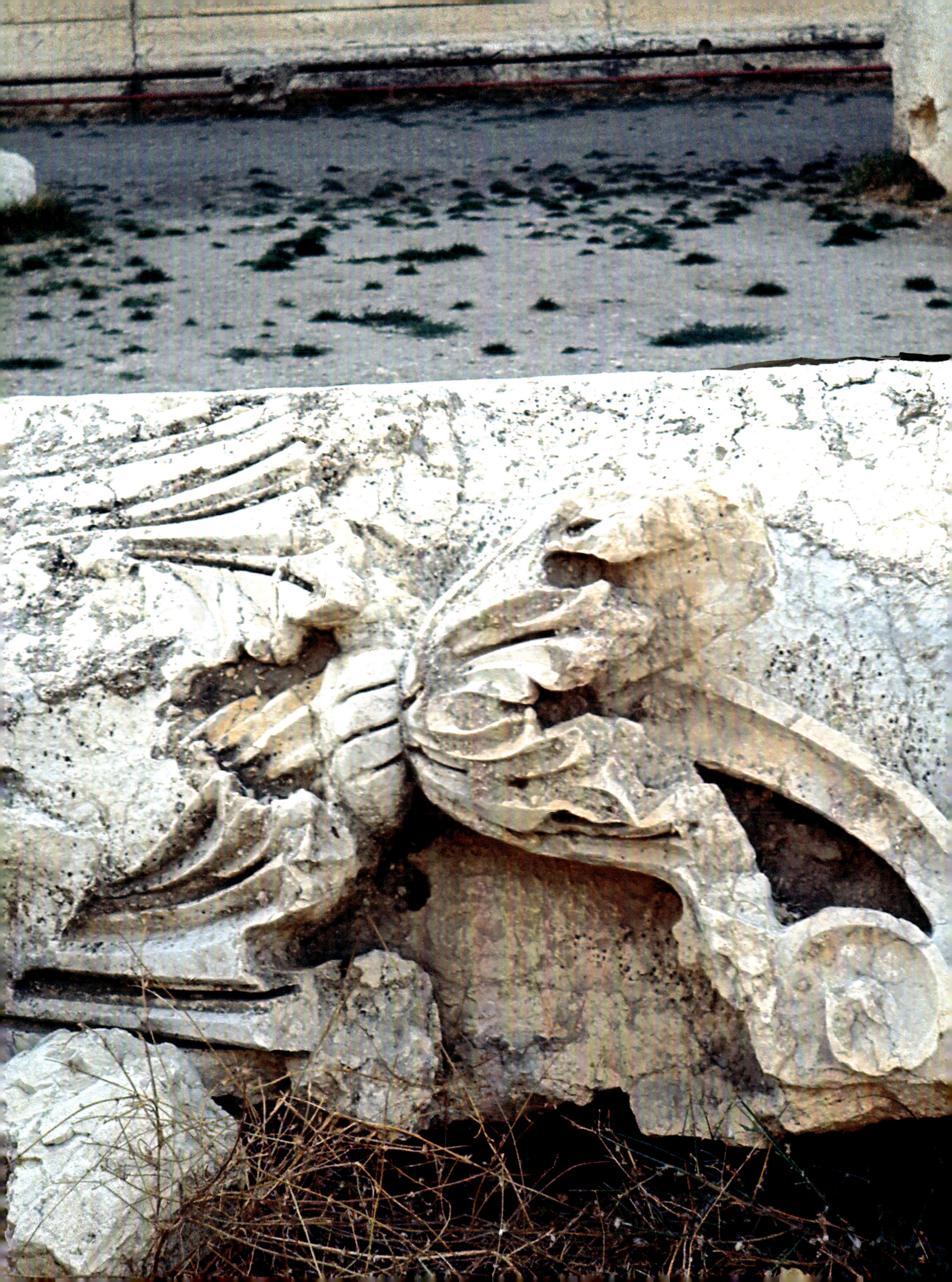

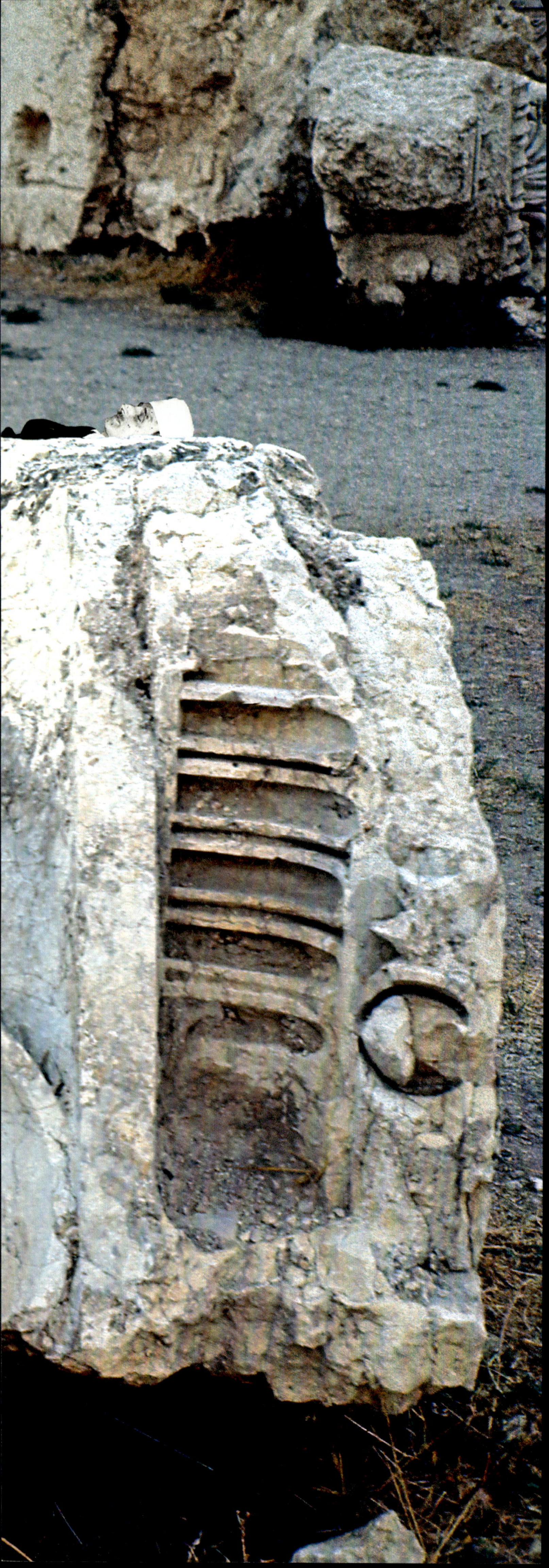

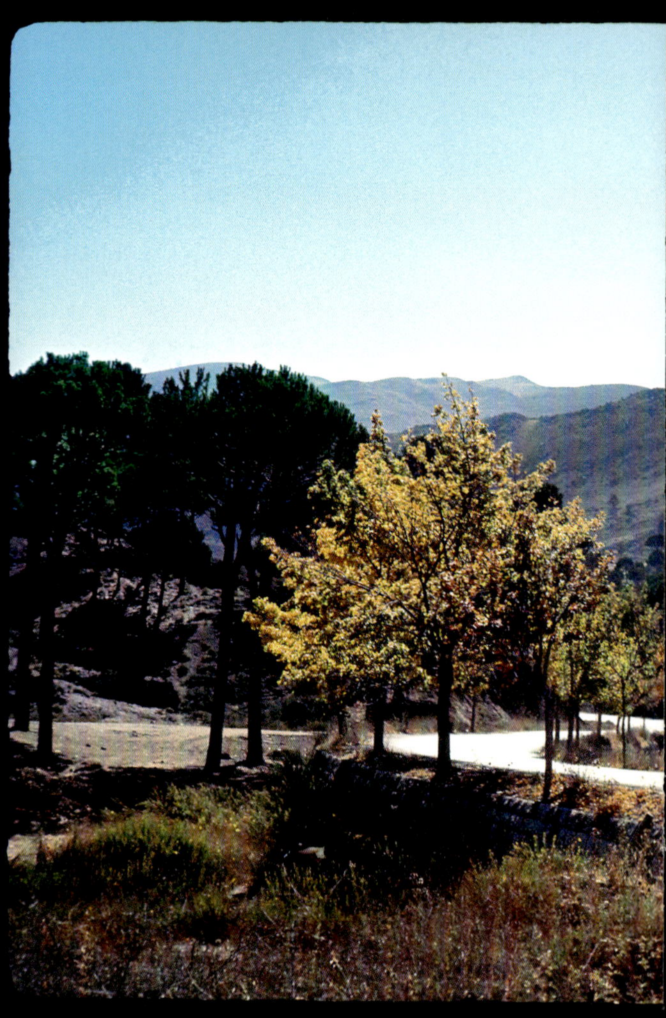

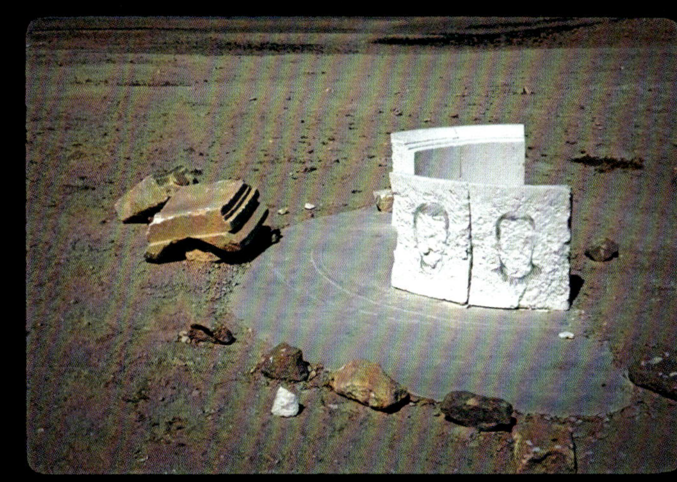

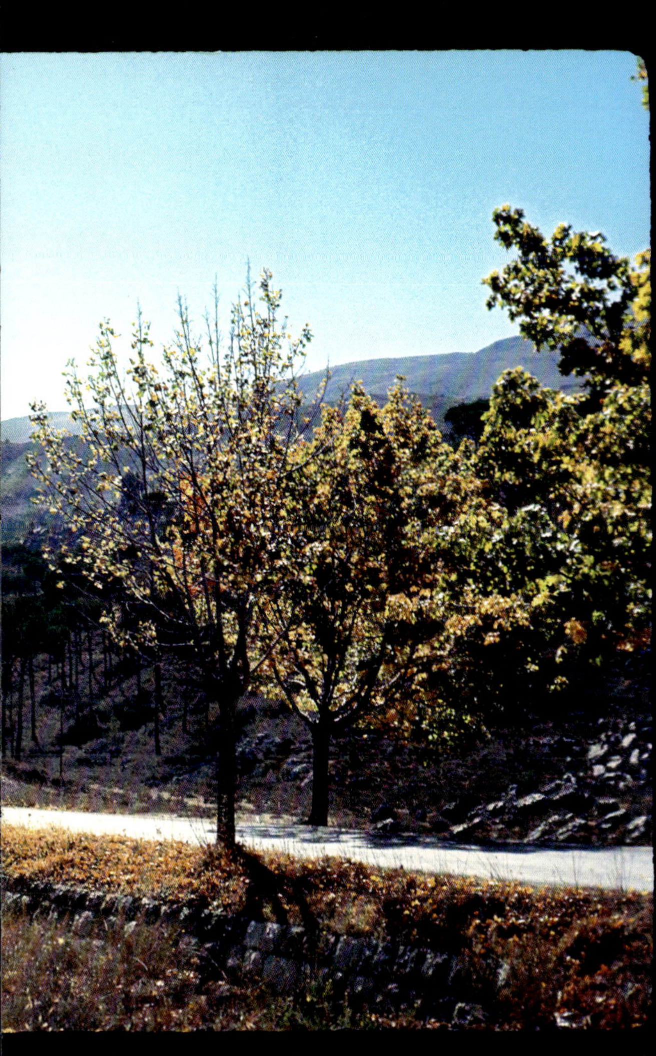

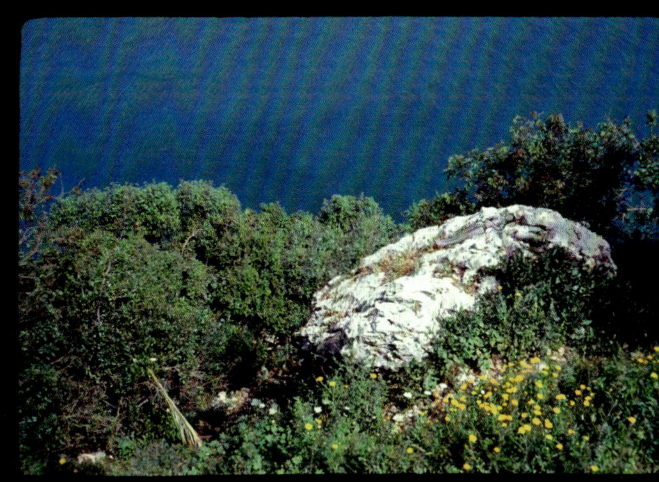

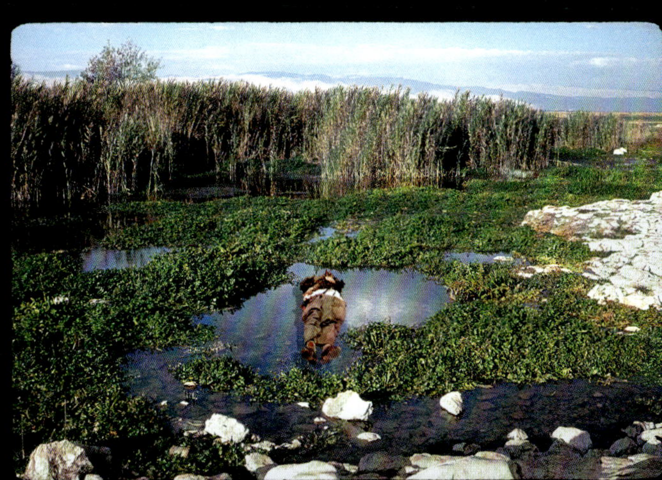

Better be watching the clouds. 2000/2015

▲ ***Trifolium s***

Woodland.

Showy clover.

Pubescent plan

leaf; purple-vi

▼▼ ***Trifoliu***

Waste ground.

Bladder trefoil.

Glabrous plant

pink corolla 10

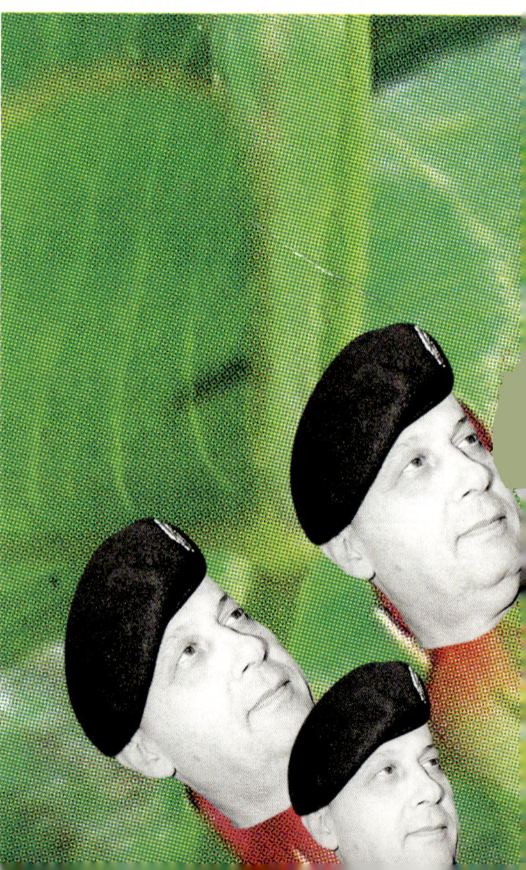

The following plates were donated to The Atlas Group in 2000. The anonymous donation came in a box labeled with the following words: *Comrade leader, Comrade leader, you'd better be watching the clouds.*

iosum Willd. **Sohmor, Aaïchiyeh**.

EFLE REMARQUABLE. **نفل بهي**

0-30 cm; elliptical and denticulate eous corolla with showy standard.

spumosum L. **Ghazir, Khaldeh**.

ÈFLE ÉCUMEUX. **نفل مزبد**

0-40 cm; oval denticulate leaves; mm; calyx with ± equal teeth.

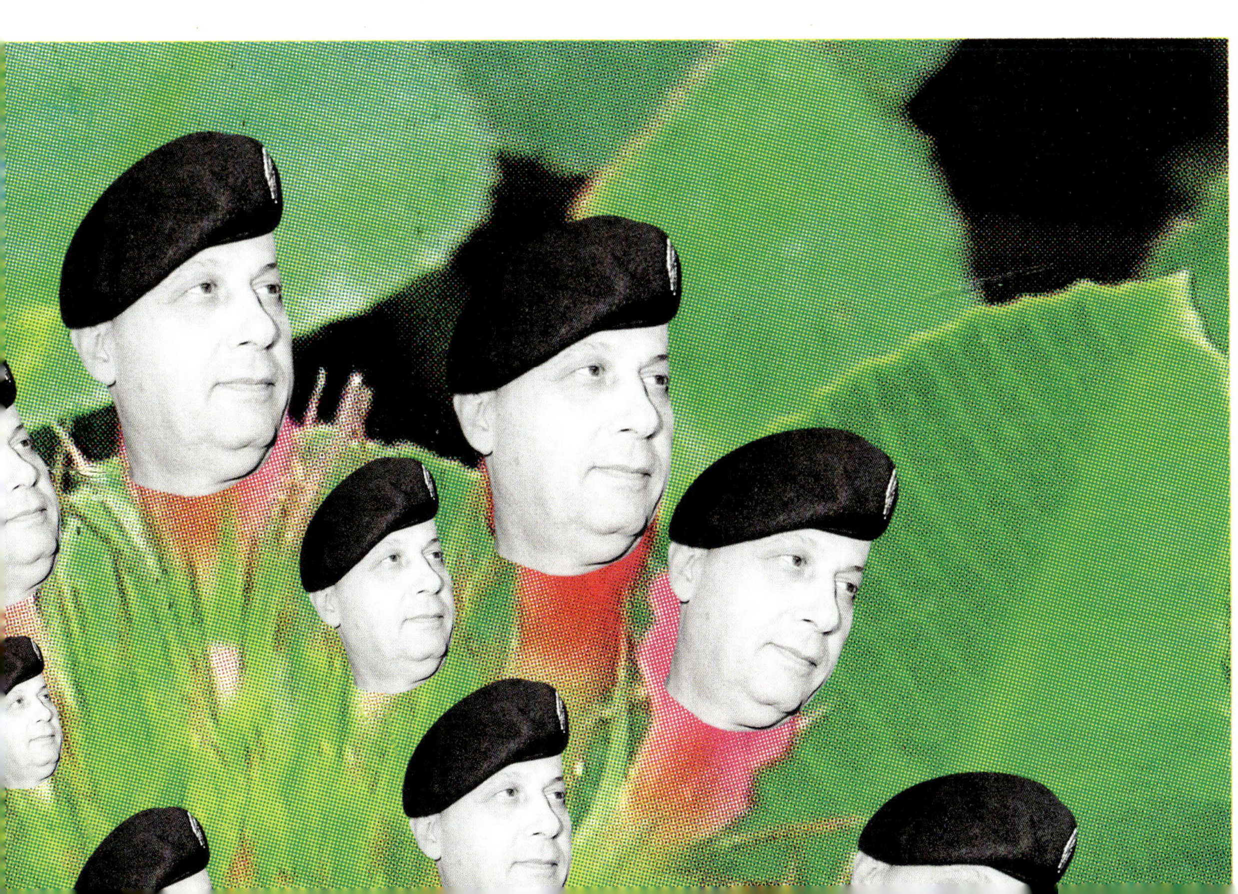

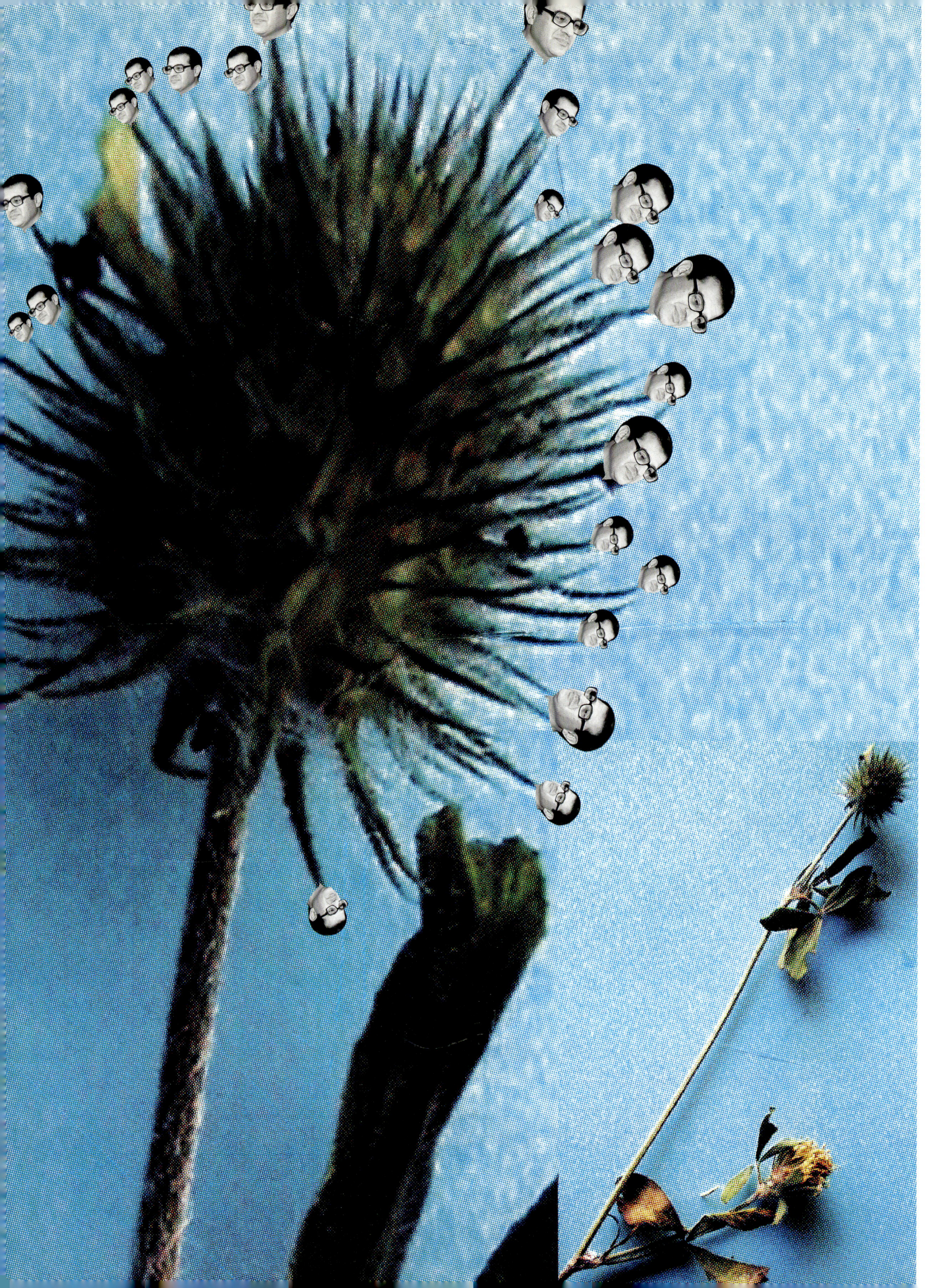

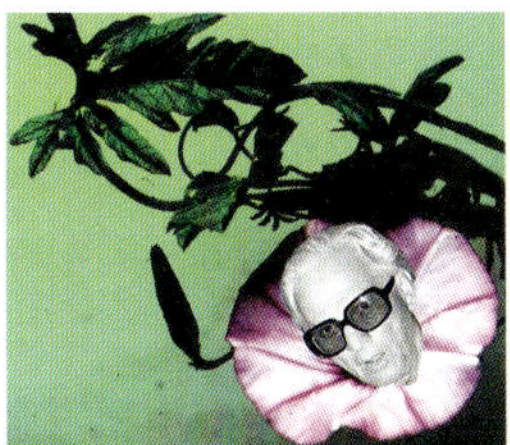

▲ *Convolvulus elegantissimus* Mill. **Daraaoun, Barja**. Stony ground.
Elegant bindweed. LISERON ARGENTÉ. لبلاب فضي
Creeping plant, silky and silvery, 50-80 cm; petiolate, cordate basal leaves; palmate upper leaves; bright pink corolla 4-5 times longer than calyx, with 5 silky bands.

▲ *Convolvulus libanoticus* Boiss. **Aïn-Swaair, Sannine**. Grass land. End (Leb+Syr).
Lebanon bindweed. LISERON DU LIBAN. لبلاب لبناني
Shrubby-tree woody rhizome, greyish 5-30 cm; oblong obtuse basal leaves; acute upper leaves; fleshy coloured corolla 10-12 mm, hairy outside. Fl: 6-8.

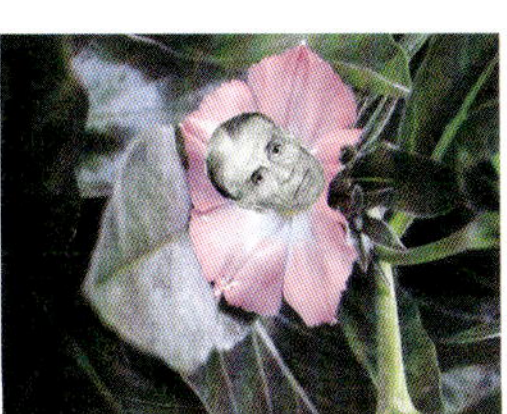

▲
▼ *Convolvulus galaticus* Rost. ex Chois, **Kfarqouq, Aayha**. Grass land, roadsides. End (Leb+Tur).
Galatian bindweed. LISERON DE GALATIE. لبلاب غلاطيا
Almost silky plant not creeping, 30-60 cm.

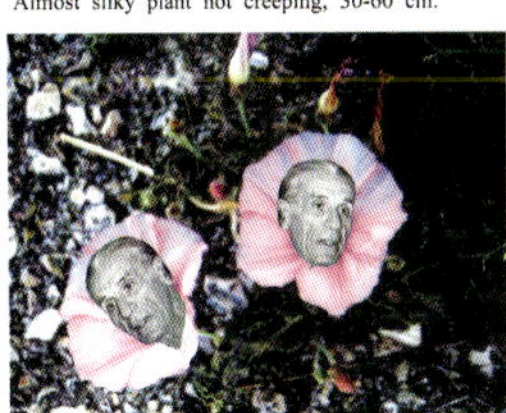

◄ *Convolvulus lineatus* (not found recently in Rachaya) silky plant, ± silvery simple stem 5-20 cm

215

NICACEAE

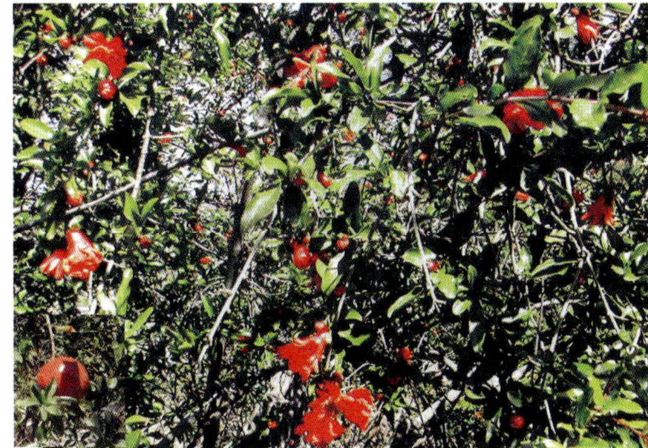

▲▲ *Punica granatum* L. From sea level to 1200 m, common tree escaped from cultivation. Several varieties.
Common pomegranate. GRENADIER COMMUN. رمان

RAFFLES

▼ *Cytinus hypocistis* L. **Zanduqa**. Parasite
Rape of cistus. CYTINET HYPOCISTE. طفيلي اللاذن
Plants without chlorophyll, with succulent stem covered by red scales, which live on roots of *Cistus*, 5-15 regular white flowers, in terminal racemes, 4-partite, (ssp *orientalis* has bright red scales and pale yellow ▼ flowers).

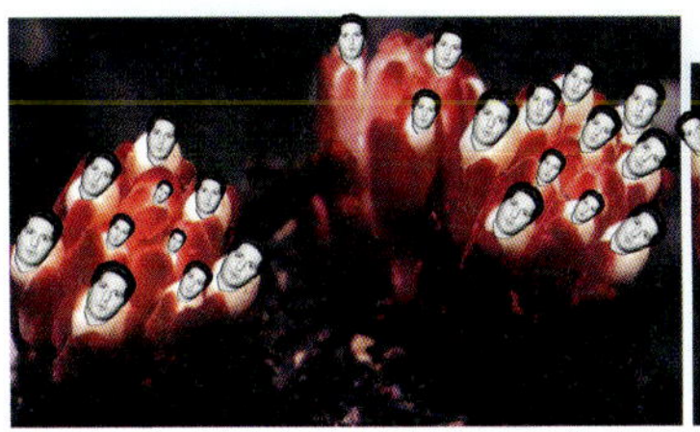

5111

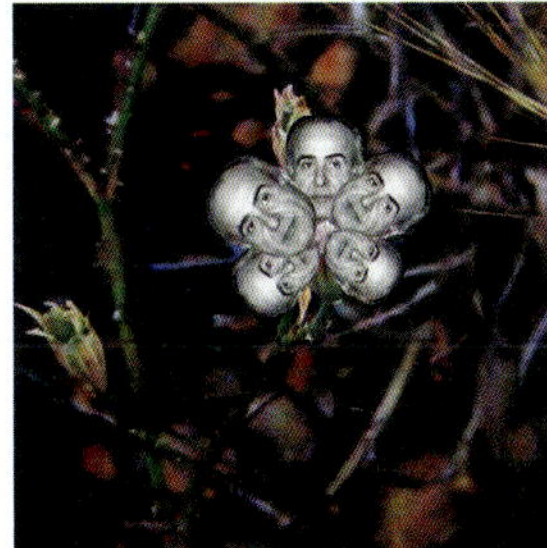

▲ *Allium curtum* Boiss. & Gaill. **Mounsef, Kaounine**. Sandy ground. EMR.
Dwarf garlic. AIL NAIN. ثوم قزم

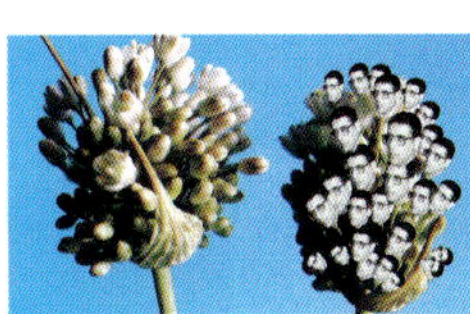

▼ *Allium descendens* Sibth. & Smith. **Qalaat Chqif**. Rocks.
Bent-flowered garlic.
AIL À FLEURS PENCHÉES. ثوم منحني الزهر
Stem spathe with prominent veins. Fl: 5-6.

▼▼ *Allium feinbergii* Oppenheimer. **Makmel, Sannine**. Scree at altitude. End (Leb+Syr).
Feinberg's garlic. AIL DE FEINBERG. ثوم فينبرغ
Black-violet and sessile small bulbs; under ground stem; narrow cylindrical leaves; umbel with 7-12 pink flowers, stamens with simple filaments, short spathe. Fl: 6-8.

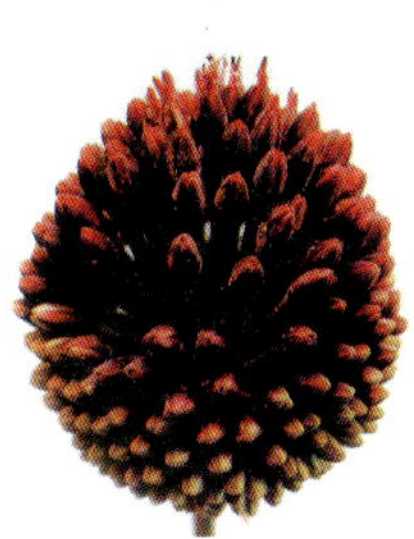

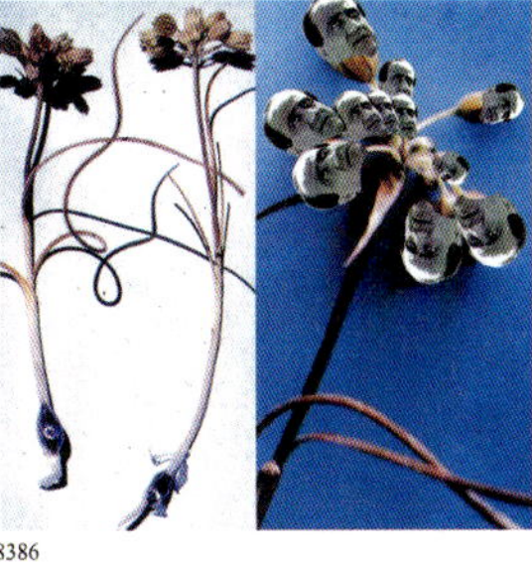

8386

In 2007 I initiated a project, *Scratching on things I could disavow*, on the history of art in the "Arab world." I began the project at the same time that the establishment of new cultural foundations, art galleries, art schools, art magazines, art prizes, art fairs, and large Western-brand museums was accelerating in cities such as Abu Dhabi, Dubai, Beirut, Cairo, Doha, Manama, Ramallah, and others. These material developments were matched by equally fraught efforts to define, sort, and stitch "Arab art" along three loosely silhouetted nodes: "Islamic," "modern," and "contemporary." When viewed alongside the political, economic, social, and military conflicts that have consumed the "Arab world" in the past few decades, such developments shape a rich yet thorny ground for creative work.

The artworks and stories I present in this project concentrate on some of the stories, forms, lines, and colors made available by these developments, especially when they are screened alongside Jalal Toufic's concept of "the withdrawal of tradition past a surpassing disaster."[1] I have so far produced two main chapters, each composed of several works.

Scratching on things I could disavow: Walkthrough chronicles some of the encounters that drove me to engage with the history of art in the "Arab world" in the first place: an invitation to join the Dubai branch of the Artist Pension Trust; the development of Saadiyat Island in Abu Dhabi; the opening of the Sfeir-Semler Gallery in Beirut, and the subsequent shrinking of my works; my "communication" with artists from the future; artworks that have lost their reflections and shadows; and the effects of the wars in Lebanon on colors, lines, and forms.

Scratching on things I could disavow: Les Louvres relates to my ongoing study of "Islamic art." More specifically, I present works that emerged out of my two-year exploration of the Louvre's newly established Département des Arts de l'Islam, its archives and new exhibition spaces. This encounter with "Islamic arts" in the Louvre in Paris was also animated by the emergence of a new Louvre in Abu Dhabi.

1
The writings of Jalal Toufic, and in particular his concept of the "withdrawal of tradition past a surpassing disaster," remain central to me and to this project. With this concept Toufic considers how certain disasters affect tradition. He pays special attention to the rare instances when artworks are affected immaterially, in more subtle and insidious ways than has hitherto been thought. He characterizes such immaterial effects as "withdrawals," meaning not that an artwork or other cultural artifact is hidden (to safeguard against its destruction, or because it does not conform to the reigning ideological and political outlook of the time) but that it is treated by sensitive artists in their own artworks as though destroyed, as unavailable to vision. In his various books, Toufic also proposes that artists have at times attempted to resurrect such withdrawn artworks, albeit with great doubt as to the success of their efforts.

Scrat
on Th
I Co
Disa

ching
hings
ould
avow

Walkthrough

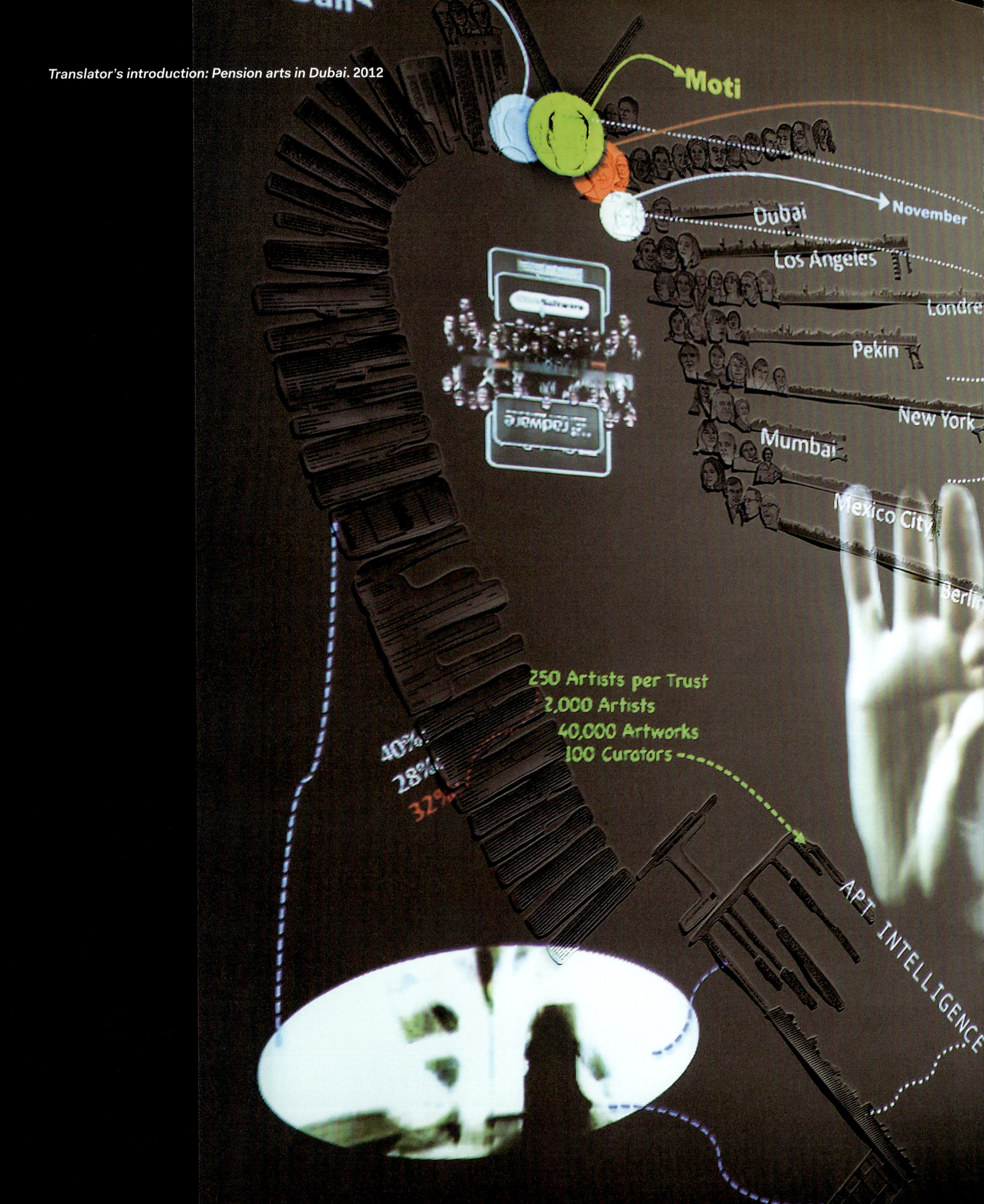

Translator's introduction: Pension arts in Dubai. 2012

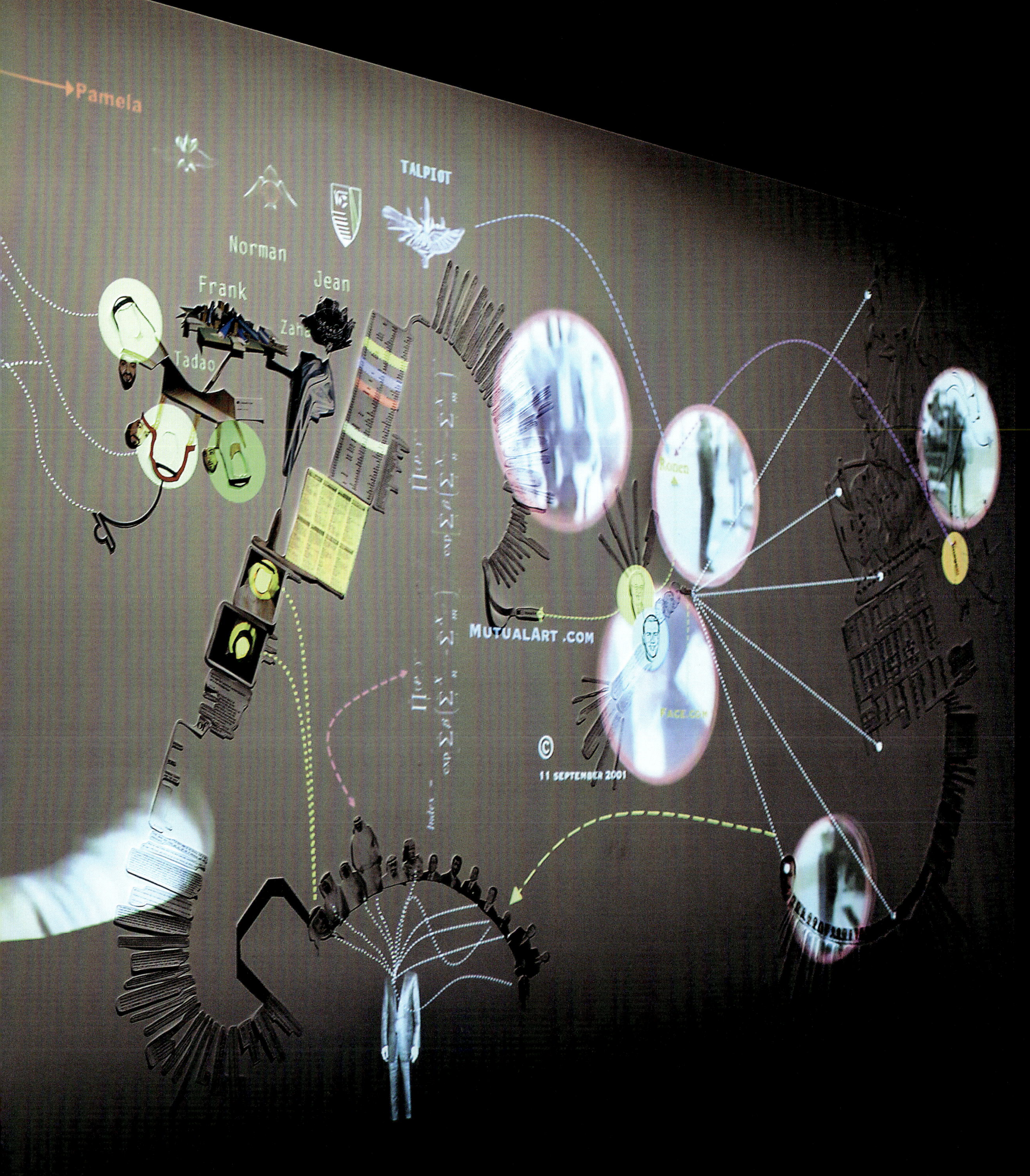

Pamela
TALPIOT
Norman
Frank
Jean
Zaha
Tadao
MUTUALART.COM
©
11 SEPTEMBER 2001

In 2007, I was asked to join the Dubai branch of the Artist Pension Trust (APT). A private company established in 2004 by a savvy entrepreneur and a risk-management guru, APT aims to select and pool artists and artworks into regional investment and pension funds, of which it has thus far established eight. APT is owned by MutualArt, a British Virgin Islands–registered company whose assets include the Web site by the same name.

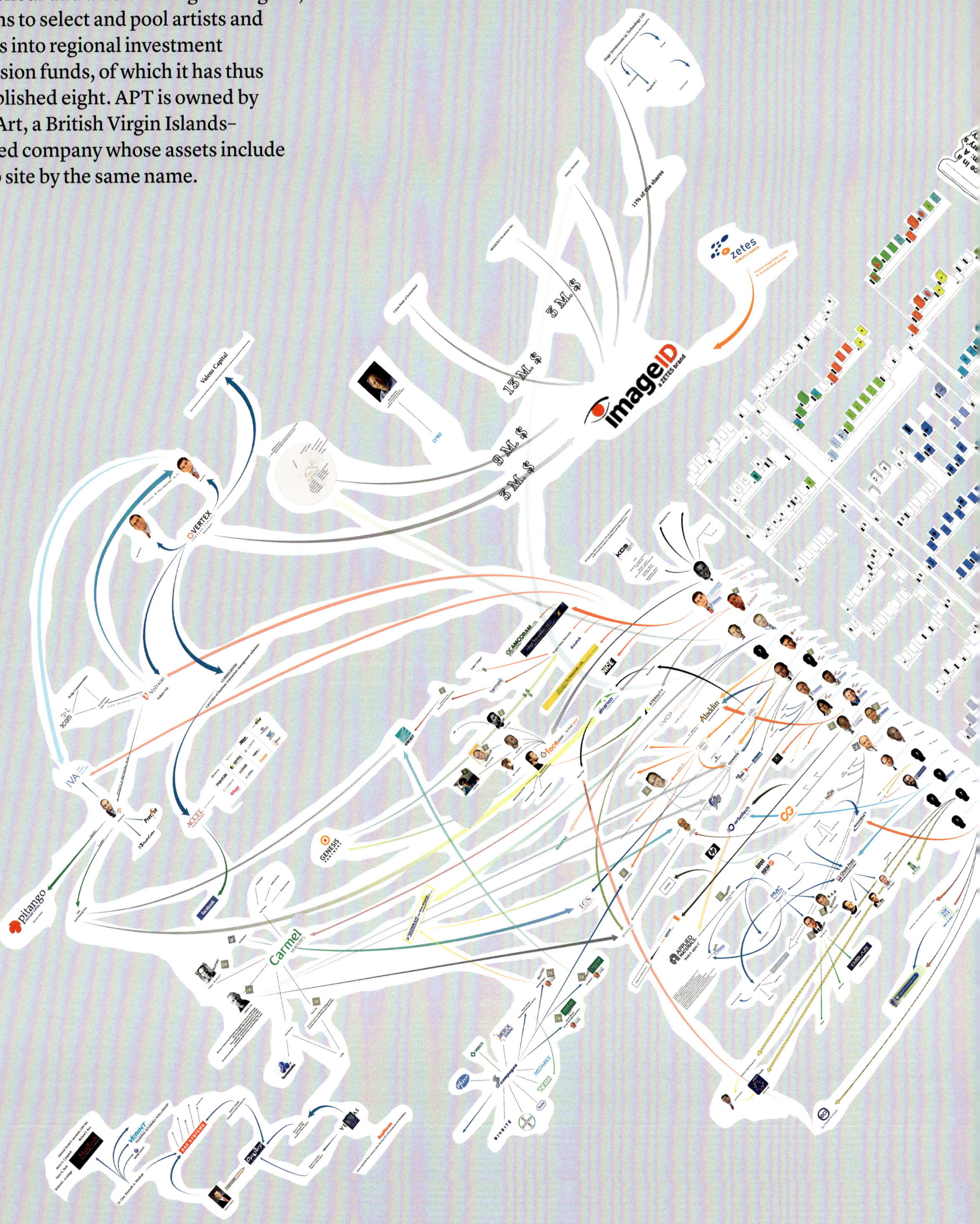

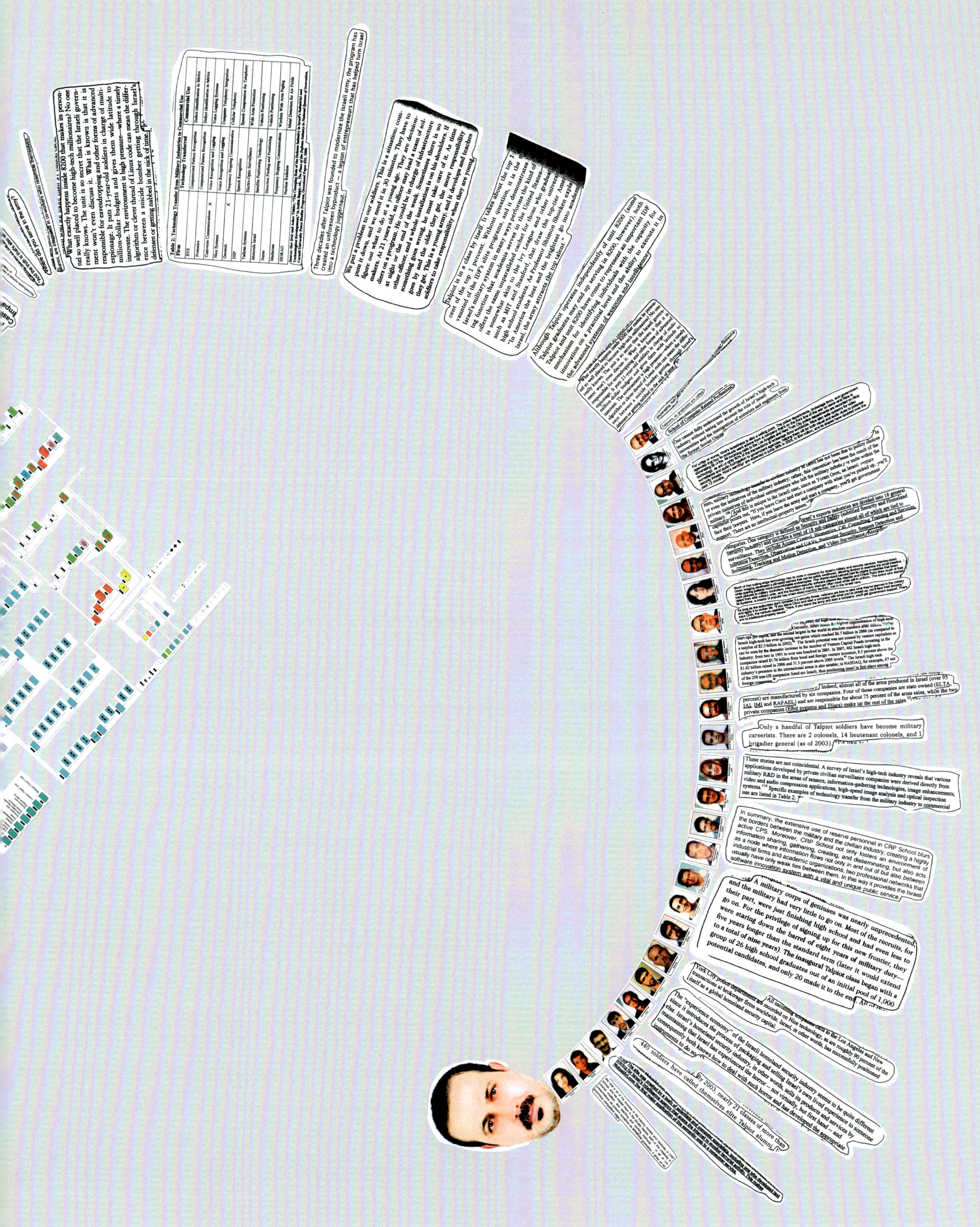

What exactly happens inside 8200 that makes its personnel so well placed to become high-tech millionaires? No one really knows. The unit is so secret that the Israeli government won't even discuss it. What is known is that it is responsible for eavesdropping and other forms of advanced espionage. It puts 21-year-old soldiers in charge of multi-million-dollar budgets and gives them wide latitude to innovate. The environment is high pressure—where a timely algorithm or clever thread of Linux code can mean the difference between a suicide bomber getting through Israel's defenses or getting nabbed in the nick of time.
Three decades after Talpiot was founded to modernize the Israeli army, the program has created an unforeseen byproduct — a legion of entrepreneurs that has helped turn Israel into a technology juggernaut.
Only a handful of Talpiot soldiers have become military careerists. There are 2 colonels, 14 lieutenant colonels, and 1 brigadier general (as of 2003)
percent) are manufactured by six companies. Four of these companies are state owned (ELTA, IAI, IMI and RAFAEL) and are responsible for about 75 percent of the arms sales, while the two private companies (Elbit systems and Elisra) make up the rest of the sales.
These stories are not coincidental. A survey of Israel's high-tech industry reveals that various applications developed by private civilian surveillance companies were derived directly from military R&D in the areas of sensors, information-gathering technologies, image enhancements, video and audio compression applications, high-speed image analysis and optical inspection systems.
In summary, the extensive use of reserve personnel in CRP School blurs the borders between the military and the civilian industry, creating a highly active CPS. Moreover,
A military corps of geniuses was nearly unprecedented, and the military had very little to go on. Most of the recruits, for their part, were just finishing high school and had even less to go on.
440 soldiers have called themselves elite Talpiot alumni

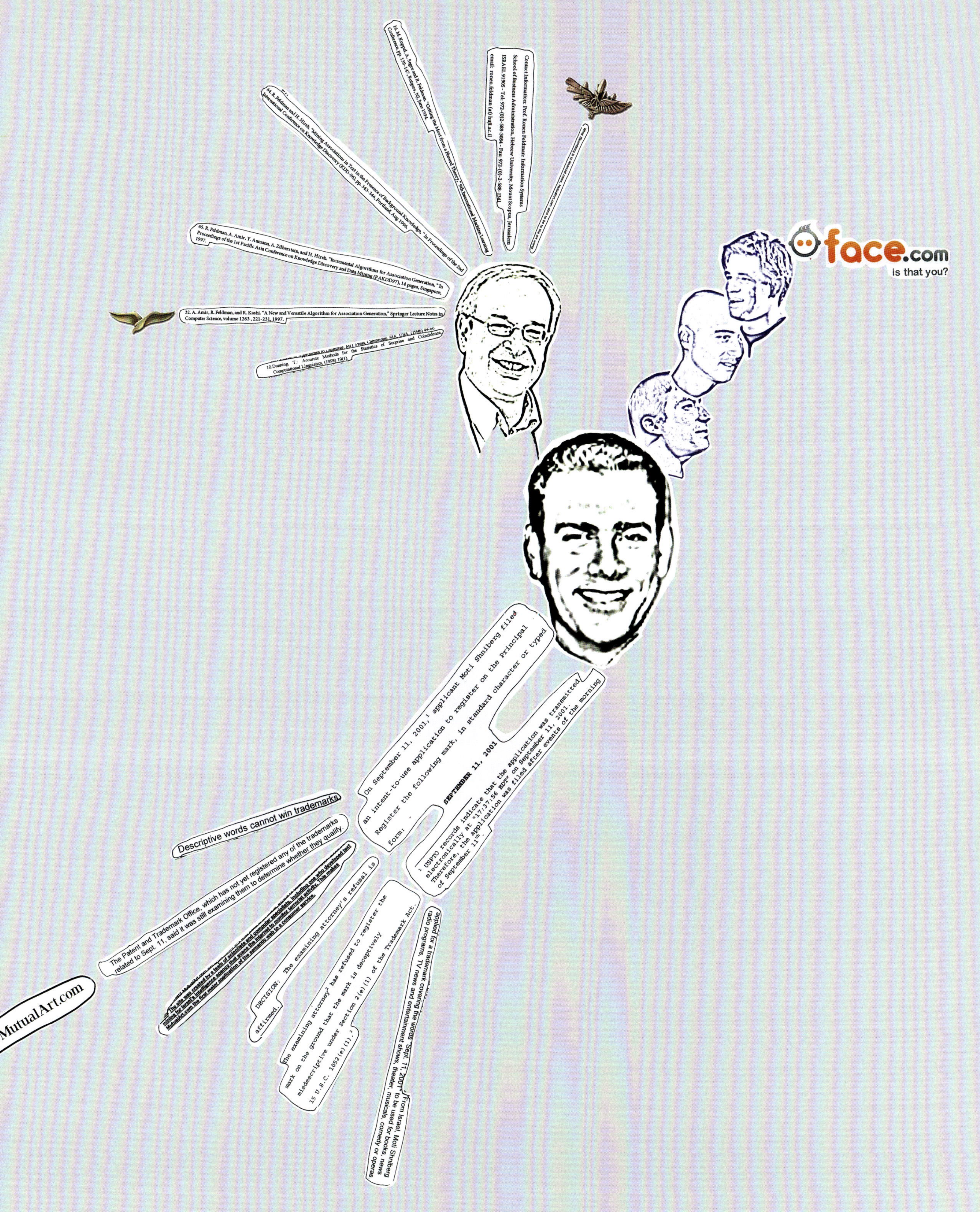

Contact Information: Prof. Ronen Feldman: Information Systems
School of Business Administration, Hebrew University, Mount Scopus, Jerusalem
ISRAEL 91905 - Tel: 972-(0)2-588-3084 - Fax: 972-(0)-2-588-1341
email: ronen.feldman (at) huji.ac.il
16. M. Koppel, A. Segre and R. Feldman. "Getting the Most from a Flawed Theory," 9th International Machine Learning Conference, pp. 139-147, Rutgers, NJ, June 1994.
64. R. Feldman and H. Hirsh. "Mining Associations in Text in the Presence of Background Knowledge, " In Proceedings of the 2nd International Conference on Knowledge Discovery (KDD-96), pp. 343-346, Portland, Aug 1996.
What Bloomberg is to financial news, MutualArt.com aims to be to the art world.
65. R. Feldman, A. Amir, Y. Aumann, A. Zilberstein, and H. Hirsh. "Incremental Algorithms for Association Generation, " In Proceedings of the 1st Pacific Asia Conference on Knowledge Discovery and Data Mining (PAKDD97), 14 pages, Singapore, 1997.
32. A. Amir, R. Feldman, and R. Kashi. "A New and Versatile Algorithm for Association Generation," Springer Lecture Notes in Computer Science, volume 1263 , 221-231, 1997.
10.Dunning, T.: Accurate Methods for the Statistics of Surprise and Coincidence. Computational Linguistics, (1993) 19(1).
face.com
is that you?
On September 11, 2001,¹ applicant Moti Shniberg filed an intent-to-use application to register on the Principal Register the following mark, in standard character or typed form:
SEPTEMBER 11, 2001
¹ USPTO records indicate that the application was transmitted electronically at "17:37:56 EDT" on September 11, 2001. Therefore, the application was filed after events of the morning of September 11th.
Descriptive words cannot win trademarks.
The Patent and Trademark Office, which has not yet registered any of the trademarks related to Sept. 11, said it was still examining them to determine whether they qualify.
The site was created by a team of scientists and computer specialists, including one who developed text mining for Israel's intelligence agency that scans the Internet to monitor terrorist activity. This makes MutualArt.com the first major application of the semantic web to a consumer service.
DECISION: The examining attorney's refusal is affirmed.
The examining attorney² has refused to register the mark on the ground that the mark is deceptively misdescriptive under Section 2(e)(1) of the Trademark Act. 15 U.S.C. 1052(e)(1).³
applied for a trademark covering the words "Sept. 11, 2001" to be used for books, news radio programs, TV news and entertainment shows, theater, musicals, comedy or operas.
From Israel, Moti Shniberg
MutualArt.com

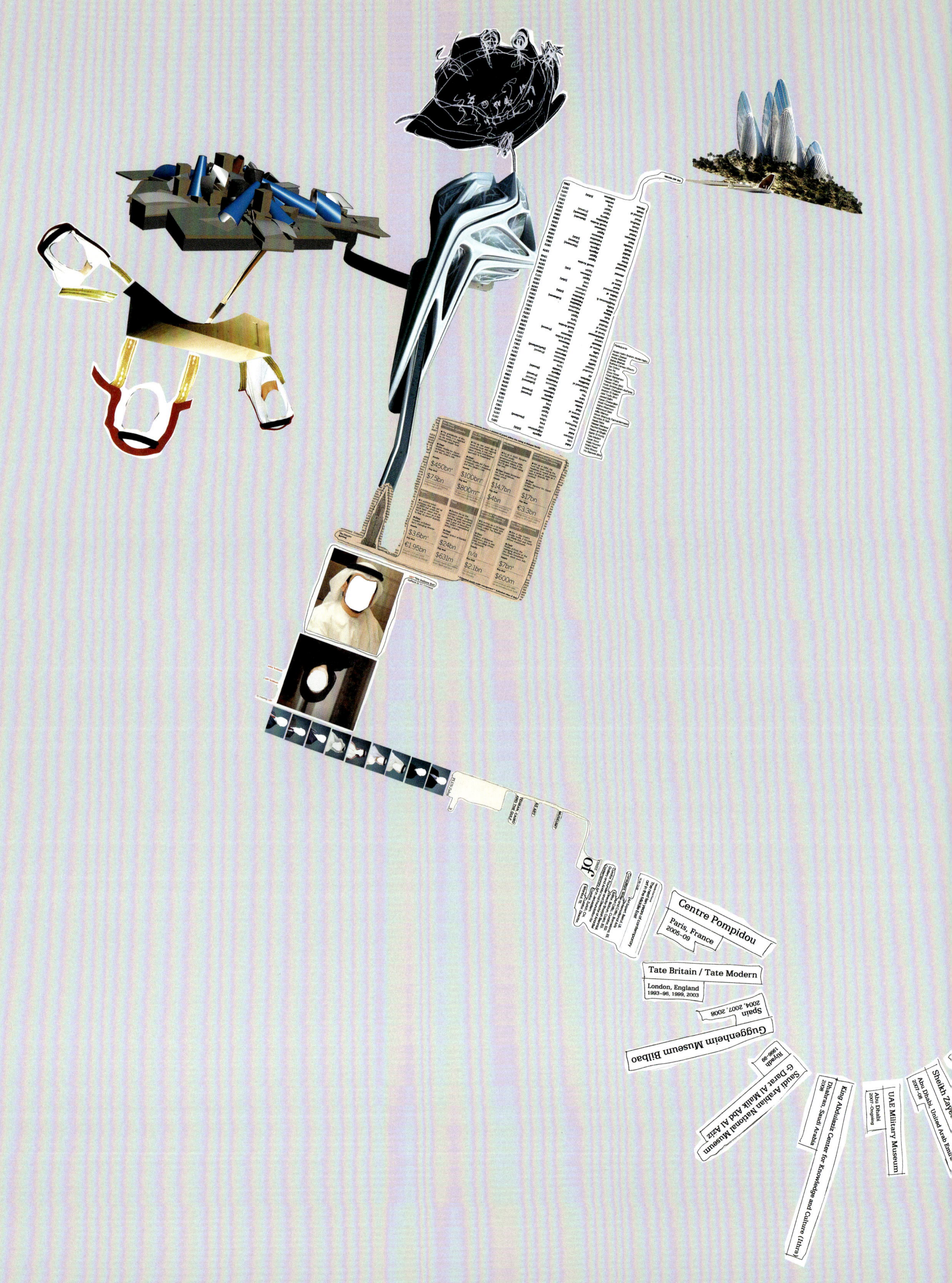
Centre Pompidou
Paris, France
2005–09
Tate Britain / Tate Modern
London, England
1993–96, 1999, 2003
Spain
2004, 2007, 2008
Guggenheim Museum Bilbao
Riyadh
1996–99
Darat Al Malik Abd Al Aziz
Saudi Arabian National Museum
King Abdulaziz Center for Knowledge and Culture (Ithra)
Dhahran, Saudi Arabia
2008
UAE Military Museum
Abu Dhabi
2007–Ongoing

To determine whether to join APT Dubai, I found myself asking who was funding APT and MutualArt, and why was APT launching a trust in the Middle East. This led me to look into technological innovations in the areas of statistics; risk-management concepts in finance; art as an alternative asset class; culture as an engine of economic growth in the Arab world and elsewhere; text, data-mining, and face-recognition algorithms; and the Israeli military and its links to the Israeli high-tech sector. All of which led to the tableau presented here, which I regard as a stage set for an accompanying oral presentation in which I narrate my findings.

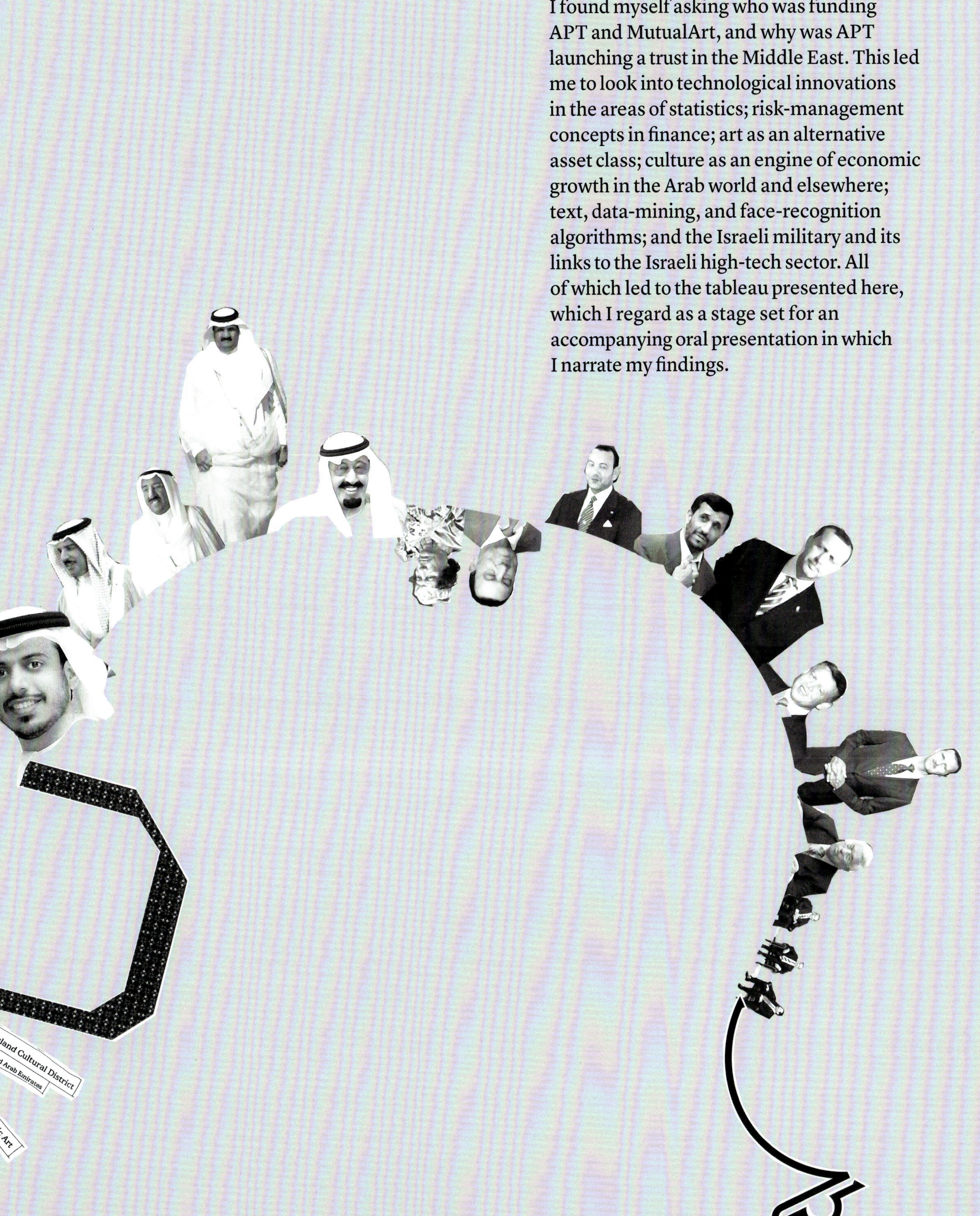

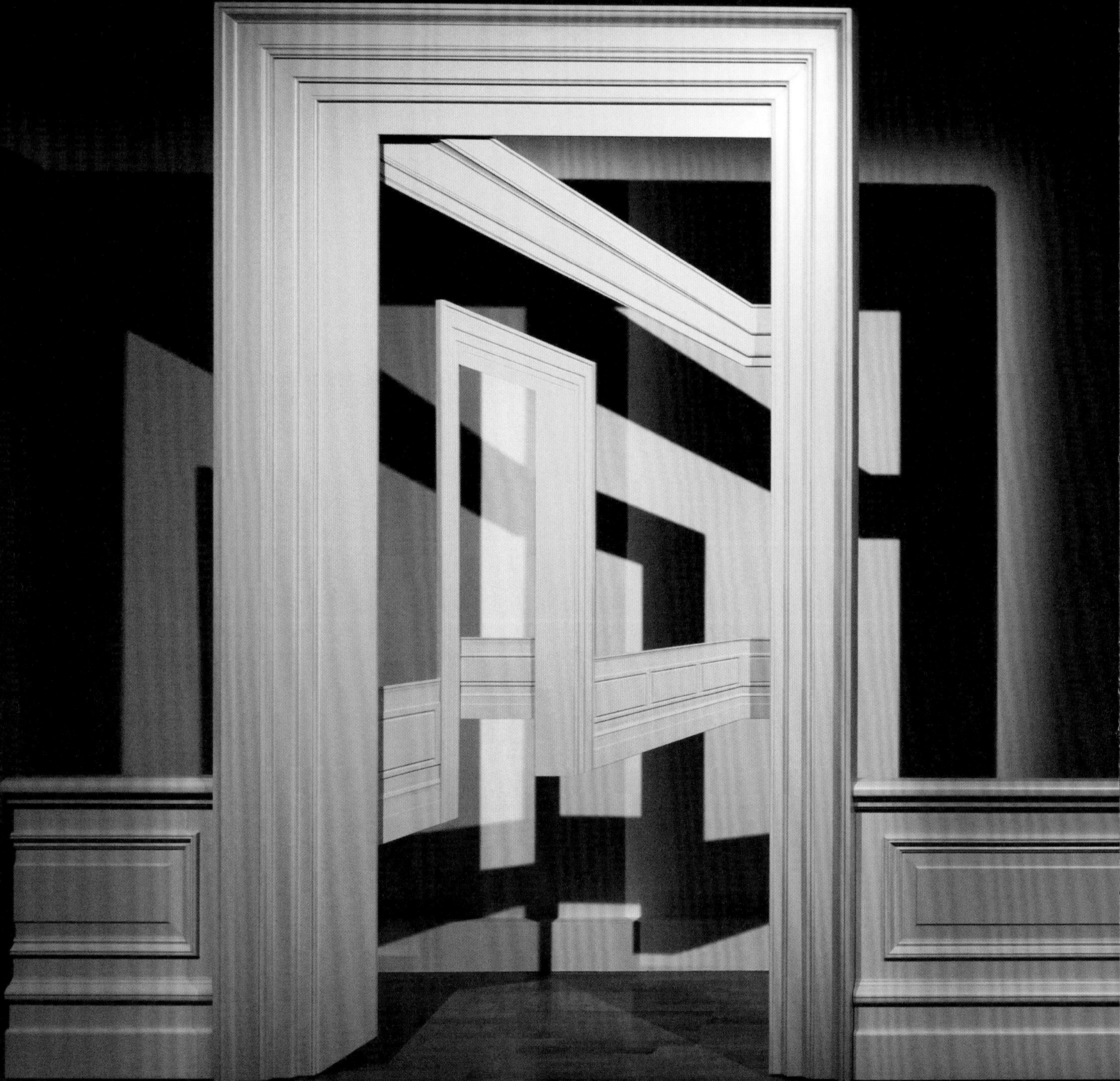

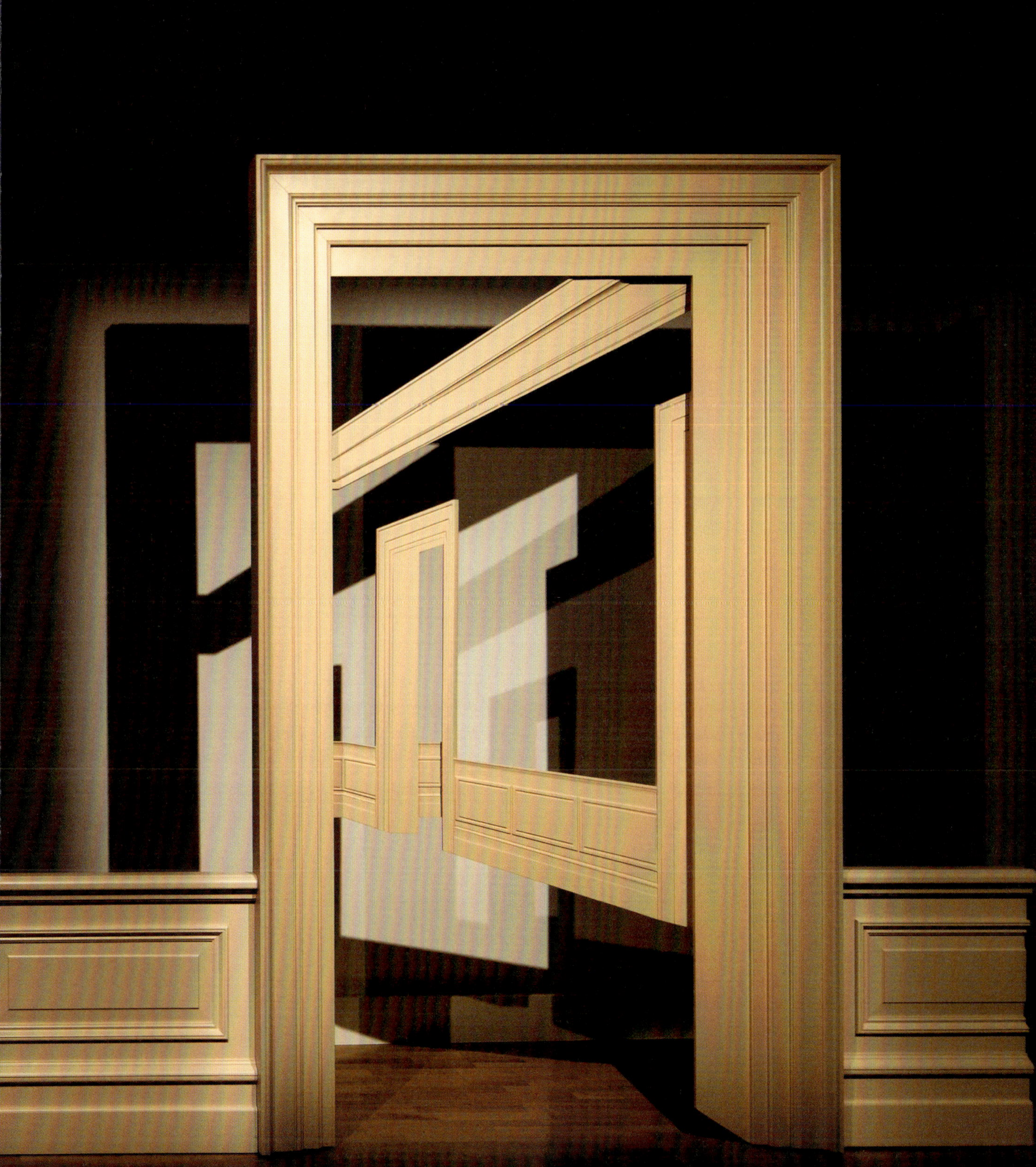

At the opening of a new museum of modern and/or contemporary art in an Arab city, a proud local resident rushes the entrance only to find that he is unable to proceed.

Is it his casual wear at an event announced as a black-tie affair? No.

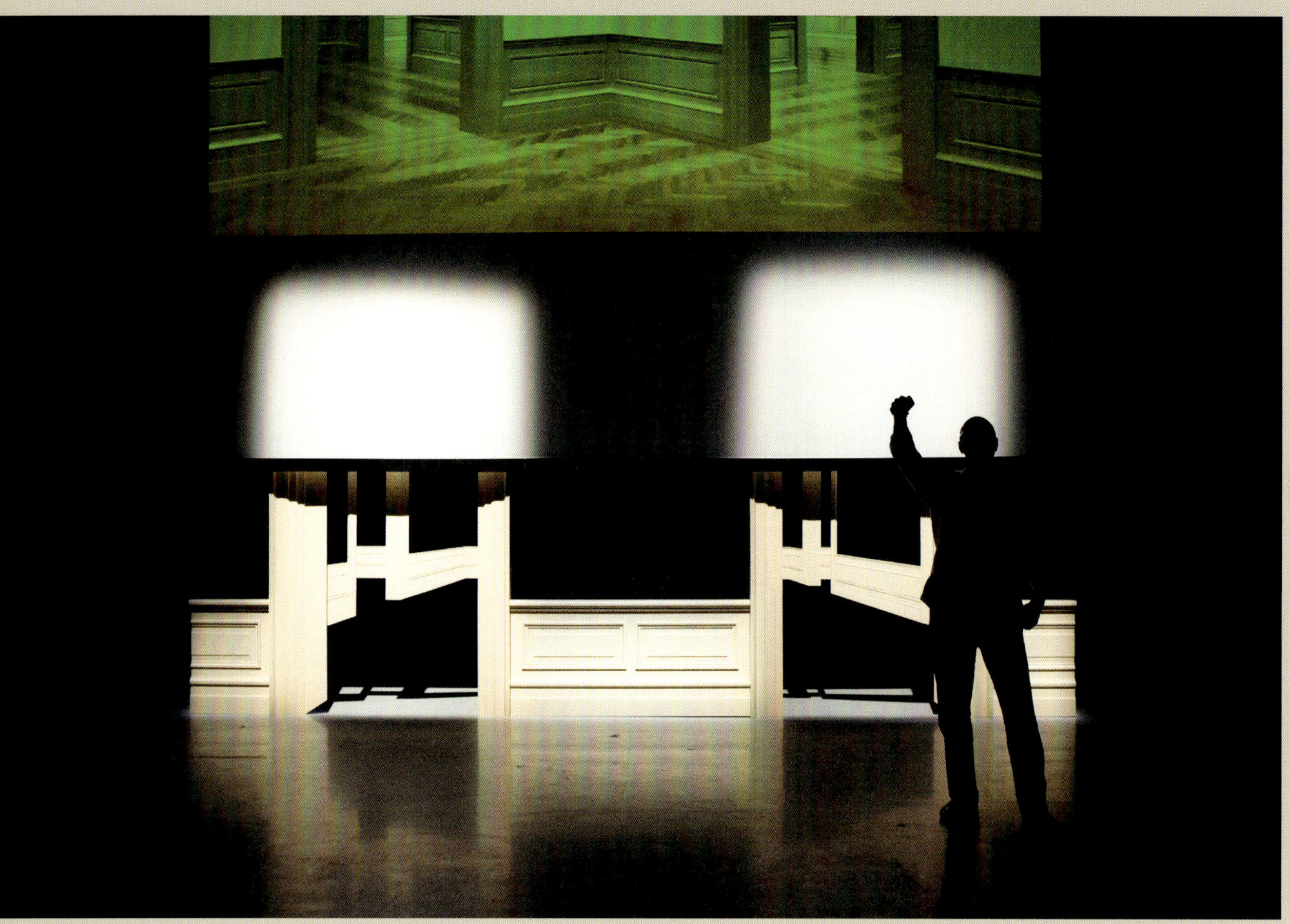

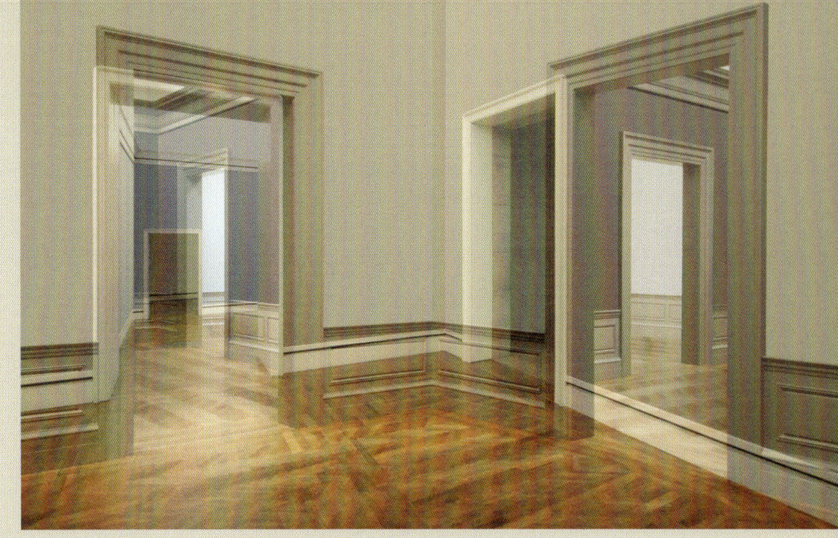

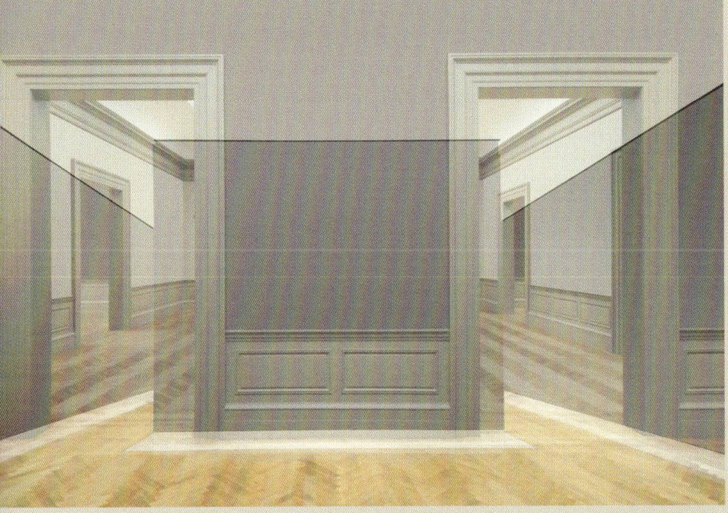

Is it the thugs who shield the ruling dynasty attending the event en masse to showcase their benevolence and refined sensibilities, pubescent future rulers in tow, who prevent his access? No.

He simply feels that were he to walk in, he would certainly "hit a wall."

On the spot, he turns to face the rushing crowd and screams: "Stop. Don't go in. Be careful."

Within seconds, he is removed from the site, severely beaten, and sent to a psychiatric facility.

These events will take place sometime between 2014 and 2024. We will certainly read in newspapers the following day the headline: "Demented Man Disturbs Opening—Claims World Is Flat."

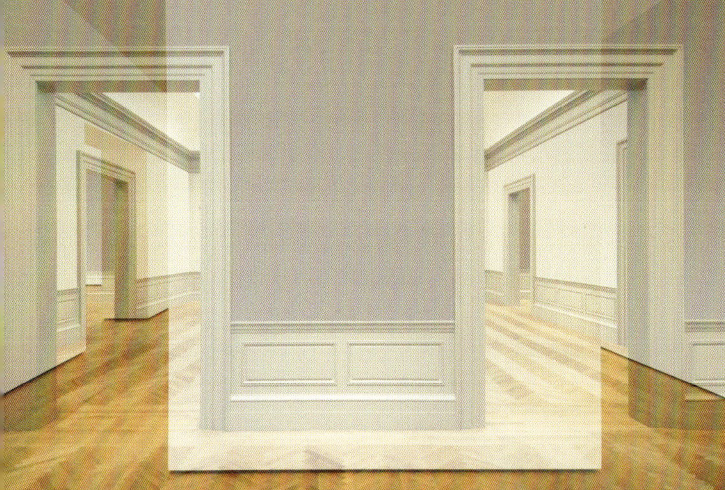

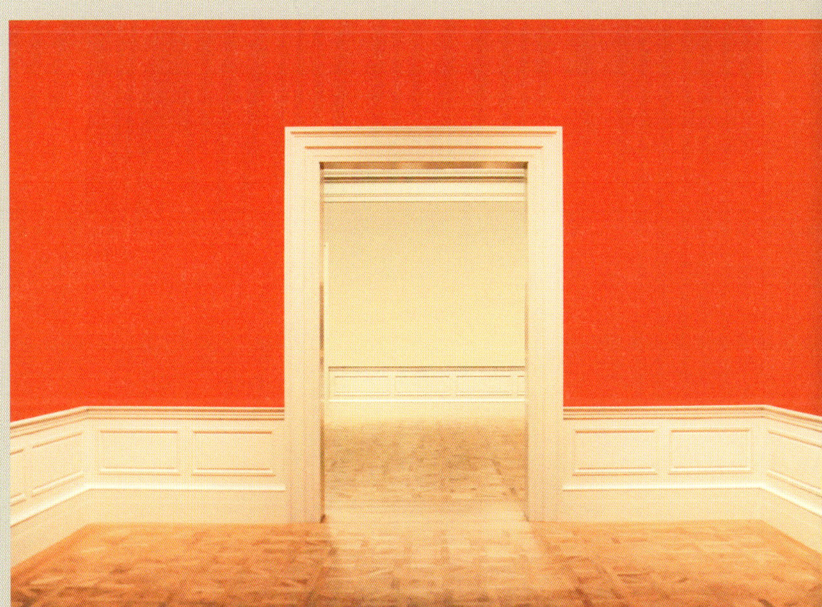

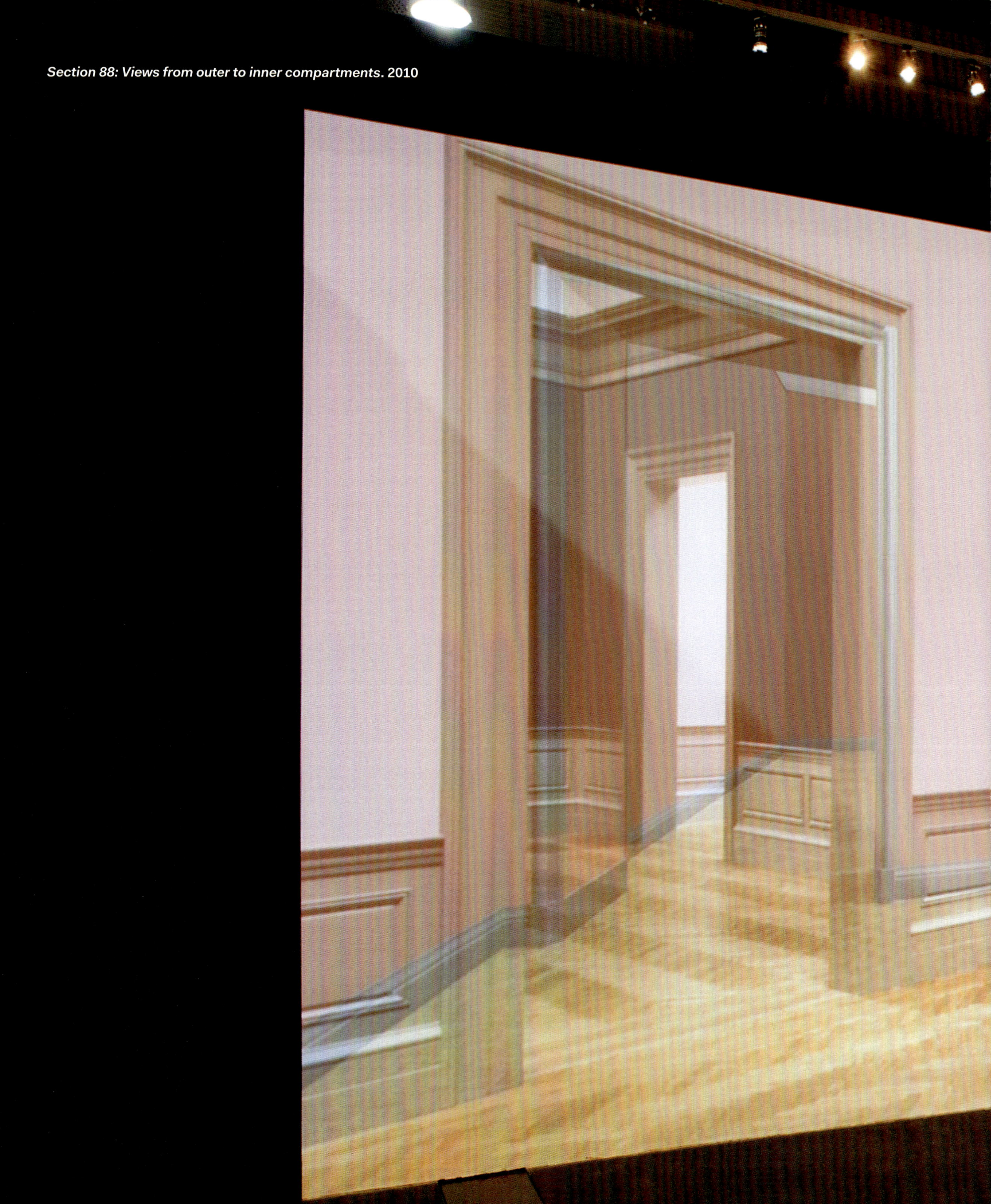

Section 88: Views from outer to inner compartments. 2010

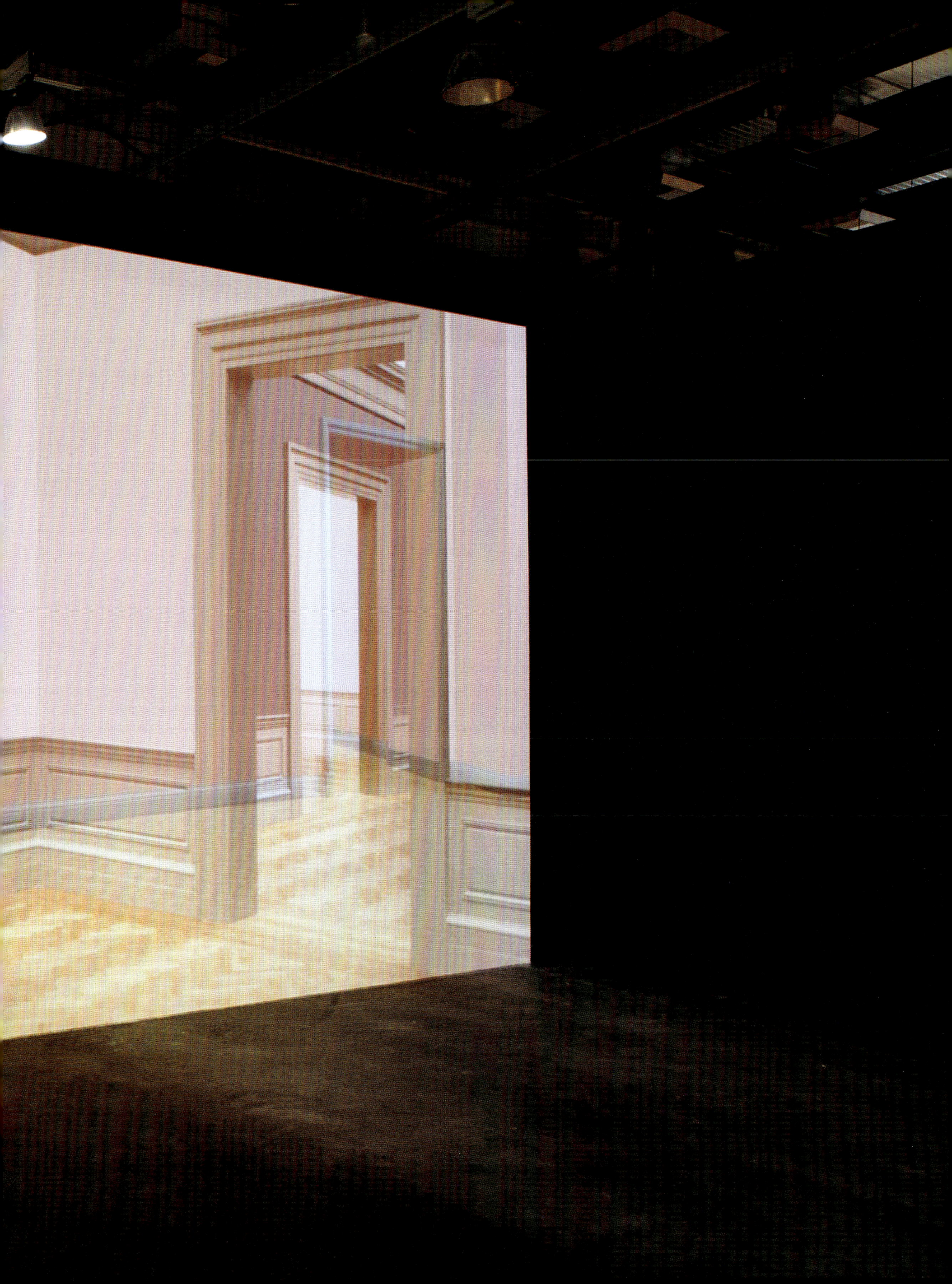

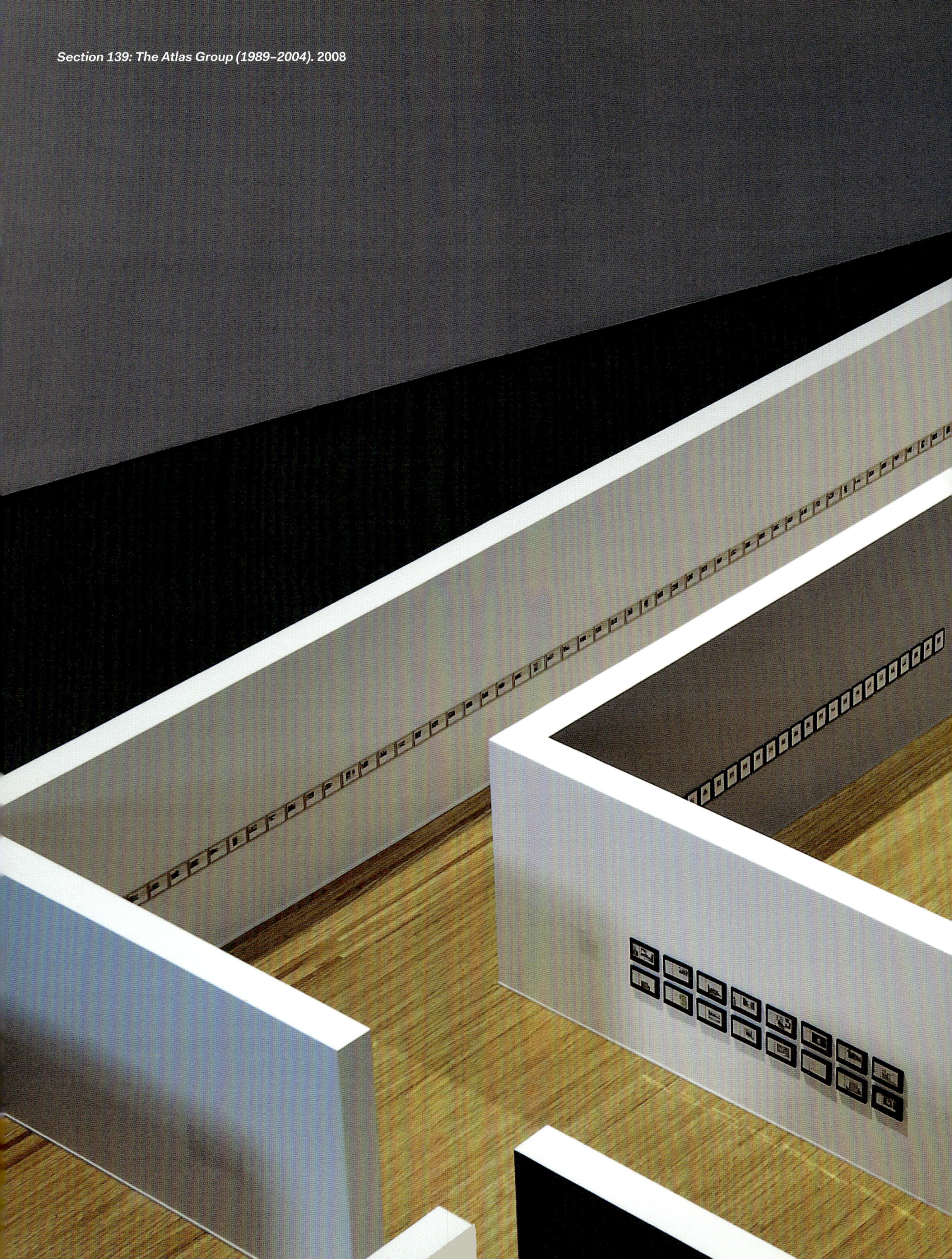

Section 139: The Atlas Group (1989–2004). 2008

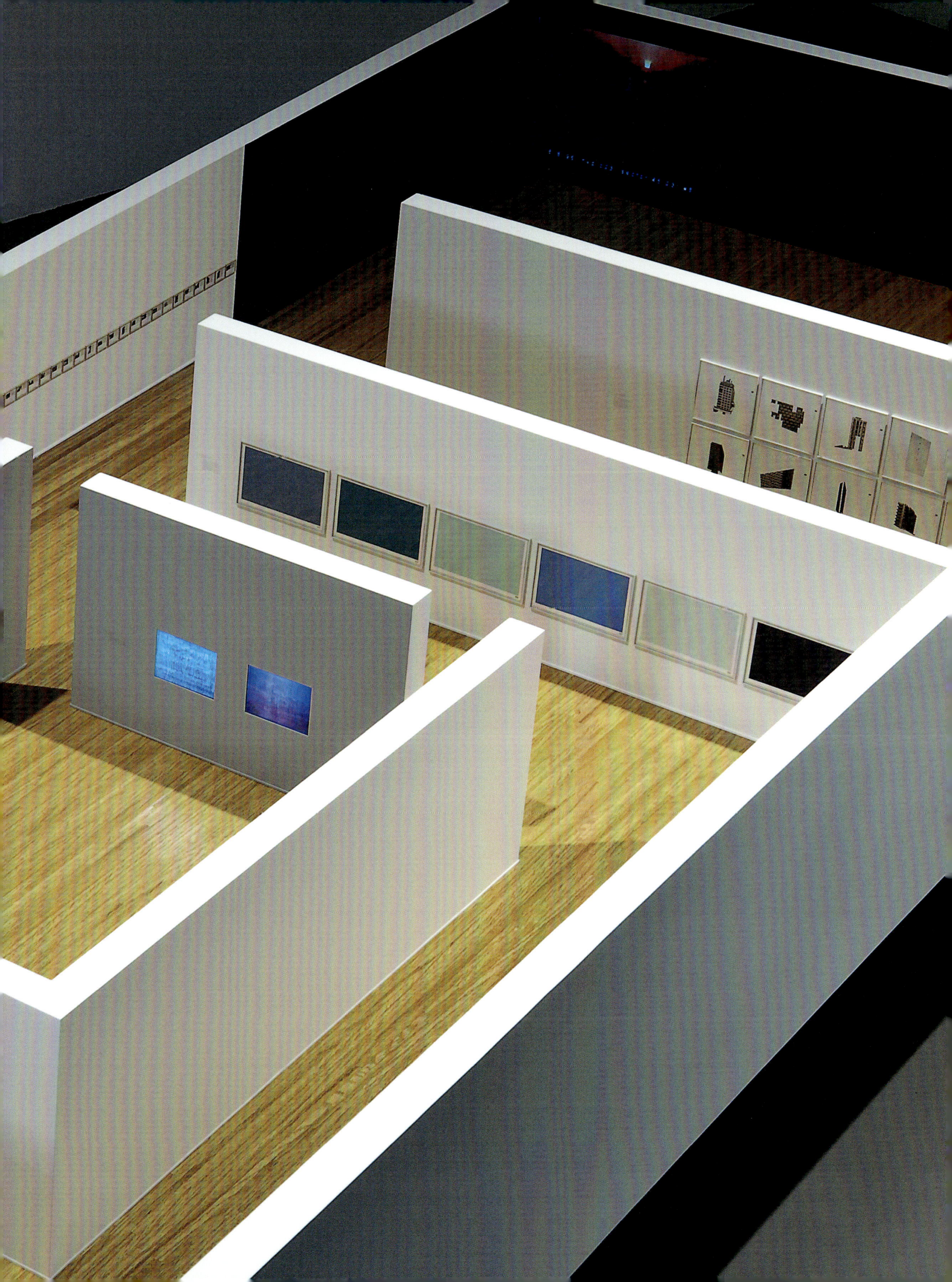

Between 1989 and 2004, I worked on a project titled "The Atlas Group." It consisted of artworks made possible by the Lebanese wars of the past few decades.

In 2005, I was asked to exhibit this project for the first time in Lebanon, in Beirut's first-of-its-kind white-cube art gallery.

For some reason this offer perturbed me and I refused.

In 2006, I was asked again. I refused again.

In 2007, I was asked again. I refused again.

In 2008, I was asked again. I agreed.

Weeks later, when I went to the gallery to inspect my exhibition before its opening, I was startled to find that all my artworks had shrunk to 1/100th of their original size.

I subsequently decided to build a smaller white cube befitting my works' new dimensions, and to display them there.

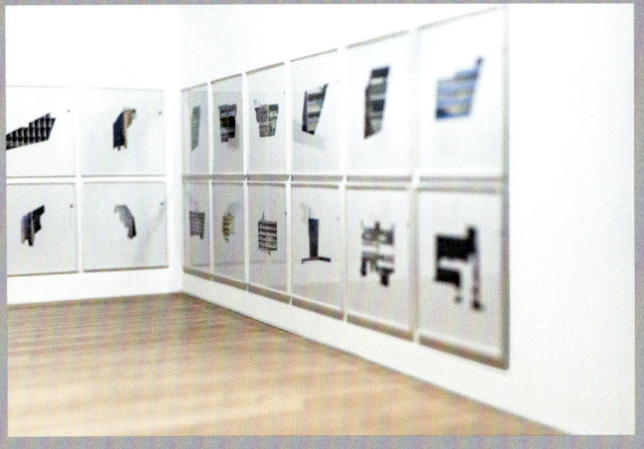

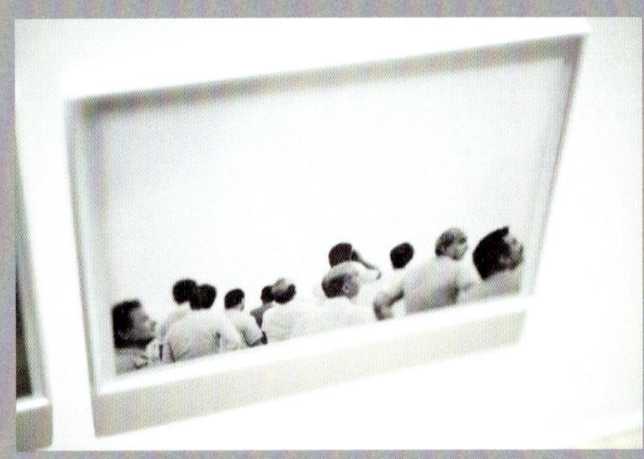

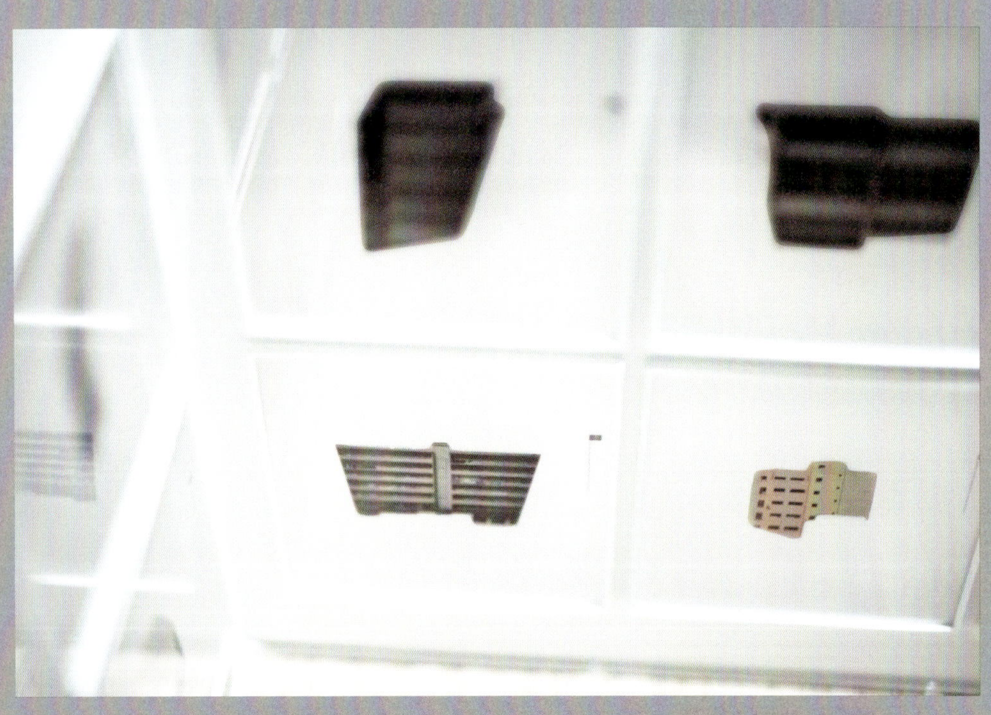

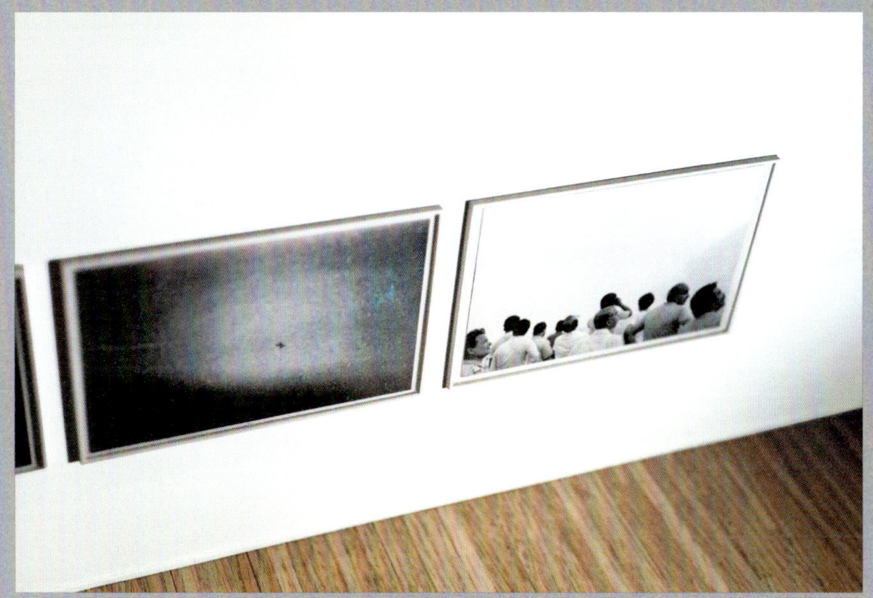

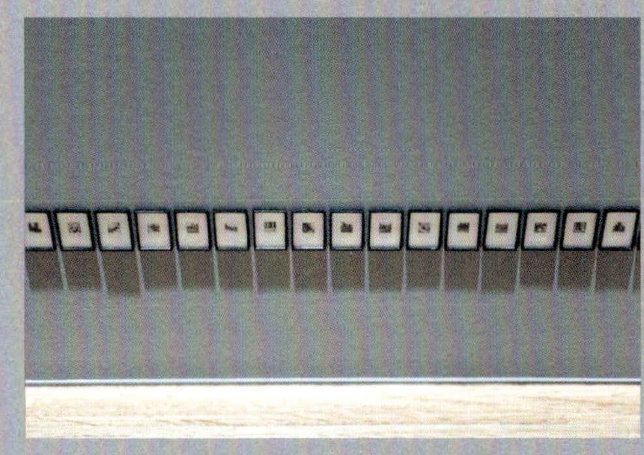

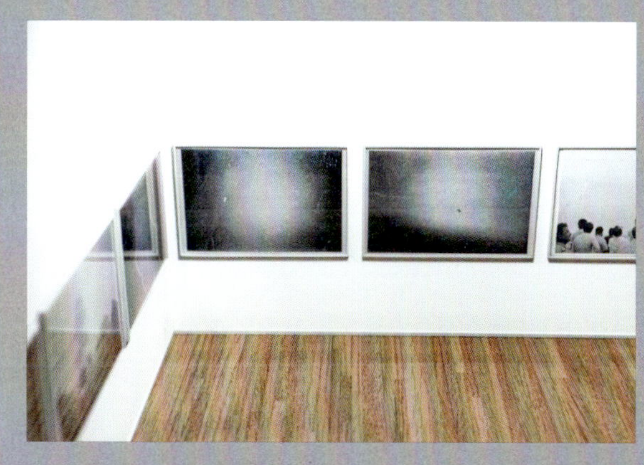

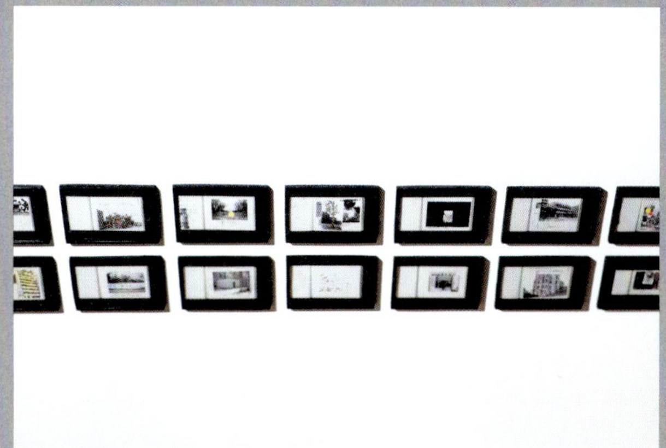

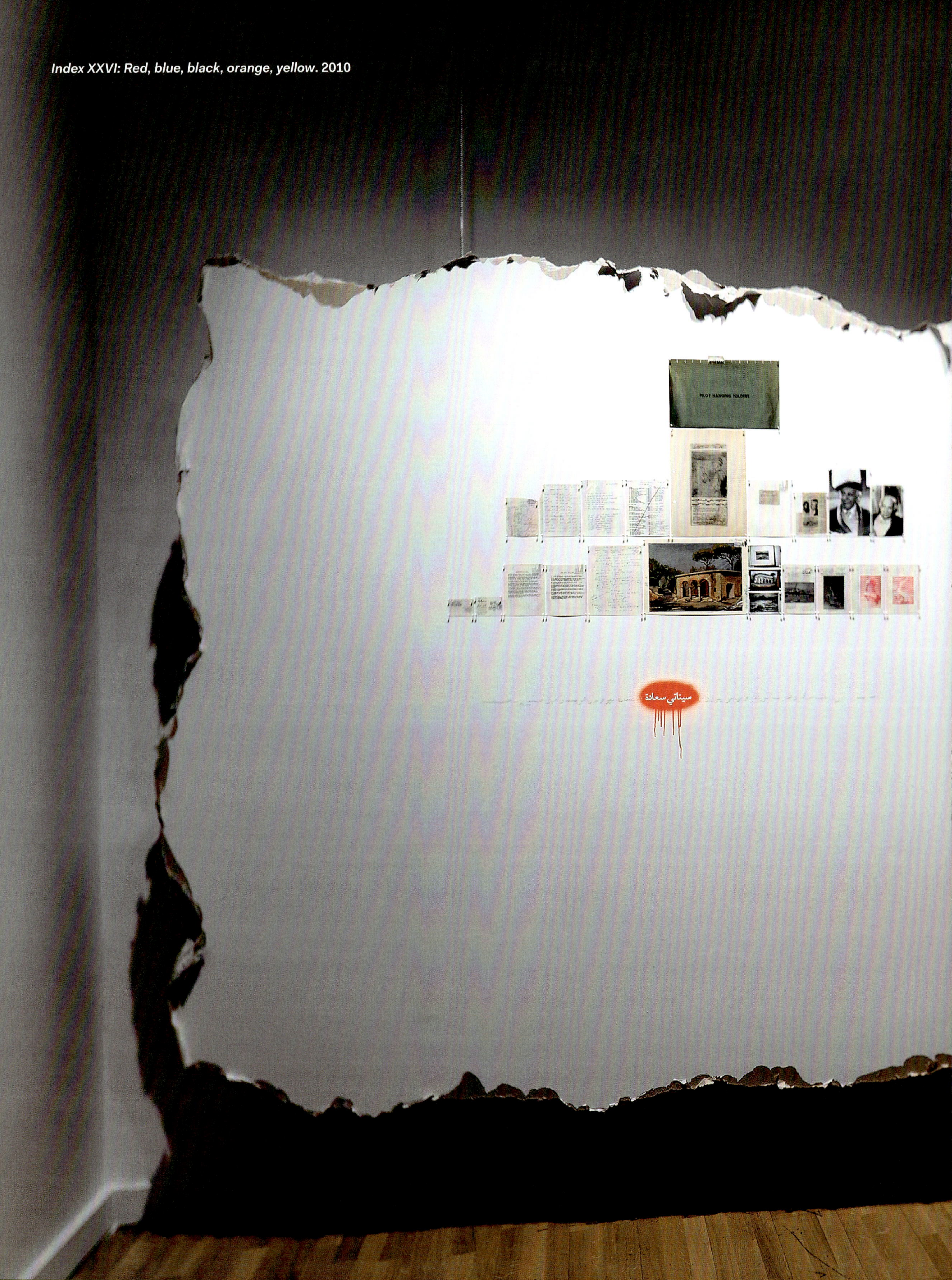

Index XXVI: Red, blue, black, orange, yellow. 2010

This work is based on the names of painters and sculptors who worked in Lebanon in the past century. Over the past few years, artists from the future have been sending me the names via telepathy.

Given my past experience with the "noise" that accompanies most telepathic signals, I decided in 2005 to make the names public by displaying them in white vinyl letters on these white walls. I was seeking confirmation from kindred spirits about the spelling of the names. What I did not expect was that this confirmation would come to me from the least sympathetic source, a renowned local dancer who considers himself a guardian of Lebanese art.

Disregarding my claims to telepathy as a fanciful conceptual conceit, the dancer unequivocally confirmed that the names displayed were those of artists and that many were indeed misspelled. He was unwilling to attribute my orthographic errors to telepathic noise, but blamed it on the impertinent attitude common to my generation of postwar Lebanese artists who not only can't even spell the names of their predecessors but choose time and again to overlook their contributions. And with a red, blue, black, orange, and yellow spray paint, the dancer "corrected" the misspelled names.

I was deeply moved by the dancer's sharp rebuke and as a result I have devoted the last few years to researching the misspelled artists' lives and works. But all along, there was something that seemed to me deceptive about the dancer's indignation. In time, I came to view it as a ruse distracting me from a more troubling scenario than merely ignoring predecessors and misspelling their names.

Today I am convinced that the artists from the future intentionally distorted the names they communicated to me telepathically. Future artists are not hailing past painters, sculptors, and their works but the colors red, blue, black, orange, and yellow that surface in the dancer's sprayed "corrections." Future artists want or need these colors because they are no longer available to them.

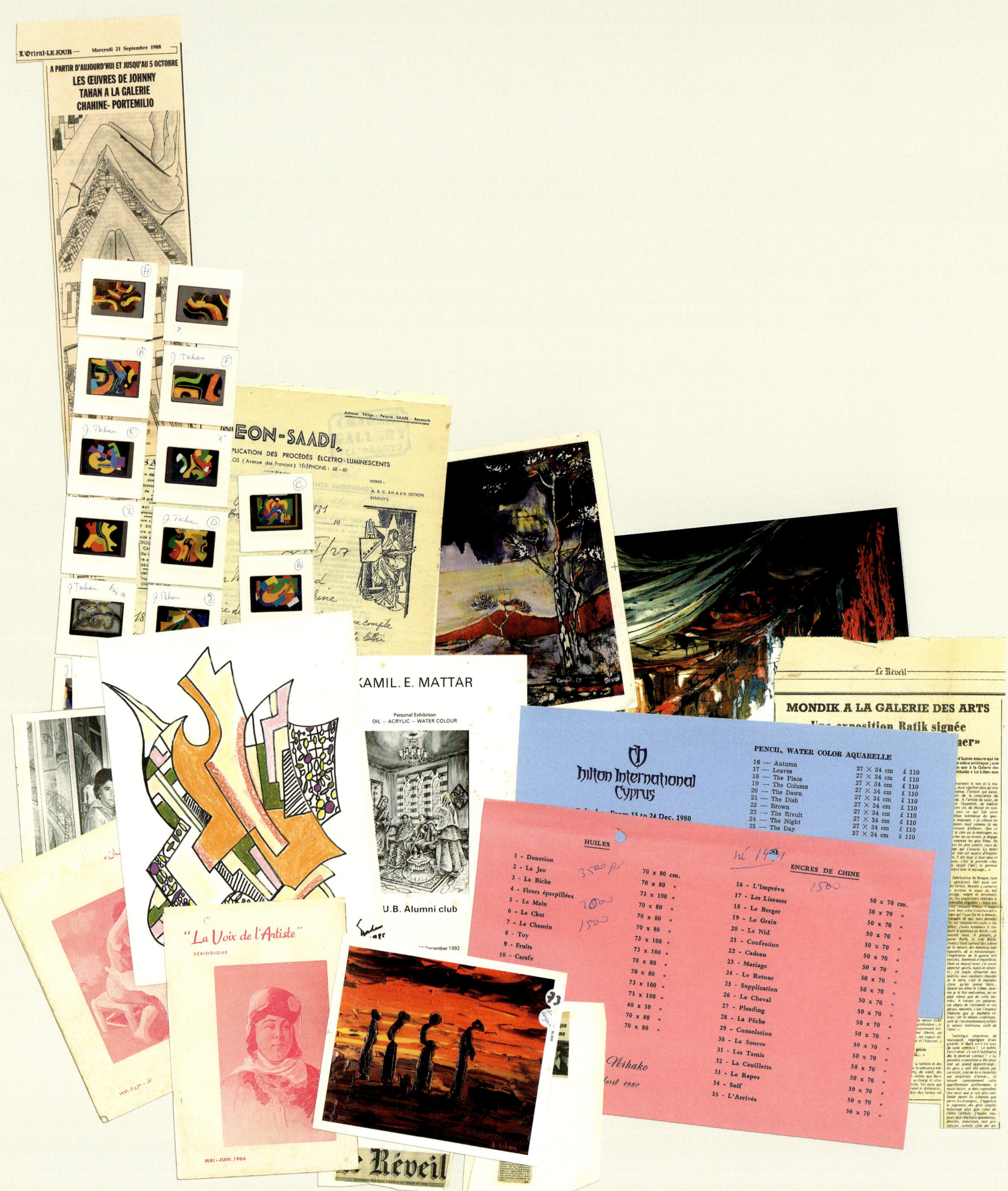

L'Orient-LE JOUR — Mercredi 21 Septembre 1988
A PARTIR D'AUJOURD'HUI ET JUSQU'AU 5 OCTOBRE
LES ŒUVRES DE JOHNNY TAHAN A LA GALERIE CHAHINE- PORTEMILIO
EON-SAADI
PLICATION DES PROCÉDÉS ÉLECTRO-LUMINESCENTS
KAMIL. E. MATTAR
Personal Exhibition
OIL – ACRYLIC – WATER COLOUR
U.B. Alumni club
Le Réveil
MONDIK A LA GALERIE DES ARTS
hilton International Cyprus
PENCIL, WATER COLOR AQUARELLE
16 — Autumn
17 — Leaves
18 — The Place
19 — The Column
20 — The Dawn
21 — The Dish
22 — Brown
23 — The Rivult
24 — The Night
25 — The Day
HUILES
1 - Donation
2 - Le Jeu
3 - La Biche
4 - Fleurs éparpillées
5 - La Main
6 - Le Chat
7 - Le Chemin
8 - Toy
9 - Fruits
10 - Carafe
ENCRES DE CHINE
16 - L'Imprévu
17 - Les Liseuses
18 - Le Berger
19 - Le Grain
20 - Le Nid
21 - Confession
22 - Cadeau
23 - Mariage
24 - Le Retour
25 - Supplication
26 - Le Cheval
27 - Pleading
28 - La Pêche
29 - Consolation
30 - La Source
31 - Les Tamis
32 - La Cueillette
33 - Le Repos
34 - Soif
35 - L'Arrivée
"La Voix de l'Artiste"
PÉRIODIQUE
MAI - JUIN 1966
Réveil

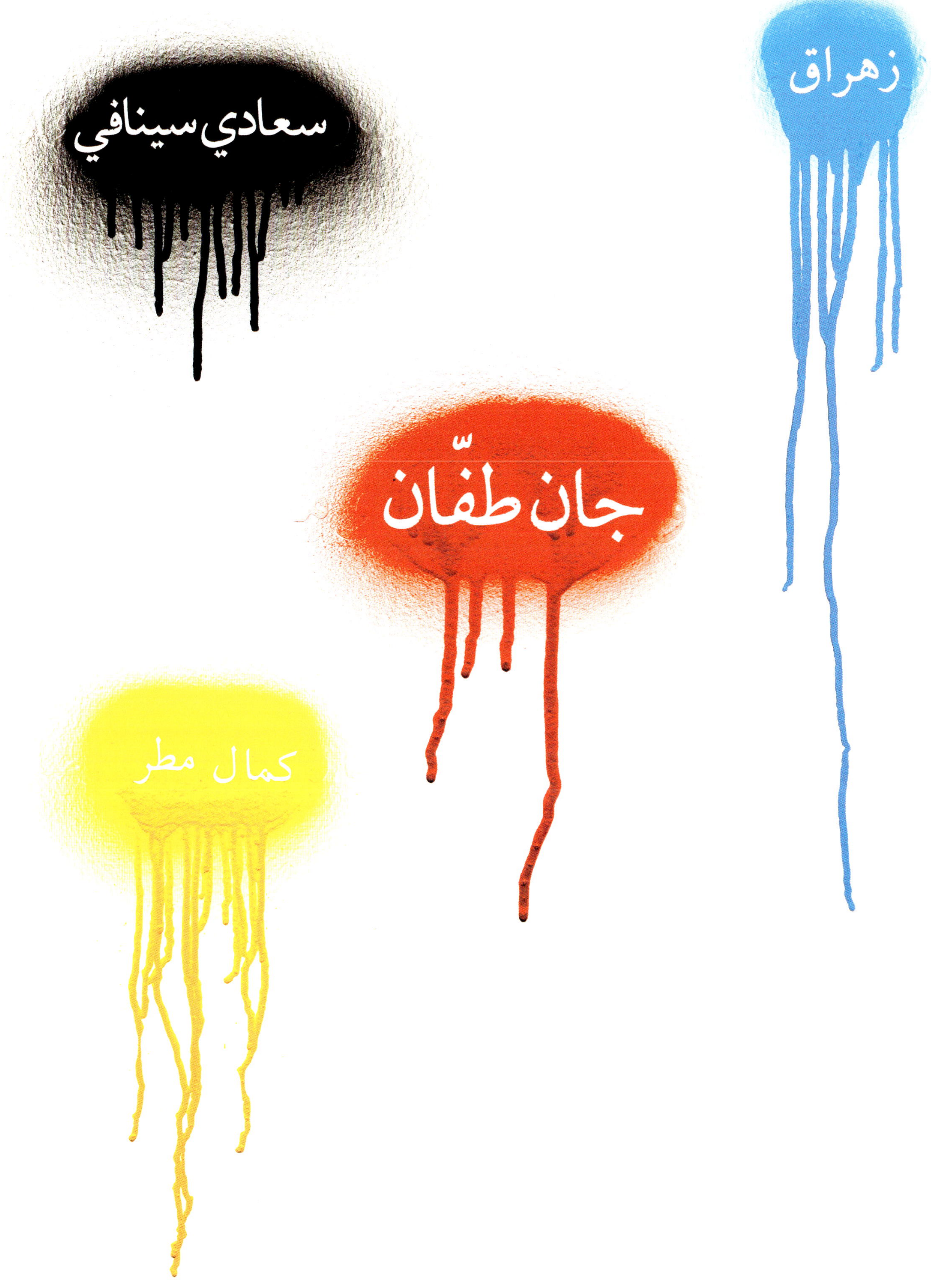
زهراق
سعادي سينافي
جان طفّان
كمال مطر

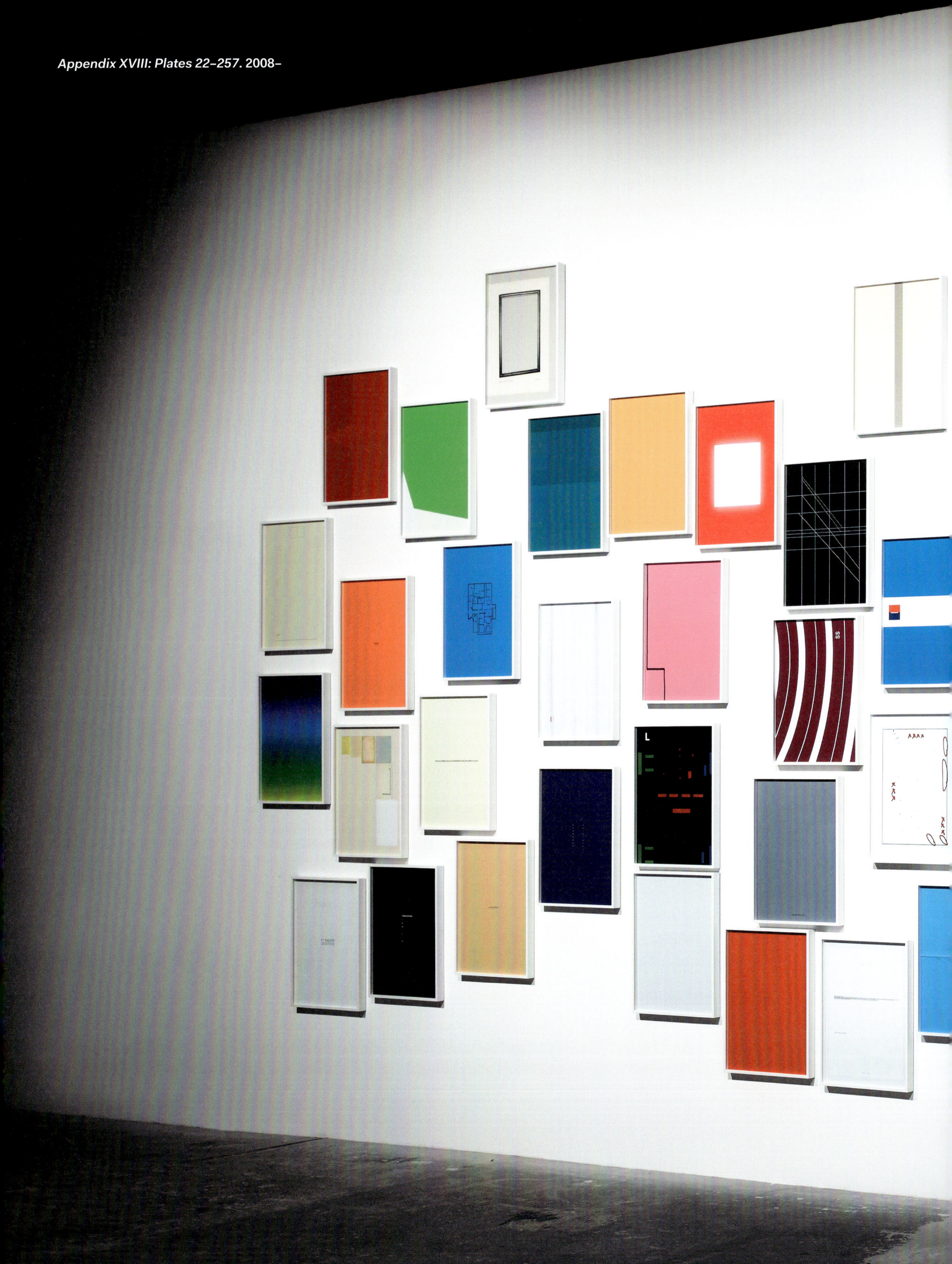

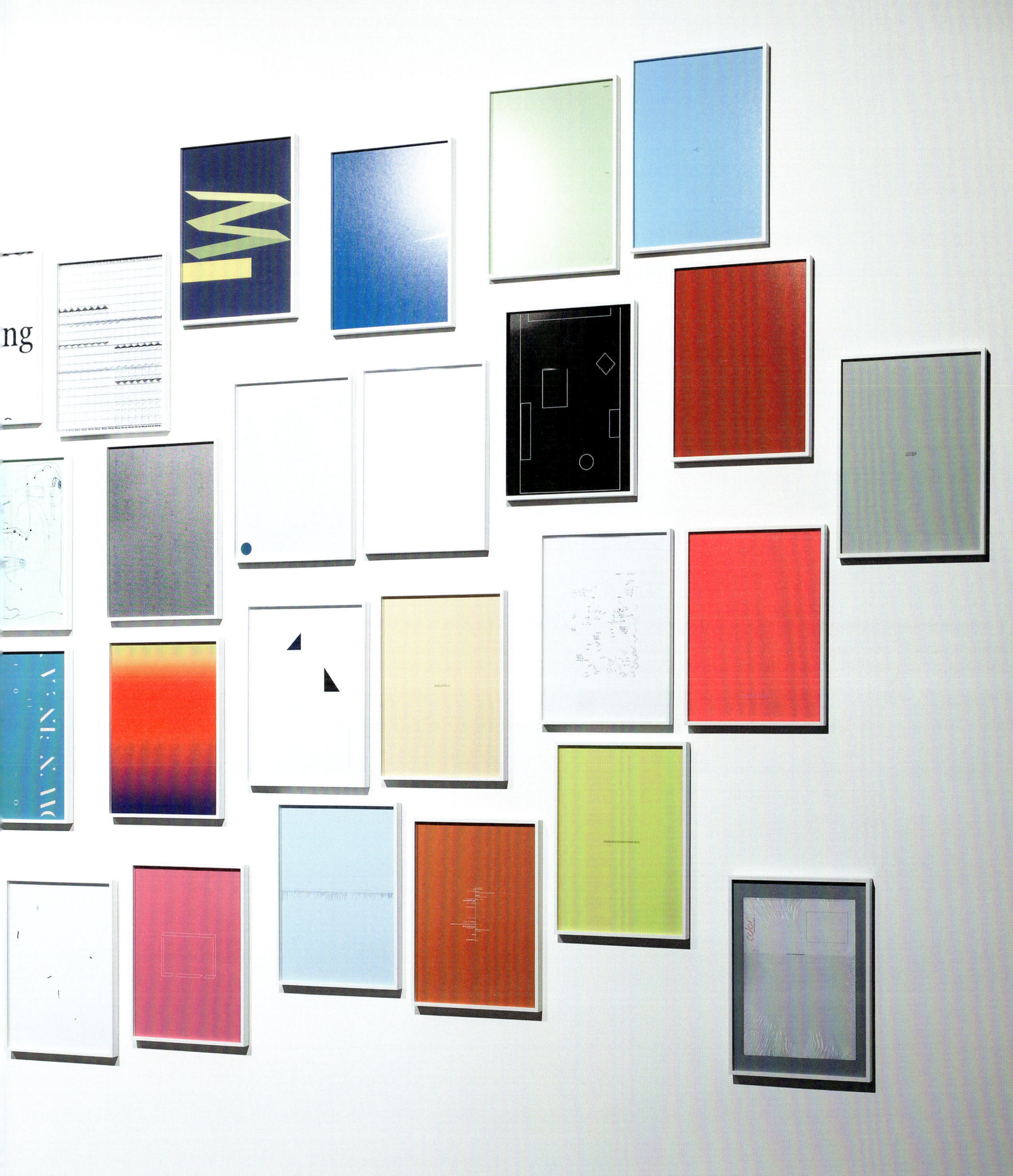

The Lebanese wars of the past three decades affected Lebanon's residents physically and psychologically: from the 100,000-plus who were killed; to the 200,000-plus who were wounded; to the 1,000,000-plus who were displaced; to the even more who were psychologically traumatized.

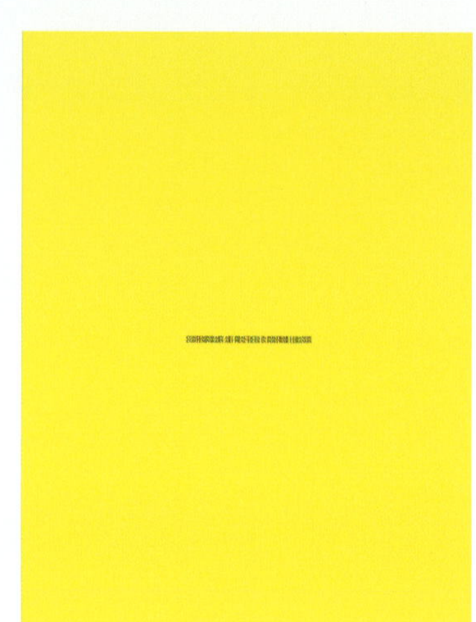

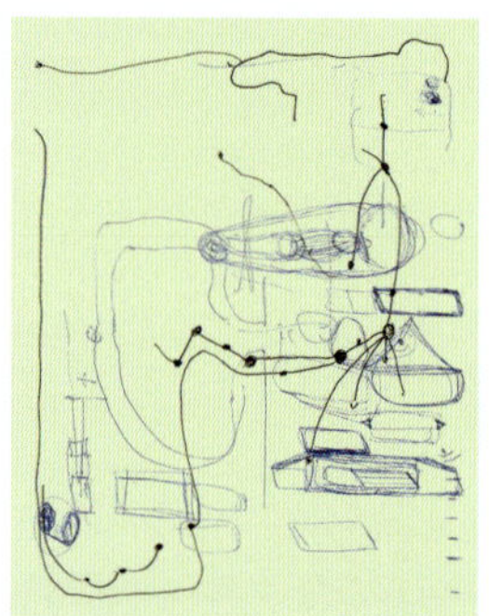

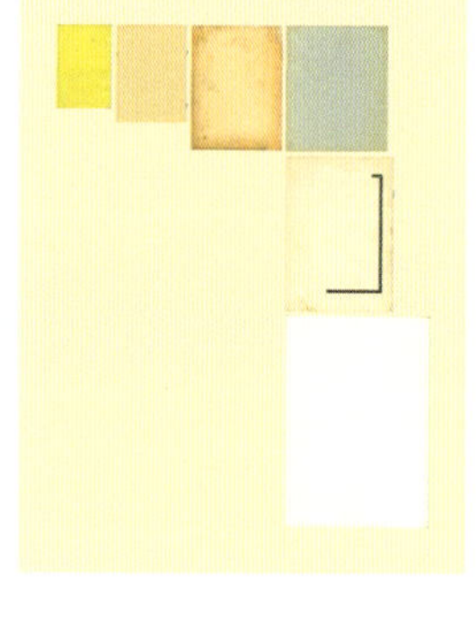

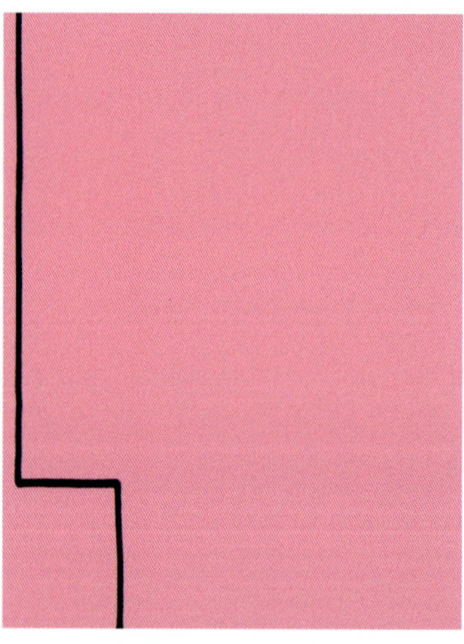

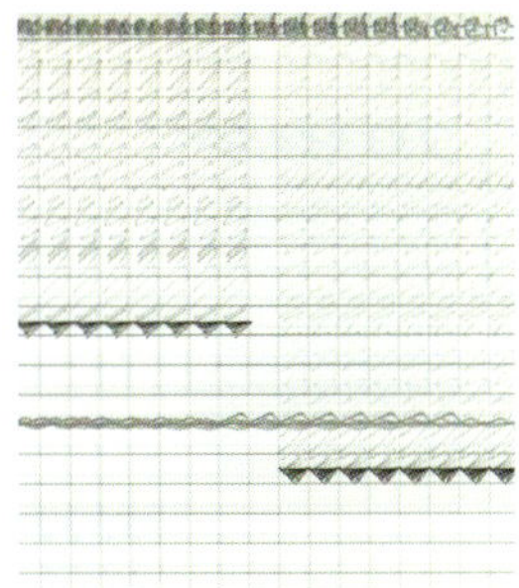

It is clear to me today that these wars also affected colors, lines, shapes, and forms. Some of these were affected in a material way, and, like burned books or razed monuments, were physically destroyed and lost forever; others, like looted treasure or politically compromised artworks, remain physically intact but are removed from view, possibly never to be seen again. And yet other colors, lines, shapes, and forms, sensing the forthcoming danger, have deployed defensive measures: they hide, take refuge, hibernate, camouflage, and/or dissimulate. I expected them to do so in the artworks of past artists, whose paintings and sculptures I thought would be their most hospitable hosts. I was wrong. Instead, colors, lines, shapes, and forms took refuge in unexpected places: they hid in Roman and Arabic letters and numbers; in circles, rectangles, and squares; in yellow, blue, and green. They dissimulated as fonts, covers, titles, and indices; as the graphic lines and footnotes of books; they camouflaged themselves as letters, price lists, dissertations, and catalogues; as diagrams and budgets. They hibernated not in but around artworks.

These are the colors, lines, shapes, and forms that compose the plates displayed here.

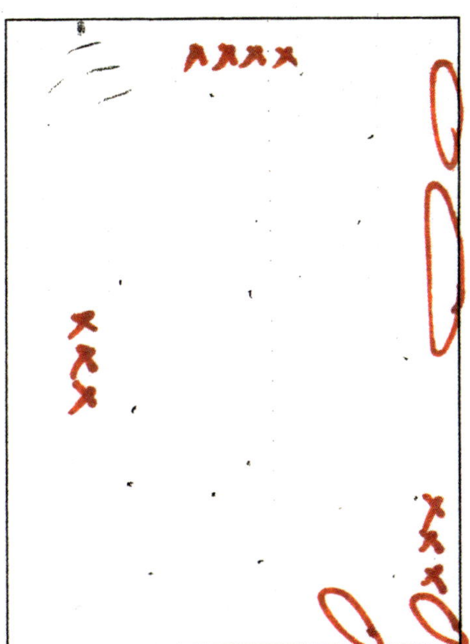

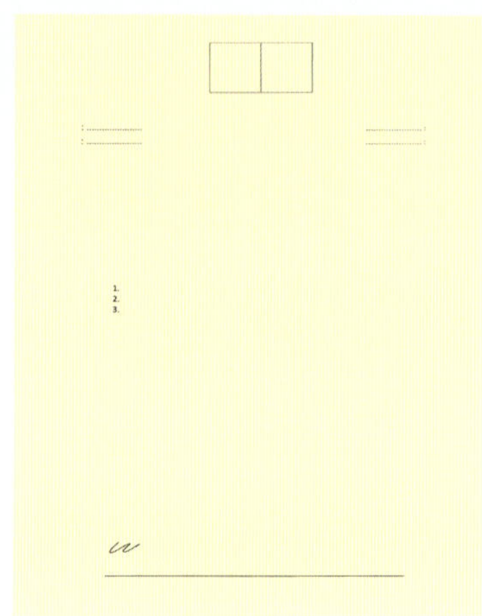

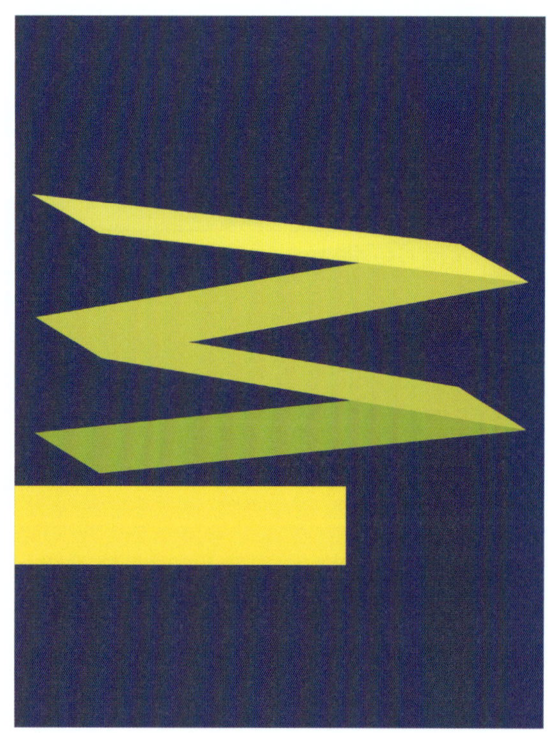

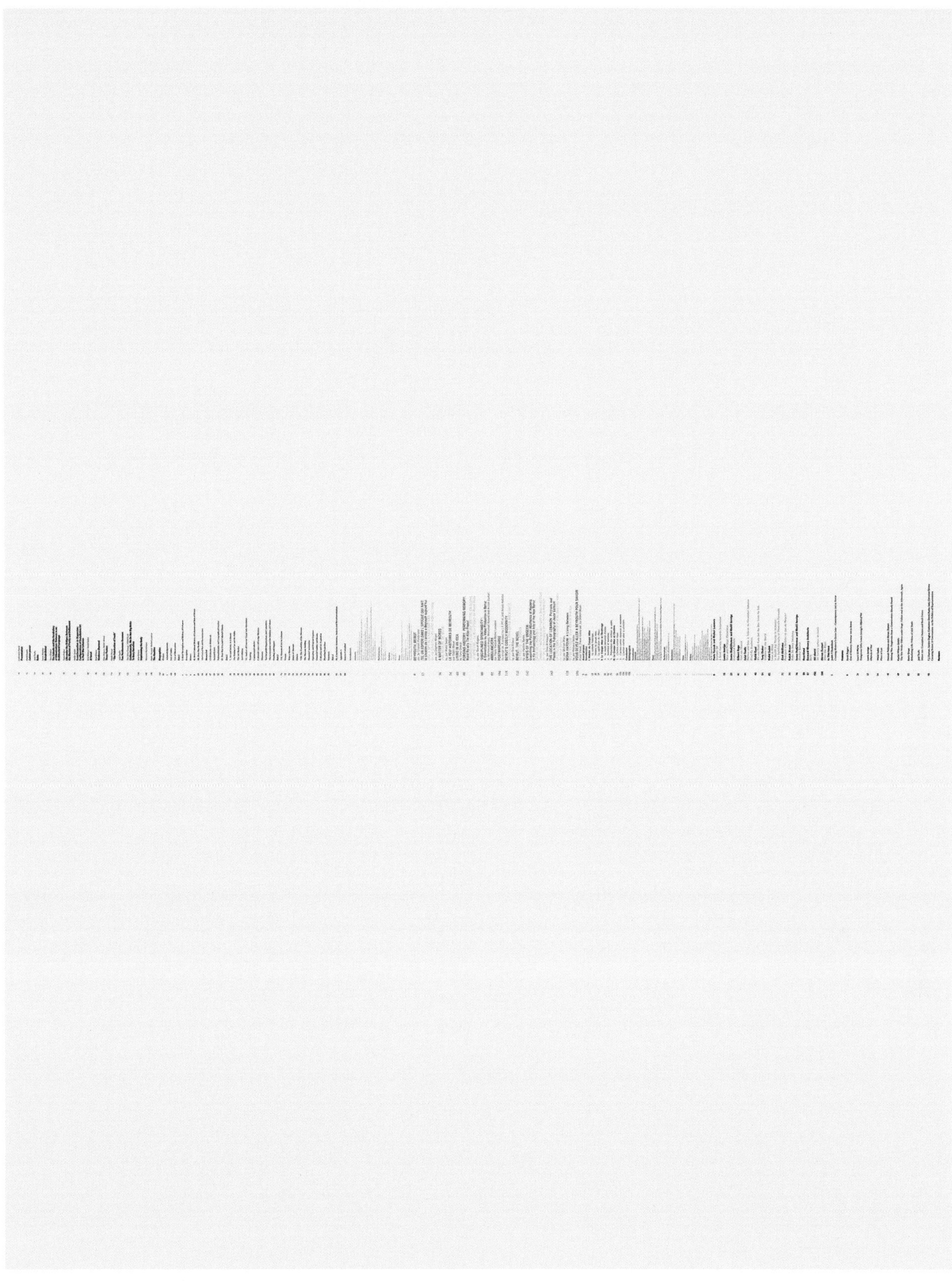

I was recently taken aback by how most paintings on display in the Arab Museum of Modern Art in Doha lack some (but not all) reflections. I decided to provide some with these works. I am hoping that the reflections in my photographs will eventually leave my works and attach themselves to the paintings in the museum.

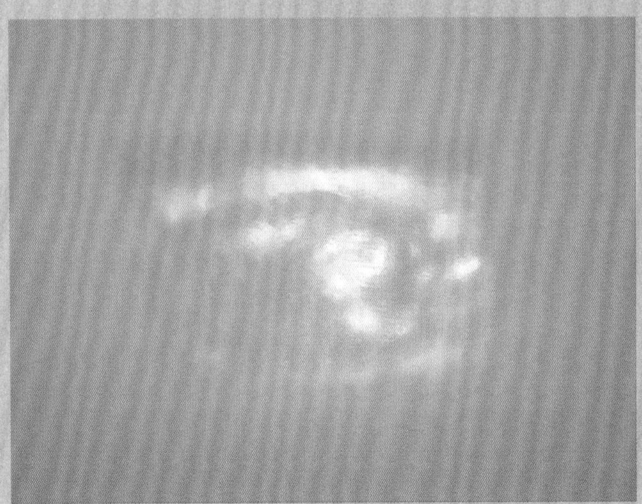

Of the nearly 18,000 objects held in the Louvre's newly established *département des Arts de l'Islam,* 294 will be loaned to the Louvre Abu Dhabi sometime between 2016 and 2046. Of the 294 objects, twenty-eight will be affected by the journey in ways that historians, curators, and conservators could not have anticipated or predicted.

While no one will doubt the subsequent changes, the reason for their onset will be contested. Most will attribute them to the weather, asserting that the "corrosion" began soon after the exquisitely crafted, climate-controlled crates were opened in the Arabian Desert. But a rare few will correctly surmise that the objects opted to dissimulate: they traded skins, limbs, faces, and organs with each other.

Here, the objects are caught in the act; moreover, and to complement their dissimulation, I decided to provide them with like-minded vitrines, notations, and shadows.

Les Louvres (Département des Arts de l’Islam)

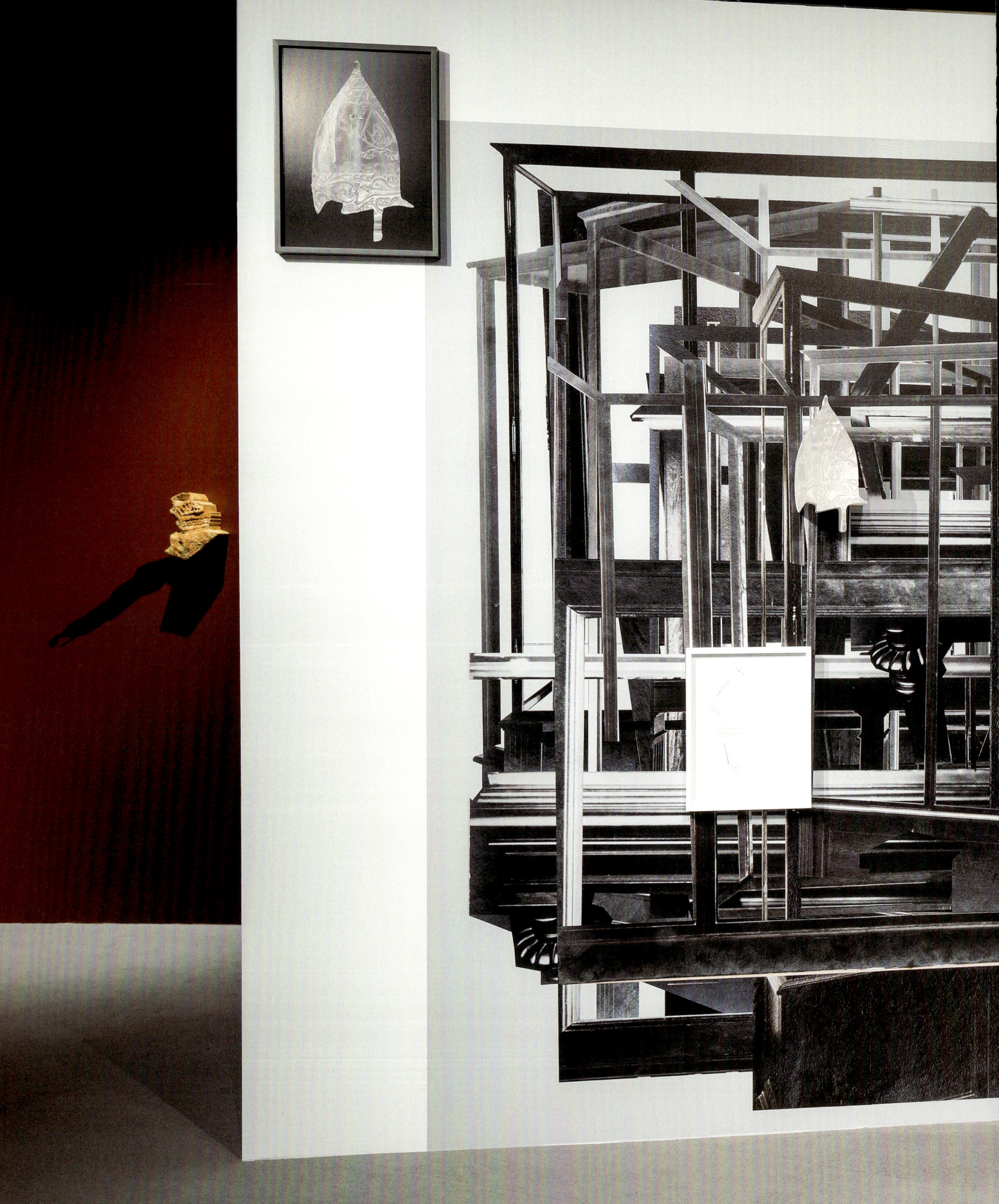

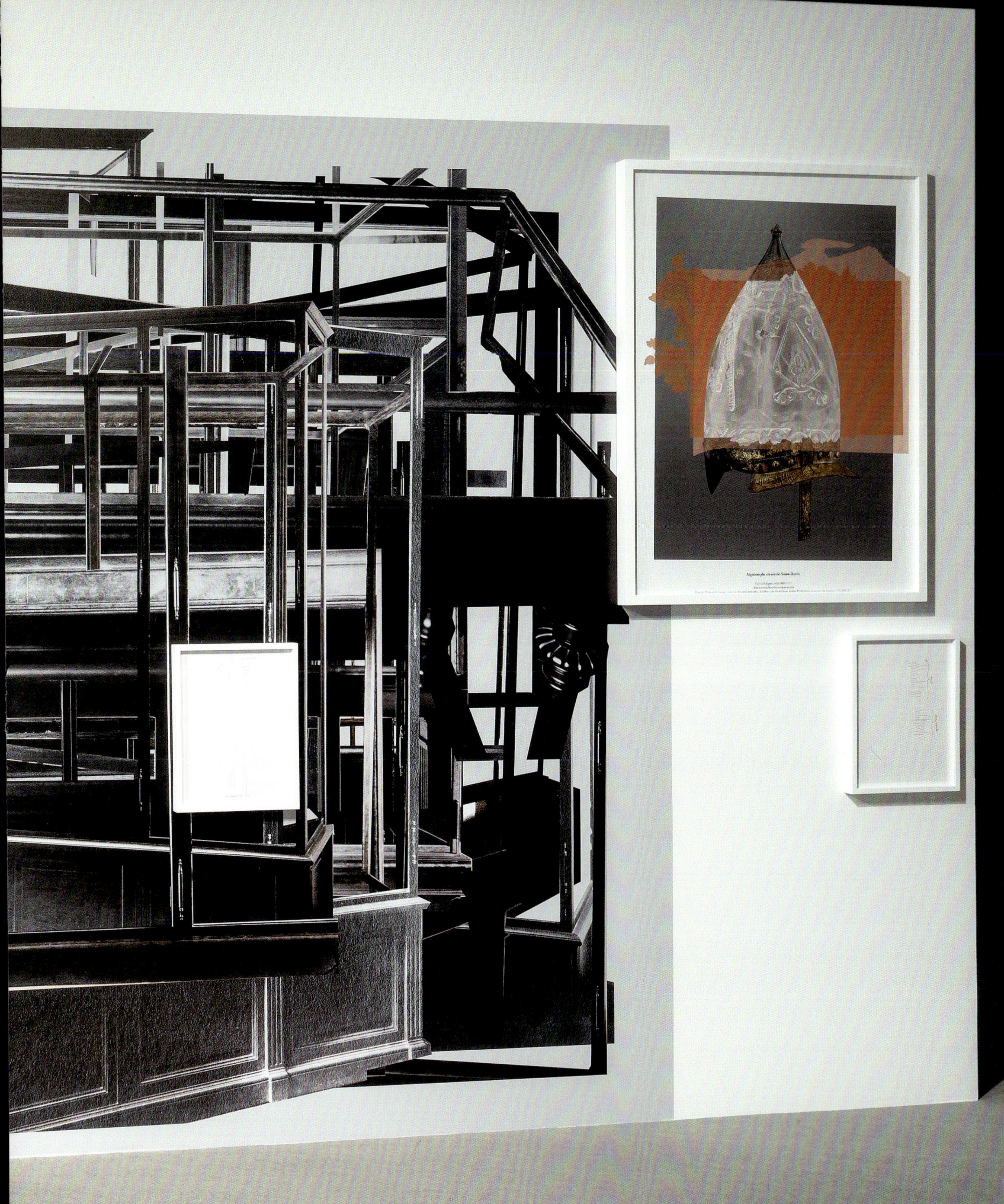

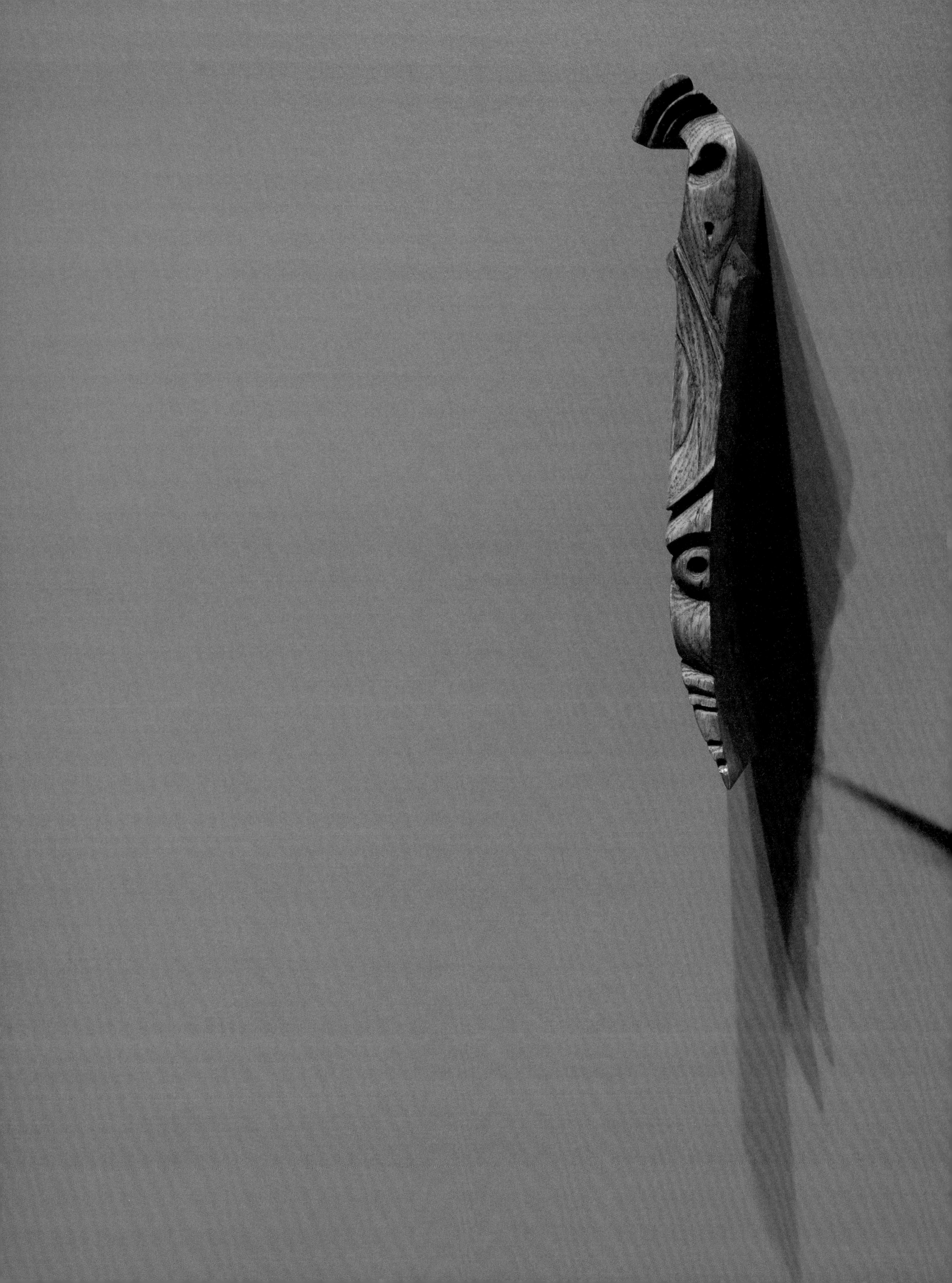

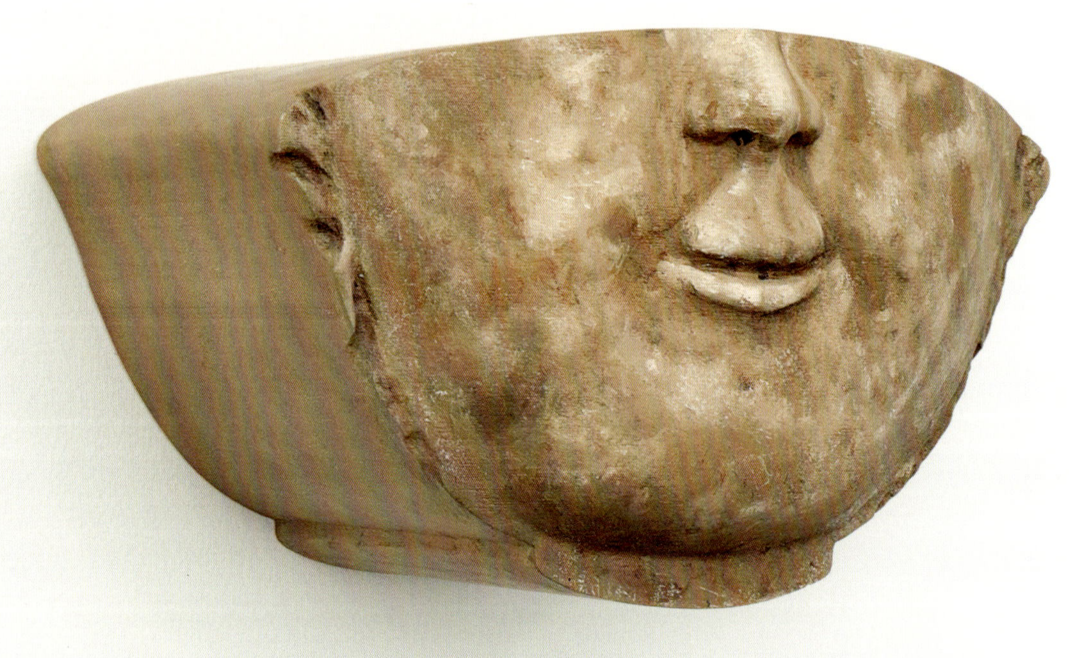

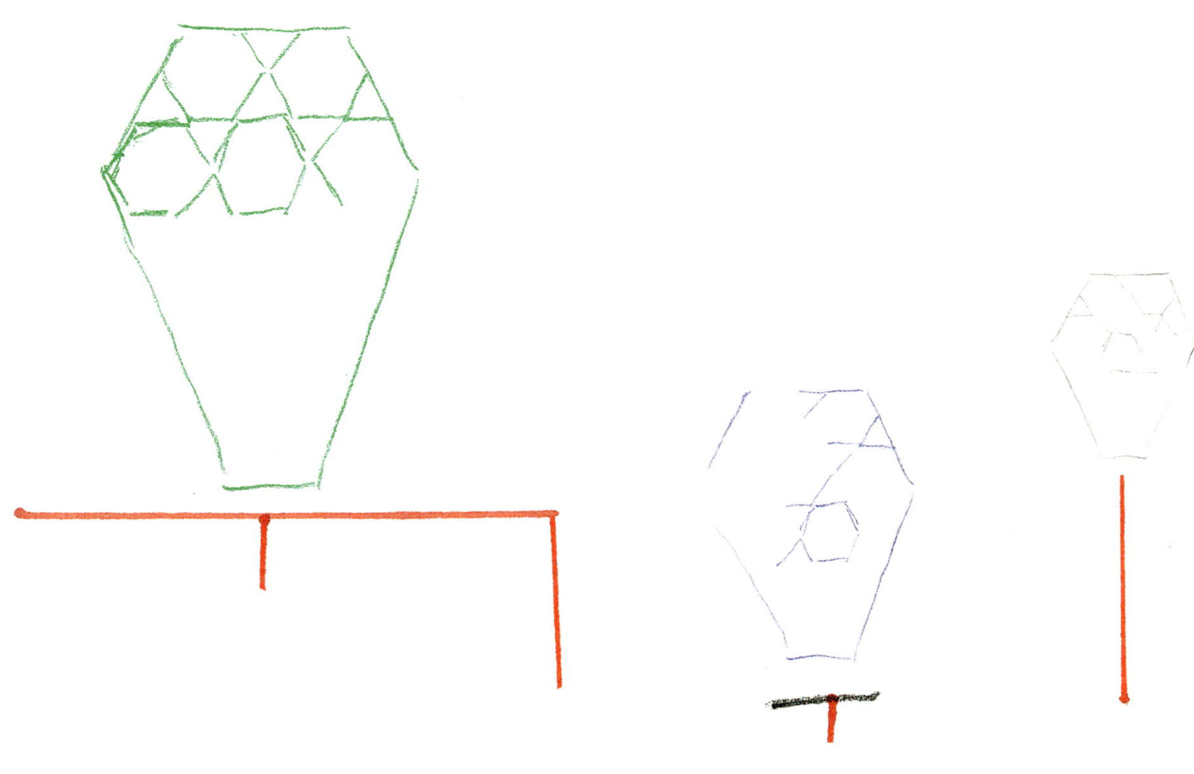

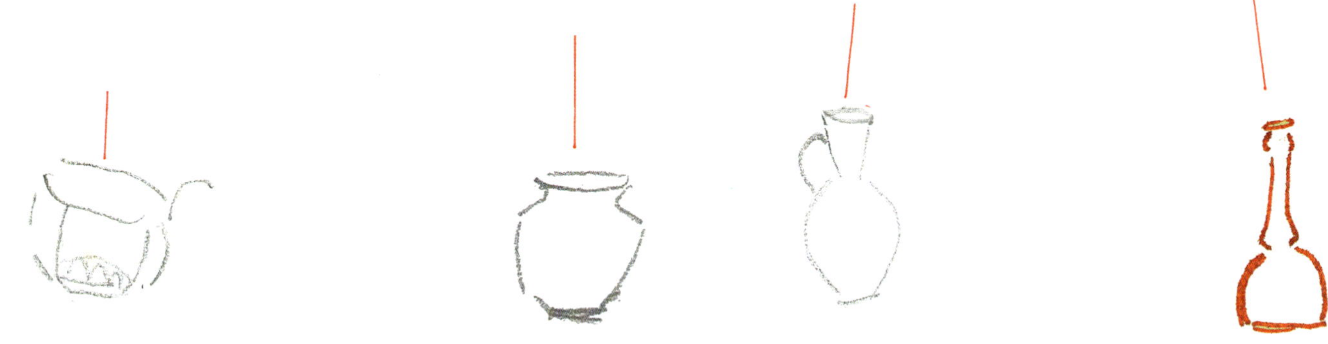

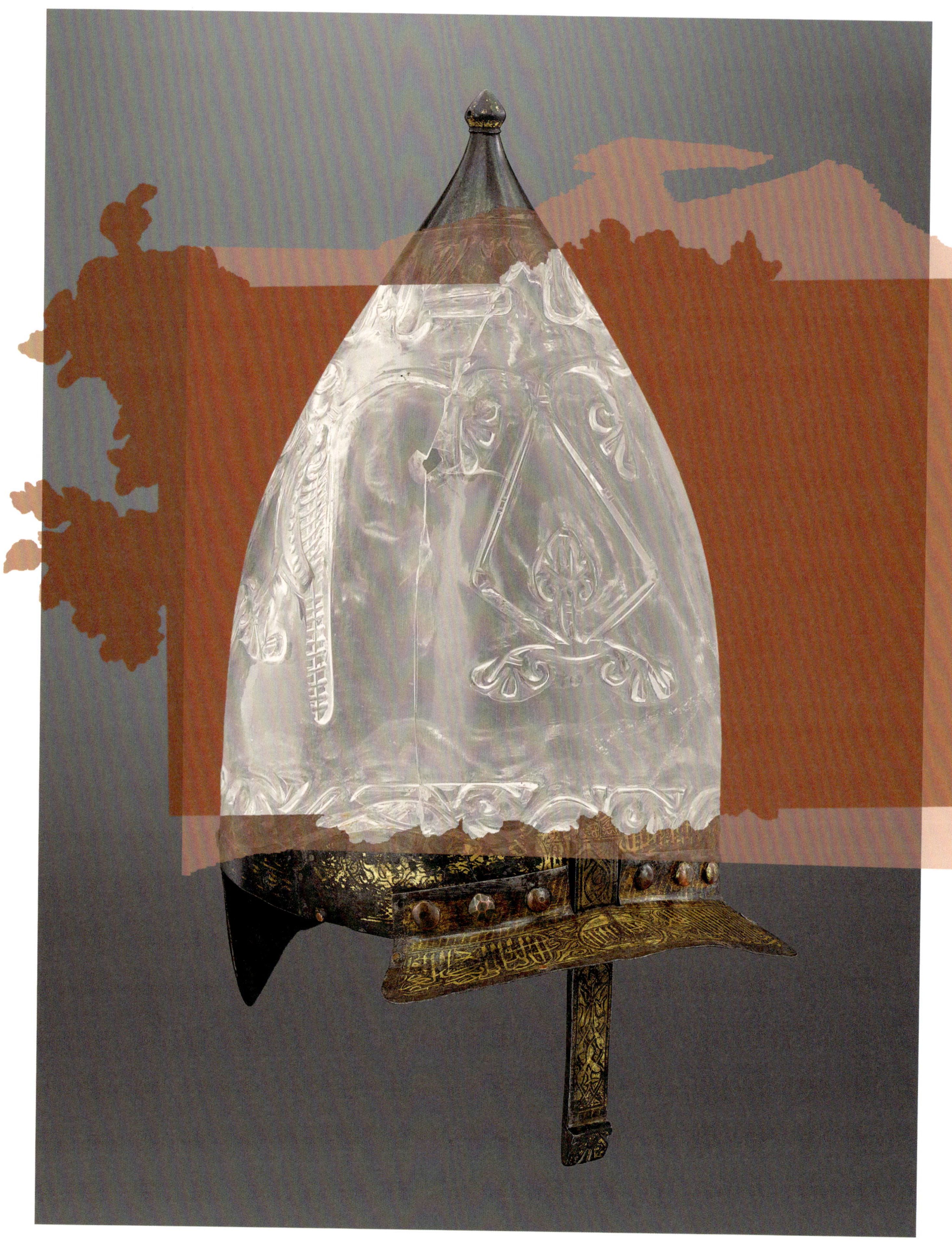

Aiguière du trésor de Saint-Denis

Vaisselle, Égypte, vers 1000-1015
Cristal de roche taillé, sculpté et poli
Don de Thibaud le Grand, comte de Blois-Champagne, à l'abbaye de Saint-Denis (avant 1152), versé au musée du Louvre, 1793, MR333

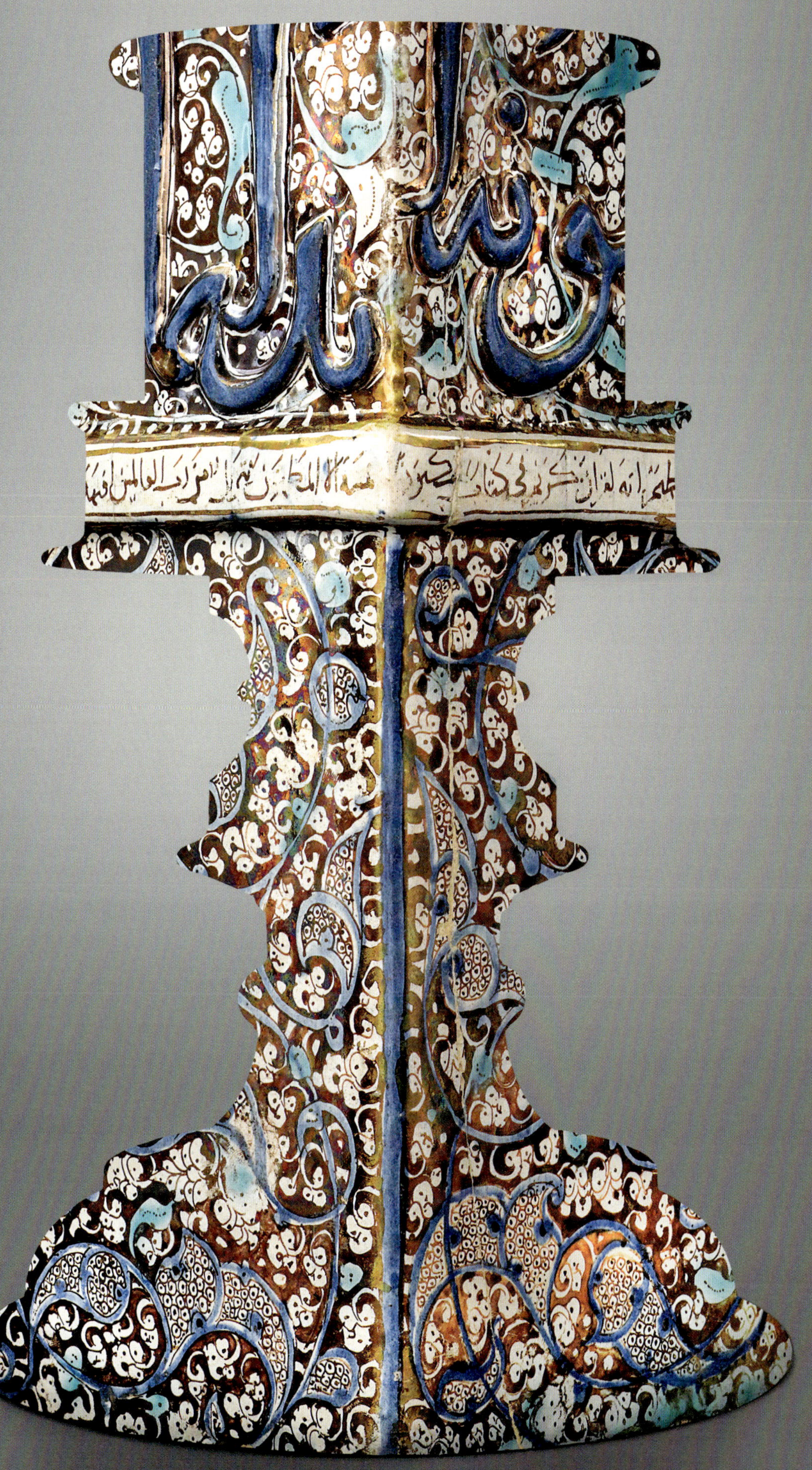

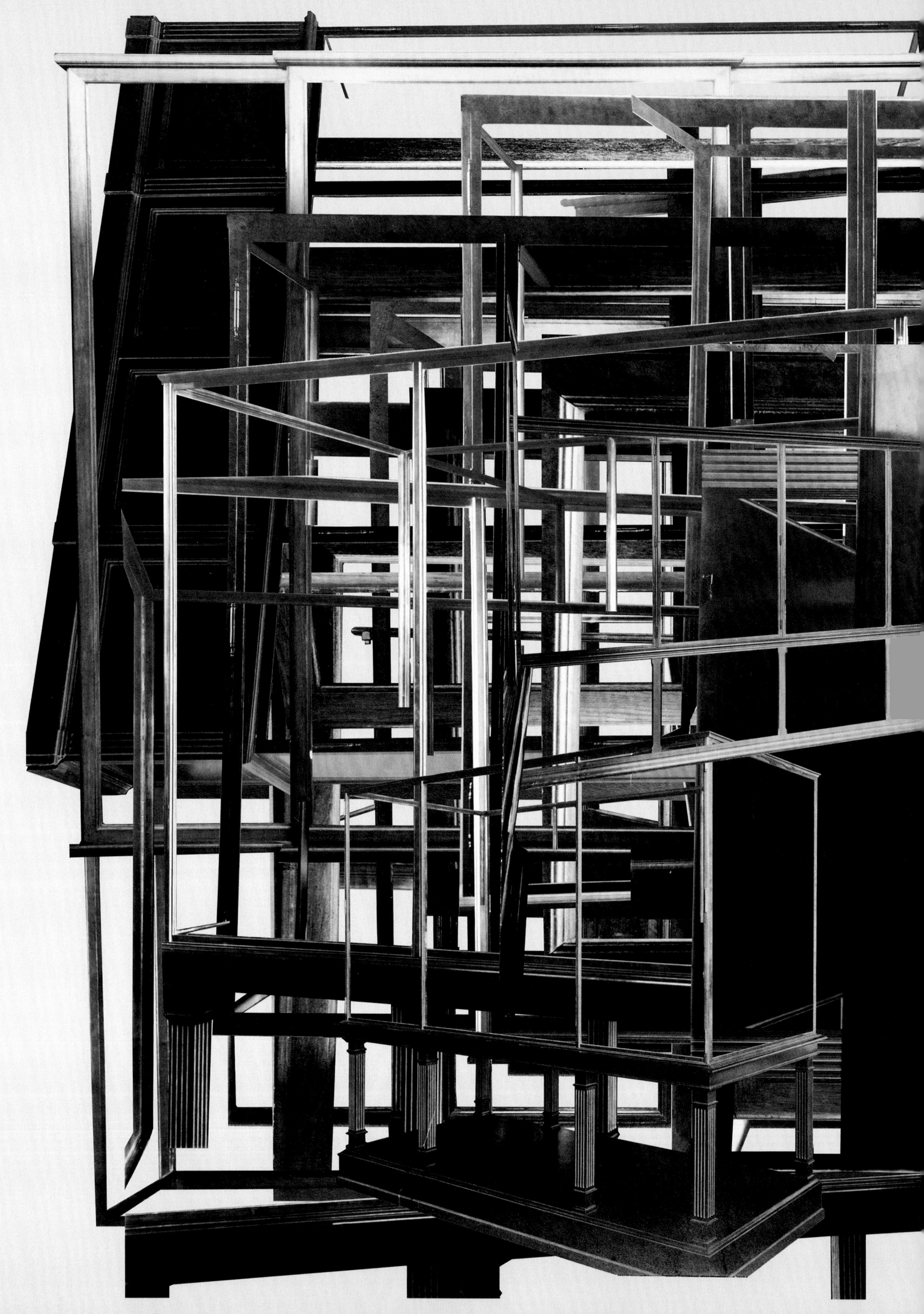

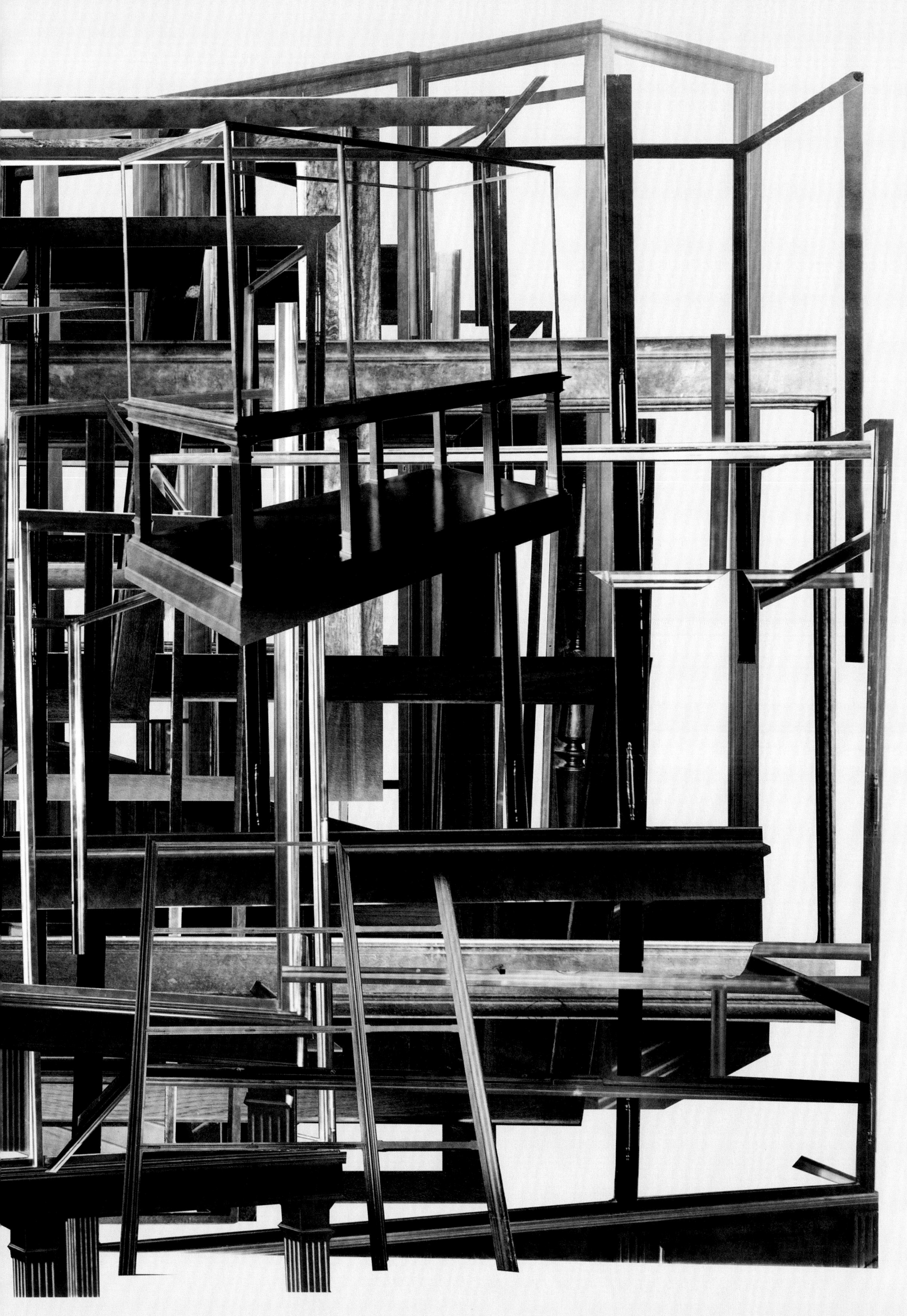

Staging Traces of Histories Not Easily Disavowed

Finbarr Barry Flood

The museum is a colossal mirror in which man contemplates himself, in short, in all his aspects, finds himself literally admirable and abandons himself to the ecstasy expressed in all the art journals.
—Georges Bataille, *Encyclopaedia Acephalica*, 1929–30

Over the past decade, major museums in Cairo, Copenhagen, Detroit, Doha, Kuwait, London, New York, and other cities have installed or reinstalled their collections of Islamic art. The results have attracted bouquets and brickbats in equal measure. Some of these museums house collections whose origins lie in nineteenth- and early-twentieth-century intersections between antiquarianism, commercialism, and orientalism. Others, especially those in the Gulf, house collections of more recent vintage, whose acquisition over the past two decades has infused the market with a giddy frisson of excess seldom previously associated with Islamic art.[1]

This reinvestment of Islamic antiquities has been paralleled by the development of Middle Eastern franchises of museums such as the Guggenheim and the Louvre in Abu Dhabi, and the global emergence of an extensive array of galleries and museums dedicated to showcasing the modern and contemporary art of the Middle East. These range from small commercial galleries and private spaces in cities such as Beirut, Cairo, London, New York, and Ramallah to national institutions such as Doha's Mathaf: Arab Museum of Modern Art, whose opening in 2010 signaled the role of the Gulf region in the vanguard of these developments. At the same time, biennials, exhibitions, and foundations for the collection and promotion of modern and contemporary "Islamic" art have proliferated in the Middle East, Europe, and the United States. Modern Middle Eastern art is enjoying an ongoing canonization as a field of collecting and study (both in its own right and as a chapter in the history of global modernism), witnessed by the establishment of professorships, the writing of doctoral dissertations, and the appointment of curators to such august institutions as the British Museum in London and The Metropolitan Museum of Art in New York.

These developments have taken place against a background of tumultuous political instability and violence in the Middle East, from the United States–led invasion of Iraq in 2003, through Israel's 2006 war on Lebanon, to the revolutions of the Arab Spring, the reassertion of a U.S.-funded military dictatorship in Egypt, and the transformation of a popular uprising against a brutal Syrian dictatorship into a proxy war fueled by the very petrodollars with which Gulf states are sponsoring their cultural infrastructures and institutions. The worlds of political violence and of the museum have occasionally intersected, with disastrous consequences: in January 2014, the Museum of Islamic Art in Cairo, the world's oldest museum of Islamic art, was seriously damaged when a car bomb detonated outside the police quarters across the road and almost entirely destroyed the museum's facade, along with many prize artifacts (fig. 1).

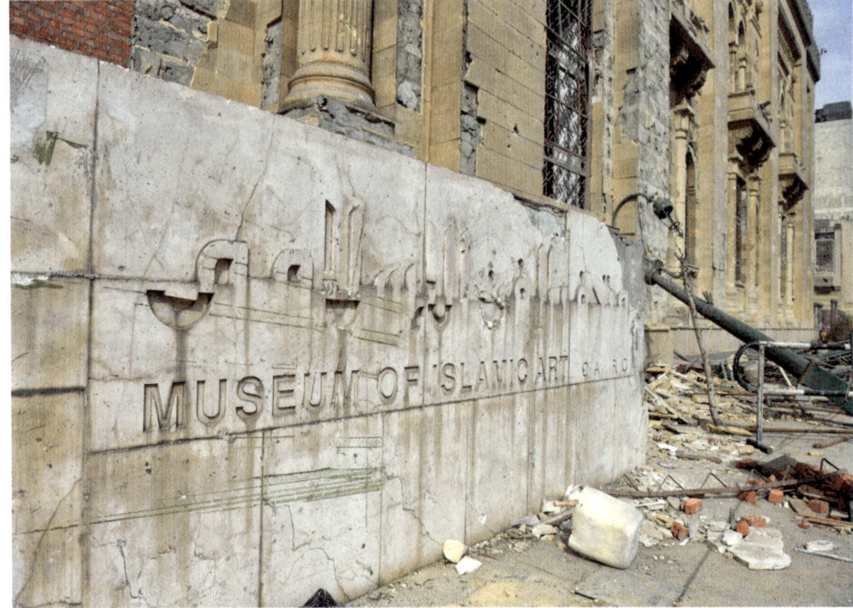

1 Damage to the Museum of Islamic Art, Cairo, after a bombing across the street on January 24, 2014

Tensions between contemporary geopolitics, the emergence of major art institutions across the Arab world, and the economic developments that underwrite both provide the background to Walid Raad's latest project. *Scratching on things I could disavow* (2007–) is an amorphous congeries of intersecting images and texts meticulously crafted to interrogate the cultural, economic, material, and political infrastructures that produce and sustain certain kinds of work *as* art, while questioning the nature of the archives that enable us to write histories of and from artworks. *Scratching . . .* is an amorphous history of Arab art staged through images, installations, tales, and texts, an assemblage perhaps best encapsulated by the Arabic word *athar*, which can be variously translated as antiquity, impression, mark, relic, remnant, ruin, or vestige. Raad's carefully staged constellations of artifacts, images, and narratives are loosely associated by their relation to the histories and historiographies of artistic production in the Arab world, both long entrenched and more recent. They include canonical artifacts of Islamic art, paradigmatic works of Arab modernism that have undergone more recent canonization, and a contemporary canon that is currently under construction and contestation.

The measured ambivalence that permeates the project is implicit both in the conditional disavowal that it evokes and in the "scratching" of the project's title, with its dual sense of surface archaeology and the relief of capitulating to the masochistic urge to rake one's fingers across an irritation. In this as in all of Raad's work, the materials of and for any history are fragmentary, disjunctive, and recalcitrant. Authoritative data presented as charts and diagrams resist easy co-option or circumscription by practices of representation, being simultaneously offered and withdrawn, asserting even while denying their own historicity. The play with statistical authority in the form of precise dates and carefully numbered captions is also typical. Titles appropriate the standard categories of teleological time while frustrating the expectations that they generate: prefaces, appendixes, interrupted sequences, random dates, partial views, and tantalizing excerpts of orphaned fascicles extracted from series that might never have been or never be—all assert the authority of the catalogue or monograph while simultaneously undermining it. The dialectic between the authority of Roman and Arabic numerals in the sequences of the titles only doubles the play.

Raad co-opts the space of the gallery or museum to autopsy the range of institutions that produce and sustain art as history. He turns his forensic gaze not only on the architectural space of the gallery but also on its sustaining infrastructures, including the institutional gestures and tics that constitute its role as part of the frame that gives work cultural and economic value: the lecture, the PowerPoint presentation, the dissertation, the catalogue essay. Like Raad's earlier Atlas Group project, *Scratching . . .* enacts the way that stories spun around objects alter their meaning and value and hence their stability as historical reifications. The project is, in effect, a meta-curation, a performative restaging of the elusive artifacts, histories, practices, and spaces that it engages, with Raad as choreographer, impresario, and medium overseeing installations marked by displacement, shape-shifting, and time travel.

This "meta" quality is enhanced by the imprimatur that *Scratching . . .* has received not only from long-established sanctuaries of Islamic art but also from newly emergent sites of pilgrimage to the modern and contemporary art of the Arab world. The reopening of the galleries of the Louvre's Département des Arts de l'Islam in 2012 (fig. 2), for example, was accompanied by a series of commissioned works by Raad, which took as their subjects the department's star objects. Among these, Raad's 2013 work *Preface to the third edition* (2013; pp. 150, 157) is a handsome portfolio containing luxurious images of twenty-eight canonical objects of Islamic art in the Louvre's collection. An accompanying text (p. 148) explains that these are among the 294 objects from the Louvre that will travel to the museum's new Abu Dhabi franchise (designed by starchitect Jean Nouvel) at some point between 2016 and 2046. On the journey, the text observes, these twenty-eight works will undergo changes whose causes will be contested but that may be material—results of the change in climate, for example; immaterial, manifesting only in the dreams and disorders of the non-Emirati workers constructing such temples of culture; or aesthetic, manifesting only once: in the portfolio's twenty-eight polychrome photos, purportedly the work of a female artist sponsored to work in the museum in 2026.

The mutations evoked in *Preface to the third edition* are multiple, from the transformation of three-dimensional artifacts into two-dimensional photographs to the superimposition of one artifact's surface patterns onto another. This latter cross-fertilization subverts function in the production of striking hybrids, as when a dense floral pattern from a lacquer book-cover comes to pattern the handle of a dagger, or the form of a metal helmet is inhabited by the delicate translucent surface of a medieval rock-crystal vessel. The helmet image is among those that reappear in *Footnote II* (2015; pp. 150–51), a recent installation in which photographs and models of Raad's transformations of the Louvre's objects are mounted against densely layered archival shots, palimpsest images of the vitrines that once constrained them. *Preface to the third edition* offers spectacularly beautiful ways of rethinking these objects, destabilizing their deployment as institutionalized representatives of singular times and spaces while presenting canonical artifacts as objets trouvés, like those that feature in Raad's Atlas Group work.

The process of materialization and transubstantiation assumes more dynamic aspects in the video *Preface to the fourth edition* (2012). Here, prime objects in the Louvre's Islamic collection—ceramics, crystals, ivories, metalwork, textiles—flick and flit by the viewer's gaze, eventually merging and morphing into a dense vortex of incoherent forms and unstable hues. This then resolves into a series of chromatic verticals of variable densities and thicknesses (fig. 3), similar to those that recur in the mixed-media *Section 88_Act XXII: Views from outer*

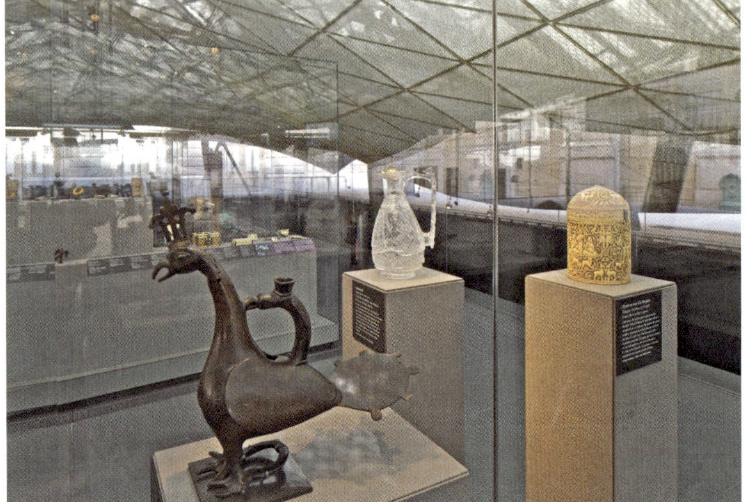

2 Département des Arts de l'Islam, Musée du Louvre, Paris. 2012. In the foreground: vitrine 9, showing, left to right, the peacock aquamanile, a ewer, and the pyxis of al-Mughira

to inner compartments (2012–). The extraction of pure color and form from images of historical objects, producing traces of traces, resonates with a core concept of *Scratching . . .* : according to a text accompanying one of its works, *Appendix XVIII: Plates 22–257* (2008– ; pp. 138–43), the Lebanese wars of the past three decades displaced lines and shapes, colors and forms, which sought refuge not in artworks but in their sustaining documentary infrastructures: budgets, catalogues, covers, diagrams, fonts and footnotes, price lists and the titles of dissertations (especially those by foreign scholars of Lebanese art)—in short, the sorts of materials that feature prominently throughout *Scratching. . . .*

The transformation of historical artifacts into chromatic abstractions suggests the unstable relation between the museum object and the institutional and material frames that produce and sustain it. Recalling the twentieth-century valorizations of Islamic art as an art of abstraction,[2] Raad's transformations also manifest one of the most original and radical aspects of *Scratching . . .* : its subversion of the temporal taxonomies that govern the presentation of art, whether in gallery or museum, lecture or text, stratifying the premodern from the modern and both from the contemporary.[3] That the historical objects of Islamic art are capable of this kind of transformation suggests more complex imbrications between past and present, underlining the fact that Raad's history of art in the Arab world neither begins nor ends with modernism. His production of fugitive color from the material certainties of historical objects is an interrogation not simply of chronology, taxonomy, the museum, or even the histories of Arab art, but of the conditions of visibility necessary for the production of histories *tout court*. In *Scratching . . .* as in much of Raad's work, questions of legibility, visibility, and temporality are mutually implicating.

As Raad has often acknowledged, his work is indebted to the writings of the Lebanese artist and philosopher Jalal Toufic. In suggesting why colors, forms, lines, and shapes may have sought refuge in unlikely places, the introductory text for *Scratching . . .* cites Toufic's idea of "the withdrawal of tradition past a surpassing disaster," an idea developed in an eponymous book of 2009.[4] Toufic suggests that in the wake of a surpassing disaster—the atomic bombings of 1945, or the series of catastrophes that have hit the Arab world since the 1980s—certain artistic, literary, and musical works remain immaterially withdrawn. Artifacts, buildings, documents, and paintings may persist in a material sense but are unavailable to those directly affected by the surpassing disaster, being seen but at the same time experienced and engaged with as if unavailable to vision. The idea owes something to a distinction between *zahir* and *batin*, between exoteric and esoteric, form and essence, in mystical strains of Islamic thought.

The notion that artworks might be both materially present and immaterially withdrawn calls into question the way histories, historical events, and memories are constituted, and by whom. The problem is the violence not simply of war (as if that

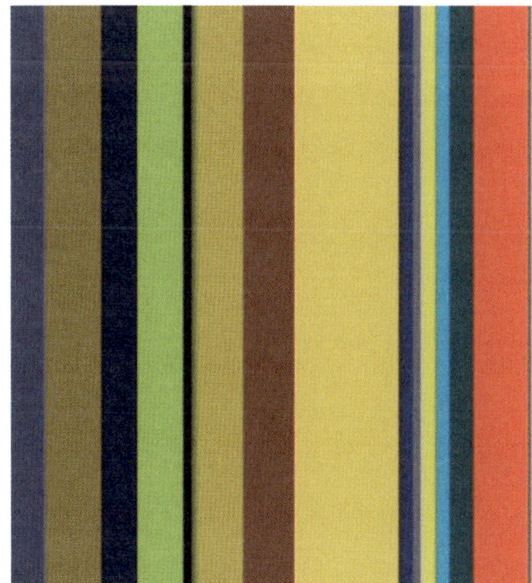
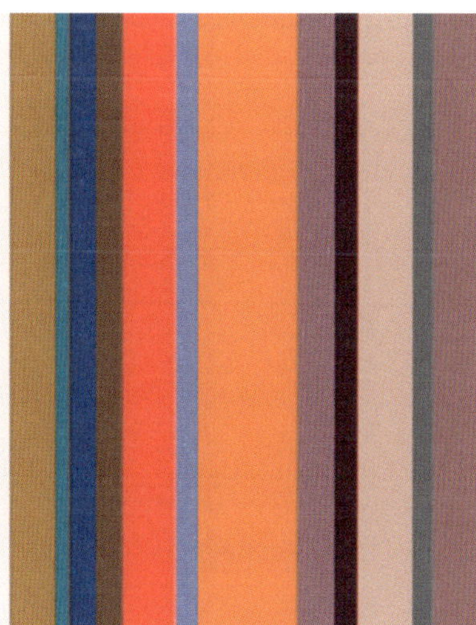

3 Walid Raad. ***Preface to the fourth edition.*** **2012. Still from single-channel video (color, silent), 12 min. 49 sec.**

were ever simple) but of the archive through which histories of war (or histories in general) are constituted—fragments worn and torn, ripped from their context in order to preserve the testimonies that they are made to instantiate. Under interrogation, all such documents are produced, valorized, valued, and enshrined through a process of stratification or winnowing that divides the wheat from the chaff, the historically significant from the apparently contingent.

Yet it is precisely in the promise or potential of the contingent, the ephemeral, that the possibility of a counterhegemonic history emerges. For Toufic, the works and documents subject to immaterial withdrawal after a surpassing disaster—books, films, monuments, photographs, paintings—remain available to the hegemonic histories promoted by perpetrators and victors, while those affected by the disaster are compelled to resurrect these same works. In *Scratching . . .*, objects, documents, and images afforded archival status as marooned instantiations of (often contested) histories are manifest not as historical documents but in ways recalling Toufic's suggestion that, following a surpassing disaster, "while the documentation of the referent is for the future, the presentation of the withdrawal is an urgent task for the present."[5] In both Toufic's writings and Raad's practice, the strategies of presenting withdrawal are multiple, including blurring, displacement, textual mediation, and temporal destabilization.[6]

In this sense Raad's move from archive to museum is a natural one. A corollary of the recent rise of interest in modern Arab art, for example, is a headlong dash not simply *to* the archive but to *constitute* it, with varying results. In an arch in-joke, Raad's *Appendix XVIII: Plates 56–58 Dr. Kirsten Scheid's Fabulous Archive* (2008) plays with the anthropologist's or art historian's need for archives in order to resurrect occluded histories and the desire that permeates that archival quest. Named after a celebrated Beirut-based scholar of modern Arab art, the work includes blurry miniature reproductions of artworks, collated and collected yet still somehow inacessible. Similarly, *Preface to the fifth edition* (2014) explores the mutually constituting relation between museum artifacts and archival ephemera, juxtaposing blurry photographs of museum objects with curatorial notes, statistical observations, and the sketches and reports of conservators.

Like much of Raad's earlier work, *Scratching . . .* suggests that the project of resurrecting past histories of art is not simply a matter of bringing them to light, of (re-)establishing them by constructing archives necessarily permeated by contingency and ephemerality. On the contrary, it is a more fundamental matter of staging the relation between the material and immaterial qualities of artworks, of interrogating the relationships between accessibility, temporality, and visibility. Here Raad's approach is clearly inspired by Toufic's idea that the ultimate goal of artists operating in the wake of a surpassing disaster is the resurrection of withdrawn works, the overcoming of their immaterial withdrawal. Pending that resurrection, however, the artist's mandate is to present a withdrawal of a kind that manifests itself only fleetingly and incompletely. It can be discerned in a film's closing credits, for example, or in the photograph that performs not in its historical role as an archival document, an index of the past available to the present, but as an index of immaterial withdrawal, capable of preserving its blurred or off-center referent only in a future time, when the work of resurrection has been completed.[7] In passages rich with resonances for *Scratching . . .* , Toufic proposes that an appropriate locus for the display of such photographic indexes of withdrawal would be the Isabella Stewart Gardner Museum, Boston, where the theft of thirteen paintings by Degas, Rembrandt, Vermeer, and others on March 18, 1990, is memorialized by the continued display of the empty frames from which they were cut (p. 45, fig. 24).[8] In this way Toufic suggests how two distinct forms of absence or unavailability might be enshrined in the gallery, with photographic indexes of immaterial withdrawal complementing frames that memorialize material evanescence.

Several component works of *Scratching . . .* , among them the mixed-media installations *Preface to the first edition* (2014; p. 44, fig. 21) and *Section 88: Views from outer to inner compartments*, literalize Raad's engagement with practices of framing, functioning as stage sets that co-opt while echoing the framing role of the gallery itself. The principle operates in a cascading series of registers, from a vista of open doorways that leads the eye from one gallery space to the next (offering the tantalizing promise of a vanishing point that never quite appears) through material frames that articulate, define, and punctuate the space of the gallery, devices ranging from elegant classical door-jambs to skirting boards, walls, and picture frames, epitomes of an entire infrastructure of enframing (pp. 122–27). A text (pp. 124–25) accompanying *Section 88: Views from outer to inner compartments* negates the invitation of these open doors and frames, telling the tale of a hypothetical resident of an unnamed Arab city who rushes toward the entrance of a new museum of modern and/or contemporary art only to find himself stopped in his tracks, frozen in place by the sense that should he proceed, he would "hit a wall."

Showcasing institutional carapaces generally occluded in the production of aesthetic or historical value, the frame functions in *Scratching . . .* as a hieroglyph for the staging not only of display but of practices of viewing and consuming. Its role in this ambivalent parsing of institutional productivity recalls Jacques Derrida's characterization of the role played by the *parergon*, the supplement that in Kant's aesthetics remains (at least in theory) exterior to the work: "The violence of framing proliferates. It confines the theory of aesthetics within a theory of the beautiful, the theory of the beautiful within a theory of taste, and the theory of taste within a theory of judgment."[9]

Little wonder, then, that like Kovalyov's nose, many of the works in *Scratching . . .* seek to break their bonds and take on a life of their own. In *Preface to the second edition* (2012; pp. 144–47), reflected images flicker as shadows cast upon the pristine floors of Mathaf. The museum's polished floor is pressed into service as a primary medium for evanescent artworks whose alienated traces morph with the physical structure of their spaces of display. Conversely, in an exhibition of Islamic art from the collection of Doris Duke held at New York's Museum of Arts and Design in 2012, Raad supplied some of the captive objects caught in the glare of museum lights with shadows, anticipating the hope expressed in a text accompanying *Preface to the second edition* (p. 146) that the reflections captured in his images will eventually join the paintings in the museum, which currently lack them. By contrast, in *Preface to the seventh edition* (2012; fig. 4) these reflections and shadows take their place as prime objects, framed as canonical examples of Arab abstraction in a hypothetical Emirati museum. An accompanying text explains that eventually archival research divulges their true nature as paintings of a painting's shadow, at which point they lose their status as paradigms of Arab abstraction and are removed from view.

As this suggests, Raad is master of the mise en abyme, his work at once archly ludic and infused with the poignant ambivalence and absurdity of contingency as a condition of life (and death).[10] The miniaturization of his past work, and of the gallery itself *as* work, in *Section 139: The Atlas Group (1989–2004)* (2008; pp. 128–31) evokes a nostalgia for craft, for careful practices of making, by no means irrelevant to Raad's own carefully constructed tableaux. The conceit underlying the work is the unexpected shrinkage of Raad's Atlas Group works to 1/100th of their actual size when displayed in a Beirut gallery; in order to display the shrunken work, Raad constructed a white-cube gallery on the same scale. This model gallery housing tiny works constitutes a whole, which is displayed in gallery spaces that appear as macro-versions of its miniature spaces. Miniaturization through modeling provides privileged vistas into shrunken gallery spaces, engaging questions of exterior and interior that recall an observation of Susan Stewart's: "miniature time transcends the duration of everyday life in such a way as to create an interior temporality of the subject."[11] At a formal level, several commentators have connected Raad's gesture of miniaturization to canonical works of twentieth-century European art, invoking Marcel Duchamp's *Boîte-en-valise* (1935–41; p. 42, fig. 18) and the miniature museums of Marcel Broodthaers, but given the nature of the *Scratching . . .* project, other histories may be equally relevant. Among the most enigmatic and compelling examples of medieval Islamic art, for example, are small-scale ceramic replicas of houses and mosques, their roofs raised to show interiors replete with human figures, furnishings, and even well-stocked tables (fig. 5).[12] Examples of these models can be found in most historical collections of Islamic art.

Similarly, Raad's penchant for micro-calligraphy recalls the miniature scale of amuletic or talismanic scripts. It may not be entirely serendipitous that to an observer familiar with Islamic art, the horizontal line of micro-calligraphy extending across the width of *Appendix XVIII: Plate 98_A History of Essays* (2009; p. 143) and other works in the *Appendix XVIII* series recalls

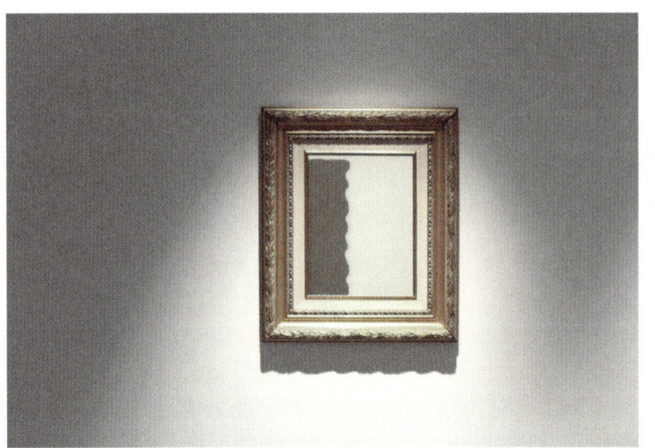

4 Walid Raad. *Preface to the seventh edition_III*. 2012. Pigmented inkjet print, 29 × 43½" (73.7 × 110.5 cm)

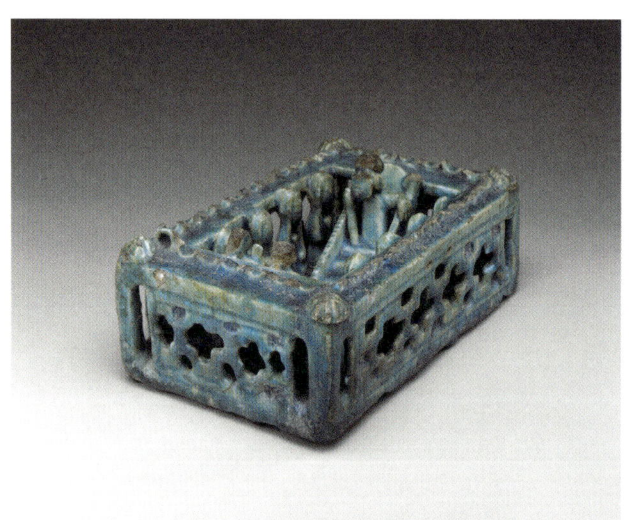

5 Model of a mosque with a preacher on a minbar. Iran, 12th–13th century. Molded, modeled, monochrome-glazed stone-paste, 2¾ × 7⅛ × 4½" (7 × 18.1 × 11.4 cm). The Metropolitan Museum of Art, New York. Rogers Fund

medieval *tiraz*, textiles inscribed with a linear band of Arabic script, often containing historical information (fig. 6). This is the case with *Appendix XVII*, where a partly miniaturized reproduction of the contents page from a 2002 issue of *Parachute* magazine dedicated to the art of Beirut is rotated through ninety degrees, so that variations in the lengths of the articles' titles register as verticals on a statistical bar chart.[13] The texts of the *Parachute* issue include an essay on Raad's Atlas Group by the art historian Sarah Rogers. Also present are writings by celebrated Beirut-based artists with whom Raad has collaborated, including Akram Zaatari, whose recent work also engages with themes of archaeology and archives, and Walid Sadek, whose work Raad has addressed in his own. Sadek's *Love Is Blind*, an installation at Modern Art Oxford in 2006, comprised a group of framed captions and verbal descriptions of the landscape paintings of the Lebanese artist Mustafa Farroukh (1901–1957), images Sadek made accessible only through this textual narration; Raad's *On Walid Sadek's Love Is Blind (Modern Art Oxford, 2006)* (2008) restages that work as a trompe l'oeil painting after a photograph of the 2006 installation. The genealogy that Raad provides for this painterly recapitulation of a photograph of another artist's work in which images are mediated by texts explicitly invokes Robert Rauschenberg's *Erased de Kooning Drawing* of 1953, an icon of transformative appropriation.[14] Less obviously, perhaps, the palimpsest qualities of the work recall the visual concatenations that produced the improbable objects of *Preface to the third edition*.

Comparisons have been made between Raad's overlays and practices of photomontage from Dada to Gerhard Richter, but the centrality of photography to his practice of morphing and layering is especially reminiscent of the work of Sherrie Levine (with whom he has exhibited). Levine's comments on her paintings after photographic reproductions of paintings in books (what she describes as "ghosts of ghosts") are worth quoting: "I wanted to make a picture which contradicted itself. I wanted to put a picture on top of a picture so that there are times when both pictures disappear and other times when they're both manifest; that vibration is basically what the work's about for me—that space in the middle where there's no picture."[15] This quality of vibration, of hovering between manifestation and occlusion, captures the defining spirit of *Preface to the third edition*, and perhaps of *Scratching . . .* more generally.

In its allusive and anachronic telling of fragments and flotsam, layered to evoke conditions of living on and practices of reading back, Raad's work has been compared to that of the art historian Aby Warburg. Warburg's fabled *Mnemosyne Atlas*—left unfinished when he died, in 1929—was designed to showcase the afterlife and transformation of antique images and motifs, and consisted of constellations of images (including Islamic astrological paintings) brought into dialogue in a precocious analogue version of the hypertext (fig. 7).[16] Similarly, in *Scratching . . .*, as in Raad's earlier work, memory and montage are mutually constituting. Proliferating visually striking hybrids, a work such as *Preface to the third edition* draws attention to

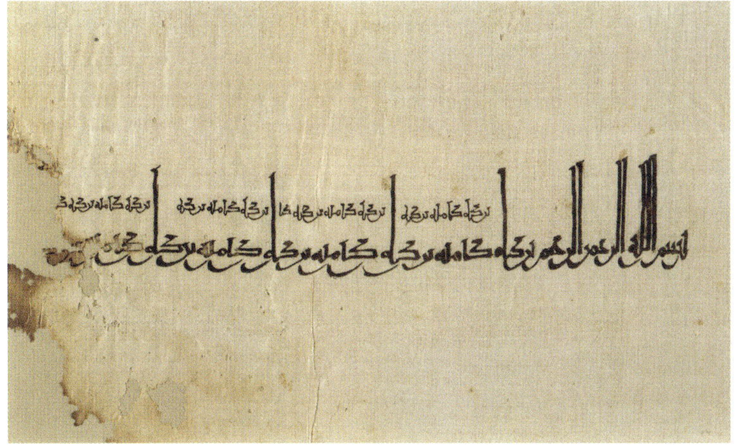

6 Tiraz (fragment). Iraq, 10th century. Linen and paint, 9 × 14" (22.9 × 35.6 cm). The Metropolitan Museum of Art, New York. Gift of George D. Pratt

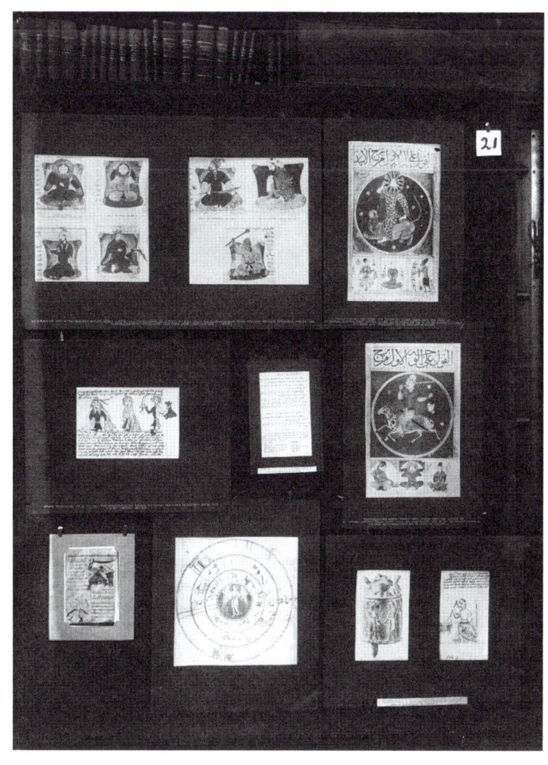

7 Aby Warburg. *Bilderatlas Mnemosyne*, plate 21. October 1929. The Warburg Institute, London

the impure temporality of artworks, materializing their temporal stratifications and sedimentations through the medium of photomontage.[17]

The visual, even ontological indeterminacy effected through photomontage points to the epistemological uncertainties of the archive and of the object histories that it underwrites. Echoing Walter Benjamin's observations on the capacity of translation to create its original, Toufic argues that it is precisely practices of re-creation and repetition, such as Levine's, that prevent earlier works from appearing as counterfeits. In Toufic's terms, these are works that have not undergone an attempted resurrection, the idea being that artistic traditions can only become fully visible *as* tradition if constituted retrospectively. In an inversion that might serve as an epigram for Raad's earlier projects, which played with the authority of photography in their exploration of the Lebanese Civil War—one reason why the work has sometimes attracted criticism for undermining the very possibility of historical documentation—Toufic asserts that it is in fact the *impression* of being counterfeit that guarantees the reliability of the events that the work documents.[18]

In Raad's earlier work, even photodocumentation is pressed into a performance of instability and uncertainty, an oscillation between states of occlusion and visibility, inner and outer, that also permeates many of the works constituting *Scratching. . . .* This dialectical quality invokes a tension between exoteric and esoteric, form and essence, a dialectic with evident relevance to the notion of withdrawal and the messianic specter of resurrection. Practices of re-creation, remaking, and repetition are integral to Raad's undertaking, engaging the peculiar temporality of withdrawal. The easy temporality implied by such titles as *Preface to the first edition* is at once belied by the doubled allusion to sequential time implied by "preface" and "first," a promise of progression consistently withheld from the reader/viewer of Raad's work, with its appendices, indices, prefaces, interrupted series, and marooned numerical sequences.

If attenuated or mediated access is one index of withdrawal, temporal instability is another. This is art history as augury enabled by time travel and telepathy: the portfolio that constitutes *Preface to the third edition* was purportedly made by a female artist working in 2026; in *Index XXVI: Red, blue, black, orange, yellow* (2010; pp. 132–37) Raad appears as both choreographer and medium, exhibiting the names of Lebanese painters working during the last century. The names appear as relief Arabic texts in white on white vinyl, their full visibility frustrated by the materials of inscription; a text accompanying *Index XXVI: Red, blue, black, orange, yellow* explains that these names have been transmitted telepathically from artists in the future (pp. 134–35). Of the work's dramatic corrections, crudely executed in colored, primarily red, paint (p. 137), the text explains that these telepathic artistic mediums have purposefully distorted the names' orthography, not to frustrate the writing of histories in the present but in the hope that the corrections necessitated by their errors will be made in colors immaterially withdrawn and unavailable to artists working in the future. The artists from the future, like the vampires that feature in Toufic's work, will then seek to harvest this blood-red pigment from the present. Their mediated and opportunistic time-travel echoes the scavengings of contemporary art historians. Equally, the corrective policing of the contemporary canon necessitated by the orthographic distortions transmitted from the future performs an authority attenuated by the multiple mediations underlying it.

That artists from the future enable the writing of histories of art in the present (even if their activities are marked by an ambivalence emblematic of *Scratching . . .* itself) is one more indication of the way in which the project ranges blithely and refreshingly across temporal taxonomies. Once again, the impact of Toufic's work is palpable: integral to the temporal disruptions that follow traumatic events, Toufic suggests, is the fact that artists who were once avant-garde are merely of their time, any future-oriented aspects of their work the results of anachronistic collaboration with artists from the future. Similarly, Toufic suggests that the eschewal of tradition often associated with a certain rhetoric of modernism leads to a form of relativism that exaggerates its own absolutist (or universal) credentials. Consequently, "Only those who fully discerned the withdrawal of tradition past a surpassing disaster, tried to resurrect tradition, failed in doing so, may become truly absolutely modern."[19] Such a scenario levels the distinctions between tradition and modernity, so that what might once have appeared traditional is revealed not to be so, while "many modernist works of art which vehemently attacked 'tradition' are, prior to any reluctant gradual canonization, revealed by their withdrawal to be part of that tradition."[20]

This question of temporality is directly related to the problematic of taxonomy engaged by *Scratching . . .* , and epitomized by ongoing debates about the value of such terms as "Modern Islamic Art" or "Contemporary Islamic Art."[21] As *Scratching . . .* suggests, despite the rigid temporal taxonomies that ensure the disaggregation of the modern from the premodern and both from the contemporary, their institutional presentation has more in common than first appears. When The Metropolitan Museum of Art's galleries of Islamic art were reinstalled in 2011, for example, they were renamed as the galleries showcasing the Art of the Arab Lands, Turkey, Iran, Central Asia, and Later South Asia. That choice was mirrored in Doha's Mathaf, the Arab Museum of Modern Art, which had opened one year earlier. Both represent a move away from the universalist aspirations or pretensions of encyclopedic museums and toward ethnically or regionally based presentations reminiscent of earlier taxonomies. Similar tensions permeate the creation of regional franchises of national museums in the Gulf in order to promote access to a cultural heritage presented in universalist terms.

In terms of Islamic art, these developments raise significant questions about the politics of representation: about whether and how the art of vast regions extending from the Atlantic to the Tigris and beyond can be adequately represented in and by one center, and about what is at stake in the authority and economic or infrastructural capacity to represent.[22] In the case of the Gulf museums, the "homecoming" of Arab or Islamic art—ranging from ceramics, metalwork, and miniature paintings to large-scale canvases and sculptures—is an aspect and effect of contemporary geopolitics that highlights the utility of art in regional constructions of transregional identity and heritage. Tensions between pan-Arabism and nationalism or regionalism seem to suffuse some of the work in *Scratching . . .*, appearing, for example, as a disjunction between title and inscription in plates 88–90 of *Appendix XVIII*, in which each "plate" has its own, universal title (*. . . . A History of Art*, *. . . A History of Museums* [p. 140], *. . . A History of Exhibitions*) at odds with the Arabic micro-texts that it bears, which signal a more specifically Lebanese orientation.

In keeping with all of Raad's earlier work, *Scratching . . .* eschews any shrill ideological position in favor of a politics of poetics. The project is nonetheless deeply implicated by questions about the possibilities and problematics of representation, questions arising from current economies of cultural production. Integral to one of the works within *Appendix XVIII* are costings—rough calculations, dollar amounts, figures and lists of beverages (for a gallery opening?) articulated around the words "Beirut" and "Cairo," foregrounding interrelations between economic and cultural capital, between the production of value and the means of production, the visibility of art and its sustaining infrastructures. *Translator's introduction: Pension arts in Dubai* (2012; pp. 114–21) unravels the global networks underpinning an unlikely investment fund for artists, laying bare the imbrications between global capital, information technology, and the Israeli military. Ultimately these global connections relate the objects of art to the bodies that shape and consume them, including those exploited in the construction of pristine architectural frames for the promotion of cultural values. Raad's involvement with Gulf Labor, a coalition of international artists working to protect migrant workers' rights during the construction and maintenance of foreign museums and universities in Abu Dhabi, makes the matter more than academic.

Collaborative endeavors between secular humanism and enlightened despotism to develop cultural infrastructures dependent on the predations of bonded labor throw into high relief the Janus-faced principles that permeate histories of the modern museum, histories and principles central to *Scratching on things I could disavow*. Such collaborations constitute a cosmopolitan coalition of the willing, a cultural coming-of-age that finds its mirror image in a recent widely circulated photograph of the United Arab Emirates' first female pilot heading north to join American, Arab, and European aircraft dropping high-tech bombs on Syria (fig. 8). Which will be the face of the future remains to be seen. What the play with fragments, frames, taxonomies, and temporalities that constitutes *Scratching on things I could disavow* suggests is that collusions and occlusions integral to the construction of archives, histories, and cultural infrastructures in general are necessarily marked by what one critic of the newly installed Louvre Islamic galleries described as "the occultation of ambiguities."[23]

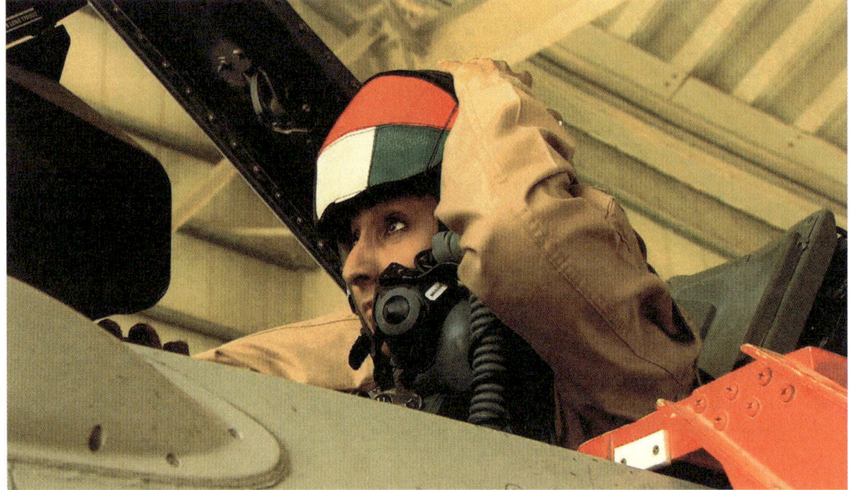

8 Mariam al-Mansouri, the first Emirati female fighter jet pilot. Video still from CNN broadcast, September 2014

1
For a review of some of these developments, albeit omitting some of the more critical voices, see Benoît Junod, Georges Khalil, Stefan Weber, and Gerhard Wolf, eds., *Islamic Art and the Museum: Approaches to Art and Archaeology of the Muslim World in the Twenty-first Century* (London: Saqi, 2012). See also the essays on collecting and the historiography of the field of Islamic art history in *Ars Orientalis* no. 30 (2000) and the *Journal of Art Historiography* no. 6 (June 2012).

2
Perhaps the most idiosyncratic articulation of this well-established idea appears in Eustache de Lorey, "Picasso et l'Orient musulman," *Gazette des Beaux-Arts* 6 per., t. 8 (1932):299–314. More recent (and orthodox) articulations include Markus Brüderlin, *Ornament and Abstraction: The Dialogue between Non-Western, Modern and Contemporary Art* (New Haven: Yale University Press, 2012).

3
See my essay "From the Prophet to Postmodernism? New World Orders and the End of Islamic Art," in Elizabeth C. Mansfield, ed., *Making Art History: A Changing Discipline and Its Institutions* (New York: Routledge, 2007), pp. 31–53. The practices of temporal alienation and stratification are directly related to the politics of display, underwriting the narratives of civilizational decline or fall that the rhetoric around Islamic art objects often promotes.

4
Jalal Toufic, *The Withdrawal of Tradition Past a Surpassing Disaster*, 2009, available online at www.jalaltoufic.com/downloads/Jalal_Toufic,_The_Withdrawal_of_Tradition_Past_a_Surpassing_Disaster.pdf (accessed February 21, 2015). A print copy of this text was included with Walid Raad's exhibition catalogue *Scratching on Things I Could Disavow: A History of Modern and Contemporary Art in the Arab World/ Part I_Volume 1_Chapter 1 (Beirut: 1992–2005)*, ed. Clara Kim (Los Angeles: California Institute of the Arts/REDCAT, 2009). For Raad's introduction to his Scratching project see his website: http://www.scratchingonthings.com/ (accessed March 12, 2015).

5
Ibid., pp. 59–60.

6
Suggestively in terms of *Scratching . . .*, Toufic imagines that, in the space of the gallery or museum, proximity to any index of immaterial withdrawal will affect the artifacts or images on display with blurring, a lack of sharpness or crispness. Ibid., pp. 66–67.

7
On the supposed indexicality of the photograph, however, see Peter Geimer, "Image as Trace: Speculations about an Undead Paradigm," in *differences: a Journal of Feminist Cultural Studies* 18, no. 1 (2007):7–28.

8
Toufic, *The Withdrawal of Tradition*, pp. 58–59. The missing Gardner paintings have been the subject of two projects by the French artist Sophie Calle, which combined texts and photographs to explore questions of absence and memory. In 2013, Calle's work was displayed in the Gardner Museum itself; see http://www.gardnermuseum.org/contemporary_art/exhibitions/past_exhibitions/sophie_calle_last_seen?filter=exhibitions:5438 (accessed March 12, 2015).

9
Jacques Derrida, "The Parergon," trans. Craig Owens, *October* no. 9 (Summer 1979):30.

10
In this as in its engagement with the archive and the museum, some of Raad's work recalls that of Barbara Bloom. See Dave Hickey, Susan Tallman, and Bloom, *The Collections of Barbara Bloom* (Göttingen: Steidl, and New York: International Center of Photography, 2008).

11
Susan Stewart, *On Longing: Narratives of the Miniature, the Gigantic, the Souvenir, the Collection* (Durham, N.C., and London: Duke University Press, 1993), p. 66.

12
See Margaret S. Graves, "Ceramic House Models from Medieval Persia: Domestic Architecture and Concealed Activities," *Iran: Journal of the British Institute of Persian Studies* no. 46 (2008):227–51.

13
Parachute no. 108 (2002).

14
See www.sfeir-semler.com/beirut/exhibitions-beirut/2008/2008-10-07-walid-raad.html. On *Erased de Kooning Drawing* see Benjamin H. D. Buchloh, "Allegorical Procedures: Appropriation and Montage in Contemporary Art," *Artforum* 21, no. 1 (September 1982):43–56.

15
Sherrie Levine, quoted in Jeanne Siegel, "After Sherrie Levine," in Sally Everett, ed., *Art Theory and Criticism: An Anthology of Formalist, Avant-Garde, Contextualist and Post-Modernist Thought* (Jefferson, N.C.: Mcfarland & Co, 1995), p. 266.

16
Aby Warburg, *L'Atlas Mnémosyne* (Paris: L'écarquillé, 2012).

17
See Georges Didi-Huberman, "Before the Image, before Time: The Sovereignty of Anachronism," trans. Peter Mason, in Claire Farago and Robert Zwijnenberg, eds., *Compelling Visuality: The Work of Art in and out of History* (Minneapolis and London: University of Minnesota Press, 2003), pp. 31–44.

18
Toufic, *The Withdrawal of Tradition*, pp. 26–27, 56. See also Bruno Latour and Adam Lowe, "The Migration of the Aura or How to Explore the Original through its Facsimiles," in Thomas Bartscherer and Roderick Coover, eds., *Switching Codes: Thinking Through Digital Technology in the Humanities and the Arts* (Chicago: at the University Press, 2011), pp. 275–98. Relevant earlier projects of Raad's include *My neck is thinner than a hair: Engines* (1996–2001) and *Let's be honest, the weather helped I* (1998/2006).

19
Toufic, *The Withdrawal of Tradition*, p. 34.

20
Ibid., p. 64.

21
See Flood, "From the Prophet to Postmodernism."

22
A case in point is the Bahrain pavilion at the Venice Biennale's 14th International Architecture Exhibition in 2014. Entitled *Fundamentalists and Other Arab Modernisms*, the pavilion presented a pan-Arab history of modernist architecture at a moment when the Bahraini government, with the help of Saudi Arabia, was brutally supressing its own Shi'i Arab population.

23
Rémi Labrusse, "Des arts de l'Islam au Louvre et de quelques ambiguïtés," *La Croix*, November 19, 2012, available online at www.la-croix.com/Archives/2012-11-19/OPINION.-Des-arts-de-l-Islam-au-Louvre-et-de-quelques-ambiguites.-Remi-Labrusse-professeur-d-histoire-de-l-art-a-l-universite-Paris-Ouest-la-Defense-_NP_-2012-11-19-877835 (accessed February 23, 2015).

Key to Plates
The Atlas Group

Each work in The Atlas Group carries two dates, the first indicating a fictional attributed date, the second the actual production date.

Pp. 50–51
The Atlas Group (1989–2004)_Archive. 1989/2003–present

Pp. 52–55
Civilizationally, we do not dig holes to bury ourselves. 1958–59/2003
Twenty-four pigmented inkjet prints, each: 10 × 8" (25.4 × 20.3 cm)
Courtesy the artist and Paula Cooper Gallery, New York

Pp. 52–54:
Civilizationally, we do not dig holes to bury ourselves_Plate 923 (detail)

P. 54, top to bottom:
Civilizationally, we do not dig holes to bury ourselves_Plate 945

Civilizationally, we do not dig holes to bury ourselves_Plate 943

P. 55, clockwise from top left:
Civilizationally, we do not dig holes to bury ourselves_Plate 922

Civilizationally, we do not dig holes to bury ourselves_Plate 924

Civilizationally, we do not dig holes to bury ourselves_Plate 941

Civilizationally, we do not dig holes to bury ourselves_Plate 942

Civilizationally, we do not dig holes to bury ourselves_Plate 935

Civilizationally, we do not dig holes to bury ourselves_Plate 925

Pp. 56–59
We decided to let them say "we are convinced" twice. It was more convincing this way. 1982/2004
Fifteen pigmented inkjet prints, each: 44 × 67" (111.8 × 170.2 cm)
Courtesy the artist and Sfeir-Semler Gallery, Beirut/Hamburg

Pp. 56–58:
We decided to let them say "we are convinced" twice. It was more convincing this way_City III (detail)

P. 58, top to bottom:
We decided to let them say "we are convinced" twice. It was more convincing this way_Plane I

We decided to let them say "we are convinced" twice. It was more convincing this way_Onlookers

P. 59, top row, left to right:
We decided to let them say "we are convinced" twice. It was more convincing this way_Soldiers I

We decided to let them say "we are convinced" twice. It was more convincing this way_Soldiers II

We decided to let them say "we are convinced" twice. It was more convincing this way_Soldiers III

P. 59, middle row, left to right:
We decided to let them say "we are convinced" twice. It was more convincing this way_Plane IV

We decided to let them say "we are convinced" twice. It was more convincing this way_Plane III

We decided to let them say "we are convinced" twice. It was more convincing this way_Plane II

P. 59, bottom row, left to right:
We decided to let them say "we are convinced" twice. It was more convincing this way_City I

We decided to let them say "we are convinced" twice. It was more convincing this way_City II

We decided to let them say "we are convinced" twice. It was more convincing this way_City IV

Pp. 60–63
Notcbook volume 72: Missing Lebanese wars. 1989/1998
Twenty-one pigmented inkjet prints, each: 13⅜ × 9¾" (34 × 24.8 cm)
Courtesy the artist and Paula Cooper Gallery, New York

Pp. 60–61:
Notebook volume 72: Missing Lebanese wars_Plate 140 (detail)

P. 62
Notebook volume 72: Missing Lebanese wars_Plate 134

P. 63, clockwise from top left:
Notebook volume 72: Missing Lebanese wars_Plate 142

Notebook volume 72: Missing Lebanese wars_Plate 132

Notebook volume 72: Missing Lebanese wars_Plate 139

Notebook volume 72: Missing Lebanese wars_Plate 137

Pp. 64–67
I might die before I get a rifle. 1993/2002
Twelve pigmented inkjet prints, each: 63" × 6' 11" (160 × 210.8 cm)
Courtesy the artist and Paula Cooper Gallery, New York

Pp. 64–66:
I might die before I get a rifle_Device IV (detail)

P. 66, top to bottom:
I might die before I get a rifle_Device I

I might die before I get a rifle_Device II

P. 67, top row, left to right:
I might die before I get a rifle_Device III

I might die before I get a rifle_Device V

I might die before I get a rifle_Device VI

P. 67, middle row, left to right:
I might die before I get a rifle_TNT

I might die before I get a rifle_Semtex

I might die before I get a rifle_Fuse I

P. 67, bottom row, left to right:
I might die before I get a rifle_Fuse II

I might die before I get a rifle_Cable I

I might die before I get a rifle_Cable II

Pp. 68–69
Miraculous beginnings/ No, illness is neither here nor there. 1993/2003
Two-channel video (color, silent), 1:50 min.
Museo Nacional Centro de Arte Reina Sofía, Madrid

Pp. 68–69:
Miraculous beginnings/No, illness is neither here nor there
Video stills

Pp. 70–73
Secrets in the open sea. 1994/2004
Six pigmented inkjet prints, each: 43¹¹⁄₁₆ × 68⅛" (111 × 173 cm)
Colección Helga de Alvear, Madrid/Cáceres

Pp. 70–72:
Secrets in the open sea_Plate 18 (detail)

P. 73, clockwise from top left:
Secrets in the open sea_Plate 16

Secrets in the open sea_Plate 17

Secrets in the open sea_Plate 21

Secrets in the open sea_Plate 19

Pp. 74–77
My neck is thinner than a hair: Engines. 1996–2001
One hundred pigmented inkjet prints, each: 9⁷⁄₁₆ × 13⅜" (24 × 34 cm)
The Museum of Modern Art, New York. Fund for the Twenty-First Century

Pp. 74–76:
My neck is thinner than a hair: Engines (14 June 1985) (detail)

P. 76, top to bottom:
My neck is thinner than a hair: Engines (4 March 1982)

My neck is thinner than a hair: Engines (8 August 1986)

P. 77, top row, left to right:
My neck is thinner than a hair: Engines (1 July 1988)

My neck is thinner than a hair: Engines (7 August 1980)

My neck is thinner than a hair: Engines (3 September 1990)

P. 77, second row, left to right:
My neck is thinner than a hair: Engines (16 June 1982)

My neck is thinner than a hair: Engines (12 April 1987)

My neck is thinner than a hair: Engines (7 August 1980)

P. 77, third row, left to right:
My neck is thinner than a hair: Engines (13 January 1989)

My neck is thinner than a hair: Engines (17 August 1985)

My neck is thinner than a hair: Engines (17 May 1985)

P. 77, fourth row, left to right:
My neck is thinner than a hair: Engines (25 December 1981)

My neck is thinner than a hair: Engines (19 August 1983)

My neck is thinner than a hair: Engines (21 August 1988)

P. 77, bottom row, left to right:
My neck is thinner than a hair: Engines (24 February 1986)

My neck is thinner than a hair: Engines (20 June 1985)

My neck is thinner than a hair: Engines (13 February 1991)

Pp. 78–83
Let's be honest, the weather helped. 1998/2006
Seventeen pigmented inkjet prints, each: 18⁷⁄₁₆ × 28½" (46.8 × 72.4 cm)
Walker Art Center, Minneapolis. T. B. Walker Acquisition Fund

Pp. 78–79:
Let's be honest, the weather helped_United Kingdom (detail)

Pp. 80–81:
Let's be honest, the weather helped_Finland

P. 82, top to bottom:
Let's be honest, the weather helped_Switzerland

Let's be honest, the weather helped_Greece

Let's be honest, the weather helped_Belgium

P. 83, top to bottom:
Let's be honest, the weather helped_United States of America

Let's be honest, the weather helped_Germany

Pp. 84–89
Notebook volume 38: Already been in a lake of fire. 1991/2003
Nine pigmented inkjet prints, each: $11\frac{13}{16}$ × 16½" (30 × 41.9 cm)
Courtesy the artist and Paula Cooper Gallery, New York

Pp. 84–85:
Notebook volume 38: Already been in a lake of fire_Plates 59–60 (detail)

Pp. 86–87:
Notebook volume 38: Already been in a lake of fire_Plates 69–70

Pp. 88–89:
Notebook volume 38: Already been in a lake of fire_Plates 61–62

Pp. 90–93
Hostage: The Bachar tapes (English version). 2001
Video (color, sound), 16:17 min.
The Museum of Modern Art, New York.
Gift of the Jerome Foundation in honor of its founder, Jerome Hill

Pp. 90–93:
Hostage: The Bachar tapes (English version). 2001
Video stills

Pp. 94–97:
I only wish that I could weep. 1997/2002
Video (color, silent), 7:40 min.
The Khalid Shoman Foundation, Amman

Pp. 94–97:
I only wish that I could weep
Video stills

Pp. 98–101
Oh God, he said, talking to a tree. 2004/2008
Thirty-one pigmented inkjet prints, each: $16\frac{15}{16}$ × 22" (43.1 × 55.9 cm)
The Museum of Modern Art, New York.
General Print Fund

Pp. 98–100:
Oh God, he said, talking to a tree_Beirut: August 6, 2006 (detail)

P. 100:
Oh God, he said, talking to a tree_Tyre: July 26, 2006

P. 101, clockwise from top left:
Oh God, he said, talking to a tree_Beirut: July 15, 2006

Oh God, he said, talking to a tree_Sidon: August 6, 2006

Oh God, he said, talking to a tree_Kfar Shouba: April 10, 2002

Oh God, he said, talking to a tree_Iqlim al-Tufah: January 12, 2000

Oh God, he said, talking to a tree_Beirut: July 20, 2006

Oh God, he said, talking to a tree_Beirut: August 4, 2006

Pp. 102–5
We are a fair people. We never speak well of one another. 1994/2013
Nine pigmented inkjet prints, each: 34 × 44" (86.4 × 111.8 cm)
Courtesy the artist and Paula Cooper Gallery, New York

Pp. 102–4:
We are a fair people. We never speak well of one another_Plate II (detail)

P. 104–5:
We are a fair people. We never speak well of one another_Plate VII

P. 105, top to bottom:
We are a fair people. We never speak well of one another_Plate V

We are a fair people. We never speak well of one another_Plate VI

We are a fair people. We never speak well of one another_Plate IX

Pp. 106–9:
Better be watching the clouds. 2000/2015
Pigmented inkjet prints, each: 24 × 36" (60.9 × 91.4 cm) Courtesy the artist and Paula Cooper Gallery, New York

Pp. 106–8:
Better be watching the clouds_Plate 313 (detail)

P. 109, clockwise from top left:
Better be watching the clouds_Plate 215

Better be watching the clouds_Plate 511

Better be watching the clouds_Plate 386

Key to Plates
Scratching on things I could disavow

I. Walkthrough

Pp. 114–15:
Translator's introduction: Pension arts in Dubai. 2012
Paper cutouts on wall, two-channel video (color, silent, looped), dimensions variable. This image installation view, *Scratching on things I could disavow*, dOCUMENTA (13), Kassel, June 9–September 16, 2012
Courtesy the artist and Paula Cooper Gallery, New York

Pp. 116–21:
Translator's introduction: Pension arts in Dubai (composite details of paper cutouts)

Pp. 122–23:
Section 88_ACT XXXI: Views from outer to inner compartments. 2010
Painted wood, 16' $4\frac{13}{16}$" × 8' $\frac{7}{16}$" × $7\frac{7}{8}$" (500 × 250 × 20 cm). This image installation view, *Scratching on things I could disavow: A history of art in the Arab world*, Thyssen-Bornemisza Art Contemporary, Vienna, May 26–June 15, 2011. Thyssen-Bornemisza Art Contemporary Collection, Vienna
Courtesy the artist and Sfeir-Semler Gallery, Beirut/Hamburg

P. 124:
Section 88: Views from outer to inner compartments, 2010, and *Section 88_ACT XXXI: Views from outer to inner compartments*, 2010 (detail).
Seen with *Scratching on things I could disavow: Walkthrough*, 2010, 55 min., performance view showing Carlos Chahine, Kunstenfestivaldesarts, Les Halles de Schaerbeek, Brussels, May 8–15, 2011

P. 125:
Section 88: Views from outer to inner compartments
Video stills

Pp. 126–27:
Section 88: Views from outer to inner compartments. 2010
Single-channel HD video (color, silent), 14:36 min.
Courtesy the artist and Paula Cooper Gallery, New York

Pp. 128–29:
Section 139: The Atlas Group (1989–2004). 2008
Plexiglass, high-density foam, LCD panels, four iPads, pigmented inkjet prints, plastic, steel, MDF, electrical supply, 12½" × 9' × 41" (31.8 × 280.4 × 104.1 cm)
Courtesy the artist and Paula Cooper Gallery, New York

Pp. 130–31:
Section 139: The Atlas Group (1989–2004) (details)

Pp. 132–33:
Index XXVI: Red, blue, black, orange, yellow. 2010
Vinyl, pencil, and inkjet prints, dimensions variable. This image installation view, *Scratching on things I could disavow: A history of art in the Arab world*, Thyssen-Bornemisza Art Contemporary, Vienna, May 26–June 15, 2011
Courtesy the artist and Paula Cooper Gallery, New York

Pp. 134–35:
Index XXVI: Red, blue, black, orange, yellow (detail)

Pp. 136–37:
Index XXVI: Red, blue, black, orange, yellow (composite details)

Pp. 138–39:
Appendix XVIII: Plates 22–257. 2008–
Pigmented inkjet prints, each: 21½ × 16½" (54.6 × 41.9 cm). This image installation view, *Scratching on things I could disavow*, dOCUMENTA (13), Kassel, June 9–September 16, 2012
Courtesy the artist and Paula Cooper Gallery, New York

P. 140, clockwise from center left:
Appendix XVIII: Plate 89_A History of Museums. 2009
The Museum of Modern Art, New York.
The Sue and Edgar Wachenheim III Endowment

Appendix XVIII: Plate 103_A History of Titles. 2009
The Museum of Modern Art, New York.
The Sue and Edgar Wachenheim III Endowment

Appendix XVIII: Plate 204_A History of a Timeline. 2012
Courtesy the artist and Paula Cooper Gallery, New York

Appendix XVIII: Plate 92_A History of Monographs. 2009
The Museum of Modern Art, New York.
The Sue and Edgar Wachenheim III Endowment

Appendix XVIII: Plate 247_A History of a Wall. 2012
Courtesy the artist and Paula Cooper Gallery, New York

P. 141, clockwise from top left:
Appendix XVIII: Plate 215_A History of a Project. 2012
Courtesy the artist and Paula Cooper Gallery, New York

Appendix XVIII: Plate 76_A History of a Triennale. 2012
Courtesy the artist and Paula Cooper Gallery, New York

Appendix XVIII: Plate 72_A History of an Anthropistorian. 2012
Courtesy the artist and Paula Cooper Gallery, New York

Appendix XVIII: Plate 200_A History of a Condition. 2012
Courtesy the artist and Paula Cooper Gallery, New York

P. 142, clockwise from center left:
Appendix XVIII: Plate 188_A History of a Biennale. 2012
Courtesy the artist and Paula Cooper Gallery, New York

Appendix XVIII: Plate 250_A History of a Contract. 2012
Courtesy the artist and Paula Cooper Gallery, New York

Appendix XVIII: Plate 91_A History of a Dissertation. 2009
The Museum of Modern Art, New York. The Sue and Edgar Wachenheim III Endowment

Appendix XVIII: Plate 136_A History of Gifts. 2009
The Museum of Modern Art, New York. The Sue and Edgar Wachenheim III Endowment

P. 143:
Appendix XVIII: Plate 98_A History of Essays. 2009
The Museum of Modern Art, New York. The Sue and Edgar Wachenheim III Endowment

Pp. 144–45:
Preface to the second edition. 2012
Five pigmented inkjet prints, each: 59 × 6' 6¾" (149.9 × 200 cm). This image installation view, *Scratching on things I could disavow*, dOCUMENTA (13), Kassel, June 9–September 16, 2012
Courtesy the artist and Paula Cooper Gallery, New York

P. 146:
Preface to the second edition_Plate III

Pp. 146–47
Preface to the second edition_Plate I

II. Les Louvres (Département des Arts de l'Islam)

Pp. 150–51:
Footnote II. 2015
Wallpaper, five pigmented inkjet prints, one object in clear cast-urethane resin, white pigment dye, overall dimensions variable. This image installation view, *Walid Raad: Postface*, University Museum of Contemporary Art, University of Massachusetts, Amherst, September 11–December 7, 2014
Courtesy the artist and Paula Cooper Gallery, New York

Footnote II includes: Wallpaper: *Prologue_Plate I*. 2015
Vinyl wallpaper, dimensions variable

Top left: *Preface to the third edition_Aiguière*. 2013
Pigmented inkjet print, 20 × 15" (50.8 × 38.1 cm)

Center left: *Preface to the third edition_Acknowledgement (Aiguière)*. 2014–15
Clear cast-urethane resin, white pigment dye, 14 × 7¾ × 7¼" (35.6 × 19.7 × 18.4 cm)

Top right: *Preface to the third edition_Édition française: Plate I*. 2012
Pigmented inkjet print, 44 × 33½" (111.8 × 85.1 cm)

In a row below: *Preface to the fifth edition_Plate II*, *Preface to the fifth edition_Plate XII*, *Preface to the fifth edition_Plate V*. 2014
Three pigmented inkjet prints, each: 16½ × 13" (41.9 × 33 cm)

Pp. 152–53:
Preface to the third edition_Remerciements (Panneau). 2014
Installation variable. As seen here: vinyl wallpaper, wooden object, and painted shadow, overall dimensions variable. This image installation view, *Walid Raad: Postface,* University Museum of Contemporary Art, University of Massachusetts, Amherst, September 11–December 7, 2014
Courtesy the artist and Paula Cooper Gallery, New York

Preface to the third edition_Remerciements (Panneau) includes:

Preface to the third edition_Acknowledgement (Panneau). 2014
Wood, 16 × 3 × 8" (40.6 × 7.6 × 20.3 cm)

Preface to the third edition_Remerciement (Panneau). 2014
Vinyl wallpaper, variable dimensions

P. 154:
Preface to the third edition_Acknowledgement (Coupe II). 2014–15
Resin, paint, 4½ × 7½ × 6" (11.4 × 19.1 × 15.2 cm)
Courtesy the artist and Paula Cooper Gallery, New York

P. 155:
Preface to the fifth edition_French edition XII (detail). 2014
Pigmented inkjet print, 16½ × 13" (41.9 × 33 cm)
Courtesy the artist and Paula Cooper Gallery, New York

P. 156:
Preface to the third edition_Édition française: Plate I (detail). 2012
Pigmented inkjet print, 44 × 33½" (111.8 × 85.1 cm)
Courtesy the artist and Paula Cooper Gallery, New York

P. 157:
Preface to the third edition_Element II. 2013
Pigmented inkjet print, 20 × 15" (50.8 × 38.1 cm)
Courtesy the artist and Paula Cooper Gallery, New York

Pp. 158–59:
Prologue_Plate II. 2015
Vinyl wallpaper, dimensions variable
Courtesy the artist and Paula Cooper Gallery, New York

Selected Bibliography
Compiled by Kristin Poor and Katerina Stathopoulou

The artist's name appears here as both Walid Raad and Walid Ra'ad, following the spelling given in the source.

Writings by Walid Raad

1994
Ra'ad, Walid, and Jayce Salloum. "Up to the South . . . Excerpts." *Documents* 2, no. 4/5 (Spring):158–61.

1996
"Bayrut ya Beyrouth: Maroun Baghdadi's *Hors la vie* and Franco-Lebanese History." *Third Text* 10, no. 36 (Autumn):65–82.

1997
Ra'ad, Walid, and Fouad Boustani. "Miraculous Beginnings." *Public* no. 16:44–53.

1999
Abdallah, Ziad, and Farah Awada. "Missing Lebanese Wars: A Project by Walid Raad." *Public Culture* 11, no. 2 (Spring):i–xiv.

"The Beirut Al-Hadath Archive." *Rethinking Marxism* 11, no. 1 (Spring):15–29.

"No, Illness Is Neither Here Nor There." *Felix: Voyeurism* 2, no. 2:60–63.

2000
The Atlas Group. "Anhang: Eine Stellungnahme der Atlas-Gruppe bezüglich 'The Dead Weight of a Quarrel Hangs.'" *Springerin* 6, no. 4 (December 2000–February 2001):47.

Boustani, Fouad. "Already Been in a Lake of Fire: Dokumente aus dem 'Atlas Group Archive.'" *Springerin* 6, no. 4 (December 2000–February 2001):42–46.

2001
"Bidayat ʿagaʾbiyya—muswwada." *Al Adab* 49, no. 1–2:64–67.

2002
The Atlas Group and Walid Raad. "Civilizationally, We Do Not Dig Holes to Bury Ourselves: Excerpts from an interview with Souheil Bachar conducted by Walid Raad of The Atlas Group." In Catherine David, ed. *Tamáss 1: Contemporary Arab Representations—Beirut/Lebanon*. Barcelona: Fundació Antoni Tàpies. Pp. 122–37. Published in German as "'In unserer Zivilisation ist es nicht üblich, Löcher auszuheben, um sich dann Selbst darin zu begraben.' Auszüge aus einem Interview mit Souheil Bachar." Trans. Gaby Gehlen. *Springerin* 8, no. 2:36–41.

"The Atlas Group Archive. Sweet Talk: A Photographic Document of Beirut." In Beatrice von Bismarck et al., eds. *Interarchive: Archival Practices and Sites in the Contemporary Art Field*. Exh. cat. Cologne: Verlag der Buchhandlung Walther König. Pp. 380–83.

The Atlas Group, Zeina Traboulsi, and Walid Ra'ad. "Sweet Talk or Photographic Documents of Beirut." *Camera Austria* no. 80:43–53.

"The Dead Weight of a Quarrel Hangs." In *After 9/11*. New York: National Video Resources. Pp. 16–17.

"I Have Already Been in a Lake of Fire." *Framework* 43, no. 2 (Fall):42–63.

"I Only Wish That I Could Weep." In Thomas Y. Levin, Ursula Frohne, and Peter Weibel, eds. *Ctrl [Space]: Rhetorics of Surveillance from Bentham to Big Brother*. Karlsruhe: ZKM Center for Art and Media, and Cambridge, Mass.: The MIT Press. Pp. 626–29.

Raad, Walid, and Akram Zaatari. "Mapping Sitting." *Camera Austria* no. 78 (June):16–25.

2003
The Atlas Group and Walid Raad. "Already Been in a Lake of Fire: Notebook Volume 38—A Document by Fadl Fakhouri from The Atlas Group Archive." *Grand Street* no. 71 (Spring):215–21.

Ra'ad, Walid, and The Atlas Group. "Civilizationally, We Do Not Dig Holes to Bury Ourselves." In Ursula Biemann, ed. *Stuff It: The Video Essay in the Digital Age*. Zurich: Edition Voldemeer Zürich, and Vienna: Springer Wien New York. Pp. 34–45.

Ra'ad, Walid, and Akram Zaatari, "On Mapping Sitting," and Ra'ad, Walid, and The Atlas Group, "Civilizationally, We Do Not Dig Holes to Bury Ourselves: An Interview with Souheil Bachar." Both in Anna Kafetsi, ed. *Synopsis 3. Testimonies: Between Fiction and Reality*. Exh. cat. Athens: The National Museum of Contemporary Art. Pp. 135–43, 154–59. "Civilizationally, We Do Not Dig Holes to Bury Ourselves . . ." appears in a Portuguese translation, as "Civilizadamente, Nós Não Cavamos Buracos Para Enterrarmos a Nós Mesmo. Fragmentos de uma entrevista com Souheil Bachar conduzida por Walid Raad do The Atlas Group," in Catherine David and Jean-Pierre Rehm, eds. *A Respeito de Situações Reais*. Exh. cat. São Paulo: Paço das Artes and Exo. Pp. 18–27.

2004
The Atlas Group. "Already Been in a Lake of Fire." *Multitudes* no. 15 (Winter):4, 18–24.

The Atlas Group in collaboration with Walid Raad. "My Neck Is Thinner Than a Hair: A History of the Car Bomb in the 1975–1991 Lebanese Wars." *Cabinet* no. 16 (Winter):26–31.

"My Neck Is Thinner Than a Hair" and "Let's Be Honest, The Rain Helped: Excerpts from an Interview with the Atlas Group." Both in Jalal Toufic, ed. *Review of Photographic Memory*. Beirut: Arab Image Foundation. Pp. 28–43, 44–47.

Ra'ad, Walid, and The Atlas Group. "My Neck Is Thinner Than a Hair: Craters, The Nassar files (Notebook 23)." In Anna Kafetsi, ed. *Transcultures*. Exh. cat. Athens: National Museum of Contemporary Art. Pp. 78–83.

"Secrets in the Open Sea: A Project by The Atlas Group and Walid Raad." In Andreas Baur and Ludwig Seyfarth, eds. *Recherche—Entdeckt! Bildarchive der Unsichtbarkeiten. 6. Internationale Foto-Triennale Esslingen 2004*. Exh. cat. Frankfurt: Revolver Archiv für aktuelle Kunst. Pp. 146–55.

Serven, Ingrid. "Portfolio." *Mouvement* no. 26 (January/February):38–45.

Untitled statement. In *Beyond East and West: Seven Transnational Artists*. Exh. cat. Champaign: Krannert Art Museum, University of Illinois at Urbana-Champaign. P. 54.

2005
The Atlas Group and Walid Raad. "My Neck Is Thinner Than a Hair: Engines. A Project by The Atlas Group in Collaboration with Walid Raad." In *Go Between*. Exh. cat. Bregenz: Bregenzer Kunstverein, and Frankfurt: Revolver. Pp. 28–37.

2006
The Atlas Group and Walid Raad. "Civilizationally, We Do Not Dig Holes to Bury Ourselves: Documents from the Fakhouri File in The Atlas Group Archive." In Fereshteh Daftari, ed. *Without Boundary: Seventeen Ways of Looking*. Exh. cat. New York: The Museum of Modern Art. Pp. 74–81.

The Atlas Group in collaboration with Fadl Fakhouri. "Vituperative Speeches." *TDR* 50, no. 1 (Spring):5, 190.

"The Atlas Group/Walid Raad." *Soft Targets* 1, no. 1:103–6.

Cooke, Lynne, Michael Craig-Martin, Linda Nochlin, Walid Raad, and Mark Godfrey. "How Has Art Changed? (2005)." In Polly Staple and Melissa Gronlund, eds. *Frieze Projects: Artists' Commissions and Talks 2003–2005*. London: Frieze. Pp. 232–41.

Kolbowski, Silvia, and Walid Raad. *Between Artists*. New York: Art Resources Transfer Press.

"'Oh God,' He Said, Talking to a Tree: A Fresh-Off-the-Boat, Throat-Clearing Preamble About the Recent Events in Lebanon. And a Question to Walid Sadek." *Artforum* 45, no. 2 (October): 242–44, 288.

"This Morning, This Evening: Beirut: 15 July 2006." In Monica Narula et al., eds. *Sarai Reader 06: Turbulence*. New Delhi: The Director, Centre for the Study of Developing Societies. Pp. 450–53.

"We Can Make Rain but No One Came to Ask." In Suzanne Cotter, ed. *Out of Beirut*. Exh. cat. Oxford: Modern Art Oxford. Pp. 48–53.

2007
"A Disclosure." *Bidoun* no. 9 (Winter):34–37.

Serven, Ingrid. "Oh God, She Said, Talking To A Tree." *Printed Project* no. 6 (February): 55–63.

2008
The Atlas Group. "Secrets in the Open Sea." *Bidoun* no. 14 (Spring/Summer):66–67.

The Atlas Group in collaboration with Walid Raad. "Secrets in the Open Sea." *Blindspot* no. 39:n.p, plates 254–59.

2009
"Civilizationally, We Do Not Dig Holes to Bury Ourselves: Documents from the Fakhouri File in the Atlas Group Archive." *Mizna* 11, no. 1:30–36.

Raad, Walid, and Farid Sarroukh. "Kan ya ma kan and Beirut (1992)." Jen Budney, ed. In *Jayce Salloum: History of the Present*. Exh. cat. Saskatoon: Mendel Art Gallery, Kamloops: Kamloops Art Gallery, and Charlottetown: Confederation Centre Art Gallery. Pp. 51–57.

2010
"Appendix XVIII: Plates 88–107." *Art Journal* 69, no. 3 (Fall):7–19.

"Sweet Talk: Commission (Beirut): 1991–1995." In Matthew Gumperg and Jalal Toufic, eds. *Thinking: The Ruin*. Istanbul: Rezan Has Museum. Pp. 67–76.

"Sweet Talk: Commissions (Beirut)." *Camera Austria* no. 111:41–49.

2011
"Scratching on Things I Could Disavow." *Springerin* 17, no. 3 (Summer):24–29.

"Scratching on Things I Could Disavow: A History of Art in the Arab World." *Kalamon* no. 2 (Spring):141–61.

2012
Raad, Walid, and Sergio Mah. "O Grupo Atlas (1989–2004)." *Zum* no. 3:130–43.

"Sous la direction." In Cosmin Costinaş, Maria Hlavajova, and Jill Winder, eds. *Rabih Mroué: A BAK Critical Reader in Artists' Practice*. Utrecht: BAK, basis voor actuele kunst. Pp. 94–97.

2013
Sarroukh, Farid. "Contribution by artist Farid Sarroukh." *Peeping Tom Digest* no. 3 (April):2–11, 204–9. A special issue on Beirut.

2014
"Letters to the Reader (1864, 1877, 1916, 1923), 2014." In Nuria Enguita Mayo and Erick Beltrán, eds. *31st Bienal de São Paulo: How to (. . .) things that don't exist*. Exh. cat. São Paulo: Fundaçao Bienal de São Paulo. P. 180.

"Walkthrough, Part II: Continued from 'Walkthrough, Part I.'" In *Shangri La: Imagined Cities*. Exh. cat. Los Angeles: Los Angeles Municipal Art Gallery and City of Los Angeles Department of Cultural Affairs. Pp. 202–5.

Interviews with Walid Raad

2002
Gilbert, Alan. "Walid Ra'ad." *Bomb* no. 81 (Fall):38–45.

2003
Weinsowski, Ingeborg. "'Fakten sagen wenig': Der libanesische Künstler Walid Raad, 35, über die scheinbare Wahrheit von Bildern." *Kultur Spiegel* no. 4 (April):30.

2004
Carlotti, Roberto. "Beirut, la guerra in autobomba." *Il Manifesto* June 16. P. 16.

Ghosn, Joseph. "Car Crash. Atlas Group: My Neck Is Thinner Than A Hair." *Les Inrockuptibles* no. 443 (May 26–June 1):80.

Gardner, Belinda Grace. "Spurensuche in den Straßen Beiruts: Interview mit Walid Raad 'The Atlas Group.'" *Kunstzeitung* no. 91 (March):6.

Imhof, Dora, and Annina Zimmermann. "Sich ein Projekt vorstellen, das es Wirklichkeit werde Walid Ra'ad und Bilal Khbeiz im Gespräch." Posted August 20 on the website Regioartonline, at www.regioartonline.org/dev/index.php?id=4&backPID=1&L=0&tt_news=585&PHPSESSID=734abcdef12c6de13758e61198c33; site unavailable as this book goes to press.

Raad, Walid, and John Menick. "Témoignages Imaginaires." *Journal des Laboratoires* no. 2 (June):42–50.

2006
Brian, Laura. "Walid Raad: Portraits and Absence." *Eye-rhyme* no. 8:30–41.

Freitag, Jan. "Die Bomben von Heute un von Morgen. Walid Raad über das Leben in Beirut, Städte in Angst und sein Projekt 'The Atlas Group.'" *Zitty* 29, no. 19:82–83.

Gothe, Karin. "Ohne Beirut kann ich nicht sein." *Süddeutsche Zeitung*. September 20. P. 15.

Lenot, Marc, and Sylvain Prudhomme. "Une autre histoire de la Guerre du Liban. Entretien avec Walid Raad." *Geste* no. 3 (Autumn):60–65.

2007
Rato, Vanessa. "Atlas Group. O projecto do artista plástico libanês Walid Raad chega finalmente a Portugal." *Público* (Edição Lisboa), September 28. Sec. ípsilon, pp. 4–10.

2009
Cerrato, Sara. "Walid Raad: 'Solo l'arte ci fa risorgere tra violenza e conflitti.'" *La Provincia di Como*, July 1. P. 61.

Morse, Marcia. "Deserving Lebanon: Shangri La's artist in residence reflects on the intersection of history, imagination and art." *Honolulu Weekly*, October 14–20. P. 5.

2010
Raad, Walid, and Achim Borchardt-Hume. "In Search of the Miraculous." In Borchardt-Hume, ed. *Miraculous Beginnings: Walid Raad*. London: Whitechapel Gallery. Pp. 9–21.

Raad, Walid, and Jalal Toufic. "'How Would You Not Ask?': An Interview by Walid Raad of Jalal Toufic." Audio recording, June 10. Available online at http://www.jalaltoufic.com/downloads/How_Would_You_Not_Ask.mp3 (accessed April 27, 2015).

Raad, Walid, and Jalal Toufic. "A Conversation Between Walid Raad and Jalal Toufic Dedicated to Walid Raad." Audio recording, June 11. Available online at http://www.jalaltoufic.com/downloads/A_Conversation_Between_Walid_Raad_and_Jalal_Toufic_Dedicated_to_Walid_Raad,_June_11,_2010.mp3 (accessed April 27, 2015).

2011
Davis, Ben. "Interview with Walid Raad About the Guggenheim Abu Dhabi." *Artinfo*, June 9. Available online at http://br.blouinartinfo.com/news/story/123954/interview-with-walid-raad-about-the-guggenheim-abu-dhabi (accessed April 27, 2015).

Iza, Fabiola. "Heterónimos y nuevas geografías—Walid Raad." *Código* no. 62 (April/May):89–93.

Morgenthaler, Daniel. "'Es geht mir nicht um Fantastereien.' Der libanesische Multimedia-Künstler Walid Raad erklärt sein komplexes Werk." *Basler Zeitung*, September 20. P. 41.

2013
Buck, Louisa. "Artist Interview, Walid Raad: A Mediator Between Worlds." *Art Newspaper* no. 242 (January):46–47.

Sand, Olivia. "Profile: Walid Raad." *Asian Art Newspaper* 16, no. 5 (March):2–6.

Solo Exhibition Catalogues, Monographs, and Artist's Books

2003
The Truth Will Be Known When the Last Witness Is Dead: Documents from the Fakhouri File in The Atlas Group Archive. Exh. brochure. Essays by Doris Chon and Jean-Pierre Rehm. Noisy-le-Sec: La Galerie.

2004
The Atlas Group and Walid Raad. *The Atlas Group. Volume 1: The Truth Will Be Known When The Last Witness Is Dead. Documents from the Fakhouri File in The Atlas Group Archive*. Ed. Hélène Chouteau and François Piron. Cologne: Verlag der Buchhandlung Walther König, Noisy-le-Sec: La Galerie de Noisy-le-Sec, and Aubervilliers: Les Laboratoires d'Aubervilliers.

2005
The Atlas Group and Walid Raad. *The Atlas Group. Volume 2: My Neck Is Thinner Than a Hair. Documents from The Atlas Group Archive*. Cologne: Verlag der Buchhandlung Walther König, Toronto: Art Gallery of York University, and Liverpool: FACT (Foundation for Art and Creative Technology).

2006
Nakas, Kassandra, and Britta Schmitz, eds. *The Atlas Group (1989–2004): A Project by Walid Raad*. Exh. cat. Essays by André Lepecki, Kassandra Nakas, Britta Schmitz, and Jalal Toufic. Cologne: Verlag der Buchhandlung Walther König.

We Can Make Rain but No One Came to Ask: Documents from the Atlas Group Project. Exh. cat. Essays by Jalal Toufic. Montreal: Leonard & Bina Ellen Art Gallery, Concordia University.

2007
The Atlas Group and Walid Raad. *The Atlas Group. Volume 3: Let's Be Honest, The Weather Helped. Documents from The Atlas Group Archive.* Cologne: Verlag der Buchhandlung Walther König, Seattle: Henry Art Gallery, and Arles: Les Rencontres d'Arles.

The Atlas Group (1989–2004). Un proyecto de Walid Raad. Exh. brochure. Essay by Paola Santoscoy. Mexico City: Museo Tamayo de Arte Contemporáneo.

Raad, Walid. *Scratching on Things I Could Disavow: Some Essays from The Atlas Group Project*. Exh. cat. Lisbon: Culturgest, and Cologne: Verlag der Buchhandlung Walther König.

2008
The Dead Weight of a Quarrel Hangs: Selections from the Atlas Group Archive. Exh. cat. Preface by Cara McCormack. Essay by Mary Leclère. Houston: Museum of Fine Arts, Houston.

We Can Make Rain But No One Came to Ask. Exh. cat. Essay by Vesela Stretenovic. Providence: Brown University.

2009
Raad, Walid. *Scratching on Things I Could Disavow: A History of Modern and Contemporary Art in the Arab World/Part I_ Volume 1_Chapter_1 (Beirut: 1992–2005).* Exh. cat. Ed. Clara Kim. Essay by Jalal Toufic. Los Angeles: California Institute of the Arts/REDCAT.

2010
Borchardt-Hume, Achim, ed. *Miraculous Beginnings: Walid Raad*. Exh. cat. Interview with Walid Raad by Achim Borchardt-Hume. Essays by Hélène Chouteau-Matikian, Alan Gilbert, and Blake Stimson. London: Whitechapel Gallery, and Paris: Festival d'Automne à Paris.

Walid Raad: Sweet Talk: Commissions (Beirut). Exh. brochure. Essay by Walid Raad. Graz: Camera Austria.

2011
Ebersberger, Eva, and Daniela Zyman, eds. *Walid Raad: Scratching on Things I Could Disavow. A History of Art in the Arab World*. Exh. cat. Essay by Jalal Toufic. Vienna: Thyssen-Bornemisza Art Contemporary.

Walid Raad: I Might Die Before I Get a Rifle. Essay by Hélène Chouteau-Matikian. Afterword by Gunilla Knape. New York: Hasselblad Foundation, and Göttingen: Steidl.

2012
Scratching on Things I Could Disavow: A History of Art in the Arab World. Exh. brochure. Kassel: dOCUMENTA (13), New York: Paula Cooper, and Beirut/Hamburg: Galerie Sfeir-Semler.

2013
Raad, Walid. *Preface to the third edition*. Paris: Musée du Louvre.

2014
Walid Raad: Walkthrough. Nîmes: Carré d'Art, Naples: MADRE (Museo d'Arte Contemporanea Donnaregina), Amherst: University Museum of Contemporary Art, and London: Black Dog Publishing.

2015
Walid Raad. Exh. cat. Essays by Eva Respini and Finbarr Barry Flood. Contribution by Walid Raad. New York: The Museum of Modern Art.

Group Exhibition Catalogues and Other Books

1996
Salloum, Jayce, ed. *East of Here: (Re) Imagining the 'Orient.'* Exh. cat. Toronto: YYZ Artists' Outlet.

2000
Anderson, Maxwell, et al. *Whitney Biennial: 2000 Biennial Exhibition*. Exh. cat. New York: Whitney Museum of American Art.

David, Catherine, and Ellen Blumenstein, eds. *L'Etat des Choses (1ère partie)/ Stand der Dinge (Teil 1)*. Exh. cat. Berlin: Kunst Werke Institute for Contemporary Art.

Tohme, Christine. *Mediterranean Metaphors II: Contemporary Art from Lebanon/Akdeniz Metaforlari II. Lübnan'dan Çağdaş Sanat.* Exh. cat. Instanbul: Borusan Art Gallery.

2001
Brouwer, Marianne, ed. *19th World Wide Video Festival*. Exh. cat. Amsterdam: Stichting World Wide Video Festival.

Gilbert, Alan. "Atlas Group (Presented by Walid Raad)." In *9th Biennial of Moving Images*. Exh. cat. Saint-Gervais, Geneva: Center for Contemporary Images. Pp. 26–29.

2002
Ander, Heike, ed. *Documenta 11_Platform 5: Exhibition Venues*. Exh. cat. Ostfildern: Hatje Cantz.

Bassil, Karl, Zeina Maasri, and Akram Zaatari in collaboration with Walid Raad. *Mapping Sitting: On Portraiture and Photography*. Exh. cat. Beirut: Mind the gap and Arab Image Foundation.

Basualdo, Carlos. "The Atlas Group." In *Documenta 11_Platform 5: Exhibition Short Guide*. Exh. cat. Ostfildern: Hatje Cantz. Pp. 26–27.

Bi-Rout: Zeitgenössische Kunst aus Beirut. Exh. cat. Berlin: Kunsthaus Tacheles.

David, Catherine, ed. *Tamáss 1: Contemporary Arab Representations—Beirut/Lebanon*. Barcelona: Fundació Antoni Tàpies.

Holmes, Steven. *This Is Then*. Exh. brochure. Hartford: Real Art Ways.

Levin, Thomas Y., Ursula Frohne, and Peter Weibel, eds. *Ctrl [Space]: Rhetorics of Surveillance from Bentham to Big Brother*. Karlsruhe: ZKM Center for Art and Media, and Cambridge, Mass.: The MIT Press.

Rinder, Lawrence, Chrissie Iles, Christiane Paul, and Debra Singer, eds. *Whitney Biennial: 2002 Biennial Exhibition*. Exh. cat. New York: Whitney Museum of American Art.

Wolff, Tom. "Truth is Complex. Walid Ra'ad, *Hostage: The Bachar Tapes*, 2001." In Barbara Könches and Peter Weibel, eds. *Bilder Codes: International Media Art Award 2002*. Exh. cat. Karlsruhe: ZKM Zentrum für Kunst und Medientechnologie. Pp. 97–102.

2003
A Short History of Performance Part II. Exh. cat. London: Whitechapel Gallery.

Berg, Stephan, and Martin Engler, eds. *Die Sehnsucht des Kartografen*. Exh. cat. Hannover: Kunstverein Hannover.

Bonami, Francesco, and Maria Luisa Frisa, eds. *Dreams and Conflicts: The Dictatorship of the Viewer. 50th International Art Exhibition*. Exh. cat. Venice: La Biennale di Venezia.

Buckley, Craig, Tanya Leighton, Sara Reisman, et al., eds. *Homeland*. Exh. cat. New York: Whitney Museum of American Art.

Christov-Bakargiev, Carolyn. "Walid Raad/ The Atlas Group." In Gilda Williams and Melissa Larner, eds. *Cream 3: Contemporary Art in Culture. 10 Curators, 100 Contemporary Artists, 10 Source Artists*. London: Phaidon. Pp. 304–7.

David, Catherine, and Jean-Pierre Rehm, eds. *A Respeito de Situações Reais*. Exh. cat. São Paulo: Paço das Artes and Exo. Pp. 18–27.

Kafetsi, Anna, ed. *Synopsis 3: Testimonies. Between Fiction and Reality*. Exh. cat. Athens: National Museum of Contemporary Art.

2004
Baur, Andreas, and Ludwig Seyfarth, eds. *Recherche—Entdeckt! Bildarchive der Unsichtbarkeiten. 6. Internationale Foto-Triennale Esslingen 2004*. Exh. cat. Frankfurt: Revolver Archiv für aktuelle Kunst.

Ethnic Marketing. Exh. cat. Geneva: Centre d'Art Contemporain.

'Ficcions' documentals. Exh. cat. Barcelona: CaixaForum.

Kafetsi, Anna, ed. *Transcultures*. Exh. cat. Athens: National Museum of Contemporary Art.

O'Brien, David, and David Prochaska. *Beyond East and West: Seven Transnational Artists*. Exh. cat. Champaign: Krannert Art Museum, University of Illinois at Urbana-Champaign.

Rehm, Jean-Pierre. "Distress at the Heart of the Project: The Atlas Group and Walid Raad." In *+Witness*. Exh. cat. Sydney: Museum of Contemporary Art. Pp. 51–52.

Stubbs, Mike, ed. *Proof: The Act of Seeing with One's Own Eyes*. Exh. cat. Melbourne: Australian Centre for the Moving Image.

Thompson, Nato, and Gregory Sholette, eds. *The Interventionists: Users' Manual for the Creative Disruption of Everyday Life*. North Adams: Massachusetts Museum of Contemporary Art.

Vanderlinden, Barbara, and Amy Huei-hua Cheng. *2004 Taipei Biennial: Do You Believe in Reality?* Exh. cat. Taipei: Taipei Fine Arts Museum.

2005
Brandtzaeg, Kari J. *Kiss the Frog: The Art of Transformation*. Exh. cat. Oslo: The National Museum of Art, Architecture and Design.

Go Between. Exh. cat. Bregenz: Bregenzer Kunstverein, and Frankfurt: Revolver.

Hyde, James. *Faith*. Exh. cat. Hartford, Conn.: Real Art Ways.

Neubauer, Susanne, ed. *Documentary Creations*. Exh. cat. Lucerne: Kunstmuseum Luzern.

Pontbriand, Chantal. "Walid Raad/The Atlas Group. Hostage: The Bachar Tapes #17 and #31, By Souheil Bachar, 2001." In *Tiempos De Vídeo, 1965–2005: Colección nouveaux médias del Centre Pompidou con la participación de la colección de arte contemporáneo, Fundación "La Caixa"*. Exh. cat. Barcelona: Fundación La Caixa, and Paris: Centre Pompidou. Pp. 146–47.

Rainer, Thomas. "Alexander's Warhorse Turned Scribe—A Parable of the *(Non) Plus Ultra*." In Stefan Bidner and Thomas Feuerstein, eds. *Plus Ultra. Jenseits der Moderne?/ Beyond Modernity?* Frankfurt: Revolver Archiv für Aktuelle Kunst. Pp. 371–87.

Respini, Eva. "The Atlas Group/Walid Raad." In Klaus Biesenbach, ed. *Greater New York 2005*. Exh. cat. Long Island City: P.S.1 Contemporary Art Center. Pp. 58–59.

Spinelli, Claudia, ed. *Reprocessing Reality*. Exh. cat. Nyon: Château de Nyon.

Wright, Stephen. *In Absentia*. Exh. cat. Brest: Centre d'art Passerelle.

2006
Ah, les belles images! . . . Renaud Auguste-Dormeuil, Joana Hadjithomas et Khalil Joreige, Walid Raad. Exh. cat. Paris: In Situ Fabienne Leclerc, and Clermont-Gerrand: La Tôlerie.

Cotter, Suzanne, ed. *Out of Beirut*. Exh. cat. Oxford: Modern Art Oxford.

Daftari, Fereshteh, ed. *Without Boundary: Seventeen Ways of Looking*. Exh. cat. New York: The Museum of Modern Art.

Funcke, Bettina, ed. *Grey Flags*. Exh. cat. Long Island City: SculptureCenter.

Gilbert, Alan. "The Atlas Group/Walid Raad." In Charles Merewether et al., eds. *Zones of Contact: Biennale of Sydney 2006*. Exh. cat. Woolloomooloo: Biennale of Sydney. P. 81.

Hochdörfer, Achim, and Matthias Michalka, eds. *Why Pictures Now: Fotografie, Film, Video heute*. Exh. cat. Nuremberg: Verlag für modern Kunst Nürnberg, and Vienna: MUMOK Museum Moderner Kunst Stifttung Ludwig.

Jarzombek, Mark. "The Post-Traumatic Turn and the Art of Walid Ra'ad and Krzysztof Wodiczko." In Lisa Saltzman and Eric Rosenberg, eds. *Trauma and Visuality in Modernity*. Hanover: Dartmouth College Press and University Press of New England. Pp. 249–71.

Kittelmann, Udo, and Klaus Görner, eds. *What's New, Pussycat? Die Neuerwerbungen New Acquisitions 2002–2005 Museum für Moderne Kunst Frankfurt am Main*. Exh. cat. Nuremberg: Verlag für modern Kunst Nürnberg, and Frankfurt: Museum für Moderne Kunst.

Leighton, Tanya, ed. *In the poem about love you don't write the word love*. Exh. cat. Berlin and New York: Sternberg Press.

New Media Collection 1965–2005. Exh. cat. Taipei: Taipei Fine Arts Museum.

Porter, Venetia. *Word into Art: Artists of the Modern Middle East*. Exh. cat. London: British Museum Press.

Wright, Stephen, ed. *Dataesthetics Reader: How to Do Things with Data*. Exh. cat. Zagreb: Arkzin d.o.o., and Frankfurt: Revolver Archiv für aktuelle Kunst.

2007

Aftershock: Conflict, Violence and Resolution in Contemporary Art. Exh. cat. Norwich: Sainsbury Centre for Visual Arts, University of East Anglia.

Bal, Mieke, and Miguel Ángel Hernández-Navarro. *2Move: Movimiento doble. Estéticas migratorias*. Exh. cat. Murcia: Comunidad Autónomia de la region de Murcia, Valencia: Fundación Bancaja, and Enkhuizen: Zuider Zeemuseum.

Bal, Mieke, and Anton Kos, eds. *2Move: Migration and Video*. Exh. cat. Enkhuizen: Zuider Zeemuseum.

Chong, Doryun. "Between Poetics and Severity: Walid Raad." In Chong and Yasmil Raymond, eds. *Brave New Worlds*. Exh. cat. Minneapolis: Walker Art Center. Pp. 190–95.

Cram, Gabrielle, and Daniela Zyman, eds. *Shooting Back*. Exh. cat. Vienna: Thyssen-Bornemisza Art Contemporary.

Cross-border: Fotografie und Videokunst aus dem MUMOK Wien. Exh. cat. Stuttgart: Kunstmuseum Stuttgart.

Deutsche Börse Photography Prize 07. Philippe Chancel, Anders Petersen, Walid Raad/The Atlas Group, Fiona Tan. Exh. cat. London: Photographers' Gallery.

Documentos. La memoria del futuro. Exh. cat. Vigo: MARCO, Museo de Arte Contemporánea de Vigo.

Fusi, Lorenzo, and Naeem Mohaiemen. *System Error: War Is a Force That Gives Us Meaning*. Exh. cat. Milan: Silvano Editoriale, and Siena: Palazzo delle Papesse.

La Chance, Michaël. *Oeuvres-Bombes et Bioterreur. L'Art au Temps des Bombes*. Quebec: Les Éditions Intervention.

Last News. Exh. cat. Gdańsk: Laznia Centre for Contemporary Art.

Lynn, Victoria. *Turbulence: 3rd Auckland Triennial 2007*. Exh. cat. Auckland: Auckland Art Gallery Toi o Tāmaki.

Seelig, Thomas. "Walid Raad/The Atlas Group." In *Forschen und Erfinden/ Research and Invention*. Exh. cat. Zürich: Scheidegger & Spiess, and Winterthur: Fotomuseum Winterthur. Pp. 62–69, 127.

2008

Albrethsen, Pernille, ed. *U-Turn. Kvadriennale for Samtidskunt/Quadrennial for Contemporary Art: Katalog/Catalogue*. Exh. cat. Copenhagen: U-Turn Kvadriennale for Samtidskunt/Quadrennial for Contemporary Art.

Bal, Mieke, and Miguel Ángel Hernández-Navarro. *2Move: Video, art, migration*. Exh. cat. Murcia: Centro de Documentación y Estudios Avanzados de Arte Contemporáneo.

Bonin, Vincent, and France Choinière, eds. *Function/Fiction: Utilitarian Images Reconfigured. Les essais*. Montreal: Dazibao.

Curating Architecture. Exh. brochure. London: The Showroom.

Deadpan: Photography, History, Politics. Exh. cat. New York: The Amie and Tony James Gallery, The Graduate Center, The City University of New York.

Doll, Martin. "'Documents' from the Atlas Group Archive. A 'Witness' Telling his Story/ History: Hostage—The Bachar Tapes." In Meike Wagner and Wolf-Dieter Ernst, eds. *Performing the Matrix: Mediating Cultural Performance*. Munich: E-podium Verlag. Pp. 321–35.

——. "'Missing Lebanese Wars': The Art Project *The Atlas Group Archive* and Its Endless Search for Means to 'Document' Traumatic Memories and Mental Realities." In Klaus Stierstorfer, ed. *Anglistentag 2007 Münster. Proceedings*. Trier: Wissenschaftlicher Verlag. Pp. 165–78.

Enwezor, Okwui, ed. *Archive Fever: Uses of the Document in Contemporary Art*. Exh. cat. New York: International Center of Photography, and Göttingen: Steidl.

Heartney, Eleanor. "Art & Globalism: Negotiating A Borderless World." In *Art & Today*. London and New York: Phaidon Press. Pp. 292–319.

Lavoie, Vincent. "The Indefinite Archive: Walid Raad and Imaginative Dimensions of the Lebanese Conflict." In Thérèse St-Gelais, ed. *L'Indécidable. Écarts et déplacements de l'art actuel/The Undecidable: Gaps and Displacements of Contemporary Art*. Montreal: Les Éditions Esse. Pp. 267–78.

Lügen.nirgends. Zwischen Fiktion, Dokumentation und Wirklichkeit. Exh. cat. Münster: Ausstellungshalle zeitgenössische Kunst.

Omlin, Sibylle, Barnaby Drabble, and Dorothee Messmer, eds. *Nichts zu deklarieren: 4 Triennale Zeitgenössischer Kunst Oberschwaben*. Exh. cat. Nuremberg: Verlag für modern Kunst Nürnberg.

Perna Foundation. *Mediterraneo 2008*. Exh. cat. Naples: Electa.

Reckitt, Helena, ed. *Not Quite How I Remember It*. Exh. cat. Toronto: The Power Plant.

Scènes du Sud. Méditerranée Orientale. Exh. cat. Nîmes: Carré d'Art.

Signals in the Dark: Art in the Shadow of War. Exh. cat. Mississauga: Blackwood Gallery, and Toronto: Justina M. Barnicke Gallery, University of Toronto.

Temkin, Ann. "Walid Raad." In *Color Chart: Reinventing Color, 1950 to Today*. Exh. cat. New York: The Museum of Modern Art. Pp. 216–19.

The Greenroom: Reconsidering the Documentary and Contemporary Art. Exh. cat. Annandale-on-Hudson: Center for Curatorial Studies and Hessel Museum of Art, Bard College.

Torp, Marianne. *Reality Check*. Exh. cat. Copenhagen: Statens Museum for Kunst.

2009

A Horse Is a Camel Designed by a Committee: Attempts at Rewriting the World. Exh. cat. Como: Fondazioni Antonio Ratti.

Amirsadeghi, Hossein, Salwa Mikdadi, and Nada Shabout, eds. *New Vision: Arab Contemporary Art in the 21st Century*. London: Thames & Hudson.

Cotton, Charlotte. *The Photograph as Contemporary Art*. London: Thames & Hudson.

Cramerotti, Alfredo. *Aesthetic Journalism: How to Inform without Informing*. Bristol: Intellect, and Chicago: Intellect, The University of Chicago Press.

Deep Images: Why We Need Images to Live? CREAM: Creativity for Arts and Media International Festival for Arts and Media Yokohama 2009. Exh. cat. Tokyo: Firumu Ātosha.

Lowry, Glenn D. *Oil and Sugar: Contemporary Art and Islamic Culture. Eva Holtby Lecture on Contemporary Culture, No. 3*. Toronto: Royal Ontario Museum.

Selby, Aimee, ed. *Art and Text*. London: Black Dog Publishing.

Stahel, Urs, ed. *Darkside II: Photographic Power and Violence, Disease and Death Photographed*. Exh. cat. Göttingen: Steidl, and Winterthur: Fotomuseum Winterthur.

Toufic, Jalal. "Lebanese Photography between Radical Closure and Surpassing Disaster." In Eva Ebersberger and Daniela Zyman, eds. *Thyssen-Bornemisza Art Contemporary The Collection Book*. Cologne: Verlag der Buchhandlung Walther König. Pp. 324–29.

2010

Bardaouil, Sam, and Til Fellrath, eds. *Told, Untold, Retold: 23 Stories of Journeys through Time and Place*. Exh. cat. Milan: Skira.

Basha, Regine, and Stuart Horodner. *Substitute Teacher*. Exh. cat. Atlanta: Atlanta Contemporary Art Center.

Blessing, Jennifer, and Nat Trotman, eds. *Haunted: Contemporary Photography/ Video/Performance*. Exh. cat. New York: Guggenheim Museum Publications.

Downey, Anthony. "The Production of Cultural Knowledge in the Middle East Today." In Hossein Amirsadeghi, ed. *Art and Patronage: The Middle East*. London: Transglobe Publishing and Thames & Hudson. Pp. 10–15.

Eigner, Saeb. *Art of the Middle East: Modern and Contemporary Art of the Arab World and Iran*. London and New York: Merrell.

Osborne, Peter. "La ficción de lo Contemporáneo. La Colectividad Especulativa de The Atlas Group, 1999–2005." In *El Arte Más Allá de la Estética. Ensayos Filosóficos Sobre Arte Contemporáneo*. Murcia: Cendeac. Pp. 257–84.

Wilson-Goldie, Kaelen. "Off the Map: Contemporary Art in the Middle East." In Chris Dercon, León Krempel, and Avinoam Shalem, eds. *The Future of Tradition— The Tradition of the Future*. Munich: Prestel. Pp. 60–67.

——. "Walid Raad: Setting the Stage." In *The Hugo Boss Prize 2010*. New York: The Solomon R. Guggenheim Foundation. Pp. 69–72.

2011

Cotter, Suzanne. "Walid Raad: The Atlas Group Archive." In *Defining Contemporary*

Art: 25 Years in 200 Pivotal Artworks. London and New York: Phaidon. Pp. 258–59.

De Jonge, Willemijn, ed. *Foam Album 11.* Exh. cat. Amsterdam: Foam Amsterdam.

Desmond, Jill, ed. *Companion to Light, Sound, and the Moving Image.* Exh. cat. Denver: Denver Art Museum.

Foster, Hal, Rosalind Krauss, Yve-Alain Bois, et al. *Art Since 1900: Modernism, Antimodernism, Postmodernism.* 2nd ed. London: Thames & Hudson.

Gaensheimer, Susanne, and Mario Kramer, eds. *The Lucid Evidence: Fotografie aus der Sammlung The Photography Collection MMK Museum für Moderne Kunst Frankfurt am Main.* Exh. cat. Nuremberg: Verlag für Moderne Kunst Nürnberg.

Himmelsbach, Sabine, and Michael Conner, eds. *Wild Sky.* Exh. cat. Oldenburg: Edith-Ruß-Haus für Medienkunst, and Ostfildern: Hatje Cantz.

Levy, Matthew. "Walid Raad." In Eungie Joo and Joseph Keehn II with Jenny Ham-Roberts, eds. *Rethinking Contemporary Art and Multicultural Education.* New York: The New Museum of Contemporary Art and Routledge. Pp. 181–83.

Paasche, Marit, and Judy Radul, eds. *A Thousand Eyes: Media Technology, Law and Aesthetics.* Oslo: Henie Onstad Art Centre, and Berlin: Sternberg Press.

Saadawi, Ghalya, ed. *Plot for a Biennial: Sharjah Biennial 10.* Exh. cat. Dubai: Sharjah Art Foundation.

Slavick, Susanne. *Out of Rubble.* Milan: Edizioni Charta.

The Luminous Interval: The Dimitris Daskalopoulos Collection. Exh. cat. New York: Guggenheim Museum Publications.

2012

Amman Journal: public/space/art. Exh. cat. Aarau: Forum Schlossplatz.

Armstrong, Elizabeth, ed. *More Real? Art in the Age of Truthiness.* Exh. cat. Minneapolis: Minneapolis Institute of Arts, and Munich, London, and New York: DelMonico Books/Prestel. With the essays "Making History: Some Thoughts on Contemporary Art and the Middle East," by Glenn D. Lowry, pp. 156–70, and "Walid Raad," by Joan Rothfuss, pp. 274–75.

Doris Duke's Shangri La: A House in Paradise. Exh. cat. New York: Skira Rizzoli Publications.

Lasch, Pedro, ed. *Grand Gestures and (Im)modest Proposals: A Project for dOCUMENTA (13)/And And And.* [Durham, N.C.]: XCO Press.

Márgenes de Silencio/Margins of Silence. Cáceres: Helga de Alvear Collection, Centro de Artes Visuales Fundación Helga de Alvear.

Rogers, Sarah A. "The Formation of the Khalid Shoman Private Collection and the founding of Darat al Funun." In Sonja Mejcher-Atassi and John Pedro Schwartz, eds. *Archives, Museums and Collecting Practices in the Modern Arab World.* Surrey: Ashgate Publishing. Pp. 159–82.

Scharrer, Eva. "Walid Raad." In *dOCUMENTA (13): Das Begleitbuch/The Guidebook.* Exh. cat. Ostfildern: Hatje Cantz. Pp. 400–401.

Weiss, Marta. *Light from the Middle East: New Photography.* Exh. cat. Göttingen: Steidl, and London: V&A Publishing.

2013

Aichi Triennale 2013: Awakening. Exh. cat. Nagoya: Aichi Triennale Organizing Committee.

Demos, T. J. *The Migrant Image: The Art and Politics of Documentary during Global Crisis.* Durham: Duke University Press.

Gade, Solveig. "Performing Histories: Archiving Practices of Rimini Protokoll and the Atlas Group." In Gunhild Borggreen and Rune Gade, eds. *Performing Archives/Archives of Performance.* Copenhagen: Museum Tusculanum Press. Pp. 386–402.

Grovier, Kelly. "The Atlas Group Archive." In *100 Works of Art That Will Define Our Age.* New York: Thames & Hudson. Pp. 228–31.

Mécaniques des Fluides (naviguer, transporter, filmer). Exh. brochure. Abidjan: la galerie Cécile Fakhoury.

Speak, Memory. Exh. brochure. New York: Miriam and Ira D. Wallach Art Gallery, Columbia University.

Squiers, Carol. "Walid Raad." In *A Different Kind of Order: The ICP Triennial.* Exh. cat. Munich, London, and New York: DelMonico Books/Prestel, and New York: International Center of Photography. Pp. 150–57.

Tripp, Charles. *The Power and the People: Paths of Resistance in the Middle East.* Cambridge: Cambridge University Press.

Vujanovic, Dragana, and Louise Wolthers, eds. *Still Life Work Life: From the Hasselblad Foundation Collection, No. 1.* Exh. cat. Gothenburg: Hasselblad Foundation, and Stockholm: Art and Theory Publishing.

Wilson-Goldie, Kaelen. "Beirut." In *Art Cities of the Future: 21st-Century Avant-Gardes.* New York/London: Phaidon Press. Pp. 10–15.

2014

Enguita Mayo, Nuria, and Erick Beltrán, eds. *31st Bienal de São Paulo: How to (. . .) things that don't exist.* Exh. cat. São Paulo: Fundaçao Bienal de São Paulo.

Khalidi, Hicham, Amanda Sarroff, and Natasha Hoare, eds. *Where Are We Now? Marrakech Biennale 5.* Exh. cat. Heijningen: Jap Sam Books, and Marrakech: Marrakech Biennale.

La Disparition des Lucioles. Exposition à la prison Sainte-Anne Avignon. Exh. cat. Avignon: Collection Lambert en Avignon, and Arles: Actes Sud.

Schaper, Rüdiger. "Bilder der Gewalt, Pixel- und Puppentheater. Rabih Mroue, Walid Raad und Wael Shawky." In *Spektakel: eine Geschichte des Theaters von Schlingensief bis Aischylos.* Munich: Siedler. Pp. 211–20.

Shangri La: Imagined Cities. Exh. cat. Los Angeles: Los Angeles Municipal Art Gallery and City of Los Angeles Department of Cultural Affairs.

Articles and Reviews

1997

Anderson, Mark K. "A Gallery of Moving Images." *Valley Advocate*, August 7–13. P. 23.

"First, ideas: Assistant Professor Walid Ra'ad examines culture and its contents." *Hampshire Reports*, Spring/Summer. Pp. 4–5.

1999

"Al-Faʾz bi-jāʾzat ʾafḍal film qaṣīr Walīd Raʿd 'lil-Fārs': ḥilmy film wathaʾqiyy ʿan kul binā ya." *Al Fares* no. 142 (November 1999):18.

Khūry, Ilyās. "Mā baʿd al-ḥadatha taqraʿ ʾabwab Beirut: mahrajan ʾylūl bayna al-tajruba wa al-tajrīb, al-mulhaq." *An-Nahar* supplement, September 4. Pp. 18–19.

"'New York Times' tuʿln fawz film al-Lubnāny Walīd Raʿd." *Al Anwar*, December 9. Pp. 1, 10.

Taubin, Amy. "Mixed Tapes." *The Village Voice*, July 20. P. 142.

Zalzal, Zéna. "Walid Raad, chercheur et philosophe de l'image." *L'Orient Le Jour*, October 22. P. 6.

——. "Walid Raad. De l'ironie de la guerre et ses consequences. . . . " *L'Orient Le Jour*, September 11. P. 6.

2000

M.G. "Colloque au musée Nicolas Sursock. Vues contradictoires sur Gibran le peintre." *L'Orient Le Jour*, January 28. P. 6.

Mroueh, Leila. "Speaking your voice in another country. Mediterranean Metaphors 2: developing Lebanon's artistic voice in Istanbul." *Daily Star*, February 14. P. 12.

N.S. "'Fishing for Documents' de Walid Raad. À la recherché des effets hystériques de la guerre.'" *L'Orient Le Jour*, September 2. P. 6.

2001

Grzonka, Patricia. "Weiner Festwochen: Die vierte Woche." *Profil* no. 24 (June 11):157.

Taubin, Amy. "Video's Fourth Dimension: Neither There nor Here." *The Village Voice*, July 17. P. 118.

Van Bogaert, Pieter. "Geschiedenissen van een stad." *De Tijd Cultuur*, May 2. P. VI.

2002

Al-Kassim, Dina. "Crisis of the Unseen: Unearthing the Political Aesthetics of Hysteria in the Archaeology and Arts of New Beirut." *Parachute* no. 108 (October–December):146–63.

Blomberg, Katja. "Die Atlas Group und ihr Archiv des Bürgerkriegs." *Frankfurter Allgemeine Zeitung*, September 5. Available online at www.faz.net/aktuell/feuilleton/documenta11-kuenstlerportraet-die-atlas-group-und-ihr-archiv-des-buergerkriegs-171743.html (accessed April 30, 2015).

Boecker, Susanne. "Mapping. Sitting. On Portraiture and Photography. Die Photographische Sammlung SK Stiftung Kultur." *Kunstforum* no. 162 (November/December):330–31.

Heartney, Eleanor. "A 600-Hour Documenta." *Art in America* 90, no. 9 (September):86–95.

Lütticken, Sven. "Contemporary Arab Representations." *De Witte Raaf* no. 100 (November–December).

Mercer, Kobena. "Documenta 11." *Frieze* no. 69 (September):86–89.

M.G.H. "La Documenta XI relève le défi de l'equilibre entre éthique et esthétique" and "Unique Libanais à Kessel, Walid Raad présente les archives du Atlas Group." *L'Orient Le Jour*, June 24. P. 6.

Rogers, Sarah. "Forging History, Performing Memory: Walid Ra'ad's *The Atlas Project.*" *Parachute* no. 108 (October–December):66–79.

Steiner, Barbara. "Some Thoughts on Documenta 11." *Flash Art* 34, no. 225 (July–September):108–9.

Tayara-Deeley, Mona. "Arab artists find haven at German festival: Documenta 11 provides forum for those caught between worlds." *Daily Star*, August 2. P. 10.

Van Bogaert, Pieter. "Desoriënterend Beiroet." *De Financieel-Economische Tijd*, September 28. P. 11.

Von Schlegell, Mark. "Documenta's Global Reach." *NYFA Quarterly* 1, no. 1 (Fall): 6–7.

Wollen, Peter. "The Last Hundred Days." *London Review of Books* 24. no. 19, October 3. Pp. 31–32.

2003

Anton, Saul. "A Secret History." *Frieze* no. 72 (January/February):68–69.

Bauer, Una. "Kaleidoskopski preparirana istinosna funkcija, ili: kako nam Ra'ad pomaže prebolimo naše ratno iskustvo." *Gordogan* no. 1 (Autumn):211–13.

Chardon, Elisabeth. "Liban: The Atlas Group réinvente l'histoire." *Le Temps Samedi Culturel*, May 3. P. 40.

Dyer, Geoff. "Reborn Yesterday." *Wallpaper* no. 62 (October):226–34.

Falconer, Morgan. "Witness." *Frieze* no. 75 (May):88–89.

Hoch, Jenny. "Das Bröckeln der Wirklichkeit. Walid Raad als Beirut stellt seine 'Atlas Group' vor." *Süddeutsche Zeitung*, October 24.

Lindgaard, Jade. "Politique fiction." *Les Inrockuptibles* no. 421 (December 24–30).

Root, Deborah. "Mapping the Disaster: Walid Ra'ad's Atlas Group Project and the Lebanese Civil Wars." *Prefix Photo* 4, no. 7 (Spring/Summer):30–41.

Shatz, Adam. "50,000 Closer Looks at Arabs." *New York Times*, March 16. Sec. 2, pp. 33–34.

Smith, Lee. "Missing in Action: The Art of The Atlas Group/Walid Raad." *Artforum* 41, no. 6 (February):124–29.

Somers, Door Maartje. "Walid Ra'ad over zijn videopersonages. Doorgestoken kaart: geen probleem." *NRC Handelsblad*, May 9. *Cultureel Supplement*, p. 23.

Stallabrass, Julian. "Take a reality check." *Evening Standard*, March 4. P. 41.

Stammen, Silvia. "Sex, Lügen, Videobänder. Spielart: Walid Ra'ad durchbricht die mediale Oberfläche." *Süddeutsche Zeitung*, November 10.

2004

Al-Tufayli, Fādy. "'ʿunqy ʿarfaʿ min shaʿraʿ: ʿarshīf bārd li-rʿub al-sayyārat al-mufakhkha." *Al-Mustaqbal Nawafez*, May 8. P. 20.

"ʿarḍ li-firqat Atlas al-lubnaniyya fi mahrajan 'Lift' fi London." *Al-Quds Al-Arabi*, October 29. P. 11.

Bédarida, Catherine. "Des archives retrouvées-inventées de la guerre à Beyrouth." *Le Monde*, January 20. P. 29.

Bouteillet, Maïa. "Les Plaies de Beyrouth. Le collectif The Atlas Group osculte l'histoire contemporaine du Liban." *Libération*, May 26. P. 34.

Freuler, Regina. "Walid Ra'ad/Atlas Group am Theaterfestival 'Welt in Basel.' Verwirrende Strategien." *Basler Zeitung*, August 20. P. 38.

Glauner, Max. "Wahrheit lässt sich nicht spielen." *Freitag*, June 4. P. 13.

Huchet, Louise. "Mapping Sitting. Photos d'identités." *Beaux Arts* no. 240 (May):25.

I.R. [Isabelle Regnier]. "Le documentaire dialogue avec l'art contemporain à Barcelone." *Le Monde*, May 26. P. 32.

Jahn, Wolf. "Atlas Group/Walid Raad." *Artforum* 42, no. 10 (Summer):260–61.

Kaplan, Janet A. "Flirtations with Evidence." *Art in America* 92, no. 9 (October):134–39, 169.

Kurd, Nadia. "Leaving Impressions: I Was Overcome by a Momentary Panic at the Thought That They Were Right: Documents from the Nasser File in the Atlas Group Archive." *York University's Critical Times* 3, no. 2 (December):n.p.

Lebovici, Elisabeth. "Petite fabrique d'archives de guerre." *Libération*, January 25. P. 36.

Lequeux, Emmanuelle. "Atlas Group, une esthétique du trauma." *Le Monde Aden* no. 293 (May 26–June 1):27.

Loxley, Anne. "Confronted with Memories of Six." *Sydney Morning Herald*, April 20. Available online at www.smh.com.au/articles/2004/04/19/1082326140399.html (accessed May 3, 2015).

Milroy, Sarah. "What's Wrong with This Picture?" *Globe and Mail*, September 30. Sec. R, pp. 1, 9.

Peeters, Jeroen. "Schimmenspel als herinneringsarbeid. Het documentaire theater van Oga de Soto, Rabih Mroué en The Atlas Group op het KunstenFESTIVALdesArts." *Etcetera* 22, no. 93 (October):38-41.

Petersson, Dag. "Archiving the Potentialities of Events." *English Studies in Canada* 30, no. 1 (March):39–50.

Schiff, Hajo. "Formen des Schreckens: The Atlas Group seziert die Bildsprache von Extremismus und Krieg." *Szene Hamburg* 31, no. 2 (January):51.

——. "The Atlas Group in Collaboration with Walid Raad." *Kunstforum International* no. 170 (May/June):271–72.

——. "The Atlas Group/Walid Raad." *Artist Kunstmagazin* no. 59 (February):26–29.

Searle, Adrian. "The Atlas Group." *The Guardian*, June 8. P. 24.

Stech, Fabian. "Synopsis 3." *Kunstforum International* no. 169 (March/April):318–19.

Temple, Kevin. "Radical Raad." *now Magazine* 24, no. 4 (September 23–29):87.

TW [Thomas Wagner]. N.t. *Frankfurter Allgemeine Zeitung*, February 14. P. 45.

Van Bogaert, Pieter. "Flarden van bomauto's in Beiroet. Atlas Group brengt stukje terreur op KunstenFestivaldesArts." *De Tijd*, May 12. P. 21

Wallach, Amei. "An Artist Explores the Inner Life of Terror." *International Herald Tribune*, June 23. P. 9.

——. "The Fine Art of Car Bombings." *New York Times*, June 20. Sec. 2, pp. 30, 33.

Whitehead, Frederika. "Transcultures: Athens." *Contemporary* no. 66:69.

Wilson-Goldie, Kaelen. "Atlas Group Brings War Documents Home." *Daily Star*, May 8. P. 12.

——. "Cityscape Beirut: Living with Ghosts." *Flash Art* 37, no. 239 (November/December):53–55.

——. "Profile: Walid Raad: The Atlas Group Opens its Archives." *Bidoun* 1, no. 2 (Fall):16–25.

Withers, Rachel. "A Short History of Performance—Part II." *Artforum* 42, no. 8 (April):171–72.

Ziltener, Alfred. "Suche nach politschen Theater." *Basellandschaftliche Zeitung*, August 20. P. 6.

2005

Baird, Daniel. "Raadical Politics: Walid Raad." *Border Crossings* 24, no. 2 (May):34–41.

Budick, Ariella. "Mideast Stock Shots—Minus War and Tyranny." *New York City Newsday*, January 14.

Cohen Hadria, Michèle. "Nothing New under the Western Sun." *Third Text* 19, no. 1 (January):33–43.

Cotter, Holland. "Turning 'Them' to 'Us,' Face by Familiar Face." *New York Times*, January 14. Sec. E., p. 42.

Darrah, Ben. "Masses appeal: Raad's Genius at Work." *The Kingston Whig-Standard*, April 16. P. 17.

Dick, Terence. "Atlas Group Archives: Nassar Files; Atlas Group Archives: Fakhouri File." *Camera Austria* no. 89:87.

Gielen, Denis. "Archiver le terrorisme. Atlas Group & Johan Grimonprez." *Dites* 3, no. 5 (Winter/Spring):64–75.

Fricke, Adrienne. "Forever Nearing the Finish Line: Heritage Policy and the Problem of Memory in Postwar Beirut." *International Journal of Cultural Property* 12: 163–81.

Hassan, Jamelie. "Building an Inventory." *Fuse Magazine* 28, no. 1 (February):34–40.

Heuer, Megan. "Mapping Sitting: On Portraiture and Photography." *The Brooklyn Rail*, April. P. 29.

Ingelevics, Vid. "The Atlas Group and Walid Raad." *Ciel Variable* no. 66 (May):31–32.

Jones, Caroline A. "Doubt Fear." *Art Papers* 29, no. 1 (January/February):24–35.

Kent, Sarah. "The Atlas Group: Anthony Reynolds." *Time Out London,* December 7–13. P. 49.

Khāṭir, Nazīh. "Al-qaṣaṣ yatalaṭa waraʿ ṣawtuh." *An-Nahar*, November 21. Pp. 1, 14.

Madrid, Andrew. "First Degree: The Walid Raad Files." *Art US* no. 8 (May/June):18–21.

Merli, Melissa. "Photos Capture Their Daily Lives." *The News-Gazette*, May 9. Sec. C., p. 1.

Noe, Nicholas. "Photography Exhibit Maps Out Uncharted Space." *Daily Star*, February 24. Available online at www.dailystar.com.lb/Culture/Art/2005/Feb-24/94661-photography-exhibit-maps-out-uncharted-space.ashx (accessed May 4, 2015).

Searle, Adrian. "True Lies." *The Guardian*, December 6. available online at www.theguardian.com/world/2005/dec/06/syria.middleeast (accessed May 4, 2015).

Speers Mears, Emily. "Mapping Sitting: On Portraiture and Photography." *Time Out New York*, February 24–March 2. P. 72.

Steiner, Rochelle. "After the Blast: Rebirth of a Nation." *Modern Painters* (September):47–53.

Stevens, Mark. "Middle Eastern Studies: A Century's Worth of Proletarian Portraits Give the Arab World a Very Different Face." *New York*, January 24–31. Pp. 84–85.

Tamir, Chen. "The Atlas Group and Walid Raad." *Ciel Variable* no. 66 (May):30.

Vali, Murtaza. "Uncovering the Arab World: Photography and Self-Representation." *The Arab Studies Journal* 13/14, no. 2/1 (Fall 2005/Spring 2006):241–46.

2006

Beasley, Mark. "Walid Raad/The Atlas Group." *Frieze* no. 97 (March):152–53.

Bellenbaum, Rainer. "The Atlas Group (1989–2004), A Project by Walid Raad: Hamburger Bahnhof." *Camera Austria* no. 96:72–73.

Berteau, Emilie. "The Atlas Group Archives: Or, How to Document History in the Margins." *Edit: Territories/Territoires* no. 3 (March 30). Available online at www.edit-revue.com/?Article=77 (accessed May 4, 2015).

Cotter, Holland. "The Collective Conscious." *New York Times*, March 5. Sec. 2, pp. 1, 29.

Delgado, Jérôme. "Dans l'évidence, abstiens-toi." *La Presse*, February 24. P. 5.

Demos, T. J. "Walid Raad/The Atlas Group." *Artforum* 44, no. 6 (February):227.

Dulguerova, Elitza. "Atlas Group en collaboration with Walid Raad. We Can Make Rain but No One Came to Ask: Documents from the Atlas Group Archive: Galerie Leonard & Ellen Bina Montreal." *Para-para-7/8/9*, no. 23:4.

Dupuis, Isabelle. "Reviews: Walid Raad/The Atlas Group." *Flash Art* 39, no. 248 (May/June):124–25.

Fahim, Kareem. "Putting Order to Acts That Defy Order." *New York Times*, March 2. Sec. B., p. 2.

Falconer, Morgan. "The Long and Wounding Road." *The London Times*, May 2. Available online at www.thetimes.co.uk/tto/arts/article2408218.ece (accessed May 4, 2015).

Gordon, Avery F. "The Disasters of War." *Camerawork* 33, no. 1 (Spring/Summer):22–29.

Lee, Pamela M. "My Enemy/My Friend." *Grey Room* no. 24 (Summer):100–109.

Lepecki, André. "'After All, This Terror Was Not Without Reason': Unfiled Notes on the Atlas Group Archive." *TDR* 50, no. 3 (Fall):88–99.

Leventis, Andreas. "Home Truths: Three Middle Eastern Artists Probe the Fact behind the Fictions." *Modern Painters* (May):88–93.

——. "The Atlas Group." *Modern Painters* (February):115.

Martens, Allison. "Filling History's Gaps with Art." *Concordia Journal*, February 9. P. 10

Nakas, Kassandra. "The Atlas Group (1989–2004). A Project by Walid Raad." *Nafas Art Magazine* (September). Available online at http://universes-in-universe.org/eng/nafas/articles/2006/the_atlas_group (accessed May 4, 2015).

Pollack, Barbara. "Walid Raad/The Atlas Group: The Kitchen." *Artnews* 105, no. 4 (April):143.

Rawlins, Jarrod. "2006 Biennale of Sidney: Zones of Contact." *Flash Art* no. 250 (October):49.

Saltz, Jerry. "Interrogation Nation." *The Village Voice*, February 15–21. Sec. C, p. 69.

Schwendener, Martha. "Grey Flags." Artforum.com, May 30. Available online at http://artforum.com/archive/id=11099 (accessed May 4, 2015).

——. "Walid Raad. 'The Dead Weight of a Quarrel Hangs: Documents from The Atlas Group Archive.' The Kitchen." *Time Out New York*, February 16–22. P. 72.

Siddiqui, Yasmeen, and Hrag Vartanian. "Histories of Violence." *The Brooklyn Rail*, March. Pp. 20–21.

Smith, Roberta. "Mixing Fact and Fiction to Open Up Larger Reality." *New York Times*, March 4. Sec. B, p. 11.

Spalding, David. "Ghosts in the Machine." *Camerawork* 33, no. 1 (Spring/Summer):4–11.

Stanhope, Zara. "An Affair to Remember." *Photofile* no. 78 (Spring):50–53.

Tilmann, Christina. "Vampir Erinnerung." *Der Tagesspiegel*, September 22. P. 31.

Van Siclen, Bill. "A Hybrid History of Terrorist-Torn Beirut." *Providence Journal*, May 1. Sec. E, pp. 5, 8.

Wallach, Amei. "Missed Signals: Nuance and the Reading of Immigrant Art." *American Art* 20, no. 2 (Summer):126–33.

Wilson-Goldie, Kaelen. "New Art for a New Middle East." *Art + Auction* (March):118–23.

——. "The Art of Frustrating Expectations." *Daily Star*, May 25. Available online at www.dailystar.com.lb/Culture/Art/2006/May-25/98848-the-art-of-frustrating-expectations.ashx (accessed May 4, 2015).

Zeppetelli, John. "Mapping Deceptions: *We Can Make Rain But No One Came to Ask* Tells Alternative Stories Walid Raad Calls His." *Hour*, March 2–8. P. 23.

Zolghadr, Tirdad, and Tony Chakar. "City Report: Beirut." *Frieze* no. 99 (May):158–63.

2007

Blank, Gil. "The Atlas Group (1989–2004): A Project by Walid Raad." *Whitewall* (Fall):48.

Demos, T. J. "On the Ground: London." *Artforum* 46, no. 4 (December):294–95, 374, 376.

Feldman, Hannah, and Akram Zaatari. "Mining War: Fragments from a Conversation Already Passed." *Art Journal* 66, no. 2 (Summer):48–67.

Gardner, Belinda Grace. "Walid Raad: (Let's Be Honest, The Weather Helped). Galerie Sfeir-Semler." *ArtAsiaPacific* no. 52 (March/April):107.

Haden-Guest, Anthony. "His Dark Materials." *Financial Times*, March 17–18. Weekend sec., p. 14.

Herbert, Martin. "Has He Got News for You?" *Time Out London*, February 21–27. P. 33.

Higgie, Jennifer. "Her(his)tory." *Frieze* no. 111 (November/December):175.

Kolbowski, Silvia. "After *Hiroshima Mon Amour*." *Art Journal* 66, no. 3 (Fall):80–84.

Raza, Sara. "Out of Beirut: Modern Art Oxford." *ArtAsiaPacific* no. 51 (Winter):119.

Rebhandl, Bert. "I Feel a Great Desire to Meet the Masses Once Again." *Frieze* no. 104 (January/February):56.

Rogers, Sarah. "Out of History: Postwar Art in Beirut." *Art Journal* 66, no. 2 (Summer):8–20.

Schwarzbart, Judith. "Walid Raad: I Only Wish. . . ." *sum* no. 1 (2007):3–17.

Scott, Andrea K. "Walid Raad." *New York Times*, March 16. Sec. E, p. 33.

Shainin, Jonathan. "Ignition Switch." *Bookforum* (June/July/August):12–13, 64.

Solis, Alberto. "Exposición del artista Walid Raad en el Museo Tamayo. La Guerra en Líbano en catorce piezas." *Milenio*, April 26. P. 49.

Sosa, Yanet Aguilar. "Antología bélica de Líbano, en imágenes." *El Universal*, April 26. Sec. F, p. 2

Steenbergen, Isabella. "Een atlas van geweld. Walid Raad over zijn 'lecture performance' over de oorlog tegen terreur." *NRC Handelsblad*, June 1. P. 25.

"Walid Raad." *The New Yorker*, March 26. P. 20.

Wilson-Goldie, Kaelen. "Lebanon Bans Tale of Fighters in Militias." *New York Times*, August 18. Sec. A, pp. 13, 17.

——. "The War Works: Videos under Siege, Online and in the Aftermath, Again." *Art Journal* 66, no. 2 (Summer):68–82.

Zolghadr, Tirdad. "Walid Raad/The Atlas Group: Berlin." *Art Papers* 31, no. 3 (May/June):57.

2008

"A History of Modern and Contemporary Arab Art_Part 1_Chapter 1: Lebanon 1992–2005. Sfeir-Semler Gallery." *Time Out Beirut*, July/August. P. 59.

ʾAby Saʿb, Bīar. "Walīd Raʿd . . . Sijil ʾkhtifaʾ: ḍamīr mostatir taqdīruhu naḥnu fi 'gallery ṣafīr-zamlr.'" *Al-Akhbar*, July 24. Pp. 18–19.

Armin, Janine. "Not Quite How I Remember It." Artforum.com, July 9. Available online at http://artforum.com/archive/id=20714 (accessed May 4, 2015).

Atkins, Christopher. "Brave New Worlds." *Art Papers* 32, no. 1 (January/February):46–47.

Auricchio, Laura. "Quiet Politics." *Time Out New York*, August 13–19. P. 54.

Briggs, Patricia. "Brave New Worlds: Walker Art Center." *Artforum* 46, no. 5 (January):287–88.

Bryan-Wilson, Julia. "Not Quite How I Remember It." *Artforum* 46, no. 9 (May):175.

Burton, Johanna, and Ann Temkin. "Primary Sources." *Artforum* 46, no. 8 (April):340–47.

Carlson, Benjamin. "Not Quite How I Remember It." *Frieze* no. 119 (November/December):217.

Carr-Harris, Dory. "An Affair to Remember." *Torontoist*, June 4. Available online at http://torontoist.com/2008/06/an_affair_to_re/ (accessed May 4, 2015).

Cook, Greg. "Fact and Fantasy: Walid Raad's Installations Seek the 'Truth.'" *The Providence Phoenix*, May 2. P. 10.

Cotter, Holland. "Well, It Looks like Truth." *New York Times*, January 18. Sec. E, pp. 31, 34.

Galligan, Gregory. "Architecture in Script: From Without Boundary to Archive Fever." *ArtAsiaPacific* no. 58 (May/June):122–29.

Ganis, William V. "Visible Disillusionment." *Afterimage* 36, no. 3 (November/December):20–21.

Khāṭir, Nazīh. "Walīd Raʿd fi gallery ṣafīr-zmlar ka-al-ʾrtimāʾ fi faḍaʾ shasha bila qaʿr." *An-Nahar*, August 5. Available online at www.annahar.com.

Lappé, Anthony. "Menassat.com Dodges Bullets, Bombs and Government Censors." *Tar Magazine* (Fall):68–72.

McLaughlin, Bryne. "Not Quite How I Remember It: Rapid Memory Gloss." *Canadian Art*, July 10. Available online at www.canadianart.ca/reviews/2008/07/10/not-quite/ (accessed May 4, 2015).

Milroy, Sarah. "The Past: A Work in Progress." *Globe and Mail*, June 25. Sec. R, pp. 1–2.

O'Neill-Butler, Lauren. "'Quiet Politics.' Zwirner & Wirth." *Artforum* 47, no. 3 (November):351.

Schechter, Fran. "Moving Modern Ideas." *now Magazine* 27, no. 47 (July 24–31):59.

Secor, Beth. "Walid Raad and his Fake Foundation Show Real Art at the Glassell School." *Houston Press*, October 29. Available online at www.houstonpress.com/2008-10-30/culture/walid-raad-and-his-fake-foundation-show-real-art-at-the-glassell-school/ (accessed May 4, 2015).

Simblist, Noah. "The Dead Weight of a Quarrel Hangs: Selection from The Atlas Group Archive." *Art Lies* no. 60 (Winter):103.

Smith, Will. "New York/Archive Fever." *Bidoun* (Spring/Summer):150–51.

Sundell, Margaret. "Archive Fever: International Center of Photography." *Artforum* 46, no. 5 (January):131.

Quilty, Jim. "One Artist's Version of Not Getting the Picture." *The Daily Star*, August 9. P. 10.

——. "Walid Raad. Galerie Sfeir-Semler, Beirut." *Art Review* no. 26 (October):171.

Vidokle, Anton. "Looking Back: Solo Shows." *Frieze* no. 112 (January/February):136.

Wilson-Goldie, Kaelen. "Art Now in Lebanon. Amman: Darat Al-Funun." *Bidoun* (Fall):178–79.

——. "Walid Raad: Galerie Sfeir-Semler." *Artforum* 47, no. 3 (November 2008):370.

Zalzal, Zéna. "L'histoire de l'art modern et contemporain arabe selon Walid Raad." *L'Orient le Jour*, August 5. P. 6.

2009

Al-khubyz, Bilal. "Walīd Raʿd ʿariḍan fi Red Cat bi Los Angeles 'ṭabīa ṣāmita' ʾkhtaft fi al-masāfah bayna madinatiyyn." *Al-Mustaqbal*, May 17. P. 13.

Banai, Nuit. “Zones of Conflict.” *Time Out New York*, January 22–28. P. 47.

Baumann, Stefanie. “Archiver ce qui aurait pu avoir lieu.” *Conserveries mémorielles* no. 6. Available online at http://cm.revues.org/381 (accessed May 4, 2015).

Borchardt-Hume, Achim. “What to See This Month: Walid Raad.” *Art Review* no. 32 (May): 36.

Casavecchia, Barbara. “L’arte ai tempi della guerra Walid Raad racconta il Libano.” *La Repubblica*, July 16. P. XII.

——. “Walid Raad at Fondazione Antonio Ratti.” Frieze.com, July 17. Available online at https://www.frieze.com/shows/review/walid_raad/ (accessed May 4, 2015).

Chong, Doryun, and Yasmil Raymond. “New York Artists Dictionary: Walid Raad.” *Flash Art* 42, no. 264 (January/February):79.

Cotter, Suzanne. “The Documentary Turn: Surpassing Tradition in the Work of Walid Raad and Akram Zaatari.” In Paul Sloman, ed. *Contemporary Art in the Middle East*. London: Black Dog Publishing. Pp. 50–57.

Depaule, Jean-Charles. “La Fondation arabe pour l’image.” *Vingtième Siècle. Revue d’histoire* no. 103 (July–September):239–42.

Gladstone, Valerie. “Review: Walid Raad.” *Modern Painters* (November):72.

Hugonnier, Marine. “What to See This Month: Walid Raad.” *Art Review* no. 34 (September):36.

Kerr, Merrily. “Walid Raad, ‘Scratching on Things I Could Disavow.’” *Time Out New York*, December 3–9. P. 9.

Lafont, Isabel. “Walid Raad viaja a la estética de la violencia.” *El Pais*, February 20. P. 37.

Lambert-Beatty, Carrie. “Make-Believe: Parafiction and Plausibility.” *October* no. 129 (Summer):51–84.

Lissoni, Andrea. “File incompleti dal Libano.” *Rolling Stone* (July):148.

Maimon, Vered. “The Third Citizen: On Models of Criticality in Contemporary Artistic Practices.” *October* no. 129 (Summer):85–112.

Masters, HG. “Those Who Lack Imagination Cannot Imagine What Is Lacking.” *ArtAsiaPacific* no. 65 (September/October):124–35.

Saadawi, Ghalya. “Photography: Walid Raad.” *Canvas: Art and Culture from the Middle East and Arab World* 5, no. 2:150–61.

Vogel, Carol. “Finalists Announced for Hugo Boss Prize.” *New York Times*, October 9. Sec. C, p. 26.

2010

Blood, Anne. “Walid Raad at the Whitechapel.” *Edel Assanti Project Space*, November 25. Available online at http://edelassantiprojectspace.wordpress.com/2010/11/25/walid-raad-at-the-whitechapel/ (accessed May 4, 2015).

Boucher, Brian. “Walid Raad: Paula Cooper.” *Art in America* 98, no. 3 (March):145–46.

Bellet, Harry. “Walid Raad inscrit l’Histoire en faux.” *Le Monde, Festival d’automne 2010*, September 11. Supplement, p. 10.

C.M.S. “Beirut-Fotografien eins Grenzgängers.” *Der Standard*, January 29. P. 28.

Charlesworth, J. J. “Walid Raad ‘Miraculous Beginnings’: Whitechapel Gallery.” *Art Review* no. 44 (October):103.

Crichton-Miller, Emma. “Chaos Theories.” *Financial Times*, October 9. P. 6.

Faucheret, Anne. “‘Acid Talk’: Walid Raad’s Ausstellung in Camera Austria.” *www.gat.st*, March 5. Available online at www.gat.st/news/acid-talk-walid-raads-ausstellung-camera-austria (accessed May 4, 2015).

Forster, Lou. “Walid Raad. L’archive en Délai.” *Art21* no. 28 (Fall):15–23.

Frankel, David. “Walid Raad. Paula Cooper Gallery.” *Artforum* 48, no. 6 (February):198–99.

Gilbert, Alan. “Walid Raad (Re)invents the Archive.” *Aperture* no. 198 (Spring):60–67.

Gladstone, Valerie. “Paris Show Comments on Arab Politics and Art.” *New York Times*, November 18. Available online at http://intransit.blogs.nytimes.com/2010/11/18/paris-show-comments-on-arab-politics-and-art/ (accessed May 4, 2015).

Hale, Louise. “Views of a city tearing itself apart.” *Eastend Life*, November 22. P. 25.

Hodgson, Francis. “Walid Raad: Whitechapel Gallery, London.” *Financial Times*, December 13. Available online at www.ft.com/cms/s/2/64d93bce-06d4-11e0-8c29-00144feabdc0.html (accessed May 4, 2015).

Istim, Brigitte. “Walid Raad’s Miraculous Beginnings.” *Collective Review*, December 2. Available online at http://thecollectivereview.com/brigitte-istim/walid-raads-miraculous-beginnings.html (accessed May 4, 2015).

Lachnit, Peter. “Das Aktiv der fiktiven Wirklichkeit.” *oe1.ofr.at*, February 6. Available online at http://oe1.orf.at/artikel/216270 (accessed May 4, 2015).

Lequeux, Emmanuelle. “Le plasticien Walid Raad fait sa ‘guerre de Golfe.’” *Le Monde*, November 19. P. 22.

Meade, Fionn. “After Images.” *Mousse* no. 26 (November):182–89.

Montazami, Morad. “Walid Raad. le théâtre nous surpasse, nous dépassons l’histoire/The Disaster Surpasses Us, We Surpass History.” *Artpress* no. 370 (September):29–33.

Moulène, Claire. “Grand atlas.” *Les Inrockuptibles* no. 783 (December 1–7):104.

Pfeiffer, Alice. “Paging Atlas Group.” artinamericamagazine.com, November 4. Available online at www.artinamericamagazine.com/news-features/news/walid-raad-whitechapel/ (accessed May 4, 2015).

Pollack, Barbara. “Making an Impact.” *Artnews* 109, no. 5 (May):84–91.

Reichart, Michaela. “Transformation im Bild.” *Kronen Zeitung*, January 29. P. 31.

Saadawi, Ghalya. “Necessary Fables: Walid Raad.” *Artinfo*, October 21. Available online at http://br.blouinartinfo.com/market-news/article/36096-necessary-fables-walid-raad (accessed May 4, 2015).

Sam-Daliri, Nadia. “In the Lebanon. . . . ” *Hackney Gazette*, December 2. P. 21.

“Scratching on Things I Could Disavow: A History of Art in the Arab World/Part I_Volume I_Chapter 1.” *ArtAsiaPacific Almanac* 5:227.

Sharro, Karl. “Traces of the future: Walid Raad: Miraculous Beginnings, Whitechapel Gallery, London.” *Culture Wars*, October 21. Available online at www.culturewars.org.uk/index.php/site/article/traces_of_the_future/ (accessed May 4, 2015).

Steer, Emily. “Walid Raad: Miraculous Beginnings.” *Art Wednesday*, November 9. http://artwednesday.com/2010/11/09/walid-raad-miraculous-beginnings/; site unavailable as this book goes to press.

Steward, Sue. “Obsessed by Lebanon’s Past.” *Evening Standard*, October 22. P. 44.

Straub, Verena. “Walid Raad—Camera Austria, Graz.” *art-in.de*, January 22. Available online at www.art-in.de/incmu2.php?id=2091 (accessed May 4, 2015).

Theiss, Nora. “Der Spaziergänger des Paris des Nahen Ostens.” *Artmagazine*, February 15. Available online at www.artmagazine.cc/content45074.html (accessed May 4, 2015).

Titz, Walter. “Camera Austria. Fotografien rasanter Umbrüche.” *Kleine Zeitung*, January 31. Pp. 80–81.

Verhagen, Marcus. “Walid Raad: Miraculous Beginnings. Whitechapel Gallery.” *Art Monthly* no. 342 (December 2010–January 2011):23.

“Museum Previews: Walid Raad.” *Art in America* 98, no. 7(August):38.

Ward, Ossian. “Walid Raad. Whitechapel Gallery.” *Time Out London*, November 25–December 1. P. 66.

Wilson-Goldie, Kaelen. “Walid Raad: Miraculous Beginnings.” *Artforum* 49, no. 1 (September):173.

2011

Al-Kassim, Dina. “Reconstructions Revisited: Unearthing the Place of the Local and the Case of Post-Civil War Beirut.” *Localities* 1: 159–82.

Bal, Mieke. “Heterochrony in the Act: The Migratory Politics of Time.” *Art and Visibility in Migratory Culture: Conflict, Resistance, and Agency*. Issue no. 23 of *Thamyris/Intersecting: Place, Sex and Race*. Pp. 211–38.

Bruckstein Çoruh, A.S. “‘Irrer stört Eröffnung. Behauptet: Welt ist flach’: Walid Raad bei TBA21, Wien, und im Theater Hebbel am Ufer, Berlin.” *Texte zur Kunst* no. 83 (September):247–51.

Crow, Kelly. “Tips from Russian Heiress, 25: Do Your Homework on Artists.” *Wall Street Journal*, June 25. Available online at http://online.wsj.com/article/SB10001424052702303936704576398110053409924.html (accessed May 4, 2015).

Gallagher, Ann. “Looking Back/Looking Forward.” *Frieze* no. 136 (January/February):85.

Herbert, Martin. “Walid Raad: *Miraculous Beginnings*.” *Bidoun* (Spring):168.

Kim, Sunjung. “Looking Back/Looking Forward.” *Frieze* no. 136 (January/February):90.

“Lebanese/American Photographer Walid Raad Announced as 2011 Hasselblad Winner.” *Artdaily.org*, March 13. Available online at http://artdaily.com/news/45684/Lebanese-American-Photographer-Walid-Raad-Announced-as-2011-Hasselblad-Award-Winner#.Us3baPu41n8 (accessed May 4, 2015).

Lewis, Ben. “Private View.” *Prospect* (January):80.

Magagnoli, Paolo. “A Method in Madness: Historical Truth in Walid Raad’s *Hostage: The Bachar Tapes*.” *Third Text* 25, no. 3 (May):311–24.

Marcus, J. S. “Artist Focus. Walid Raad: A Prize born in Violence.” *Wall Street Journal*, November 5–6. Sec. C, p. 14.

McConnell, Jonathan. “Walid Raad: 2011 Hasselblad Award Winner.” *Designboom*, March 17. Available online at www.designboom.com/weblog/Cat/10/view/13685/walid-raad-2011-hasselblad-award-winner.html (accessed May 8, 2015).

Morgenthaler, Daniel. “Schrumpfkunst im kleinteiligen Wohnmuseum. Eine Ausstellung in der Kunsthalle Zürich zeigt Walid Raad als brillanten Fingierer.” *Basler Zeitung*, September 20. P. 41.

Muller, Hans-Joachim. “Aktivist? Poet? Archivar? Walid Raad schlüpft in Zürich durch alle Raster.” *Monopol Magazine für Kunst and Leben* (October):109.

Oberländer, Jan. “Versteckte Farben: Der Performancekünstler Walid Raad eklärt im HAU Geschichte und Gegenwart der arabischen Kunst.” *Der Tagespiel,* June 26. P. 26.

Ouroussoff, Nicolai. “Abu Dhabi Guggenheim Faces Protest.” *New York Times*, March 17. Sec. C, pp. 1, 7.

Robinson, Wayne. “Guggenheim: Protest Jeopardizes Abu Dhabi Project.” artnet.com, March 24. Available online at www.artnet.com/magazineus/news/artnetnews/guggenheim-abu-dhabi-protest-3-24-11.asp (accessed May 4, 2015).

Scheller, Jörg. “Walid Raad in der Kunsthalle Zürich: Zwischen den Zeichen.” Artnet.de, September 13. Available online at www.artnet.de/magazine/walid-raad-in-der-kunsthalle-zurich/; site unavailable as this book goes to press.

Smith, Sarah-Neel, and Sam Thorne. “New Museums.” *Frieze* no. 137 (March):24–25.

Solomon-Godeau, Abigail. “The Phantom Photographer.” *Art in America* 99, *no. 10* (November):128–33.

Stoilas, Helen. “Abu Dhabi: Artists back Guggenheim boycott.” *The Art Newspaper* no. 223 (April):14.

———. “Artists boycott Guggenheim Abu Dhabi project.” *The Art Newspaper*, March 17. Available online at www.theartnewspaper.com/Articles/Artists+boycott+Guggenheim+Abu+Dhabi+project/23383; site unavailable as this book goes to press.

Suliyman, Hazim. “Walīd Raʿd . . . al-taʾrīkh bi al-ṣuwar al-mufakhkha: ʿJāʾizat hasselblad’ al-sūīdiyya li-mashrūʿuh ‘ʾṭlas ghurūb.’” *Al-Akhbar*, March 24. Available online at www.al-akhbar.com/node/7361 (accessed May 4, 2015).

“The Power 100: Walid Raad.” *Art Review* no. 54 (November):138.

Tremeau, Tristan. “Implicit Connections: The Magic Words of the 1990s.” *Esse Arts + Opinions* no. 73 (September):4–11.

Ulmer, Brigitte. “Ersatzhandlungen und Legendenbildungen. Walid Raad in der Kunsthalle Zürich im Museum Bärengasse.” *Neue Zürcher Zeitung*, August 27. P. 23.

Van der Lint, Roos. “Wetenschap als poëzie.” *Kunstbeeld* no. 9:42–45.

Wallen, Jeffrey. “The Lure of the Archive: The Atlas Project of Walid Raad.” *Comparative Critical Studies* 8, nos. 2–3:277–93.

Wilson-Goldie, Kaelen. “A Line between Public and Private Space.” *Daily Star*, June 25. P. 16.

Wroczynski, Emily. “Walid Raad and the Atlas Group: Mapping Catastrophe and the Architecture of Destruction.” *Third Text* 25, no. 6 (November):763–73.

2012

Borchardt-Hume, Achim. “Walid Raad: Symptoms of Withdrawal.” *Cura* (Winter): 86–99.

Bourriaud, Nicolas. “Hétéro Chronie.” *L’Officiel Art* no. 1 (April–June):98–107, 287.

Byrd, David. “MoMA Director Lowry Explores Middle East Art.” *Voice of America*, December 7. Available online at www.voanews.com/content/moma_director_explores_contemporary_artists_vision_of_middle_east/1560819.html (accessed May 4, 2015).

Cotter, Holland. “Walid Raad and David Diao.” *New York Times*, October 26. Sec. C, p. 25.

D’Avout, Shannon. “Structural Mutations, Cinnamon-Scented Speculation, the Twenty-First Century and the Artist Pension Trust.” *C: International Contemporary Art* no. 116 (Winter):16–19.

Lee, Stephen. “Museum Show Part 1 & Part 2: Arnolfini Bristol.” *Art Monthly* no. 353 (February):31–32.

Masters, H. G. “Five Plus One: Walid Raad.” *ArtAsiaPacific Almanac* 7:85.

McKenna, Caitlin. “The Many Authoritative Faces of Walid Raad: Thoughts from the Lecture Hall at the IFA.” *IFA Contemporary*, March 20. Available online at https://ifacontemporary.wordpress.com/2012/03/20/the-many-authoritative-faces-of-walid-raad-thoughts-from-the-lecture-hall-at-the-ifa/ (accessed May 4, 2015).

Minicucci, Andria. “Blind Spots, Caesurae and Other Archival Lacunae.” *Esse Arts + Opinions* no. 76 (Autumn):24–29.

Moran, Jason. “Best of 2012.” *Artforum* 51, no. 4 (December):70.

Rice, Shelley. “Postcard from Documenta 13: Walid Raad, Arabian Nights and the Pitfalls of Pilgrimages.” *Jeu de Paume Le Magazine*, June 22. Available online at http://lemagazine.jeudepaume.org/blogs/shelleyrice/2012/06/22/post-card-from-documenta-13-walid-raad-arabian-nights-and-the-pitfalls-of-pilgrimages/ (accessed May 4, 2015).

Singldinger, Josef. “Offen—freizügig—kommunikativ. Mitten drin im Augenblick—dOCUMENTA (13).” *Kommune* 30, no. 4 (August/September):88–89.

“The Power 100: Walid Raad.” *Art Review* no. 63 (November):144.

Von Naso, Rüdiger. “1 + 12 = d (13).” *Madame* no. 8 (August):58–65.

Wilson-Goldie, Kaelen. “Get Together.” *Frieze* no. 149 (September):157–60.

2013

Aletti, Vince. “Out of Order.” *The New Yorker*, July 1. P. 10.

Al-mul, Duḥa ʿabdul-raʾūf. “Maʿraḍ, al-farāghāt al-ḍawūʾiyya bayna al-wahm wa al-ḥaqīqa.” *Aliwaa*, March 8. Available online at www.aliwaa.com/Article.aspx?ArticleId=156934 (accessed May 8, 2015).

Bonacorsi, Ivo. “Preface to the First Edition.” *Domus*, February 26. Available online at www.domusweb.it/en/art/2013/02/26/preface-to-the-first-edition.html (accessed May 8, 2015).

Bonnet, Frédéric. “Mutations optiques.” *Le Journal des Arts* no. 385 (February 15):14.

Considine, Liam. “Art in the Age of Truthiness.” *Art Review* no. 65 (January/February):121.

Dīb, Rūiyy. “Walīd Raʿd ṣawtun ṣārkhun fi qifār al-nifṭ.” *Al-Akhbar*, February 6. Available online at www.al-akhbar.com/node/176966 (accessed May 8, 2015).

Dillon, Brian. “Philosophy of Art.” *Modern Painters* (July/August):40–41.

Holert, Tom. “Burden of Proof,” *Artforum* 51, no. 7 (March):250–59, 298.

“ʾʿmāl al-fanān al-Lubnāny Walīd Raʿd fi matḥaf al-Louvre.” *Ṣayda Al-Yaum*, January 27. Available online at http://saidaalyawm.com.

Meier, Allison. “Countdown to Abu Dhabi Begins in Paris.” *Hyperallergic*, April 19. Available online at http://hyperallergic.com/69224/countdown-to-abu-dhabi-begins-in-paris/ (accessed May 8, 2015).

Pawson, Lara. “Eye Witness.” *Frieze* no. 156 (June–August):156–61.

Takahashi, Tess. “Walid Ra’ad and The Atlas Group: The Photograph and the Archive in Experimental Documentary.” *Moving Image Review & Art Journal* 2, no. 1:68–78.

Wilson-Goldie, Kaelen. “The Web of Intrigue about Walid Raad.” *Daily Star*, January 8. P. 16.

2014

Bonnet, Frédéric. “La lisibilité faite oeuvre.” *Le Journal des Arts* no. 417 (July 4). Available online at www.lejournaldesarts.fr/jda/archives/docs_article/121918/la-lisibilite-faite-oeuvre.php (accessed May 8, 2015).

Dagen, Philippe. “Walid Raad joue avec les forms et la réalité.” *Le Monde*, Available online at www.lemonde.fr/culture/article/2014/07/03/walid-raad-joue-avec-les-formes-et-la-realite_4449914_3246.html (accessed May 8, 2015).

Désanges, Guillaume. “Performing the Document: New Political Theatricalities.” *Esse Arts + Opinions* no. 81 (Spring/Summer):40–47.

Feldman, Hannah. “Walid Raad: Preface.” *Artforum* 52, no. 9 (May):196.

De la Fresnaye, Marie. “Walid Raad au Carré d’Art de Nîmes.” *Artaïssime* (Summer):15.

Holland, Laura. “True Lies.” *Preview Massachusetts* (November):10, 14.

Lequeux, Emmanuelle. “Walid Raad, le vrai et le faux au Carré d’Art à Nîmes.” *Le Quotidien de l’Art*, July 2–August 15. P. 5.

Loret, Eric. “Walid Raad, reflets et réflexion.” *Libération*, June 14–15. Available online at http://next.liberation.fr/arts/2014/06/13/walid-raad-reflets-et-reflexions_1040705 (accessed May 8, 2015).

Marchand, Antoine. “Inside Information.” *02* no. 71 (Autumn):16–20.

Martí, Silas. “Pedra no sapato do Guggenheim, Walid Raad vem à Bienal.” *Folha de S. Paulo*, February 2. Sec. E, p. 3.

Moynihan, Colin. “Protesters Renew Criticism of Guggenheim’s Abu Dhabi Plans.” *New York Times*, November 7. Sec. A, p. 25.

Muṣṭafa, Muṣṭafa. “Walīd Raʿd: riḥla fi tārīkh ‘al-fann al-ʾslāmy.’” *Al-Akhbar*, March 22. Available online at www.al-akhbar.com/node/203146 (accessed May 8, 2015).

Souriau, Judith. “Elusive but Truthful.” *Canvas* 10, no. 4 (July/August):42–44.

Watier le Borgne, Julie. “Walid Raad: recompose l’histoire.” *Beaux Arts* no. 363 (September):124.

2015

Masters, H. G. “Carré d’Art: Walid Raad.” *ArtAsiaPacific Almanac* 10:231.

Streitberger, Alexander. “Photography, History and Memory in contemporary video art.” *Eikon* no. 89:48–53.

Wilson-Goldie, Kaelen. “By All Accounts.” *Artforum* 53, no. 9 (May):324–29.

Selected Exhibition History
Compiled by Katerina Stathopoulou

Solo Exhibitions

1985
Beaver Country Day School, Chestnut Hill, Mass. *Walid Raad: Photographs*. October 9–November 8.

2003
Anthony Reynolds Gallery, London. *The Complete Fakhouri File*. November 21–December 20.

La Galerie, Noisy-Le-Sec. *The Truth Will Be Known When the Last Witness Is Dead: Documents From The Fakhouri File in The Atlas Group Archive*. November 29, 2003–February 7, 2004. Exh. brochure.

World Wide Video Festival, Passenger Terminal Amsterdam. *World Wide Solo: Walid Ra'ad–The Atlas Group Project*. May 8–25.

2004
Sfeir-Semler Gallery, Hamburg. *My Neck Is Thinner Than a Hair*. January 23–March 20.

Art Gallery of York University, Toronto. *I Was Overcome by a Momentary Panic at the Thought That They Were Right: Documents from the Nassar Files in The Atlas Group Archive*. September 15–November 14.

Prefix Institute of Contemporary Art, Toronto. *The Truth Will Be Known When the Last Witness Is Dead: Documents from The Fakhouri File in The Atlas Group Archive*. September 16–November 27.

2005
Agnes Etherington Art Center, Queen's University, Kingston, Ont. *I Feel a Great Desire to Meet the Masses Once Again: A Project by Walid Raad and The Atlas Group*. February 5–April 24.

FACT, Liverpool. *Funny How Thin the Line Is: Documents from The Atlas Group Archive*. November 11, 2005–January 8, 2006.

Anthony Reynolds Gallery, London. *We Are a Fair People. We Never Speak Well of One Another*. November 18–December 22.

2006
The Kitchen, New York. *The Dead Weight of A Quarrel Hangs: Documents from The Atlas Group Archive*. January 7–March 11.

Leonard & Bina Ellen Gallery, Concordia University, Montreal. *We Can Make Rain but No One Came to Ask: Documents from The Atlas Group Archive*. January 26–March 4. Exh. cat.

Sfeir-Semler Gallery, Hamburg. *Let's Be Honest, The Weather Helped*. September 9–October 21.

Nationalgalerie im Hamburger Bahnhof–Museum für Gegenwart–Berlin. *The Atlas Group (1989–2004): A Project by Walid Raad*. September 22, 2006–January 7, 2007. Exh. cat. Traveled to: Culturgest, Lisbon, September 28–December 30, 2007 (exh. cat.).

Henry Art Gallery, Seattle. *(We Decided to Let Them Say "We Are Convinced" Twice. It Was More Convincing This Way.) A Project by Walid Raad*. November 10, 2006–February 11, 2007.

2007
Paula Cooper Gallery, New York. *Walid Raad*. February 17–March 24.

Museo Tamayo Arte Contemporáneo, Mexico City. *The Atlas Group (1989–2004). Un proyecto de Walid Raad*. April 26–July 29. Exh. brochure.

2008
David Winton Bell Gallery, List Art Center, Brown University, Providence. *We Can Make Rain but No One Came to Ask*. April 10–May 25. Exh. cat.

Sfeir-Semler Gallery, Beirut. *A History of Modern and Contemporary Arab Art_Part I_Chapter 1: Beirut 1992–2005*. July 17–November 7.

Glassell School of Art, The Museum of Fine Arts, Houston. *The Dead Weight of a Quarrel Hangs: Selections from The Atlas Group Archive*. September 12–November 23. Exh. brochure.

Heidelberger Kunstverein, Heidelberger. *I Might Die Before I Get a Rifle (1989)*. November 22, 2008–February 1, 2009.

2009
REDCAT, Los Angeles. *Scratching on Things I Could Disavow: A History of Art in the Arab World, Part 1_Volume1_Chapter 1 (Beirut: 1992-2005)*. April 10–June 14. Exh. cat.

Museo Nacional Centro de Arte Reina Sofía, Madrid. *The Atlas Group (1989–2004). Un Proyecto de Walid Raad*. June 3–August 31. Organized by the Museo Nacional Centro de Arte Reina Sofía in collaboration with Festival Internacional de Fotografía y Artes Visuales PhotoEspaña 2009.

Fondazione Antonio Ratti, Como. *Scratching on Things I Could Disavow: A History of Art in the Arab World, Part I_Volume 1_Chapter 1: Beirut (1992–2005)*. July 3–August 20.

Anthony Reynolds Gallery, London. *Scratching on Things I Could Disavow*. September 25–October 31.

Paula Cooper Gallery, New York. *Scratching on Things I Could Disavow: A History of Art in the Arab World/Part I_Volume 1_Chapter 1 (Beirut: 1992–2005)*. November 6–December 19.

Sfeir-Semler Gallery, Hamburg. *Scratching on Things I Could Disavow: A History of Art in the Arab World: Part I_Volume 1_Chapter 1 (Beirut: 1992–2005)*. November 13, 2009–January 16, 2010.

2010
Camera Austria, Graz. *Sweet Talk: Commissions (Beirut)*. January 29–April 5. Exh. brochure.

Whitechapel Gallery, London. *Walid Raad: Miraculous Beginnings*. October 14, 2010–January 2, 2011. Exh. cat. Traveled to: Bildmuseet, Umeå University, February 20–April 25, 2011; Kunsthalle Zürich, August 26–October 30, 2011.

Le Centquatre, Paris. *Scratching on things I could disavow: A history of art in the Arab world*. November 6–December 5. Traveled to: Wiener Festwochen at Thyssen-Bornemisza Art Contemporary, Vienna, May 26–June 15, 2011 (exh. cat.); Kunstenfestivaldesarts, Les Halles de Schaerbeek, Brussels, May 6–28, 2011; Hebbel am Ufer, Berlin, June 24–26 and June 28–30, 2011.

2011
Hasselblad Centre, Göteborgs Konstmuseum, Gothenburg. *Walid Raad–2011 Hasselblad Award Winner*. November 12, 2011–January 15, 2012. Exh. cat.

2012
Sfeir-Semler Gallery, Beirut. *Scratching on Things I Could Disavow*. November 29, 2012–March 23, 2013.

2013
Musée du Louvre, Paris. *Préface à la première édition*. January 19–April 8. Exh. cat.

2014
Anthony Reynolds Gallery, London. *Preface to the First English Edition*. March 1–April 5.

Carré d'Art, Nîmes. *Walid Raad/Préface*. May 23–September 14. Traveled to: MADRE (Museo d'Arte Contemporanea Donnaregina), Naples, October 11, 2014–January 19, 2015, as *Walid Raad: Prefazione*.

University Museum of Contemporary Art, University of Massachusetts, Amherst. *Walid Raad: Postface*. September 11–December 7.

2015
The Museum of Modern Art, New York. *Walid Raad*. October 12, 2015–January 31, 2016. Exh. cat.

Group Exhibitions

1994
Hartnett Gallery, University of Rochester, N.Y. *Visual Sights/Visual Signs*. November 21–December 16.

1995
Théâtre de Beyrouth, Beirut. *Image/Quest—A Film and Video Exhibition*. June 21–28.

1996
YYZ Artists' Outlet, Toronto. *. . East of Here . . (Re)Imagining the 'Orient'*. November 20–December 14. Exh. cat.

1997
DeCordova Museum and Sculpture Park, Lincoln, Mass. *Pioneer Valley Videos: Video Art from Western New England*. June 14–September 1.

2000
Borusan Kültür Sanat, Istanbul. *Akdeniz Metaforlari II–Lübnan'dan Çağdaş Sanat*. February 4–March 5. Exh. cat.

Whitney Museum of American Art, New York. Whitney Biennial. March 23–June 4. Exh. cat.

Kunst-Werke Institute for Contemporary Art, Berlin. *Stand der Dinge*. December 10, 2000–February 4, 2001. Exh. cat.

2001
Wiener Festwochen, Künstlerhaus Wien, Vienna. *Du Bist die Welt: 24 Episodes about Life Today*. June 1–June 24.

CEPA Gallery, Buffalo, N.Y. *Paradise In Search of a Future*. June 22–August 24.

19th World Wide Video Festival, Amsterdam. October 10–November 11. Exh. cat.

Zentrum für Kunst und Medientechnologie Karlsruhe, Karlsruhe. *CTRL [SPACE]: Rhetorics of Surveillance from Bentham to Big Brother*. October 12, 2001–February 24, 2002. Exh. cat.

2002
Atlanta Contemporary Art Center. *Paradise in Search of a Future*. January 25–March 23.

Whitney Museum of American Art, New York. Whitney Biennial. March 7–May 26. Exh. cat.

Documenta 11, Kassel. June 8–September 15. Exh. cat.

Kunsthaus Tacheles, Berlin. *Bi-Rout*. May. Exh. cat.

Fundació Antoni Tàpies, Barcelona. *Representacions Àrabs Contemporànies. Beirut/Liban*. May 3–July 14. Exh. cat. Traveled to: Witte de With Center for Contemporary Art, Rotterdam, September 15–November 24, as *Contemporary Arab Representations*; Bildmuseet, Umeå University, February 9–April 21, 2003.

Palais des Beaux-Arts, Brussels (co-produced by the Arab Image Foundation, Beirut). May 4–May 26. *Mapping Sitting: On Portraiture and Photography*. Exh. cat. Traveled to: Die Photographische Sammlung, Cologne, September 2002; Kunstnernes Hus, Oslo, February 2003; Haus der Kulturen der Welt, Berlin, March 2003; World Wide Video Festival, Amsterdam, May 2003; Videobasil Festival, São Paulo; Centro de Estudios Juan de Mariana, Toledo, November 2003; National Museum of Contemporary Art, Athens, January 2004; Musée Nicéphore Niépce, Chalon-sur-Saône, March 2004; Centre pour l'Image Contemporaine, Geneva, April 2004; Beiteddine Art Festival, July 2004; Singapore Contemporary Art Museum, October–November 2004; Grey Art Gallery, New York University, New York, January 11–April 2, 2005; Krannert Art Museum, University of Illinois at Urbana-Champaign, April

15–June 5, 2005; Douglas F. Cooley Memorial Art Gallery, Reed College, Portland, Ore., August 22–September 30, 2005; Carleton College, Northfield, Minn., October–November 2006.

Watson Institute for International Studies, Brown University, Providence. *The Perplexities of Security. 911+1.* September 8–20.

Memling Museum, Bruges. *What? A Tale in Free Images.* October.

Rhode Island School of Design Museum, Providence. *Crisis Response.* November 8, 2002–January 12, 2003.

Zentrum für Kunst und Medientechnologie, Karlsruhe. *Bilder Codes: Internationaler Medien Kunstpreis.* November 9, 2002–January 6, 2003. Exh. cat.

Real Art Ways, Hartford, Conn. *This Is Then.* November 23, 2002–February 15, 2003. Exh. brochure.

2003
Neue Galerie, Graz. M_ARS–KUNST UND KRIEG. January 10–March 26.

The Curve, Barbican Centre, London. *Witness: Contemporary Artists Document Our Time.* February 13–April 27.

Carnegie Art Center, North Tonawanda, N.Y. *Art of the Encyclopedic.* February 15–March 29.

Haus der Kulturen der Welt, Berlin. *DisORIENTation.* March 20–May 11.

Paço das Artes, São Paulo. *A Respeito de Situações Reais.* April 29–June 1. Exh. cat.

50th Biennale di Venezia, Venice. *Dreams and Conflicts: The Dictatorship of the Viewer.* June 15–November 2. Exh. cat.

Galerie Christian Nagel, Cologne. *Haupt- und Nebenwege.* June 28–August 15.

CEPA Gallery, Buffalo, N.Y. *Fresh Meat.* September 19–December 20.

Herter Art Gallery, University of Massachusetts, Amherst. *Global Priority.* October 27–November 23.

Whitechapel Gallery, London. *A Short History of Performance Part II.* November 18–23. Exh. cat.

National Museum of Contemporary Art, Athens. *Synopsis 3: Testimonies. Between Fiction and Reality.* December 10, 2003–February 29, 2004. Exh. cat.

Kunstverein Hannover. *Die Sehnsucht des Kartografen.* December 13, 2003–February 1, 2004. Exh. cat.

2004
Krannert Art Museum, University of Illinois at Urbana-Champaign. *Beyond East and West: Seven Transnational Artists.* January 23–April 4. Exh. cat. Traveled to: Louisiana State University Museum of Art, Baton Rouge, April 16–September 4; Hood Museum of Art, Dartmouth College, Hanover, N.H., October 9–December 12; Williams College Museum of Art, Williamstown, Mass., February 19–May 15, 2005.

Fundació "la Caixa", Barcelona. *'Ficcions' documentals.* March 10–June 27. Exh. cat.

Museum of Contemporary Art, Sydney. *+Witness.* March 12–May 16. Exh. cat.

Massachusetts Museum of Contemporary Art, North Adams. *The Interventionists: Art in the Social Sphere.* May 2004–March 2005. Exh. cat.

National Museum of Contemporary Art, Athens. *Transcultures.* July 6–December 31. Exh. cat.

6. Internationale Foto-Triennale 2004, Esslingen. *Recherche—Entdeckt!: Bildarchive der Unsichtbarkeiten.* July 18–October 3. Exh. cat.

Centre d'Art Contemporain, Geneva. *Ethnic Marketing.* October 21–December 5. Exh. cat.

Taipei Biennial 2004, Taipei Fine Arts Museum. *Do You Believe in Reality?* October 23, 2004–January 23, 2005. Exh. cat.

Australian Centre for the Moving Image, Melbourne. *Proof: The Act of Seeing with One's Own Eyes.* December 9, 2004–February 13, 2005. Exh. cat.

2005
Contemporary Arts Center, Cincinnati. *Incorporated: A Recent (Incomplete) History of Infiltrations, Actions and Propositions Utilizing Contemporary Art.* February 11–May 8.

P.S. 1 Contemporary Art Center, a MoMA affiliate, Long Island City, N.Y. *Greater New York 2005.* March 13–September 26. Exh. cat.

Museum für Moderne Kunst, Frankfurt am Main. *What's New Pussycat? die Neuerwerbungen 2002–2005.* March 19–July 31. Exh. cat.

Centre for Contemporary Arts, Glasgow. *Risk: Creative Action in Political Culture.* March 26–May 14.

Sfeir-Semler Gallery, Beirut. *Flight 405.* April 9–June 18.

Château de Nyon, Nyon. *Reprocessing Reality.* April 18–May 29. Exh. cat.

Alexander and Bonin, New York. *Mirage.* June 4–July 29.

Passerelle Centre d'art contemporain, Brest. *In Absentia.* June 22–October 15. Exh. cat.

The Museum of Modern Art, New York. *New Work/New Acquisitions.* June 29–September 26.

Künstlerhaus Palais Thurn & Taxis, Bregenz. *Go Between.* Organized by the Bregenzer Kunstverein/Magazin 4, Bregenz. July 17–September 4. Exh. cat.

CaixaForum Barcelona. *Tiempos de vídeo, 1965–2005. Colección nouveaux médias del Centre Pompidou con la participación de la colección de arte contemporáneo, Fundación "La Caixa".* September 28, 2005–January 8, 2006. Exh. cat. Traveled to: Taipei Fine Arts Museum, April 29–July 23, 2006, as *New Media Collection 1965–2005 Centre Pompidou* (exh. cat.); Miami Art Central, Miami, September 20–December 10, 2006, as *Video: An Art, a History, 1965–2005*; Museum of Contemporary Art Australia, Sydney, December 15, 2006–February 25, 2007, as *Centre Pompidou Video Art: 1965–2005*; Australian Center for the Moving Image, Melbourne, March 22–May 27, 2007, as *Centre Pompidou Video Art: 1965–2005*; Museu Nacional de Arte Contemporânea do Chiado, Lisbon, October 19, 2007–January 6, 2008, as *Centre Pompidou Novos Media 1965-2003*; Nicosia Municipal Arts Center, March–May 2008; Honolulu Academy of Arts, June–September 2008; Musée Fabre, Montpellier, October 2008–January 2009.

Center for Contemporary Art, Glasgow. *In the Poem about Love You Don't Write the Word Love.* November 12, 2005–January 28, 2006. Exh. cat. Traveled to: Overgaden Institute of Contemporary Art, Copenhagen, November 10, 2007–January 20, 2008.

Extra City Kunsthal, Antwerp. *Information/Transformation.* November 17–December 4.

2006
La Maison Rouge, Paris. *Une vision du monde—la collection video d'Jean-Conrad et Isabel Lemaître.* February 19–May 14.

The Museum of Modern Art, New York. *Without Boundary: Seventeen Ways of Looking.* February 26–May 22. Exh. cat.

La Maison des Arts, Malakoff. *Vidéos Séquence 2.* March 22–May 7.

SculptureCenter, New York. *Grey Flags.* May 7–July 30. Exh. cat. Traveled to: Musée d'Art Contemporain de Bordeaux, December 20, 2006–March 18, 2007.

Modern Art Oxford. *Out of Beirut.* May 13–July 16. Exh. cat.

La Tôlerie, Clermont-Ferrand. *Ah, les belles images! . . .* May 15–July 13. Exh. cat.

The British Museum, London. *Word into Art: Artists of the Modern Middle East.* May 18–September 3. Exh. cat.

Museum Moderner Kunst, Vienna. *Why Pictures Now.* June 9–October 1. Exh. cat.

Heidelberger Kunstverein. *100 Tage = 100 Videos.* September 1–December 31.

Det Nationale Fotomuseum, Copenhagen. *Under the Same Sky.* September 5, 2006–January 27, 2007.

2006 Biennale of Sydney. *Zones of Contact.* September 15–October 22. Exh. cat.

San Francisco Camerawork. *Ghost in the Machine.* September 16–November 18.

Real Art Ways, Hartford, Conn. *Faith.* 2005–6. Exh. cat.

Gallery Nova, Zagreb. *Dataesthetics.* December 1, 2006–January 6, 2007. Exh. cat.

2007
De Appel Arts Centre, Amsterdam. *Het Schaduwkabinet: 'Distorted Fabric.'* January 19–28.

Koldo Mitxelena Kulturunea, San Sebastián. *Documentos. La memoria del futuro.* January 25–March 17. Traveled to: Museo de Arte Contemporáneo de Vigo, March 30–June 24 (exh. cat.).

Palazzo delle Papesse, Siena. *System Error: War Is a Force That Gives Us Meaning.* February 3–May 6. Exh. cat.

The Photographers' Gallery, London. *Deutsche Börse Photography Prize 07.* February 9–April 9. Exh. cat. Traveled to: C/O Berlin, May 10–July 8; Deutsche Börse Group headquarters, Frankfurt, September 3–October 19.

Sala Verónicas and Centro Párraga, Murcia. *2Move: Estéticas Migratorias.* March 8–May 13. Traveled to: Zuiderzee Museum, Enkhuizen, September 20 2007–January 6, 2008 (exh. cat.), as *2Move: Migration + Video*; Stenersenmuseet, Oslo, March 27–May 11, 2008, as *2Move/Migratory Aesthetics*; Solstice Arts Centre, Navan, May 3–June 2, 2008; Belfast Exposed, Belfast, May 3–June 6, 2008. Exh. cat.

Fundación Bancaja, Valencia. *2Move. Movimiento Doble, Estéticas Migratorias.* March 8–May 13. Exh. cat.

Auckland Art Gallery. *Turbulence: 3rd Auckland Triennial 2007.* March 9–June 3. Exh. cat.

Kunstmuseum Stuttgart. *Cross-border. Fotografie und Videokunst aus dem MUMOK Wien.* March 24–June 17. Exh. cat.

Casino Luxembourg Forum d'Art Contemporain. *L'oeil-écran ou la nouvelle image. 100 vidéos pour repenser le monde.* March 24–June 17.

aMAZE Cultural Lab, Milan. *Re-Thinking Beirut.* March 27–May 13.

Centrum Sztuki Współczesnej Łaźn, Gdańsk. *Last News.* April 13–May 20. Exh. cat.

Solomon R. Guggenheim Museum, New York. *The Shapes of Space*. April 14–September 5.

Museum of Cycladic Art, Athens. *Her(his)tory*. May 22–September 29.

Fotomuseum Winterthur. *Forschen und Erfinden. Die Recherche mit Bildern in der zeitgenössischen Fotografie/Research and Invention–Investigations with Images in Contemporary Photography*. June 2–August 19. Exh. cat.

Thyssen-Bornemisza Art Contemporary, Vienna. *Shooting Back*. June 6–October 28. Exh. cat.

6th Mercosul Biennial, Porto Alegre. September 1–November 18.

Sainsbury Centre for Visual Arts, Norwich. *AfterShock: Conflict, Violence and Resolution in Contemporary Art*. July 14–September 2. Exh. cat. Traveled to: University of Hertfordshire Galleries, September 20–October 28.

Walker Art Center, Minneapolis. *Brave New Worlds*. October 4, 2007–February 17, 2008. Exh. cat.

2008

Ausstellungshalle Zeitgenössische Kunst Münster. *Lügen.nirgends. Zwischen Fiktion, Dokumentation und Wirklichkeit*. January 12–March 30. Exh. cat.

International Center of Photography, New York. *Archive Fever: Uses of the Document in Contemporary Art*. January 18–May 4. Exh. cat.

4 Triennale Zeitgenössischer Kunst Oberschwaben. *Nichts zu deklarieren*. April 4–June 22. Exh. cat.

The Museum of Modern Art, New York. *Color Chart: Reinventing Color, 1950 to Today*. March 2–May 12. Exh. cat. Traveled to: Tate Liverpool, May 29–September 13.

The Amie and Tony James Gallery, The Graduate Center, The City University of New York. *Deadpan: Photography, History, Politics*. May 16–June 28. Exh. cat.

The Power Plant, Toronto. *Not Quite How I Remember It*. June 7–September 1. Exh. cat.

Carré d'Art-Musée d'art contemporain de Nîmes. *Scènes du Sud II. Méditerranée orientale*. June 13–September 21. Exh. cat.

Zwirner & Wirth, New York. *Quiet Politics*. June 26–August 29.

Villa Rufolo, Ravelo. *Mediterraneo 2008*. Organized by the Perna Foundation. June 27–August 24. Exh. cat.

Nikolaj Kunsthallen, Copenhagen. *U-Turn: Quadrennial for Contemporary Art*. September 5–November 9. Exh. cat.

Statens Museum for Kunst, Copenhagen. *Reality Check*. September 6, 2008–January 4, 2009. Exh. cat.

FRAC Provence-Alpes-Côtes d'Azur. *Éclats de frontières*. September 19–December 13.

New York Center for Art and Media Studies. *Other Certainties*. September 19–October 24.

Center for Curatorial Studies, Bard Galleries, and Hessel Museum of Art, Bard College, Annandale-on-Hudson, N.Y. *The Greenroom: Reconsidering the Documentary and Contemporary Art*. September 27, 2008–February 1, 2009. Exh. cat.

Pratt Manhattan Gallery, New York. *Zones of Conflict*. November 19, 2008–February 7, 2009.

The Showroom, London. *Curating Architecture*. Organized as part of the Curating Architecture research project, Department of Arts, Goldsmiths, University of London. November 20–December 14. Exh. brochure.

2009

Paula Cooper Gallery, New York. *Commentary*. February 19–March 14.

Fotomuseum Winterthur. *Darkside II–Fotografische Macht und fotografierte Gewalt, Krankheit und Tod*. September 5–November 15. Exh. cat.

CREAM: International Festival for Arts and Media Yokohama 2009. *Deep Images: Why We Need Images to Live?* October 31–November 29. Exh. cat.

Martin-Gropius-Bau, Berlin. *Taswir–Pictorial Mapping of Islam and Modernity*. November 5, 2009–January 18, 2010.

Hockney Gallery, Royal College of Art, London. *Suns Neither Rise Nor Set*. December 9–18.

2010

Atlanta Contemporary Art Center. *Substitute Teacher*. March 5–May 16. Exh. cat.

Paula Cooper Gallery, New York. *Reprise*. April 29–May 28.

Invisible Exports, New York. *A Vernacular of Violence: Eric Baudelaire, Rita Sobral Campos, Claire Fontaine, Lisa Kirk, Sylvère Lotringer, and Walid Raad*. May 14–June 20.

Centro de Artes Visuales de Cáceres, Fundación Helga de Alvear. *Márgenes de Silencio*. June 3, 2010–February 20, 2011. Exh. cat.

Country Club, Cincinnati. *Pictures and Statues*. June 11–July 31.

La Virreina Centre de la Imatge, Barcelona. *Antiphotojournalism*. July 5–October 10.

John Hansard Gallery, Southampton. *Ground Level: Hayward Touring Curatorial Open II*. June 29–August 21. Traveled to: QUAD, Derby, September 18–October 31; Mostyn, Llandudno, November 20, 2010–January 3, 2011; Leamington Spa Art Gallery & Museum, February 17–April 10, 2011.

Haus der Kunst, Munich. *The Future of Tradition—the Tradition of Future 100 Years after the Exhibition "Masterpieces of Muhammadan Art" in Munich*. September 17, 2010–January 9, 2011.

MMK Museum für Moderne Kunst, Frankfurt am Main. *The Lucid Evidence. Fotographie aus der Sammlung des MMK*. September 25, 2010–April 25, 2011. Exh. cat.

Scotland's Centre for Photography, Stills Gallery, Edinburgh. *Social Documents: The Ethics of Encounter*. November 6–28.

Mathaf: Arab Museum of Modern Art, Doha. *Told, Untold, Retold: 23 Stories of Journeys through Time and Place*. December 30, 2010–May 28, 2011. Exh. cat.

Guggenheim Museum Bilbao. *Haunted: Contemporary Photography, Video, Performance*. November 6, 2010–March 13, 2011. Exh. cat.

2011

Museo Tamayo de Arte Contemporáneo, Mexico City. *Abstract Possible*. March 10–August 28.

Sharjah Biennial 10. *Plot For A Biennial*. March 16–May 16. Exh. cat.

Denver Art Museum. *BLINK! Light, Sound, and the Moving Image*. March 13–May 01. Exh. cat.

Foam Fotografiemuseum Amsterdam. *Antiphotojournalism*. April 1–June 8. Exh. cat.

Guggenheim Museum Bilbao. *The Luminous Interval: The D. Daskalopoulos Collection*. April 12–September 11. Exh. cat.

Paula Cooper Gallery, New York. *Locations*. April 28–July 1.

Krakow Photomonth Festival 2011. *Alias*. May 13–June 12.

Edith-Russ-Haus für Medienkunst, Oldenburg. *Wild Sky*. May 27–August 14. Exh. cat.

QUAD, Derby. *All That Fits: The Aesthetics of Journalism*. May 28–July 31.

Arnolfini, Bristol. *Museum Show Part 1*. September 24–November 19.

2012

Paula Cooper Gallery, New York. *Sophie Calle, Christian Marclay, Paul Pfeiffer, Walid Raad, Michael Sailstorfer, Carey Young*. January 7–February 25.

The Museum of Modern Art, New York. *The Shaping of New Visions: Photography, Film, Photobook*. April 16, 2012–April 21, 2013.

Jüdisches Museum Wein, Vienna. FREMDE ÜBERALL/FOREIGNERS EVERYWHERE. May 24–October 7.

DOCUMENTA (13), Kassel. *Scratching on Things I Could Disavow*. June 9–September 16. Exh. cat. and exh. brochure.

SITE Santa Fe, N.M. *More Real? Art in the Age of Truthiness*. July 8, 2012–January 6, 2013. Traveled to: Minneapolis Institute of Arts, March 3–June 9, 2013. Exh. cat.

Anthony Reynolds Gallery, London. *Summer Show*. July 26–September 8.

Museum of Arts and Design, New York. *Doris Duke's Shangri La: Architecture, Landscape, and Islamic Art*. September 7, 2012–February 17, 2013. Organized by the Doris Duke Foundation for Islamic Art, New York. Exh. cat. Traveled to: The Norton Museum of Art, West Palm Beach, March 16–July 15, 2013; Nasher Museum of Art at Duke University, Durham, N.C., August 29, 2013–January 5, 2014; University of Michigan Museum of Art, Ann Arbor, January 25–May 4, 2014; Nevada Museum of Art, Reno, May 31–September 7, 2014; Los Angeles Municipal Art Gallery, October 26–December 28, 2014; Honolulu Museum of Art, February 12–June 7, 2015.

Paula Cooper Gallery, New York. *Walid Raad and David Diao*. September 22–November 3.

Victoria and Albert Museum, London. *Light from the Middle East: New Photography*. November 13, 2012–April 7, 2013. Exh. cat.

Forum Schlossplatz Aarau. *Amman Journal: Public, Space, Art*. November 10, 2012–January 27, 2013. Exh. cat.

2013

Hasselblad Center, Göteborgs Konstmuseum, Gothenburg. *Still Life/Work Life: From the Hasselblad Foundation Collection*. March 23–May 19. Exh. cat.

The Wallach Art Gallery, Columbia University, New York. *Speak, Memory*. May 1–June 8. Exh. brochure.

International Center of Photography, New York. *A Different Kind of Order: The ICP Triennial*. May 17–September 22. Exh. cat.

Ashkal Alwan, Beirut. *Home Works 6*. May 17–June 10.

Galerie Cécile Fakhoury, Abidjan. *Mécaniques des Fluides (Naviguer, Transporter, Filmer)*. June 14–July 27. Exh. brochure.

Art Basel. *Unlimited*. June 13–16.

Aichi Triennial 2013. *Awakening—Where Are We Standing?—Earth, Memory and Resurrection*. August 10–October 27. Exh. cat.

Peninsula Arts Gallery, Plymouth University, Devon. *Document*. September 13–October 12.

Performance Chronology
Compiled by Kristin Poor

Paula Cooper Gallery, New York. *Jonathan Borofsky, Sam Durant, Charles Gaines, Wayne Gonzales, Liz Glynn, Hans Haacke, Walid Raad, Andres Serrano*. October 10–26.

2014
Murray Guy, New York. *Someone Like You*. January 16–February 22.

Marrakech Bienniale 5. WHERE ARE WE NOW? February 26–March 31. Exh. cat.

Townhouse Gallery, Cairo. *A Guest without a Host Is a Ghost*. May 5–June 18.

Prison Sainte-Anne, Avignon. *La Disparition des Lucioles*. May 18–November 25. Exh. cat.

Fundação de Serralves, Porto. *Histories: Works from the Serralves Collection*. May 29–September 21.

Centre Pompidou, Paris. *Une Histoire, art, architecture et design, des années 80 à aujourd'hui*. July 2, 2014–March 7, 2016.

Museum der Moderne, Salzburg. *Art/Histories*. July 26–October 26.

Pérez Art Museum Miami. *Global Positioning Systems*. August 19, 2014–August 15, 2015.

31st Bienal de São Paulo. *How to Talk about Things That Don't Exist*. September 6–December 7. Exh. cat.

Contemporary Arts Center, Cincinnati. *Memory Palace*. September 12, 2014–February 22, 2015.

2015
Muzeum Sztuki Nowoczesnej w Warszawie, Warsaw. *Lest the Two Seas Meet*. February 12–August 23.

Sfeir-Semler Gallery, Beirut. *Gallery 3010*. April 2–August 1.

MAK–Austrian Museum of Applied Arts/Contemporary Art, Vienna. Vienna Biennale 2015: *Ideas for Change*. June 11–October 4.

Walid Raad's performances developed out of the form of the artist talk and the question-and-answer discussions following his video screenings, as well as from his teaching experience as a professor. He initially called them "lecture/performances," in fact, but no longer finds the name productive and stopped using it around 2008. He used that term when appearing in the spaces of art, experimental theater, and performance; he has also called his performances "presentations," when staging them in academic or conference settings, and "artist talks," when presenting them in art schools. These designations may all refer to the same work; the same scripts, images, videos, and PowerPoint displays have reappeared across these different settings, even while their titles, exact scripts, and durations may have remained in flux.

The entries below are grouped first by performance, then chronologically by performance date.

Fishing for documents: Case studies from The Atlas Group Archive (1999–2001)

70 minutes
The Atlas Group in collaboration with Walid Raad

"Fishing for Documents" was the title of a symposium Raad had attended in Berlin in 1992 organized by the artist group Botschaft e.V. Raad liked the conference title and used it. At some point, he recalls, the conference organizers rightly objected to his using the title, so he renamed the performance *The loudest muttering is over*. (Unless otherwise noted, the source for such notes as these is a conversation with the artist, February 11, 2015.)

1999
"Building City and Nation: Space, History, Memory and Identity" conference. Center for Behavioral Studies, American University of Beirut. July 1–3.

Department of Visual Arts, Notre Dame University, Beirut. Date uncertain.

2000
Department of Architecture, American University of Beirut. May 22.

Ayloul Festival, Samaha House, Beirut. September 2.

"Rethinking Marxism 2000" conference, University of Massachusetts, Amherst. September 21–24.

Kunst-Werke Institute for Contemporary Art, Berlin. December 10.

2001
Palais des Beaux-Arts, Brussels. May 16.

Bibliothèque Solvay, Brussels. May 24.

B-SPACE.BE, Brussels. May 26.

Du bist die Welt: 24 Episodes about Life Today. Wiener Festwochen, Künstlerhaus Wien, Vienna. June 1–3.

The loudest muttering is over: Documents from The Atlas Group Archive (2001–5)

75 minutes
The Atlas Group in collaboration with Walid Raad

The loudest muttering is over continued to evolve as works were added to and deleted from The Atlas Group Archive. In addition to images and texts from other Atlas Group works, it included at various points the videos *Miraculous beginnings/No, illness is neither here nor there* (pp. 68–69), *Hostage: The Bachar tapes (English version)* (pp. 90–93), and *I only wish that I could weep* (pp. 94–97).

2001
9e Biennale de l'Image en Mouvement, Geneva. November 8 and 9.

University of Buffalo. November 26.

2002
Fondation Cartier, Paris. January 10.

"Contemporary Arab Representations" colloquium. Akademie Schloss Solitude, Stuttgart. February 7–9.

Saratoga Springs Public Library, N.Y. March 8.

Whitney Biennial. Whitney Museum of American Art, New York. March 27 and April 10.

The Cooper Union, New York. April 19.

Representacions Àrabs Contemporànies. Fondació Antoni Tàpies, Barcelona. June 21.

Eurokaz festival, ZKM, Zagreb. June 27 and 28.

Documenta 11. Kassel. July 26 or 27.

The Truth about the Nearly Real. 4. Internationale Sommerakademie, Künstlerhaus Mousonturm, Frankfurt. August 28 and 29.

Middle Eastern Studies Association, CUNY Graduate Center, New York. September 27.

This Is Then. Real Art Ways, Hartford, Conn. December 6.

2003
Columbia University, New York. February.

Kunstnernes Hus, Oslo. February 8.

Carnegie Mellon University, Pittsburgh. April 17.

World Wide Video Festival, Amsterdam. May 10.

Hammer Museum, University of California, Los Angeles. June 3.

In Transit 03 Festival, Haus der Kulturen der Welt, Berlin. June 13.

Belluard Bollwerk International Festival, Fribourg. July 4.

Laokoon Festival 2003, Kampnagel, Hamburg. August 29.

Possible Narratives—Art Practices in Lebanon and 14º Festival Internacional de Arte Eletrônica Videobrasil, São Paulo. September 28.

Spiel Art Theater Festival. Gasteig Black Box, Munich. November 7.

A Short History of Performance Part II: The Lecture as a Work of Art. Whitechapel Gallery, London. November 22.

The Truth Will Be Known When The Last Witness Is Dead: Documents From The Fakhouri File in The Atlas Group Archive. La Galerie, Noisy-le Sec. November 29.

Portland Institute of Contemporary Art, Portland, Ore. December 12.

Arts International, New York. Date uncertain.

2004
"Artists at the Institute." Institute of Fine Arts, New York University, 2003–4 academic year, likely spring semester.

International School of New Media (ISNM), St. Petri, Lübeck. Between January 20 and February 7.

Hochschule für bildende Künste, Hamburg. January 22.

Die Sehnsucht des Kartografen. Kunstverein Hannover. January 28.

Les Laboratoires d'Aubervilliers. January 30.

BIT Teatergarasjen, Bergen. February 4 and 5.

"Beyond East and West: Transnational Art Today" conference. Krannert Art Museum, University of Illinois, Champaign-Urbana. February 7.

Sculpture Department, Yale University, New Haven, Conn. February 18.

School of the Art Institute of Chicago. February 25.

Department of Art History, Visual Art & Theory, University of British Columbia, Vancouver. March 17.

Rensselaer Polytechnic Institute (RPI), Albany, N.Y. April 7.

Wexner Center for the Arts, Ohio State University, Columbus. April 15.

Indoor Fireworks. London International Festival of Theater (LIFT) and Forced Entertainment. Riverside Studios, London. October 29 and 30.

Kodak Lecture Series. Reyerson University, Toronto. November 26.

2005
I Feel a Great Desire to Meet the Masses Once Again: A Project by Walid Raad and The Atlas Group. Agnes Etherington Art Centre, Queen's University, Kingston, Ont. February 5.

University of Cincinnati. March 17.

Reed College, Portland, Ore. September 23.

Funny How Thin the Line Is: Documents from The Atlas Group Archive. FACT, Liverpool. November 11.

In the poem about love you don't write the word love. Centre for Contemporary Arts, Glasgow. November 12.

2006
The Dead Weight of a Quarrel Hangs: Documents from The Atlas Group Archive. The Kitchen, New York. January 7.

Montreal Museum of Fine Arts. January 25.

University of Wisconsin in Milwaukee. February 10.

Théâtre 71, Malakoff. March 14 and 15.

Centre dramatique national de Normandie (CDN), Caen. March 17–19.

Le Lieu Unique, Nantes. March 21 and 22.

Herbert F. Johnson Museum of Art, Cornell University, Ithaca, N.Y. October 16.

2007
School of Art, California State University, Long Beach. Spring.

Auckland Triennale, Auckland. March 12.

Haudenschild Garage in collaboration with the University of California, San Diego, La Jolla. April 10.

The Atlas Group (1989–2004). Un proyecto de Walid Raad. Museo Tamayo Arte Contemporáneo, Mexico City. April 26.

Brave New Worlds. Walker Art Center, Minneapolis. October 25.

Art Papers, Emory University, Atlanta. November 7.

Meeting Points 5, Townhouse Factory, Cairo. November 15.

Meeting Points 5, Ness El fen, Tunis. November 17.

2008
University of California, Davis. January 14.

Crossroads Theatre, Rutgers University, New Brunswick, N.J. April 30.

U-Turn Quadrennial. Camp X Aveny, Copenhagen. November 7.

2009
Modern Art Museum of Fort Worth. February 10.

Festival Escena Contemporánea. Museo Nacional Centro de Arte Reina Sofía, Madrid. February 18 and 19.

2011
Phillips Collection, Washington, D.C. April 13.

Walid Raad—2011 Hasselblad Award Winner. Hasselblad Centre, Göteborgs Konstmuseum, Gothenburg. November 11.

Civilizationally, we do not dig holes to bury ourselves: An interview with Souheil Bachar (2002)

60 minutes
The Atlas Group in collaboration with Walid Raad

This performance included a screening of *Hostage: The Bachar tapes (English version)* (pp. 90–93) followed by a scripted question-and-answer session with planted and regular audience members.

2002
Representacions Àrabs Contemporànies. Fondació Antoni Tàpies, Barcelona. June 20.

Documenta 11, Kassel. July 26 or 27.

The Truth about the Nearly Real. 4. Internationale Sommerakademie. Künstlerhaus Mousonturm, Frankfurt. August 30 and 31.

2003
World Wide Video Festival, Amsterdam. May 10.

In Transit 03 Festival. Haus der Kulturen der Welt, Berlin. June 14.

Laokoon Festival 2003. Kampnagel, Hamburg. August 30 and 31.

Spiel Art Festival. Gasteig Black Box, Munich. November 8.

Cinema Project, Portland, Ore. December 13.

We can make rain but no one came to ask (2003)

60 minutes
Walid Raad with Tony Chakar

This performance included a video and a PowerPoint presentation.

2003
Künstlerhaus Mousonturm, Frankfurt. November 30.

My neck is thinner than a hair: A history of the car bomb in the 1975–1991 Lebanese Wars_Volume 1 (2004–6)

70 minutes
The Atlas Group in collaboration with Bilal Khbeiz, Tony Chakar, and Walid Raad

The performance, which included a video of the same title, emerged from the project *My neck is thinner than a hair: Engines* (pp. 74–77), here expanded to focus on a single car bomb. According to the program notes for the January 28, 2006, performance at The Kitchen, New York, "This work is part of an on-going investigation by The Atlas Group into the events and experiences surrounding the use of car bombs in the 1975–91 Lebanese wars. The Atlas Group examines the multiple dimensions—social, political, economic, military, technological, psychological and epistemic—of the wars and investigates the public and private discourses surrounding the 3,600 car bombs that were detonated during this period. For the past year, Tony Chakar, Bilal Khbeiz, and Walid Raad have been working on the first volume of this multi-volume project. This research will result in a 70-minute mixed media presentation/performance about and around the events, experiences, forms, and objects of a car bomb that was detonated on January 21, 1986 in the Furn Ech Chubak area of Beirut."

2004
MediaScope. The Museum of Modern Art, New York. March 15.

Ashkal Alwan, Beirut. May 6 and 7.

Kunstenfestivaldesarts. Kaaitheater, Brussels. May 12–15.

Spectacles Vivants. Centre Pompidou, Paris. May 26 and 27.

In Transit Festival 04. Haus der Kulturen der Welt, Berlin. June 5.

London International Festival of Theater (LIFT). Institute of Contemporary Art, London. June 7 and 8.

Theaterfestival "Welt in Basel." Kasernenareal, Basel. August 18–20.

Flying Circus Project. Theaterworks, Singapore. December 17 and 18.

2005
California College of the Arts, San Francisco. February 24.

Hamburger Kunsthalle, Hamburg. March 30.

Kampnagel, Hamburg. June 2 and 3.

Kiss the Frog: The Art of Transformation. Nasjonalmuseet for Konst, Oslo. August 26 and 27.

Teaterhuset Avant Garden, Trondheim. August 31 and September 1.

BIT Teatergarasjen, Bergen. September 3 and 4.

The New School, New York. December 6.

2006
The Kitchen, New York. February 28.

Biennale of Sydney. Sydney Opera House, Sydney. June 10 and 11.

2007
Auckland Triennale, Auckland. March 10.

"America and Its Wars" conference. University of California, Berkeley. April 13.

University of Minnesota, Minneapolis. October 26.

2008
REDCAT, Los Angeles. January 16.

List Art Center, Brown University, Providence. April 9.

"Visual Memories" symposium. University of Rochester, N.Y. May 8.

U-Turn Quadrennial. Camp X Aveny, Copenhagen. November 8.

2009
Istanbul International Contemporary Dance & Performance Festival (iDANS). Garajistanbul, Istanbul. May 21 and 22.

I feel a great desire to meet the masses once again (2005–7)

45 minutes
Walid Raad

From the program notes by Walid Raad: "In November 2004, returning to New York City from a family visit to Rochester (New York—upstate New York), I am detained and interrogated by the police and the FBI for several hours at the Rochester International Airport. As my luggage is unpacked in front of me, I am baffled by what I had packed and by what I am shown (photographs, videotapes, essays and books, bank statements, etc), and by the circumstances that put me in this situation. This encounter is the diluted version of others, such those experienced by Khaled el-Masri, Maher Arar or Mamdouh Habib. Masri, for example, was kidnapped in 2003 by Macedonian police, drugged and shipped to Afghanistan where he was detained, tortured and interrogated by U.S. intelligence officers and subsequently released to a German government that thinks he made it all up. This form of government-sponsored kidnapping, known as rendition, began in the 1990s by the CIA but has increased dramatically in the past four years. *I Feel a Great Desire to Meet the Masses Once Again* will offer narratives, thoughts and reflections on detention and rendition."

The presentations in 2005 were collaborations with the Visible Collective and the artist Naeem Mohaiemen, who came on stage after Raad to give a five-minute presentation. This was followed by a question-and-answer session with both Mohaiemen and Raad.

2005
Theater der Welt 2005. Kunstmuseum Stuttgart. June 22 and 26.

Homeworks III, Ashkal Alwan, Beirut. November 20 and 22.

2006
Hebbel am Ufer, Berlin. October 24–26.

Teaterhuset Avant Garden, Trondheim. October 28 and 29.

Black Box Teater, Oslo. November 1 and 2.

BIT Teatergarasjen, Bergen. November 4 and 5.

2007
The Holland Festival. Theater Bellevue, Amsterdam. June 1 and 2.

Les Halles de Schaerbeek, Brussels. October 4 and 5.

Festival d'Automne, Centre Pompidou, Paris. October 12 and 13.

Scratching on things I could disavow: Walkthrough (2008–ongoing)

70 minutes
Walid Raad

Raad has presented this performance both in gallery spaces, within an installation of related sculptural and video works, and in theater spaces, in the format of a lecture with a PowerPoint slide show. See pp. 110–47.

2009
Scratching on Things I Could Disavow: A History of Art in the Arab World, Part 1_Volume 1_Chapter 1 (Beirut: 1992–2005). REDCAT, Los Angeles. April 9.

Scratching on Things I Could Disavow: A History of Art in the Arab World, Part I_Volume 1_Chapter 1: Beirut (1992–2005). Fondazione Antonio Ratti, Como. July 2.

Scratching on Things I Could Disavow. Anthony Reynolds Gallery, London. September 23–26.

Scratching on Things I Could Disavow: A History of Art in the Arab World/Part I_ Volume 1_Chapter 1 (Beirut: 1992–2005). Paula Cooper Gallery, New York. November 5–7.

Scratching on Things I Could Disavow: A History of Art in the Arab World: Part I_Volume 1_Chapter 1 (Beirut: 1992–2005). Sfeir-Semler Gallery, Hamburg. November 12–14.

2010
Festival d'Automne, Le Centquatre, Paris. With Carlos Chahine. November 6 and 7, November 9–14, November 16–21, November 23–28, November 30, December 1–5.

2011
Bildmuseet, Umeå University, Umeå. February 19.

Kunstenfestivaldesarts. Les Halles de Schaerbeek, Brussels. With Carlos Chahine. May 8–15.

Wiener Festwochen. Thyssen-Bornemisza Art Contemporary, Vienna. May 26–28, June 7–12 (with Walid Raad), May 29–31, June 1–6, 11, and 13–15 (with Markus Reymann).

Hebbel am Ufer, Berlin. June 24–26 and 28–30.

2012
Institute of Fine Arts, New York University. February 23.

Carpenter Center, Harvard University, Cambridge, Mass. March 1.

Tensta Konsthall, Tensta, Sweden. March 24.

Scratching on things I could disavow. DOCUMENTA (13), Kassel. June 7–10 and 12–16, July 10–15, September 10–16.

2014
Eurokaz festival, Muzej suvremene umjetnosti, Zagreb. January 11.

Binghamton University, State University of New York, Binghamton. April 24.

Walid Raad: Postface. University Museum of Contemporary Art, University of Massachusetts, Amherst. September 17.

"Eikones." Schaulager, Basel. November 14.

2015
Walid Raad. The Museum of Modern Art, New York.

Other

2000
Miraculous Beginnings. Kahlil Gibran colloquium, Nicolas Sursock Museum, Beirut. January 27.

During this event Raad presented archival material on Kahlil Gibran as annotated by The Atlas Group's fictional historian Dr. Fadl Fakhouri. It is described in M.G., "Colloque au musée Nicolas Sursock: Vues contradictoires sur Gibran le peintre," *L'Orient Le Jour*, January 28, 2000, p. 6.

2010
Lecture on Bernd and Hilla Becher. Dia Art Foundation, New York. January 11.

Photograph Credits

All works by Walid Raad © 2015 Walid Raad.

© 2015 Artists Rights Society (ARS), New York/ADAGP, Paris/Estate of Marcel Duchamp: p. 42 fig. 18. © 2015 John Baldessari: p. 37 fig. 12. Courtesy CNN: p. 172. Photograph by Hughes Dubois, © Musée du Louvre, dist. RMN-Grand Palais/ Hughes Dubois/Art Resource, New York: p. 44 fig. 22, p. 45 fig. 23. Photograph by Leo Eloy/Fundação Bienal de São Paulo: p. 46. Photograph by Paolo Gasparini, courtesy Instituto Lina Bo e P. M. Bardi and Paolo Gasparini: p. 43. Photograph by Maria Gilissen, © 2015 Maria Gilissen/Artists Rights Society (ARS), New York/SABAM, Brussels, © Département des Aigles: p. 42 fig. 19. © Hans Haacke/Artists Rights Society (ARS), New York, courtesy the artist and Paula Cooper Gallery, New York, photograph by Fred Scruton: p. 40 fig. 16. © 2015 Ilya Kabakov/Artists Rights Society (ARS), New York: p. 47. © Matjaž Kačičnik: p. 162. Photograph by Kelly & Massa Photography, Philadelphia, courtesy Andrea Fraser and Galerie Nagel Draxler, Berlin/Cologne: p. 41. © Piet Janssens: p. 124. © Zoe Leonard, courtesy Galerie Gisela Capitain, Cologne, photograph by Geoffrey Clements: p. 35. © 2015 Sherrie Levine: p. 31 fig. 3. © The Metropolitan Museum of Art, New York, image source Art Resource, New York: p. 168 fig. 5, p. 169 fig. 6. © Lutz Meyer/ Sfeir-Semler Gallery, Hamburg, courtesy Rabih Mroué and Sfeir-Semler Gallery, Beirut/Hamburg: p. 33 fig. 5. The Museum of Modern Art, New York, Department of Imaging and Visual Resources. Photograph by David Allison: p. 31 fig. 3; photograph by Robert Kastler: pp. 90–92; photograph by Kate Keller: p. 42 fig. 18; photograph by Paige Knight: p. 37 fig. 12; photographs by John Wronn: pp. 34, 36; photograph by Imaging and Visual Resource Studio: p. 47. Photographs by Stephen Petegorsky: pp. 150–53. © Jakob Polacsek/TBA21, 2011: pp. 122–23, 130–33. Courtesy Walid Raad and Paula Cooper Gallery, New York: p. 154. Courtesy Walid Raad, Paula Cooper Gallery, New York, and Sfeir-Semler Gallery, Beirut/ Hamburg: pp. 10–27, p. 37 fig. 13, pp. 50–89, 93–109, 116–21, 125–27, 134–37, 140–43, 146–47, 155–59, p. 168 fig. 4. Photograph by Philippe Rualt, © RMN-Grand Palais/Art Resource, New York: p. 164. Courtesy Walid Raad and Sfeir-Semler Gallery, Beirut/Hamburg: p. 165. Courtesy Jayce Salloum and Walid Raad: p. 30 fig. 1 . © Herman Sorgeloos; Courtesy Walid Raad: p. 32. Isabella Stewart Gardner Museum, Boston: p. 45 fig. 24. Photograph by Rodney Todd-White and Son; Courtesy Anthony Reynolds Gallery, London: pp. 128–29. ©Telegrau.com; Courtesy Walid Raad and Sfeir-Semler Gallery, Beirut/Hamburg: pp. 114–15, 138–39, 144–45. © The Warburg Institute, London: p. 169 fig. 7. Courtesy Akram Zaatari and Sfeir-Semler Gallery, Beirut/Hamburg: pp. 30–31 fig. 2. Courtesy David Zwirner, New York/London: p. 38.

Lenders to the Exhibition

Colección Helga de Alvear, Madrid/Cáceres

Museo Nacional Centro de Arte Reina Sofía, Madrid

Paula Cooper Gallery, New York

Sfeir-Semler Gallery, Beirut/Hamburg

The Khalid Shoman Foundation, Amman

The Museum of Modern Art, New York

Walid Raad

Walker Art Center, Minneapolis

Trustees of The Museum of Modern Art